全国翻译硕士专业学位(MTI)系列教

北京市高等教育精品教材立项项目

总主编：何其莘 仲伟合 许 钧

英汉视译

English-Chinese
Sight Interpreting

秦亚青 何 群 编著

外语教学与研究出版社
FOREIGN LANGUAGE TEACHING AND RESEARCH PRESS
北京　BEIJING

图书在版编目（CIP）数据

英汉视译 = English-Chinese Sight Interpreting ／ 秦亚青，何群编著 . — 北京：外语教学与研究出版社，2009.2（2020.10 重印）
（全国翻译硕士专业学位(MTI)系列教材 ／ 何其莘，仲伟合，许钧主编）
ISBN 978-7-5600-8191-5

Ⅰ.①英… Ⅱ.①秦… ②何… Ⅲ.①英语－翻译－研究生－教材 Ⅳ.①H315.9

中国版本图书馆 CIP 数据核字（2009）第 023210 号

出 版 人　徐建忠
项目负责　都帮森
责任编辑　邓付华　骆 为
封面设计　刘 冬
版式设计　付玉梅
出版发行　外语教学与研究出版社
社　　址　北京市西三环北路 19 号（100089）
网　　址　http://www.fltrp.com
印　　刷　三河市紫恒印装有限公司
开　　本　787×1092　1/16
印　　张　27
版　　次　2009 年 3 月第 1 版 2020 年 10 月第 19 次印刷
书　　号　ISBN 978-7-5600-8191-5
定　　价　41.90 元

购书咨询：（010）88819926　电子邮箱：club@fltrp.com
外研书店：https://waiyants.tmall.com
凡印刷、装订质量问题，请联系我社印制部
联系电话：（010）61207896　电子邮箱：zhijian@fltrp.com
凡侵权、盗版书籍线索，请联系我社法律事务部
举报电话：（010）88817519　电子邮箱：banquan@fltrp.com
法律顾问：立方律师事务所　刘旭东律师
　　　　　中咨律师事务所　殷 斌律师
物料号：181910001

记载人类文明
沟通世界文化
www.fltrp.com

全国翻译硕士专业学位（MTI）系列教材编写委员会

总主编：

何其莘　　仲伟合　　许　钧

编　委：（以姓氏笔画为序）

文　军	王克非	王宏印	王维东
王斌华	仲伟合	任　文	孙致礼
许　钧	何　群	何刚强	何其莘
李　力	李长栓	陈宏薇	陈建平
姜秋霞	胡显耀	赵军峰	柴明颎
秦亚青	傅勇林	谢天振	詹　成
廖七一	穆　雷		

总　序

　　改革开放 30 年，助推中国翻译事业的大发展、大繁荣，勃勃生机，蔚为壮观。今天的翻译，无论在规模、范围上，还是在质量、水平上，以及对中国社会发展的贡献上都是史无前例的。随着我国经济持续、健康、快速的发展和改革开放的不断深入，我国综合国力不断增强，政治、经济、文化等各方面的国际交往日益频繁。作为服务于改革开放的先导力量和与世界沟通的桥梁，翻译的作用愈发突出。然而，在翻译需求不断攀升的同时，作为翻译人员主要培养阵地的高校，却日益暴露出其在翻译教学与实践之间的脱节问题。毕业生翻译技能不扎实，知识面狭窄，往往难以胜任不同专业领域所需的高层次翻译工作，致使翻译领域特别是高级翻译领域的供需矛盾日益突出，不能满足目前的经济和社会发展需要。这从数量上和质量上，都对高水平翻译人才的培养提出了迫切的要求。

　　为适应我国改革开放和社会主义现代化建设事业发展的需要，促进中外交流，培养高层次、应用型高级翻译专门人才，国务院学位委员会 2007 年 1 月23 日第 23 次会议审议通过设置翻译硕士专业学位（MTI）。翻译硕士专业学位是我国第 18 个硕士层次的专业学位，其设立无疑是继 2006 年教育部批准试办翻译本科专业后我国翻译学科建设取得的又一里程碑式的成果，为我国培养高层次、应用型、职业化的翻译人才提供了重要途径，为我国翻译学的学科发展奠定了基础，同时也给我国的外语学科发展带来了机遇与挑战。

　　翻译硕士专业学位培养德、智、体全面发展，能适应全球经济一体化及提高国家国际竞争力的需要，适应国家经济、文化、社会建设需要的高层次、应用型、专业性口笔译人才。翻译硕士专业学位教育在培养目标、师资要求、教学内容以及教学方法和手段这四点上都与传统的翻译方向研究生教育有很大的不同。首先，翻译硕士专业学位教育注重对学生实践能力的培养，按口译或笔译方向训练学生的口笔译实际操作能力、跨文化交际能力，并为满足翻译实践积累所需要的百科知识。这一点与传统的外国语言文学学科中的翻译研究方向侧重培养学生的外国语言文学理论研究能力、学术研究能力以及就业为导向的教学能力的培养目标差别很大。第二，对学生实践能力的高要求和培养目标的应用型导向，也要求承担翻译硕士专业学位教学任务的教师必须具有丰富的口译或笔译实践经验，并了解翻译教学的原则。第三，翻译硕士专业学位教育中的翻译教学有别于外语教学中的教学翻译。翻译训练不是作为一种检测学生语言能力、水平的手段，而是建立在学生双语交际能力基础之上的职业技能训练，包括译前准备、笔记方法、分析方法、记忆方法、表达方法、术语库的建立等，专门训练学生借助语言知识、主题知识和百科知识对源语信息进行逻辑分析，并用另一种语言将理解的信息表达出来。最后，在教学方法和手段上，专业化的翻译教学需要的是双语交际环境、特定的交际对象和交际主题，还要考虑到翻译用人单位的需求等，要求学生不仅要具备扎实的中文基础和至少通晓一门外语，同时还要具备广博的其他学科（如经济、管理、法律、金融等）知识和实际翻译操作技能。另外，专业翻译人员培养还特别强调要忠实地表达讲话人／作者的想法或信息。因此，翻译作为一个职业（无论是兼职还是全职），专业化程度高，应用性和操作性都很强。要培养职业化高级翻译人才，现行外语教学体制是难以完成的。

职业化的翻译教育也因此需要专门化的教材。该教材体系应根据职业翻译人才的知识结构"双语知识、百科知识、翻译技能知识"三个部分来设计。专业翻译课程的设置也都是根据培养单位的师资特点及教学资源围绕上述三个板块安排的。因此，专业翻译教材应该至少包括口译技能类、笔译技能类、通识教育类、口笔译理论类等类别。正是在上述原则及《翻译硕士专业学位研究生指导性培养方案》的指导下，我们在 2007 年底组织国内多位了解翻译硕士专业学位并一直从事翻译教学与研究的专家、学者进行研讨，并着手编写国内第一套专门面向翻译硕士专业学位教育的系列教材。该套教材包括口译技能、笔译技能、翻译理论、通识教育及翻译工具书五个类别。整套教材以翻译职业技能训练为核心，以适当的应用型翻译理论为指导，配合不同学科领域的专题训练，旨在完善学生翻译学科知识结构，提高学生口笔译实践能力。在本系列教材全体编委的努力下，呈现在读者面前的这套"全国翻译硕士专业学位（MTI）系列教材"具备以下特点：

（1）口笔译训练的技能化。全面介绍翻译技能。以口译类教材为例，包括口译的记忆、笔记、数字口译、口译语篇分析、口译预测、语义识别、口译译前准备等技能；同声传译则介绍同声传译的概论、视译、应对策略等。

（2）口笔译训练的实战性。笔译的选材基本是社会、经济、文化、教育等领域的真实文本材料；口译则尽可能选用全真会议资料，而且题材范围涉及政治、外交、经济、文化、高科技、法律等多方面。

（3）口笔译训练的专业化。所介绍的口译技能、笔译技能等均为目前国内外口笔译质量评估及口笔译专业认证考试测试的主要方面，通过对本系列教材的学习可以了解职业化翻译培训的程序与内容。

（4）**口笔译理论的指导性。**对应用型的高水平翻译人才来说，树立正确的翻译观，掌握相关的翻译基础理论是非常重要的。本系列教材所涵盖的翻译基础知识和口笔译理论应努力领会和掌握。

（5）**通识教育的融通化。**口笔译实践要求掌握英汉两种语言的相关知识及跨文化交际知识，本系列教材中的通识类各分册对拓宽学生的知识面、提高其跨文化交际的意识和能力将起到重要的促进作用。

MTI职业化人才培养的教学理念和面向实践的教学导向在目前的翻译教学界还是新事物，对其进行不断的探讨、丰富并开展教与学的交流是必要的，也将对翻译硕士专业学位发展大有裨益。外研社这套翻译硕士专业学位系列教材在开发之初就考虑到了这一点，在教材出版的同时，也将推出翻译硕士专业学位教学资源网，不仅指导系列教材的科学使用，也希望能够汇教学实时动态、集各方意见反馈、倡教学经验交流、促学科长远发展。

中国职业化翻译人才的培养才刚刚起步，需要译界、学界同仁"筚路蓝缕，以启山林"。教材建设是专业建设的核心任务之一，我们也希望借编写本套翻译硕士专业学位教材的机会为刚刚起步的中国职业翻译教育尽一份绵薄之力。本套教材的编写力求科学性、指导性和前瞻性，但内容等方面也难免有不尽完善的地方。希望通过本系列教材的编写，与关心中国翻译事业和从事翻译职业的同仁、同行一起关注我国翻译和翻译教学事业的发展现状，以及翻译硕士专业学位教育的实施和发展，进一步探讨高层次专业化翻译人才培养的模式和途径。

全国翻译硕士专业学位（MTI）系列教材编写委员会

2009 年 3 月

目　录

绪 论

改革开放以来，中国全面地融入了国际社会，国际交流日趋频繁，国际会议日益增多，使得翻译成为需求量很高的行业。对翻译的需求，尤其是对会议翻译的需求，极大地推动了翻译的教育和训练。视译是会议翻译的重要形式，而视译译员需要专门的训练。视译是一种比较特殊的翻译类型，但到目前为止，国内还没有出版过专门的视译教材，所以，我们希望这本《英汉视译》能够成为培训会议翻译人员的基本教材之一。

一、什么是视译？

视译（on-sight interpreting，简称 sight interpreting）即视稿翻译，就是一面听着发言人的发言，一面看着稿子，同时跟着发言人的速度，口头翻译出稿件的内容。视译与交替传译（consecutive interpreting，简称交传）和同声传译（simultaneous interpreting，简称同传）都属于口译的范畴，其中视译和同传又属于会议口译（conference interpreting）。所以，视译与同传有很多相似的地方。由于二者都是同步翻译，有人也将同传和视译都称为同声传译，认为视译只是同传的一种特殊形式。

视译和同传有同有异。两者最大共同点是都有时间限制，译员在翻译时都在不断地抢时间。视译要求译员在几乎无所准备的情况下，跟着发言者的速度，将发言内容用另一种语言译出。所以，在翻译速度和节奏上面，与同传是完全一样的，这也意味着视译和同传的基本原理和技巧是一样的。但是，视译与同传又有不同的地方。做同传时译员完全依靠听力理解获取信息，视译时译员则是有稿可依。同传是三步骤翻译，即听、译、说；视译是四步骤翻译，即听、看、译、说。也就是说，同传人员只是凭着发言人口头表达的内容进行翻译，而视译则是一面听着发言人的发言，一面看着发言稿，一面做翻译。有稿可依虽然可以方便译员对内容的把握，但要求译员的译出率和准确率更高，所以难度依然很大。

视译的应用范围很广。在国际会议上，发言人可能在即将发言的时候向译员提供发言稿，这就需要译员进行视译。另外，如果发言人使用投影仪或 PPT 在大屏幕上演示发言内容要点，边讲边放，译员也需要视译。在商务洽谈和法庭翻译中，其中一方出示的书面材料往往需要现场视译。除了这些实际需要之外，对于同传教学，视译更是必不可少的一部分。视译训练是从交替传译教学转入同传教学的过渡阶段，可以帮助学生理解同传的基本原理，掌握同传的重要技巧，练习同传的思维方式，既为学生学习同传打下良好的基础，也是他们同传训练的一部分。

二、视译的基本要求和首要原则

视译的基本要求是翻译的速度与发言者的速度保持同步，视译的首要原则是译出语语序与译入语语序基本保持一致。

做到这两点，从某种意义上说，是对中国传统翻译理论和技巧的革命。我们知道，翻译是国际交流不可或缺的工具。自从西学东渐以来，中国的仁人志士就翻译了许多西方的著作。如今，翻译已经成为一门显学，翻译作品也越来越多。中国改革开放以来，口译也逐渐成为一种技能和职业。随着需求的增大，各种讨论翻译理论、翻译技巧的专门论述也随之产生。

在讨论翻译的著述中，不少是讨论英汉两种语言的句子结构的。英汉两种语言句子结构差异很大，这种差异又突出表现在部分句子的语序上。按照传统的翻译理论，翻译要做到"信"、"达"、"雅"，就需要调整英语语序，有时甚至要将句末的内容调整到句首，把句子中间的成分置于句末。所以，严复在译完《天演论》时曾发出"西文句法，少则二三字，多则数十百言"的感慨。他认为，如果根据原句法而译，必然不通。所以，译者必须将"全文神理，融会于心"，然后再下笔，才算佳品。这样就把翻译单位定位为整篇文章。后来，林语堂专门就英汉句法的不同谈翻译，认为翻译有字译和句译，字译就是以字为主体的翻译，句译是以句为主体的翻译。林语堂认为，字译是不对的，句译是对的，因为句译是理解了整句再翻译，译文必然准确通达。所以他提出以"句译为本位"，也就是以句子为基本的翻译单位。

其实，后来的学者对英汉句法和句子结构的思考大致也是如此。如此一来，翻译的过程也就在相当程度上成为调整句子结构的过程。严复和林语堂的观点对于笔译来说无疑是正确的，对于交传也没错。但是，在做同传和视译的时候就行不通了。大幅度的调整译入语和译出语句子结构，只有在翻译人员有充裕的时间时才能做到。对于会议翻译，无论是视译还是同传，颠来倒去的语序调整却是大忌，因为这样做势必耗费时间，而翻译速度恰恰是视译和同传的生命。如果译员跟不上发言人的速度，即便是翻译得再准确，也没有任何意义。所以翻译速度是做好视译和同传的必备条件。从这个意义上讲，视译人员不但无法做到"全文神理，融会于心"，即便以句译为本位也是不可能的。一般来说，发言人说到第三至五个词的时候，译员就要开始翻译了。所以，在保持翻译正确的情况下，速度就成为视译和同传的基本要求。

由于这种翻译性质的要求，视译译员就不得不对传统或笔译的原则和技巧进行革命了。这种革命的核心就是保持译出语语序，目的是跟上发言人的速度。一般来说，发言人的速度在每分钟 120 个单词左右，视译的速度也必须保持这个速度。那么，在部分句子英汉语序差异较大的情况下，要保持较快的翻译速度，视译时就要尽可能地避免调整英语原文的语序。由于汉语是灵活的语言，汉语句子结构的特点是"意合"（parataxis），一个汉语句子即便没有关联词明显地表明它的内在逻辑关系，也不会影响人们对它的理解。英语亦如此。所以，视译时基本保持英文原来的顺序是完全可能的。再者，视译是口头翻译，语言表达可以相对松散些。因此，译员如果能够充分地利用这些特点，便可以减少语序方面的调整，在基本保持原文语序的情况下，跟上发言人的讲话速度，做好视译。当然，在视译中为了尽量保持原文语序、确保翻译速度所作的一些调整，有时可能会对原文的意思有所影响，会出现意义重心略有偏移的情况，但是，这些调整在总体上不影响发言人的原意，在视译和同传允许的"忠实度"之内，因此，是可以接受的。

三、本书的结构和内容

视译课，作为会议翻译教学和培训的一门课程，需要专门教材，以便使教学更为系统、更为科学。外交学院英语系在培养高级翻译人才方面教学经验丰富，为外交部翻译室、国家各大部委及其他外事单位输送了很多高级翻译人才。视译课在外交学院开设已有 15 年，属于翻译系列中的一门主要口译课程，教学方法独特，教学效果也相当明显。我们希望通过《英汉视译》一书，与翻译教学的同行分享教学经验，并填补国内会议口译教学中视译课程教材建设方面的空白。

教育部已经批准设立翻译硕士专业学位（MTI），将翻译列为一个专门的科目进行教学和训练，这对于中国的翻译教学和翻译学科发展具有重要的意义。《英汉视译》是一本以翻译专业硕士生为主要教学对象的实用型教材，强调实践和实用，重视同步习惯的培养，适用于翻译专业教学和训练。它既可以供已经学过交传的学生作为翻译专业研究生阶段的技巧训练教材，也可以作为有本科基础，有志于做会议翻译人员的自学教材。教材设计为 15 个单元，每周两学时可使用一个学期。每单元又分为技巧讲解、语段视译、实战练习和自主训练四个部分。各部分都有详细的分析，练习部分附有译文，讲解部分十分详细，方便自学者学习和使用。

技巧讲解部分从视译的原理和原则开始，逐步将学生引入学习视译和同传的轨道，使学生明白视译和同传不仅是可能的，而且是完全可以做得很好的。所以，在开始阶段，讲解重点在于告诉学生视译的原理、原则和基本要求。之后，则将重点转移到具体的视译技巧上。对于视译必须掌握的重要技巧，每单元突出一个重点，分别介绍不同类型的句型在视译中常用的翻译技巧，也对一些特别实用的句型进行了讲解，同时还使用了大量实例进行示范。

语段视译是技巧讲解之后的实际练习。所选语段都是口语化较强的内容，语言相对简单，要求学生按照视译的基本原则来进行翻译，并在练习过程中逐步提高速度，期待学生在修完该课程后达到每分钟 80 至 100 个英文单词的翻译速度。在段落翻译方面，我们既提供了笔译译文又提供了视译译文，并就两者的不同之处做了比较详细的点评，讲解具体的处理方法。这样做的目的，主要是希望学生在做完段落视译之后能够将这两种译文进行比较，逐步克服多年养成的笔译习惯，能够在做视译和同传的时候做到上口快、适应能力强。

实战练习的目的是使学生在做过比较容易的段落练习之后，能够以实际的素材做视译练习。实战练习的材料大多来自国际会议上的发言稿或公众人物的讲演词。在实战练习阶段，我们对难句做了详细的分解，告诉学生这些句子怎样才能依照视译的原则译成中文，怎样在这些难句中使用我们学过的技巧。建议教师可以根据学生的实际水平，先练习难句，然后再进行全篇的实战。

最后是自主训练，选篇均来自实际的讲演和会议发言。课堂讲解和练习的时间毕竟有限，要想成为一名合格的会议翻译，就要像一个好的运动员或飞行员一样进行大量的、有目的的训练。因此，课下自主训练必不可少。我们提供的自主训练材料就是为了加大学生的训练量。在翻译专业的教学中，我们建议学生的自主训练要进一步加大。

四、如何使用这本教材

如何使用《英汉视译》进行视译教学呢？就此，我们提出以下建议：

首先，培养习惯。开始的时候，学生会很不适应，甚至做不下来。在某种程度上，视译和同传更是一种习惯。许多人做不了或是做不好同传和视译，并不是因为他们在语言上有重大障碍，而是他们没有同步使用耳、目、脑、口的习惯。即便是有些中英文都很好的人，初做视译和同传的时候也会很不适应，甚至发懵。所以，在开始阶段，教师要利用教材的讲解和例句的练习部分，有意识地训练学生耳、目、脑、口同步活动的习惯。经过一段时间的训练，学生要在拿到一段文稿的时候，习惯地做出同步反应。

第二，控制时间。视译和同传的时间要求是让学生感到压力最大的。其实，养成时间感和紧迫感是同传人员素质的重要表现。所以，在语段视译和实战练习部分，要控制学生的翻译时间。比如在做语段视译的时候，可先给学生三分钟，让他们默读一下原文。这样做的目的有两个：其一，使学生对内容有一个大致的了解；其二，使学生有强烈的时间感和紧迫感。第二条尤为重要，因为时间感和紧迫感是练出来的，而它们最初是被逼出来的。逐渐，学生内化了这种感觉，在上场的时候就会积极进入状态。

第三，强调实践。讲解部分要简明扼要，讲解内容是针对视译教学的特殊需要设计的，每单元试图说明一个问题。这些问题需要大量的例句来演示，以便学生能够理解和掌握。但是理解和掌握必须在实践过程中完成。所以，对于提供的例句，教师可以先让学生根据视译的基本原则译出，然后再讲解如何译好这个句子，这样可以加强学生的能动性。对于语段视译和实战练习这两部分内容，教师可让学生先尝试视译，然后可依照视译单位的划分原则，将原文改为断句后的视译格式，要求学生依照断句后的格式进行视译。实践证明，这种独特的教学方式非常有利于训练学生的同步反应能力，帮助他们学会在尽可能保持原文语序不变的条件下，迅速顺畅地做好视译。课堂上进行实战练习时，要强调其实战性，教师应该要求学生在限定时间内完成视译，帮助他们体会并学会适应实际工作的现场压力。每单元的自主训练是供学生课后巩固所学技巧专门配备的练习，要求学生或结成对子或个人单独完成，对其中的难句可要求学生在视译练习后以笔头形式记录下解决方案，相互交流视译体会和经验。另外，我们建议教员使用配备多媒体教学设备的教室或在语言实验室进行教学，并尽可能做到讲解简明扼要，加强师生互动。教师在讲解重点技巧时要演示视译实例。

第1单元

视译语序

基本技巧：

• 依序顺译，即译入语和译出语在语序上尽量保持一致。

一、技巧讲解：视译语序

这一单元主要讨论视译的一个重要原则——使译入语尽量保持译出语语序。这也是视译的第一原则。这里的译出语指原文所使用的语言，译入语指的则是译文所使用的语言。

速度是同声传译的生命，也是视译的生命。如果译员跟不上发言人的速度，即便翻译得再准确，也没有意义。

翻译速度与很多因素有关，比如说讲话的语速习惯。有的人讲话快，有的人讲话慢，人的语速还可以根据环境和情绪进行调整。对于同声传译人员来说，只要不是自己天生语速过慢，一般都是可以跟上发言人语速的。要保持较快的翻译速度，关键还是语序。也就是说，如果能在翻译时保持译出语的语序，或是基本保持译出语的语序，就可以大大节省时间，加快速度。正因为如此，我们说视译的第一原则是尽量保持译出语语序。对于英汉视译来说，就是要使翻译出来的中文尽量保持英语原文的语序。

英汉两种语言的句子结构差异较大，这种差异又突出表现在部分句子的语序上。如果像笔译那样大幅度调整句子的语序，视译就根本无法进行。因为译者可能需要将句末的内容调整到句首，把句子中间的成分置于句末，颠来倒去，时间消耗殆尽，速度无法提高。所以，语序是英汉视译的重点，也是难点。

语序固然是难点，但并非无法逾越。以下三个基本特点表明：在英汉视译的过程中，保持英语句子原来的顺序是可能的。第一，英语和汉语都是十分灵活的语言，调整语序之后仍然能保持原来的意思。比如汉语中的"一条板凳坐两个人"和"两个人坐一条板凳"，虽然二者的顺序几乎完全颠倒，但意思并没有改变。第二，汉语句子结构的特点是"意合"，虽然句子之间往往没有关联词语明显地表明内在逻辑关系，但是读者或听众都能根据特定的语境对话语的语义作出正确的判断。比如"大小餐馆今晚爆满，人们现在都喜欢在外面吃年夜饭"，这个句子与"因为人们现在都喜欢在外面吃年夜饭，所以大小餐馆今晚爆满"的意思是一样的，不会让人产生因果关系上的误解。第三，口译属于口语范畴，允许一定的松散性，这也为视译的语序安排提供了比笔译更大的回旋余地。英汉视译时，如果能够充分利用这些特点，就可以减少由句子结构差异造成的困难，在基本保持原语序的情况下做好翻译。下面，我们举几个例子说明视译中保持语序的可能性。

例 1： There will come a day when people the world over will live a happy life under the sun of socialism.

译文 1[1]：全世界人民在社会主义阳光下过幸福生活的一天是会到来的。

【讲解】 分解这个句子，比较英语原文和汉语译文的语序：

There will come a day // when people the world over will live a happy life
————————————   ————————————————————————————————
     1   2

under the sun of socialism.
————————————————
        2

可以看出，英语原文的语序是：1+2。我们再来分解一下汉语译文：

全世界人民在社会主义阳光下过幸福生活的一天 // 是会到来的。
————————————————————————————————   ——————————
                       2   1

比照英语语序，汉语译文的语序是：2+1，亦即完全颠倒了英文的语序。所以，译出语和译入语的语序往往有着很大的不同，汉语译文把原句语序几乎完全颠倒过来，这是典型的笔译译法，不考虑时间和速度因素，因为这两种因素对于笔译而言的确不是问题。但是，笔译的这种做法在视译中是行不通的。

虽然以上例子说明典型的汉语译文语序与英语原文语序是有很大差异的，但是这并不说明译文的语序非要做如此大的调整不可。只要充分利用上面说到的几个特点和汉语的灵活性，译入语的语序就可能接近译出语语序。下面

---

1 全书中的译文 1 均为笔译译文，译文 2 均为视译译文。

我们换一种方法把原句再译一遍：

译文 2：终究会有一天，// 世界人民将在社会主义阳光下过着幸福的生活。

　　　　　　　1　　　　　　　　　　2

　　这个例句说明，许多在笔译中往往要调换位置的句子成分，实际上是可以基本保持原顺序不动的。为了说明问题，我们还可以将例句进一步分解一下。分解之后，视译译文的语序仍然可以保持原文语序。请看以下对照译文：

原文语序	视译语序
There will come a day	终将有一天，
when people the world over	全世界人民
will live a happy life	会过上幸福的生活，
under the sun of socialism.	沐浴着社会主义的阳光。

　　我们将例句 1 分成四个部分，然后分别译出，每一部分的顺序不变，译文干净利落。[1] 这样处理，原句就成了一个非常便利于视译的句型。

例 2：　On the average, male students score higher on tests that measure mathematical reasoning, mechanical ability, and problem solving skills.

译文 1：总的来说，男生在数学推理、机械技术和解决问题等方面的测试中成绩较高。

【讲解】　该例句可分解如下：

On the average, // male students score higher on tests // that measure

　　　1　　　　　　　　　　　2　　　　　　　　　　　　3

mathematical reasoning, // mechanical ability, // and problem solving skills.

　　　　3　　　　　　　　　4　　　　　　　　　5

该句的英文语序是：1+2+3+4+5。汉语译文分解如下：

总的来说，// 男生 // 在数学推理、// 机械技术 // 和解决问题等方面 //

　　1　　　　2A　　　3　　　　　4　　　　　5

的测试中成绩较高。

　　2B

1　当然，这里需要说明一点，就是这种句式使得原来的意义重心有所偏移。比如，最后一部分"沐浴着社会主义的阳光"，在译文中比在原文中的分量要重一些。但这是在视译和同声传译允许的"忠实度"之内的。

3

这样一来，汉语译文的语序就成为：1+2A+3+4+5+2B。这样的语序调整是很大的，因此不符合视译要求。下面我们将英文句子进一步分解开来，按照尽量保持原文语序的原则，把它翻译出来：

原文语序	视译语序
On the average,	总的来说，
male students score higher on tests	男生成绩较高的测试有
that measure mathematical reasoning,	数学推理、
mechanical ability	机械技术
and problem solving skills.	和解决问题的技巧。

例 3： Eugene Rostow was director of the US Arms Control and Disarmament Agency until January 1983 when he was fired after repeated clashes with the White House over the conduct of strategic weapons talks with the Soviets in Geneva.

译文 1： 尤金·罗斯托在 1983 年 1 月以前一直担任美国军控和裁军署署长，当时由于他多次就苏美日内瓦战略武器会谈的方式与白宫发生争执而被解职。

【讲解】 该例句可分解如下：

Eugene Rostow was director of the US Arms Control and Disarmament Agency //
　　　　　　　　　　　　　　　1

until January 1983 // when he was fired // after repeated clashes with the White
　　2　　　　　　　　　3　　　　　　　　　4

House // over the conduct of strategic weapons talks with the Soviets in Geneva.
　4　　　　　　　　　　　　　　　5

英文语序为：1+2+3+4+5。汉语译文分解如下：

尤金·罗斯托 // 在 1983 年 1 月以前 // 一直担任美国军控和裁军署署长，//
　1A　　　　　　　2　　　　　　　　　　　1B

当时由于他多次 // 就苏美日内瓦战略武器会谈的方式 // 与白宫发生争执 //
　4A　　　　　　　　　5　　　　　　　　　　　　　　　4B

而被解职。
　3

可以看出，汉语译文的语序为：1A+2+1B+4A+5+4B+3。这是个比较难做视译的句子，即便如此，也是有办法的。我们将英文句子分解开来，用视译的方法译出如下：

原文语序	视译语序
Eugene Rostow was director of the US Arms Control and Disarmament Agency	尤金·罗斯托曾任美国军控和裁军署署长，
until January 1983	1983 年 1 月
when he was fired	他被解职，
after repeated clashes with the White House	原因是他多次与白宫发生争执，
over the conduct of strategic weapons talks with the Soviets in Geneva.	争执涉及如何与苏联在日内瓦举行战略武器会谈。

比较例 1、例 2、例 3 的译文 1 和视译译文，就会发现以下几点：

1）译文 1 打破了英语原句语序，而视译译文基本保持了原文语序；

2）译文 1 结构紧凑，而视译译文结构较松散、较口语化；

3）译文 1 与视译译文传达的内容信息基本相同。

译文 1 采取的是一般笔译的句式，读起来不会有误解。但在同传箱里做视译，用这种句式基本上是行不通的。因为如果要在语序上动这样的大手术，就根本无法跟上发言者的速度。其次，听众也由于句子太长而无法一听即懂。而视译译文的结构适应速度要求，语序大致不变，每个断句部分短而上口，意思表达清楚。这不但为口译人员赢得了宝贵的时间，也使听众感觉舒服得多。虽然视译译文结构稍显松散，又加了一些原文没有的连接语，但这并未从根本上影响到对原文的"信"，因为这些较灵活的变动是在口语和口译允许的范围之内的。

从以上几个例子看，译入语大致保持译出语的语序是可能的。同时，作为视译译员，这是我们为保证速度、完成翻译任务必须遵守的一条基本原则。

二、语段视译

1 词汇与表达

在进行语段视译前，请先预习以下词汇与表达。

scholarly treatise	学术论文
bureaucracy	政府部门
rational	合乎情理的
courteous	有礼貌的
Internal Revenue Service	（美国）国内收入署，缩写为 IRS
welfare department	福利部门
bungle	弄糟，搞坏
discriminatory	带有歧视的
insensitive	冷漠的
rev up	加速

2 视译语段

请在 3 分钟之内迅速阅读下面的语段，了解大意，然后结合所学要点进行视译练习。视译时要保持正常语速，译文要顺畅达意。

Most ironic was the image of government that was born of these experiences. As any scholarly treatise on the subject will tell you, the great advantage bureaucracy is supposed to offer for a complex, modern society like ours is efficient, rational, uniform and courteous treatment for the citizens it deals with. Yet not only did these qualities not come through to the people I talked with, it was their very opposites that seemed more characteristic. People of all classes—the rich man dealing with the Internal Revenue Service as well as the poor woman struggling with the welfare department—felt that the treatment they had received had been bungled, not efficient; unpredictable, not rational; discriminatory, not uniform; all too often, insensitive, rather than courteous. It was as if they had bought a big new car that not only did not run when they wanted it to, but periodically revved itself up and drove all around their yards.

原译文：这些经历给人们的政府形象是最有讽刺意味的。任何一篇论述这个问题的学术论文都会说，对一个像我们这样复杂的现代化社会，政府部门应当提供的一大优点是在和公民打交道的时候表现出富有效率、合乎情理、公平一致和文明礼貌的办事方法。但是，和我谈过话的人并没有感觉到这些品质，倒是恰恰相反的情况更具有代表性。各阶层的人，从与国内收入署打交道的富人到与福利部门交涉的可怜的妇人，都觉得他们受到的对待是糟糕的，而不是有效的；是捉摸不定的，而不是合情合理的；是带有歧视的，而不是公平的；而且经常是冷漠的，而不是有礼貌的。就像是买了一辆新的大轿车，不仅要它走的时候不走，而且不时会自行加速，在院子里到处乱跑。(蔡基刚，2001：12)

3　视译译文

	断　句	译　文
1	Most ironic was the image of government	最具讽刺意义的是政府的形象，
2	that was born of these experiences.	它来自人们的亲身感受。
3	As any scholarly treatise on the subject	任何一篇学术论文谈及这个问题，
4	will tell you,	都会告诉你
5	the great advantage bureaucracy is supposed to offer	政府部门有一大好处，
6	for a complex, modern society like ours	对于我们这样复杂的现代社会来说，
7	is efficient, rational, uniform and courteous treatment	它富有效率、充满理性、一视同仁、文明礼貌，
8	for the citizens it deals with.	它会以这样的方式与公民打交道。
9	Yet not only did these qualities not come through	但是，这些品质并没有表现出来，
10	to the people I talked with,	和我谈过话的人都有同感。
11	it was their very opposites that seemed more characteristic.	恰恰相反的品质倒是更为常见。

（待续）

（续上表）

	断 句	译 文
12	People of all classes—	各个阶层的人士，
13	the rich man dealing with the Internal Revenue Service	无论是与国内收入署打交道的富人，
14	as well as the poor woman struggling with the welfare department—	还是同福利部门交涉的贫穷妇女，
15	felt that the treatment they had received	都感到他们受到的对待
16	had been bungled, not efficient;	糟糕透顶，而不是富有效率；
17	unpredictable, not rational;	变化无常，而不是有条有理；
18	discriminatory, not uniform;	带有歧视，而不是一视同仁；
19	all too often, insensitive,	并且往往是一张冷面孔，
20	rather than courteous.	而不是文明礼貌。
21	It was as if they had bought a big new car	正像是买了一辆崭新的大轿车，
22	that not only did not run when they wanted it to,	让它走时它偏偏不走，
23	but periodically revved itself up	却又不时地无端加速，
24	and drove all around their yards.	满院子乱跑。

4 视译点评

1. 原文第一句：Most ironic was the image of government // that was born of these experiences.

　　视译译文没有像原译文一样调整语序，而是按照原语序把句子译成两个汉语分句，然后保持原语序译出，并通过增添代词"它"作为连接语，使译语听起来通顺，即："最具讽刺意义的是政府的形象，它来自人们的亲身感受。"

2. 原文第二句：As any scholarly treatise on the subject will tell you, // the great advantage bureaucracy is supposed to offer // for a complex, modern society like ours // is efficient, rational, uniform and courteous treatment // for the citizens it deals with.

视译按照原句语序，把原句中的状语从句 As any scholarly treatise on the subject will tell you 译成汉语分句，把 the great advantage bureaucracy is supposed to offer 这个带有后置定语从句的名词词组通过增加"有"字译成汉语分句"政府部门有一大好处"，然后将后面的部分通过增加连接语译成三个汉语分句："对于我们这样复杂的现代社会来说，// 它富有效率、充满理性、一视同仁、文明礼貌，// 它会以这样的方式与公民打交道。"整体上说，译文基本保持了原文的语序。

3. 原文第三句：Yet not only did these qualities not come through // to the people I talked with, // it was their very opposites that seemed more characteristic.

视译时没有像原译文那样调整 not only 引导的分句的语序，而是把这个分句一分为二，将 to the people I talked with 单独处理成一个分句，即："和我谈过话的人都有同感。"

三、实战练习

1 词汇与表达

请先熟悉以下词汇与表达，并适当地运用在视译中。

international rule of law	国际法治
human right	人权（通常为复数）
APEC (Asia-Pacific Economic Cooperation)	亚太经合组织
in a confrontational mode	以对抗的方式
proliferation	扩散
candid	坦率的
international standard	国际标准
bilateral relations	双边关系
strategic partnership	战略伙伴关系
international institution	国际制度，国际体制
strategic competitor	战略竞争对手

2 实战课文

请在 15 分钟之内迅速阅读下面的专访，了解大意。视译时要保持正常语速，译文要顺畅达意。

Interview of Secretary of State Colin Powell by CCTV (Excerpt 1)

Interviewer: We are now half a year into Bush's presidency and there have been some ups and downs and even some setbacks in Sino-US relations. **Many Chinese people feel a little bit puzzled when they see a series of events that the US government seems to have taken a more confrontational approach toward China.** （句 1） So that is a very big question among millions of Chinese people. What exactly is in the mind of the US government toward or on our relationship, or so to say, what kind of relationship does the US wish to see?

Secretary: We want a relationship that is a friendly relationship. The word I would convey to the Chinese people today is that we want friendship with the people of China. And six months into our administration, as you noted, there had been a few ups and downs, but for the most part I think we are now moving forward in a positive direction. My trip is an example of that, and President Bush is looking very much forward to visiting China later this fall. **And I think what I would like to say to the Chinese people is that we view China as a very important nation that is going through a period of transformation.** （句 2） We want to help with that transformation. We have very, very important common interests: economic interests, trade interests. There will be areas where there will be disagreements and where we will say things that perhaps might not be well received in China, but it will always be in the context of trying to build a strong relationship with China and welcoming China into the international community—a community of international economics, a community of international rule of law, a community of international standards of human rights. And we have been very, very impressed how far China has come in recent years and we view China as a friend, not as an adversary. But I think when we have two mature countries like China and the United States with long histories and different political systems, there will be ups and downs. But it is important that we work through these ups and downs and always keep the relationship moving forward and upward.

Interviewer: And you're here mainly to prepare for President Bush's visit over here. About this trip, what can you tell us now?

Secretary: Well, he is very much looking forward to the APEC Meeting in Shanghai and then from there to Beijing, and I think he wants to form a personal relationship with President Jiang Zemin and the other leaders. **President Bush very much believes in getting to meet other leaders and to talk to them face to face and convey that American attitude of friendship and the American attitude of "let's see if we can work together to solve any problems that exist between us, and let's always be doing what we can to improve the relationship between our two countries".** (句 3) So he is excited about coming to China. He is looking forward to it very, very much.

Interviewer: Did he tell you anything before you left Washington?

Secretary: He said to make sure that in my conversations with the Chinese leaders I conveyed what I just said—Washington is not in a confrontational mode. Why would we want to be in a confrontational mode? We are one of the best trading partners that China has. Forty percent of your products come to the United States. American consumers depend to a large extent on products that come from China to help them go about their lives. The products that come are at a reasonable cost. American businesses are investing in China. This is the basis for a positive relationship, a relationship that grows, not the basis for a confrontational relationship. **The areas that we will have some difficulty with, and the President will be candid about this, have to do with human rights, and we do have some concerns about proliferation issues.** (句 4) But this isn't the only basis of our relationship. These are the things we are talking our way through.

Interviewer: But it seems that here is a little confusion in terms of definitions of bilateral relations. For example, it seems to me that President Bush does not follow very much the idea of strategic partnership that was defined by our two governments a few years ago. While, at the same time we notice that just on the eve of your visit you said that the United States is not trying to view China as an enemy. So, Mr. Powell, between "partner" and "enemy", if I may ask you, which word would you like to choose?

Secretary: Neither. **Because the relationship between the United States and**

China is so complex and it has so many pieces to it that it doesn't do it justice to try to capture it with a single word. (句 5) It is a complex relationship. **But it is a relationship that increasingly will be based on friendship, on trust, on working together, on working through problems, on being candid with each other when we have disagreements, and some people have called it a partnership in the past.** (句 6) I've even occasionally called it strategic competitors, not in the sense that we're enemies, just that we have areas of disagreement and difference, where we compete on certain issues.

Interviewer: Yes, but to many Chinese, competitor has some kind of an indication of a rivalry or even confrontation, while at the same time many people believe that cooperation between two such countries is very, very fundamental and of great importance.

Secretary: Cooperation is a good word. When we cooperate to improve trade, that's good for both of us. When we cooperate to encourage regional stability in the area so people can trade without being worried about conflicts, when we cooperate on looking at some of the more difficult issues, like Taiwan and our one-China policy and we have a common understanding what we're talking about, then we can move forward in the spirit of friendship. But we should make it clear here and now that from the American standpoint we don't need enemies, we're not looking for enemies, we don't want an enemy. America is a peaceful nation that wishes to be at peace with any other nations in the world that wishes to be at peace with us. And right now we have peaceful relations with China. And we want to do everything we can to build on this basis of friendship and peaceful relationship and work together.

Interviewer: Just as you mentioned, America is a nation for peace and American people love peace. I think that the situation is the same for the Chinese people.

Secretary: I agree.

Interviewer: And, just as the Chinese people are talking about China's bilateral relations, China-US relations, many people believe that China has been putting great importance to relations between our two countries. But there are some confusions or questions again that people in China feel that why there are always some people in America who always disregard the progress that has taken place in China, in areas like economic development, like culture, and human rights. These we understand, to some extent harm our bilateral relations.

So people will say why can't we agree on some points, on something, while we disagree on the other things.

Secretary: Well, in a democratic system such as ours you will always have different points of view and in a political system such as ours, which is very, very diverse, you will always have different points of view. But there are some things we can agree on. And as I indicated earlier, we have seen it's obvious that China has transformed greatly in the last 20 years with respect to your economy, and you have been blessed with a great deal of success as a result of this transformation. And we certainly take note that there has been change in the human rights situation in China as measured against international standards, and I know that the Chinese people should take great credit for that. But that does not mean that we should not point out there are areas where we believe that in accordance with international standards you should continue to move forward, ... So we take note of all that has happened that is very, very positive. But as your friend, and as someone who wants to see China play a more active role in the world—I'm not trying to contain China—we think it's important for us to point out where improvements are appropriate.

Interviewer: Personally, I think that maybe we need some more dialog while at the same time the ordinary Chinese people will feel uncomfortable if America is always pointing the finger at China saying you should do this and do that.

3 难句分析与视译处理

句 1： Many Chinese people feel a little bit puzzled when they see a series of events that the US government seems to have taken a more confrontational approach toward China.

笔译译文： 当中国人在发生的一系列事件中看到美国政府似乎对中国采取了更加对抗的态度时，他们很多人都感到有些迷惑。

视译译文[1]：

断　句	译　文
Many Chinese people feel a little bit puzzled	许多中国人感到困惑不解，

（待续）

1　难句分析与视译处理部分的视译译文均以表格对照形式给出。其中表格左栏为按视译单位断开的英文原文，右栏为对应的视译译文。

（续上表）

断　句	译　文
when they see a series of events	因为他们看到了一系列的事件,
that the US government seems to have taken	说明美国政府似乎采取了
a more confrontational approach	更加对抗的方式,
toward China.	来对待中国。

句2：　　　And I think what I would like to say to the Chinese people is that we view China as a very important nation that is going through a period of transformation.

笔译译文：我想告诉中国人民，我们认为中国是一个正在经历变革的非常重要的国家。

视译译文：

断　句	译　文
And I think what I would like to say to the Chinese people	我想我要告诉中国人民,
is that we view China as a very important nation	我们认为中国是一个非常重要的国家,
that is going through a period of transformation.	中国正在经历变革。

句3：　　　President Bush very much believes in getting to meet other leaders and to talk to them face to face and convey that American attitude of friendship and the American attitude of "let's see if we can work together to solve any problems that exist between us, and let's always be doing what we can to improve the relationship between our two countries".

笔译译文：布什总统相信与其他国家领导人的见面，与他们面对面的交谈，传达美国的友好态度和美国"让我们看看能否一起努力解决我们之间存在的问题，并且让我们永远努力改善两国关系"的态度是很重要的。

视译译文：

断 句	译 文
President Bush very much believes in	布什总统极其重视
getting to meet other leaders	会见其他国家领导人，
and to talk to them face to face	与他们面对面交谈，
and convey that American attitude of friendship	传达美国的友好态度，
and the American attitude	也传达美国的另一种态度，
of "let's see if we can work together	那就是"让我们看看能否共同努力
to solve any problems that exist between us,	解决我们之间存在的问题，
and let's always be doing what we can	让我们不断努力
to improve the relationship between our two countries".	改进我们两国之间的关系。"

句4： The areas that we will have some difficulty with, and the President will be candid about this, have to do with human rights, and we do have some concerns about proliferation issues.

笔译译文： 总统将坦诚提出的是：我们将存在困难的领域是在人权方面，在扩散方面我们也有一些关注。

视译译文：

断 句	译 文
The areas that we will have some difficulty with,	在有些领域我们面临一些困难，
and the President will be candid about this,	总统对此将会十分坦率，
have to do with human rights,	也就是人权领域，
and we do have some concerns	我们也关注
about proliferation issues.	扩散问题。

句5： Because the relationship between the United States and China is so complex and it has so many pieces to it that it doesn't do it justice to capture it with a single word.

笔译译文： 美中关系是如此复杂，又包括很多方面，所以简单地用一个词来涵盖是不合适的。

视译译文：

断　句	译　文
Because the relationship between the United States and China	因为美中关系
is so complex	非常复杂，
and it has so many pieces to it	包括很多方面，
that it doesn't do it justice to	所以无法恰当地
capture it with a single word.	用一个词来涵盖。

句6： But it is a relationship that increasingly will be based on friendship, on trust, on working together, on working through problems, on being candid with each other when we have disagreements, and some people have called it a partnership in the past.

笔译译文： 但也是一个越来越建立在友谊和信任基础之上的关系、建立在共同努力解决问题的基础上的关系，在遇到分歧时双方相互坦诚，过去有人把这种关系称为伙伴关系。

视译译文：

断　句	译　文
But it is a relationship	但这种关系
that increasingly will be based on friendship,	越来越基于友谊、
on trust,	信任、
on working together,	共同努力
on working through problems,	和解决问题；
on being candid with each other	基于相互坦诚相待，
when we have disagreements,	直面我们的分歧，
and some people have called it a partnership in the past.	有人曾把这种关系叫做伙伴关系。

4 参考译文[1]

美国国务卿科林·鲍威尔
接受中央电视台专访（节选 1）

主持人　布什总统上任半年多来，中美关系有起有落，甚至有些挫折。在发生的一系列事件中，当中国人在发生的一系列事件中看到美国政府似乎对中国采取了更加对抗性的态度时，他们很多人都感到有些迷惑。所以这使众多的中国人有一个很大的疑问。美国政府对两国关系到底怎么看，或者说，美国希望看到一个什么样的两国关系？

国务卿　我们希望有一个友好的关系。今天我想传达给中国人民的信息是我们希望与中国人民友好。正如你所说的那样，我们的新政府上任六个月以来，美中关系确实有起伏。但是总的来说我们的关系现在是向积极的方向发展。我的中国之行就是一个例子，而且布什总统也非常期待着在今年秋天访问中国。我想告诉中国人民，我们认为中国是一个正在经历变革的非常重要的国家。我们希望能对中国的变革提供帮助。我们有非常非常重要的共同利益：经济利益、贸易利益。我们在某些领域上也会有分歧，在这些领域，我们所说的也许不被中国所接受，但是这些都是在致力于与中国建立一种牢固的关系，欢迎中国进入国际社会的大环境之中，包括国际经济社会、国际法治社会、国际人权准则社会。并且我们对中国近年来所取得的成就印象非常深刻。我们把中国看成是朋友，不是敌人。但是我认为像美国和中国这样两个成熟国家，有着很长的历史和不同的政治体系，两国关系当然会有起伏。但重要的是我们一起解决这些起伏，不断把我们的关系向前向上推进。

主持人　您此次访华主要是为布什总统的访问做准备。关于这次访问，您能告诉我们什么信息？

国务卿　总统非常期待着参加上海的亚太经合组织会议及之后对北京的访问。我想他希望与江泽民主席和其他中国领导人建立个人关系。布什总统相信与其他国家的领导人的见面，与他们面对面地交谈，传达美国的友好态度和美国"让我们看看能否一起努力解决我们之间存在的问题，并且让我们永远努力改善两国关系"的态度是很重要的。

1　参考译文均为笔译版本，请读者思考如何用视译的方式将原文译出。

所以他对此次中国之行很兴奋。他非常期待着对中国的访问。

主持人　您在离开华盛顿之前布什总统跟您说什么了吗？

国务卿　总统要我在与中国领导人见面时一定要转达我刚才所说的那番话——华盛顿并不是准备对抗。我们为什么要对抗呢？我们是中国最好的贸易伙伴之一。你们40%的产品到了美国。美国消费者在很大程度上依赖于从中国进口的产品，以便他们生活的运转。这些产品价格合理。美国企业也在华投资。这是一个积极的、发展的关系的基础，而不是对抗关系的基础。总统将坦诚地提出：我们将存在困难的领域是在人权方面，在扩散方面我们也有一些关注。但这不是我们关系的唯一基础。这些是我们正在讨论寻求解决的问题。

主持人　但在双边关系的定义上似乎还有一些困惑，例如，布什总统好像并没有继续几年前中美两国政府所定义的战略伙伴关系的想法。同时，我们也注意到，就在您访问前，您说过美国并没有试图视中国为敌。所以，鲍威尔先生，请允许我问您一个问题：在"伙伴"和"敌人"这两个词之间，您选择哪一个？

国务卿　两个都不。美中关系是如此复杂，又包括很多方面，所以简单地用一个词涵盖是不合适的。这是一个复杂的关系。但也是一个越来越将建立在友谊和信任的基础上的关系、建立在共同努力解决问题的基础上的关系，在遇到分歧时双方相互坦诚，过去有人把它叫做伙伴关系。有时我称它为战略竞争者关系，这并不意味着我们是敌人，只是说我们有存在分歧的领域，在这些问题上我们相互竞赛。

主持人　您说的没错，但是对很多中国人来说竞争者有敌对甚至对抗的意味，而同时很多人认为两国之间的合作是最根本的，也是最重要的。

国务卿　合作是一个好词。如果我们的合作促进贸易，这对我们两国都有益。当我们合作推进地区稳定以使人们从事贸易活动而不必担忧冲突时；当我们合作审视一些更难的议题，诸如台湾问题以及我们的"一个中国"政策，并就我们谈论的问题达成共识的时候，那么我们的关系就能友好地向前发展。但我们应该阐明一点：美国的观点是，我们不需要敌人，我们并没有在寻找敌人，我们不需要敌人。美国是一个和平国家，希望与世界上任何一个愿与我们和平相处的国家和平相处。现在，我们与中国建立了和平的关系，我们愿意竭尽所能在这个友好与和平关系的基础上有所发展，共同合作。

主持人　正如你所言，美国是一个热爱和平的国家，美国人民爱好和平。我认为中国和中国人民也一样。

国务卿　我同意。

主持人　当中国人民谈到双边关系、中美关系时，许多人认为，中国非常重视我们两国之间的关系。当然有一些疑惑和问题使中国人感到不解：为什么在美国总是有人无视中国已取得的成就，如在经济发展、文化和在人权方面的成就。我们认为这在某种程度上损害了我们的双边关系。所以，人们要问，我们为什么不能求同存异呢？

国务卿　在像我们这样的民主制度中，你总会遇到不同观点。在像我们这样的一个非常多元化的政治制度中，你也总会遇到不同观点。但是我们也有意见一致的领域。像我刚才所说的，在过去的 20 年里中国在经济方面发生了巨大的变化，变革为中国人带来了巨大的成功。我们当然也注意到按照国际标准衡量中国在人权领域也发生了变化，我知道这归功于中国人民。但是这并不意味着我们就不应该指出那些根据国际标准你们应该继续前进的地方，……我们注意到了中国所有积极方面的发展。但是作为你们的朋友，作为一个希望看到中国在世界上发挥更积极作用的人，对我们来说，指出中国应该在哪些方面做出合适的改进是非常重要的。

主持人　我个人认为，也许我们需要更多对话，而同时如果美国总是指责中国，说中国应该做这个，应该做那个，中国普通百姓会感觉不舒服。

四、自主训练

　　请在 15 分钟之内迅速阅读下面的专访，了解大意。学生可组成对子练习，互相监控对视译技巧的掌握情况、视译质量和现场表现，或以边视译边录音的形式进行个人练习。视译时要保持正常语速，译文要顺畅达意。如遇难句，可在首次视译后参照"实战练习"中难句分析与视译处理的方法进行练习，找出解决方法。

Interview of Secretary of State Colin Powell by CCTV (Excerpt 2)

Secretary: Well, we don't want to point the finger at China and say you must do it our way. We think there are international standards that would benefit China to adhere to. We believe that China should do this not because we're pointing the finger at China, but because we think it's in the interest of the Chinese people and in the interest of China to work fully into the standards of the international community. We point fingers at ourselves. America is a country that has had its problems over the years with respect to human rights. I'm a perfect example of it. As a black man 40 years ago it would have been unthinkable for me to dream about becoming Secretary of State, but here I am. So we have changed because our people have decided that if we were going to be faithful to the values we believe in then it must apply to all Americans. And we think these are international standards—these are standards that follow a higher purpose and a higher order. And we think it will benefit the Chinese people. Not that we are trying to lecture to the Chinese people. And I hope that the Chinese people will see that our occasional pushes on these various issues are not for the purpose of being critical or punishing, but for the purpose of encouraging China to move in a way that we believe will benefit China and the Chinese people.

Interviewer: Well, I think that we do need some more dialog. Maybe today's talk will help that long process.

Secretary: And with the discussions I'll be having with your leaders, we'll be talking about human rights and opportunities that we have to start up a dialog again on human rights issues between the two sides.

Interviewer: Mr. Secretary, China wishes to establish a constructive relationship of cooperation with the United States and we also attach a great deal of importance to the whole series of communiqués that have been between the United States and China which have been signed since President Nixon first visited China in the early 1970s. And, in 1998, the US government reiterated its position toward Taiwan with the "three no's". So my question is, can you explicitly tell us, has that position been changed or not?

Secretary: The position of the United States government in the Bush administration is that we believe the Taiwan Relations Act and the three communiqués that subsequently followed that act are the basis of our relationship with China and are a sound enough basis for us to move forward in a positive way.

Interviewer: Moving to some global issues, we understand that some experts and analysts are saying that the American strategy on global issues tended to become a little more rigid on some issues like the Kyoto Protocol, like anti-ballistic missiles, NMD, and others. My question is, what is the American government looking upon today's world?

Secretary: We are looking on a world as increasingly interconnected economically, politically. We are not withdrawing behind our borders and we're not becoming unilateral as some people have suggested. We remain active members of NATO, the United Nations, and the World Trade Organization. We have active alliances, we are a nation that has a Pacific presence, a European presence, so we are not withdrawing and we are not moving in the direction of unilateralism. At the same time, when issues come along such as the Kyoto Protocol, where we do not believe our adherence to such protocol or ratification of such protocol would be in the best interest of the United States, or frankly in the best interest of the world because we don't think the Kyoto Protocol is the right solution to the problem of global warming, we think we should speak out and take a position, even if it looks like we are isolating ourselves. If you believe in your position, you should state it, even though you will be criticized for going against what most other nations think. And that's one of the roles that was given to us by our political system. And because of who we are when we make these kinds of judgments, we get a lot of attention because people say America is trying to be unilateral, but that's not the case. But where our interests diverge from the interests of others, I think it is important for us to say so and try to explain our views.

The same situation applies to missile defense. It's not just missile defense. We've taken a look at the world and we realize that the world we're living in, the cold war world, is over and the large numbers of nuclear weapons that we all are pointing at each other, that large number is no longer necessary. So working with the Russians we want to reduce the number of strategic offensive weapons that exist in each of our inventories and at the same time we have noticed that there are other dangers from the countries that, for reasons of their own, have started to develop weapons of mass destruction and the missiles to deliver them. And we think it is wise to develop defenses against such systems. And so that is why we are moving forward with missiles defense, but it is constrained by this 30-year old treaty, the Anti-Ballistic Missile Treaty of 1972. So we are working with the Russians to get out of the constraints of this treaty so we can develop missile defenses that will be stabilizing and deal with these new threats.

Interviewer: But some people feel that by doing that the American, let's say the

United States, is sort of dreaming, kind of an, you know, enemy which is maybe not so imminent. And, at the same time, doing away with the 1972 agreement will have very serious consequences in the global arms control situation.

Secretary: We don't think it will. We think the 1972 Treaty was designed for another time when we were trying to stop the growth of strategic offensive weapons, but that growth has already stopped. It's now going in the other direction, and as President Putin and President Bush discussed just a week ago in Genoa, it can go even lower, the number of offensive weapons we have. But it's going lower not because of the existence of the ABM Treaty, but because they are not needed in those quantities any more. So the ABM Treaty was for another time, another set of political circumstances which no longer exist now. And we shouldn't use this treaty as an obstacle to do something sensible with respect to missile defense. I think we will be able to persuade the Russian leadership and I hope the Chinese leadership, that our missile defense programs are no threat to their nuclear deterrent forces.

Interviewer: Are you going to talk about this with the Chinese leaders?

Secretary: I'm confident the subject will come up in the course of my discussions.

Interviewer: So, Mr. Secretary, with me here I have a small gift or a small secret here. I'm not going to give it to you. That's your autobiography, *My American Journey*. It's in the Chinese version. I think it's a little bit too expensive for me. It's almost 30 *yuan*, Chinese Renminbi. In this book I read what you wrote about your experience. It seems to me that what you are trying to say is that for a military person, for a soldier, war is not the utmost, peace is. So my question here is, for you, who have been in the military for more than 30 years and as a soldier, what is the relationship between war and peace—between a soldier and peace? Could you give me some very simple ideas?

Secretary: I don't know of any sane soldier who wants to see war, because soldiers know the consequences of war, the destruction that is brought about, the lives that are lost. So the philosophy of the American Army is to be strong for the purpose of preserving peace and avoiding war. If one has to fight a war because one has no choice, then do it quickly and get it over with minimum casualties in order not to cause more destruction than is necessary. Soldiers really look for peace. Now I look for peace, not wearing a uniform, but wearing a suit. But it is the same philosophy and I am trying to use everything I learnt in the military about leadership, about management, and my experience as a soldier around the world, and my experience as a National Security Advisor, now using it to help me be Secretary of State looking for peace.

Interviewer: Has it helped to change some of your personal philosophy and the way you look on the world and life?

Secretary: No, I've always looked upon the world and life in the same way, looking for peace, looking for friends, looking for hope, trying to do everything I can as a person and everything my nation can do as a nation to help people who are still hurt in this world—people who don't have enough to eat, people who are suffering from disease, people who don't have a roof over their heads. America is one of the most generous nations on the face of the earth. America, and as I said earlier, needs no enemies. We need no enemies, we want no enemies, we want to help people. We want to help China and we want to help China take advantage of the new 21st century world of information technology, access to international markets. Trade with us, let American products come here, Chinese products come to the United States. Let's share each other's cultures and values, not for the sake of one overwhelming the other, but in an atmosphere of respect for each other. We have an understanding of the importance of the rule of law, human rights. This is a bright future that is ahead of us if people like me and your leaders and President Bush and all the other leaders are ready to take advantage of it, by cooperation and not by confrontation. So to come back to your original question, the answer is friendship, cooperation, coordination, getting along, finding areas where we have common interests and can move together, and where we have disagreements, let's discuss those disagreements and make them areas of common interest.

Interviewer: Mr. Secretary, I found out that, in this book, you first came to China almost 30 years ago, in the early 1970s. That's a long time ago. Now you have come here as Secretary of State. Do you think that you have a very good and complete picture of China? In the end, finally, eventually China has been developing so drastically and so many considerable changes during the past 20 or 30 years in China.

Secretary: There has been enormous change in the almost 30 years since I visited last. Well, I visited for the first time. I was also here in 1983. Even then one could start to see the changes but nothing like what has happened between

1983 and 2001. I congratulate the Chinese people, Chinese leadership for the energy they have shown, for their willingness to take risks, for their willingness to move into a new world and leave behind some of the processes and some of the ways of doing business that didn't work and were not serving the Chinese people. And I just look forward to that transformation continuing as your leadership grapples with the challenges of the 21st century. And you can be sure that the United States stands ready to cooperate and work with the Chinese leadership as we both move forward together.

第2单元

视译单位

基本技巧：
- 断句是保持译出语语序的关键；
- 断句的关键在于采取可行的断句方法；
- 断句的基本方法是使用类意群作为视译单位。

一、技巧讲解：视译单位——类意群

视译中要基本保持原文语序，就要有一种切实可行的断句方法。所以，合理断句成为视译的重要手段。要掌握视译的断句方法，首先需要看一看英文句子的构成。

首先是单词。句子都是由单词按照语法规律构成的。但是任何两种语言的互译都不可能是词对词的翻译，所以，完全凭单词断句是不可行的。英文和中文是两种十分不同的语言，就更难以做字对字、词对词的翻译了。在实际的视译过程中，我们是不能以单词为单位断句的，如果这样断句，连"October 25, 1945"这样一个短语也无法译成通顺的中文，因为我们必须说"1945 年 10 月 25 日"，而不会说"10 月 25 日 1945 年"。

其次是意群。意群指具有相对独立意义的词组或短语。句子可以被看作是由意群构成的，因此意群是断句常常使用的一种单位。句中关系紧密的词结合起来构成的较为完整的意义整体，有时是一个短语，有时是一个短句，这就是一个意群。有的时候，一个单独的词也可以成为一个意群。一个意群是一个意义单位，同时也是一个语言单位。如"我们的国家是一个历史悠久的国家"这句话包含两个意群，第一个是"我们的国家"，第二个是"是一个历史悠久的国家"。两个意群分别具有相对独立的意义，放在一起便成为一个完整的句子。意群是一个重要的概念，在不少情况下可以作为划分视译单位的基本依据。但是，完全依赖意群也是不行的。例如，The problem of possible genetic damage to human populations from radiation exposures, including those resulting from the fallout from testing of atomic weapons, has quite properly claimed much popular attention in recent years. （蔡基刚,2001：149）这个句子的典型笔译译文是："辐射暴露，包括原子武器试验产生的放射性散落物所造成的辐射暴露，很可能对人类造成基因损伤，这一问题近年来已经理所当然地引起人们的广泛重视。"但我们可以把英文原句断成四个意群：The problem of possible genetic damage to human populations from radiation exposures, // including those resulting from the fallout from testing of atomic weapons, // has quite properly claimed much popular attention // in recent years. 可见，按照上面意群的划分仍然很难做到既保持原文语序，又将全句译成通顺的中文。以第一个意群 The problem of possible genetic damage to human populations from radiation exposures 为例，这个意群仍然太长，不对意群中的语序进行调整，就无法使译文顺畅达意。

再次就是整句。这是笔译依赖的基本单位。在笔译中，一般要求通读原文，然后逐句译出。有的时候，为了文章的连贯，或是为了保持对原文的忠实，甚至是为了翻译的通顺或是"神似"，还需要打破原来的句子结构，重新编排译入语的句子结构。但在视译中，水平再高的译员也无法做到一目十行。有的句子很长，来回看几遍都难以做出恰当的语序调整，更不用说做视译了。所以，完全以句子为翻译单位进行视译更是行不通的。

所以，在视译中，完全凭单词、词组或意群、整句来断句都是不可行的。另外，有的学者列举了六种翻译单位，包括音位、词素、单词、词组、句子、语段（方梦之，2008：67-74）。但是，完全符合这些概念定义的六种单位也很难直接用来做视译单位。所以我们必须找到一种切实可行的、可以依赖的视译单位。从上面的分析来看，意群仍然是一个最可能在视译或同传断句中使用的单位。虽然在视译中无法严守意群的定义，但大量的视译实践和教学都表明可以采用一种类似意群却又比它更加灵活的单位，我们可以将其称为类意群，也就是说我们可以将类意群作为视译的基本单位。

类意群是构成一个较完整的内容信息的基本单位。根据视译的要求，类意群应该具备三个特征：1) 相对独立的意义概念；2) 在一目可及的范围之内；3) 能够通过连接语较灵活地与前后的视译单位结合。下面我们分别解释这三个特征。

"相对独立的意义概念"指一个具有相对独立意义的词组或短语，这也是意群的基本特征。它可以被独立翻译出来而不会产生意义上的误会或不完整。比如，May I ask you to attend the meeting? 这句话中包含了两个相对独立的概念：1) May I ask you；2) to attend the meeting。译成中文，也可以分作这样两个概念：1）"我可以请你"；2）"出席会议吗"。使用相对独立的概念是十分重要的一个要求，因为它保证了视译译文可以坚持"信"的原则。

　　"在一目可及的范围之内"是指译员可以一目扫过而尽收眼中的长度，这是不同于意群的特征。一般来说，句子中相对独立的概念不会很长，是在译员一目可及的范围内。但有的时候，一个独立的概念仍然很长，再按照意群来断句就没有办法做下去，因为一目不可及，难以迅速看完。但相对独立的概念不同于意群的相对独立意义，它有时在意义上可能不尽完整，但更灵活，需要单独处理。在这类情况下，只能再度划断。比如句子 The moment when all the people in the organization became angry and began to argue with one another as to who should take the responsibility was exactly the time when an even more serious event took place. 在这里，如果 moment 只是一个作为主语的名词，没有后面定语从句的内容，这个词就没有任何独立意义，不是意群。但是，如果不将其先行处理，则下文难以翻译。原因是后面的从句太长，其中又包含了许多修饰成分，不在译员一目可及的范围之内。所以，我们可以这样来断句：The moment // when all the people in the organization // became angry // and began to argue with one another // as to who should take the responsibility // was exactly the time // when an even more serious event took place. 然后根据这种断句来做视译："当时，// 组织的所有成员 // 都愤怒了，// 他们争执不休，// 试图辨明谁要对此负责任。// 恰恰在这个时候，// 一个更加严重的事件发生了。"

　　"在一目可及的范围之内"是重要的因素，因为它可以保证译员的视译速度。"能够通过连接语较灵活地与前后的视译单位结合"则是指在增加一个连接词之后，就可以比较顺畅地将一个句子的意思完整地表达出来。这并不是意群的特征，但只有具备这个特征，断句之后的翻译才不至于支离破碎而难以表达原文的整体意义。我们来看这个句子：Indeed, we hope to intensify work with a China that not only adjusts to the international rules developed over the last century, but also joins us and others to address the challenges of the new century. 这种句子在按类意群断句后需要加上适当的连接语，使翻译出来的句子上下连贯，听起来有整体感。我们先根据类意群断句：Indeed, // we hope to intensify work with a China // that not only adjusts to the international rules // developed over the last century, // but also joins us and others // to address the challenges of the new century. 然后根据视译原则译出："的确，// 我们希望加强与中国合作，// 希望中国不仅能够适应国际规则，// 适应过去一个世纪发展起来的国际规则，// 而且希望中国能与我们和其他国家一道，// 迎接新世纪的挑战。"我们在视译中加上了"希望"、"适应"、"希望"等词，使整个句子完整通顺。通过连接语灵活地与前后视译单位结合，可以帮助译员坚持"顺"的翻译原则。

视译单位类意群的三条性质缺一不可。具有"相对独立的意义概念"可以从大处保持原文语序，给断句提供极大的方便，使译文口语化，易译易懂；每个类意群均"在一目可及的范围之内"，使译员在一个单位内进行迅速的语序调整成为可能，不致于使译文支离破碎；能"较灵活地与前后的视译单位结合"，主要是让一个较完整的内容信息能够流畅地得以传达，同时也给增益留有充分的余地。

以类意群为视译单位是训练断句的基础和译员的基本功。它近似意群，但又比意群灵活；基于词组，但又不拘泥于词组。使用类意群断句，目的是在保证"信"和"顺"的同时，也保证视译的速度，使译入语更好地保持译出语的语序。下面我们举几个例子，说明类意群是怎样被用来断句的。

例 1： The General Assembly recognized the importance of international cooperation in devising measures effectively to prevent their (terrorist acts) occurrence and of studying their underlying causes with a view to finding just and peaceful solutions as quickly as possible.

译文 1： 联合国大会认识到在为防止国际恐怖主义行为的发生制定有效措施时开展国际合作是重要的，也认识到研究发生国际恐怖主义行为的根本原因，以便尽快找出公正、和平的解决方法也是重要的。

【讲解】 可以看出，译文 1 对原语序进行了很大的调整。在视译中这样做是不可行的。即便是在笔译中，这个句子也显得太长，读起来不舒服。我们可以按照类意群的基本原则断句，把这个句子分为八个视译单位：

1) The General Assembly recognized

2) the importance of

3) international cooperation

4) in devising measures effectively

5) to prevent their (terrorist acts) occurrence

6) and of studying their underlying causes

7) with a view to finding just and peaceful solutions

8) as quickly as possible.

以上每个视译单位均是相对独立的概念，长度都在一目可及的范围之内。下面是我们使用视译单位将句子断开之后再逐个单位进行翻译的情景：

28

类意群	译　文
The General Assembly recognized	联合国大会认识到
the importance of	重要性
international cooperation	国际合作
in devising measures effectively	制定有效的措施
to prevent their (terrorist acts) occurrence	防止国际恐怖主义行为的发生
and of studying their underlying causes	研究其根本原因的重要性
with a view to finding just and peaceful solutions	为了找出公正、和平的解决方法
as quickly as possible.	越快越好。

每一个视译单位表达了一个意思，但是表格右半部分的对应译文还并不能连成一个有意义的句子，所以我们可以比较简单地使用一些连接语将这些视译单位连接起来：

类意群	译　文
The General Assembly recognized	联合国大会认识到，
the importance of	重要的是
international cooperation	要进行国际合作，
in devising measures effectively	制定有效的措施，
to prevent their (terrorist acts) occurrence	以防止国际恐怖主义行为的发生；
and of studying their underlying causes	同样重要的是要研究其根本原因，
with a view to finding just and peaceful solutions	以便找出公正、和平的解决方法，
as quickly as possible.	越快越好。

对应译文中加入了划底线部分的连接成分，就译出了以下这个完整的句子：

译文 2：联合国大会认识到，重要的是要进行国际合作，制定有效的措施，以防止国际恐怖主义行为的发生；同样重要的是要研究其根本原因，以便找出公正、和平的解决方法，越快越好。

例 2：　The moment when the United States took its place as a leader and a permanent actor on the stage of international politics—at the end of the Second World War—coincided with the dawn of the nuclear age.

译文1： 第二次世界大战结束之际美国开始作为领导者和长期活跃的角色出现在国际政治的舞台上，而此时恰恰也是核时代的开始。

【讲解】 此句可以分为六个类意群：

1) The moment

2) when the United States took its place

3) as a leader and a permanent actor

4) on the stage of international politics—

5) at the end of the Second World War—

6) coincided with the dawn of the nuclear age.

由于这个句子包含较多的修饰、插入成分，笔译时一般会对语序做较大的调整。上面的译文正是这样做的，如把"第二次世界大战结束之际"置于句子的开头等。在视译中，若能较好地把握类意群，按照基本原则划定视译单位进行断句，仍然可以在忠实于原文的前提下，基本上依照原文语序，把句子译得通顺易懂。

类意群	译文
The moment	当时
when the United States took its place	美国开始作为
as a leader and a permanent actor	领导者和长期活跃的角色
on the stage of international politics—	在国际政治的舞台上
at the end of the Second World War—	第二次世界大战结束之际
coincided with the dawn of the nuclear age.	恰逢核时代的开始

同样，我们通过加入一些连接语将这些视译单位连接起来：

类意群	译文
The moment	当时
when the United States took its place	美国开始作为
as a leader and a permanent actor	领导者和长期活跃的角色
on the stage of international politics—	出现在国际政治的舞台上，
at the end of the Second World War—	那正是第二次世界大战结束之际，
coincided with the dawn of the nuclear age.	恰恰也是核时代的开始。

这样我们可以按照视译单位依次译出，就得到了下面这样的句子：

译文 2：当时美国开始作为领导者和长期活跃的角色出现在国际政治的舞台上，那正是第二次世界大战结束之际，恰恰也是核时代的开始。

以上两例说明用类意群作视译单位，再使用恰当的连接语，便可以使译入语基本保持译出语的语序。

二、语段视译

1 词汇与表达

在进行语段视译前，请先预习以下词汇与表达。

Communications Department	交通处
station	驻扎
billet	安顿
partisan school	党校
radio operator	无线电报务员
unleavened	不发酵的
whole-wheat bread	保麸馒头，全麦馒头
millet	小米
famish	挨饿
nonchalant	冷淡的
bill	帽舌
flap	（帽边等）垂下
provoke	激起，引起，惹
embolden	使有胆量，使（更）勇敢

2 视译语段

请在 3 分钟之内迅速阅读下面的语段，了解大意，然后结合所学要点进行视译练习。视译时要保持正常语速，译文要顺畅达意。

After I talked for a few minutes with Chou Enlai, and explained who I was, he arranged for me to spend the night in Pai Chia Ping, and asked me to come next morning to his headquarters, in a nearby village. I sat down to dinner with a section of the Communications Department, which was stationed here, and I met a dozen young men who were billeted in Pai Chia Ping. Some of them were teachers in the partisan school, one was a radio operator, and some were officers of the Red Army. Our meal consisted of boiled chicken, unleavened whole-wheat bread, cabbages, millet, and potatoes, of which I ate heartedly. But, as usual, there was nothing to drink but hot water and I could not touch it. I am famished with thirst. The food was served—delivered is the word—by two nonchalant young lads wearing uniforms several sizes too large for them, and peaked Red Caps with long bills that kept flapping down over their eyes. They looked at me sourly at first, but after a few minutes I managed to provoke a friendly grin from one of them. Emboldened by this success, I called to him as he went past. (From Edgar Snow, *Red Star over China*)

原译文：我和周恩来谈了几分钟，向他说明了我的身份之后，他就替我安排在百家坪过夜，叫我在第二天早晨到他设在附近的一个村庄里的司令部去。我坐下来和驻扎在这里的交通处的一部分人一起吃饭，见到了十几个宿在百家坪的青年。他们有些是游击队学校里的教员，一个是无线电报务员，有几个是红军军官。我们吃的有炖鸡、不发酵的保麸馒头、白菜、小米和我放量大吃的马铃薯。可是像平常一样，除了热开水之外，没有别的喝的，而开水又烫得不能进口。因此我口渴得要命。饭是由两个态度冷淡的孩子伺候的，确切地说是他们端来的。他们穿着大几号的制服，戴着红军八角帽，帽舌很长，不断掉下来遮住他们的眼睛。他们最初不高兴地看着我，可是在几分钟后，我设法惹起了其中一个孩子友善地微笑。这使我的胆子大了一些，他从我身边走过时，我就招呼他。（摘自董乐山译《西行漫记》）

3 视译译文

	断 句	译 文
1	After I talked for a few minutes with Chou Enlai,	我和周恩来谈了几分钟，
2	and explained who I was,	告诉他我是谁。
3	he arranged for me to spend the night in Pai Chia Ping,	他安排我在百家坪过夜，

（待续）

（续上表）

	断　句	译　文
4	and asked me to come next morning to his headquarters,	并让我第二天早晨到他的司令部去，
5	in a nearby village.	司令部就在附近的村庄里。
6	I sat down to dinner	我坐下来吃饭，
7	with a section of the Communications Department,	一起吃饭的还有交通处的人。
8	which was stationed here,	他们驻扎在这里。
9	and I met a dozen young men	我见到了十几个年轻人，
10	who were billeted in Pai Chia Ping.	他们驻扎在百家坪。
11	Some of them were teachers in the partisan school,	有几个是党校的教员，
12	one was a radio operator,	一个是报务员，
13	and some were officers of the Red Army.	还有几个是红军军官。
14	Our meal consisted of boiled chicken,	我们吃的是炖鸡，
15	unleavened whole-wheat bread,	未发酵的全麦馒头，
16	cabbages, millet, and potatoes,	白菜，小米，还有马铃薯。
17	of which I ate heartedly.	我吃得很开心。
18	But, as usual, there was nothing to drink	但像往常一样，没有喝的东西，
19	but hot water	只有热开水。
20	and I could not touch it.	我喝不下去，
21	I am famished with thirst.	渴得难受。
22	The food was served—	伺候吃饭的，
23	delivered is the word—	确切地说应该是端饭的，
24	by two nonchalant young lads	是两个态度冷淡的小兵，
25	wearing uniforms several sizes too large for them,	他们穿的军装大好几号，

（待续）

（续上表）

	断　句	译　文
26	and peaked Red Caps with long bills	戴着红军八角帽，帽沿太长
27	that kept flapping down over their eyes.	老拉下来遮住了眼皮。
28	They looked at me sourly at first,	他们起初满怀敌意地看着我，
29	but after a few minutes	但几分钟后，
30	I managed to provoke a friendly grin from one of them.	我想法逗得其中一个友善地笑了笑。
31	Emboldened by this success,	于是我胆子大了一些，
32	I called to him as he went past.	他走过我身旁时就向他打招呼。

4　视译点评

1. 原文第一句：After I talked for a few minutes with Chou Enlai, // and explained who I was, // he arranged for me to spend the night in Pai Chia Ping, // and asked me to come next morning to his headquarters, // in a nearby village.

此句是主从句结构，其中主句和从句中又都有并列成分。视译时，在一目可及的范围内，以类意群为基础把主从句结构按原语序分成五个视译单位，每个单位都具有相对独立的意思，并能够比较灵活地与前后的单位连接，使译语听起来逻辑清楚，连接自然，符合汉语的表达习惯。例如，句子开头的从句 After I talked for a few minutes with Chou Enlai，视译时删减了 after，被译成一个独立的分句"我和周恩来谈了几分钟"，这样更易于与后面的视译单位连接顺畅，符合汉语的"意合"规则，逻辑清楚。再如本句结尾的介词词组 in a nearby village 断句为一个独立的视译单位，灵活地根据原文上下文增添了主语"司令部"，然后译成一个独立的分句："司令部就在附近的村庄里。"

2. 原文第二句：I sat down to dinner // with a section of the Communications Department, // which was stationed here, // and I met a dozen young men // who were billeted in Pai Chia Ping.

此句是并列句，两个并列主句均带有非限定性或限定性定语从句。视译时，按原语序中的类意群将此句分成五个具有相对独立的概念的视译单位。在原句中本身就是主句或从句的视译单位，能够被方便地译成独立的分句，相互顺畅连接。但是原句中的第二个视译单位 with a section of the

Communications Department 是一个介词词组，这个词组如果单独翻译成"和交通处的人一起（吃饭）"的话，让人感觉句子不完整，所以视译时，可以通过增添主语"一起吃饭的"和谓语"还有"将它译成一个分句："一起吃饭的还有交通处的人。"

3. 原文第三句：The food was served— // delivered is the word— // by two nonchalant young lads // wearing uniforms several sizes too large for them, // and peaked Red Caps with long bills // that kept flapping down over their eyes.

这是一个难处理的句子，我们先来分析一下这个句子。此句中 The food was served 是被动式主句，很简短，后面跟一个插入成分 delivered is the word，但是 by 后面的部分很长，带有现在分词 wearing 引导的定语修饰成分，其宾语 uniforms 和 peaked Red Caps with long bills 又都分别带有后置定语短语 several sizes too large for them 和定语从句 that kept flapping down over their eyes。

视译时，原句的第一个类意群 The food was served 被译成汉语的名词词组"伺候吃饭的"，这种"的"字结构可以灵活地与后面的视译单位 by two nonchalant young lads 连接，再把介词 by 译成谓语"是"，这两个视译单位就成了一个句子："伺候吃饭的，确切地说应该是端饭的，是两个态度冷淡的小兵。"原句的第二个视译单位 delivered is the word 具有相对独立的意义，可译为一句话："确切地说应该是端饭的。"这样一个分句与前面的视译单位 The food was served（伺候吃饭的）和后面的视译单位 by two nonchalant young lads（是两个态度冷淡的小兵）可以比较自然地连接起来，译文听起来很通顺。原句的后面几个类意群 wearing uniforms several sizes too large for them，peaked Red Caps with long bills 和 that kept flapping down over their eyes 也通过为定语成分 wearing… 增加"他们"，把 wearing 的宾语 peaked Red Caps with long bills 这一名词词组译成独立短语"帽沿太长"等方法译成几个较短的分句，即："他们穿的军装大好几号，戴着红军八角帽，帽沿太长，耷拉下来遮住了眼皮。"

从这个句子可以看出，由于中文的短句很好使用，中文的意合特色又可以使前后意义通过断句的逻辑顺序清楚地表达出来，所以，在视译中，要充分使用中文的短句。在可能的情况下，将英文中的从句和长短语尽量以中文短句的形式翻译出来。这样做不但可以便利译员的翻译，还可以使听众听起来也更清楚和舒服。

三、实战练习

1 词汇与表达

请先熟悉以下词汇与表达，并适当地运用在视译中。

SAIS (School of Advanced International Studies)	（美国约翰·霍普金斯大学）高等国际研究院
dislocation	动荡
deleverage	去杠杆化
liquidity provision	流动资金供给
public balance sheet	公共资产负债表
policy rate	政策利率
reserve requirement	准备金要求
one-off	一次性的
pro-cyclical	顺景气循环
debt sustainability	债务可持续性
solvency	清偿能力
liquidity squeeze	流动性紧缩
pegged exchange rate	固定汇率
short-term liquidity facility	短期流动贷款工具，缩写为 SLF
ex post	事后的
swap line	货币互换协议

2 实战课文

请在 15 分钟之内迅速阅读下面的讲话，了解大意。视译时要保持正常语速，译文要顺畅达意。

Toward a Post-Crisis World Economy (Excerpt 1)
John Lipsky First Deputy Managing Director of International Monetary Fund
SAIS, John Hopkins University
November 17, 2008

Introduction

I am grateful to SAIS for the opportunity to address this distinguished audience on such a challenging, critical and timely topic. Over the past few weeks, a consensus has emerged regarding the seriousness of the near-term threats to the global economy, with the advanced economies already close in or near recession. **At the same time, there is no sign yet of a fundamental reversal of the financial market dislocation and deleveraging that represents both a sign of and a contributor to the still unfolding global economic strains.**（句 1）To the contrary, the virulent combination of financial stress and shrinking advanced economy demand is impacting emerging economies, with potentially significant negative effect.

The G-20 Summit on Financial Markets and the World Economy that took place here in Washington last weekend was both an unprecedented response to the daunting near-term challenges, and an explicit symbol of the evolving world economic order. The Summit confirmed that the most senior political authorities recognize the urgent need to address credibly the underlying causes of the current crisis, even while acting aggressively to reverse its near-term impact. **It is notable that the underlying premise of the Summit—as captured explicitly in the Communiqué—was that success in these efforts will only be possible through international cooperation, and that the scope of that cooperation will have to be broader—both in terms of the policies and the countries involved—than has been the case in the past.**（句 2）

In several important ways, therefore, the coming months will represent both a test and a turning point for the global economy, for international financial markets and for global governance. While the efforts agreed last weekend may fall short of something that could be given as grandiose a label as a new international financial architecture, nonetheless their scope and importance shouldn't be underestimated. **The Working Groups that are being formed as a result of the Summit, with a specific deadline for reaching conclusions, together with the Summit participants' explicit commitment to reconvene by next year's second quarter, are intended to impart momentum to the reform efforts.**（句 3）

The Summit also reflected an underlying consensus about the intended nature of the future global system. In particular, the Summit Communiqué states that proposed reforms "will only be successful if grounded in a commitment to free market principles, including the rule of law, respect for private property, open trade and investment, competitive markets and efficient, effectively regulated financial systems". **Moreover, the level of consensus and political commitment regarding**

the need to act exhibited at the Summit justify hope and even optimism that the opportunity that is being created by the current crisis for implementing significant structural improvements in the global economy, and in international financial markets, will not be missed. （句 4）Finally, the G-20 leaders pledged to initiate a new push to reach agreement on the Doha Round of multilateral trade negotiations before the end of this year, ignoring the widespread skepticism that a deal would or could be reached in the foreseeable future.

The Deepening Challenges

That government leaders and finance ministers from economies representing about 85% of global GDP could agree to assemble in Washington on only a few weeks' advance notice has no precedent. （句 5 ）In fact, White House sources indicated that they could find no previous case of so many leaders meeting there for a working session. The motivation of the attendees was clear: economic prospects have deteriorated notably during the past two months, and the global financial crisis has taken a sharp turn for the worse. In the advanced economies, consumer and business confidence have dropped to levels not seen in decades, and activity is slowing sharply or even contracting in many economies. Most worrisome has been the sudden—and severe—toll that the crisis has begun to take on emerging economies, where in many cases deleveraging and asset sales have led to capital flow reversals, a sharp widening of spreads on sovereign and corporate debt, and abrupt currency depreciations.

As a result, we now project that the world economy will grow by only 2.25% in 2009. This reflects a reduction of three-quarters of a percentage point from the October *World Economic Outlook* forecast that was finalized only weeks ago. In the new forecast, the advanced economies are expected to contract by 0.25% on an annual basis in 2009. This would mark the first annual contraction in the postwar period for these countries as a group.

Growth prospects for emerging economies also have been undermined by the latest developments. Still, the new IMF forecast anticipates that activity in emerging economies will expand by 5% in 2009, although with considerable regional variation. Thus, it is expected that emerging economies will account for 100% of global growth next year. It is also true, however, that even this newly reduced forecast can't be taken for granted, as the downside risks to growth, even for the emerging economies, remain significant. **Thus, actions to be taken by emerging economy authorities to bolster confidence in the appropriateness of their policies, as well as efforts by the international community to provide necessary financial support in this moment of crisis, will be critical in order to attain the hoped-for revival of global growth by 2010.**（句 6）

In the remainder of my presentation, I will review the undertakings of last weekend's Summit from the point of view of my IMF colleagues and myself regarding the near-term actions that we view as crucial to restoring growth and financial sector soundness, as well as those measures that we consider to be essential for improving the medium-term performance of the global financial system and for reducing the risk of future crises.（句 7）Before concluding, I will summarize the role of the IMF envisioned by the Summit Communiqué, and briefly discuss what the IMF is doing to help our members through the crisis.

Sustaining Global Demand

Given the speed with which growth prospects have deteriorated, it is not surprising that there was broad agreement at last weekend's Summit that new monetary and fiscal policy initiatives will be needed to support global demand. For sure, recent policy actions in advanced countries to use the public balance sheet to recapitalize financial institutions, to provide comprehensive government guarantees, and to extend liquidity provision were important and necessary steps. Their swift and effective implementation will be crucial to restoring confidence. However, these measures will not be sufficient by themselves to halt the slide in global output.

With inflation receding, many advanced and emerging economies can further ease monetary policy.

—Many central banks already have taken decisive action in this regard, including aggressive Fed action to reduce policy rates, the recent sizeable cut in interest rates by the Bank of England, and a clear shift toward policy easing by the European Central Bank and other advanced economies, including Australia and Switzerland among others. In many key emerging economies, central banks also have cut interest rates and eased reserve requirements.

Generally speaking, however, monetary easing is likely to be less effective at stimulating demand while financial conditions remain disrupted. More specifically, survey-based data show that banks have tightened credit standards significantly since the onset of the crisis last year. The impact of such a tightening of lending standards on credit aggregates typically occurs only with a lag. Thus, the negative effects of the current tightening of credit standards likely will be felt for some time to come. Put another way, the deleveraging process is likely to shift from widening risk spreads to actual reduced volumes of credit. In emerging economies that have relied on capital inflows to finance an expansion of bank credit, the effectiveness of monetary policy may also be limited.

It is appropriate, therefore, that fiscal expansion will play a central role in helping to sustain domestic demand. This view was endorsed explicitly by the Summit Communiqué.

—Several countries, including the United States, China and various European economies, already have announced fiscal stimulus plans. In an environment of sagging confidence, the impact of various fiscal measures—both in terms of their timing and their effectiveness at boosting output—requires careful consideration. Any fiscal stimulus should be timely in its impact, as the need to cushion demand is immediate. As a result, innovative measures could be helpful. For example, measures to support low-income households would be particularly helpful in boosting demand, and would be targeted at those most in need. Also, one-off transfers to states in federal systems such as the United States could be helpful in preventing pro-cyclical fiscal tightening at the state level.

More broadly, our research suggests that global fiscal stimulus on the order of 2% of GDP is justified. Moreover, fiscal policy action would be more effective if it were implemented in key trading partner countries more or less simultaneously. That said, fiscal action may not be advisable in countries with greater vulnerabilities, or those where debt sustainability is a major concern. Thus, countries with the strongest fiscal policy frameworks, those best able to finance new fiscal efforts, and those with clearly sustainable debt positions should take the lead.

Preventing a Liquidity Shock from Becoming a Solvency Crisis

While macroeconomic policies are crucial to sustaining demand, emerging economies face an important challenge in ensuring that the unfolding liquidity squeeze does not transform itself into a solvency crisis. Deleveraging is beginning to have an increasingly striking impact on these economies following a period of exceptional growth. Countries with significant vulnerabilities are being hit hard, but even some countries with strong fundamentals are being affected. In particular, some countries with liquid domestic financial markets that previously received large capital inflows have experienced abrupt reversals of external financing flows. Past experience indicates that dealing with these challenges will require efforts by both advanced and emerging economies. For the affected emerging economies, the focus must be dealing with immediate liquidity and exchange rate pressures created by the capital flow reversals. So far, measures taken by policymakers in emerging economies to improve liquidity appear to be having only a limited impact in restoring confidence, even in countries with large reserve buffers.

In emerging economies with flexible exchange rate regimes, exchange rate adjustment can help to absorb the pressures arising from capital outflows. Of course, countries with pegged exchange rates face a different set of challenges, as they lack this degree of policy freedom.

At the same time, emerging economies with large reserve buffers may provide foreign currency liquidity as needed by their own economies.

Regardless, emerging economies likely will remain under pressure for some time from global financial deleveraging, even under the most favorable plausible scenarios. As a result, liquidity provision will continue to be critical to emerging economies' ability to weather this storm.

The IMF Executive Board recently approved a short-term liquidity facility (SLF) designed to provide substantial liquidity support to emerging countries with good policies and good track records that are experiencing liquidity shortages because of deteriorating external market conditions. (句 8)　This innovative facility is designed to be accessible on very short notice, and carries no ex post conditionality. If it proves useful, this facility will become a regular part of the Fund's policy toolkit. The Federal Reserve also established swap lines with the central banks of Brazil, Republic of Korea, Mexico, and Singapore, in an attempt to ease current dollar funding shortages. These lines will remain open until April 2009.

Regional initiatives also can be helpful. Efforts aimed at a regional pooling of international reserves, such as in Asia through bilateral swaps, provide a further backup for individual countries facing significant external funding pressures. These arrangements could be broadened, for example by linking them with use of the new SLF.

3 难句分析与视译处理

句1： At the same time, there is no sign yet of a fundamental reversal of the financial market dislocation and deleveraging that represents both a sign of and a contributor to the still unfolding global economic strains.

笔译译文： 同时，尚未有迹象表明金融市场动荡和去杠杆化的局面已发生根本性转变。其中去杠杆化是不断显现的全球经济困境的一种表象，同时也是其成因。

视译译文：

按照类意群断句[1]	视译译文[2]
At the same time,	同时，
there is no sign yet	仍然没有迹象表明
of a fundamental reversal	发生了任何根本性的转变。
of the financial market dislocation	金融市场仍然动荡，
and deleveraging	去杠杆化还在继续，
that represents both a sign of	而后者既反映了
and a contributor to	同时也造成了
the still unfolding global economic strains.	不断显现的全球经济困境。

句2： It is notable that the underlying premise of the Summit—as captured explicitly in the Communiqué—was that success in these efforts will only be possible through international cooperation, and that the scope of that cooperation will have to be broader—both in terms of the policies and the countries involved—than has been the case in the past.

笔译译文： 值得注意的是，此次峰会的重要前提是只有通过国际合作，这些努力才能奏效，同时合作的范围无论在政策上还是在参与国家方面都应比此前更为宽泛。本次峰会的公报已经明确地体现了这一前提。

---

1 以下均简称为"断句"。

2 以下均简称为"译文"。

视译译文：

断　句	译　文
It is notable that	值得注意的是，
the underlying premise of the Summit—	此次峰会的重要前提
as captured explicitly in the Communiqué—	已经在峰会公报里得以阐明，
was that	那就是
success in these efforts will only be possible	这些努力要取得成功，
through international cooperation,	就必须开展国际合作，
and that the scope of that cooperation	合作的范围
will have to be broader—	应该更为宽泛，
both in terms of the policies	无论在政策上
and the countries involved—	还是在参与国家方面
than has been the case in the past.	都应超过此前的规模。

句 3： The Working Groups that are being formed as a result of the Summit, with a specific deadline for reaching conclusions, together with the Summit participants' explicit commitment to reconvene by next year's second quarter, are intended to impart momentum to the reform efforts.

笔译译文： 为了大力推动改革，峰会决定成立工作组，并具体设定了工作组达成共识的期限，同时与会国还明确承诺于明年第二季度前再次聚首。

视译译文：

断　句	译　文
The Working Groups that are being formed	工作组正在组建，
as a result of the Summit,	这是峰会取得的成果，
with a specific deadline for reaching conclusions,	峰会还设定了工作组达成共识的期限。
together with the Summit participants' explicit commitment	此外，与会国还明确承诺，
to reconvene by next year's second quarter,	再次开会时间为明年第二季度之前。
are intended to impart momentum to the reform efforts.	这些举措都是为了大力推动改革。

句4：   Moreover, the level of consensus and political commitment regarding the need to act exhibited at the Summit justify hope and even optimism that the opportunity that is being created by the current crisis for implementing significant structural improvements in the global economy, and in international financial markets, will not be missed.

笔译译文：   此外，峰会上各国对采取行动的必要性的认同程度之高，政治意愿之强，都使我们有理由满怀希望，甚至可以乐观地认为当前的金融危机为全球经济以及国际金融市场重大结构性变革创造了机遇，我们绝不会错失良机。

视译译文：

断　句	译　文
Moreover,	此外，
the level of consensus and political commitment	还表现出高度的共识和政治意愿，
regarding the need to act	认为有必要采取行动，
exhibited at the Summit	这一点在峰会上明确地反映出来。
justify hope and even optimism	这使我们有理由希望、甚至可以乐观地认为
that the opportunity that is being created	机会就要来临，
by the current crisis	而创造机遇的正是当前的危机。
for implementing significant structural improvements	它促使我们实施重大的结构性改革，
in the global economy, and in international financial markets,	改善世界经济和国际金融市场。
will not be missed.	我们绝不会错失良机。

句5：   That government leaders and finance ministers from economies representing about 85% of global GDP could agree to assemble in Washington on only a few weeks' advance notice has no precedent.

笔译译文：   来自占全球国民生产总值 85% 的各个经济体的政府领导人与财政部长仅在几星期前才得到通知，在此情况下能够同意聚首华盛顿，堪称史无前例。

视译译文：

断　句	译　文
That government leaders and finance ministers	这些政府领导人与财政部长，
from economies representing about 85% of global GDP	来自占全球国民生产总值 85% 的各个经济体，
could agree to assemble in Washington	他们能够同意聚首华盛顿，
on only a few weeks' advance notice	尽管几个星期前才得到通知，
has no precedent.	这堪称史无前例。

句 6：　Thus, actions to be taken by emerging economy authorities to bolster confidence in the appropriateness of their policies, as well as efforts by the international community to provide necessary financial support in this moment of crisis, will be critical in order to attain the hoped-for revival of global growth by 2010.

笔译译文：　因此，各新兴经济体为增强人们对于政府政策的合理性的信心采取何种行动，国际社会在此危机时刻给予何种必要的金融支持，对于到 2010 年实现普遍企盼的全球经济复苏显得尤为重要。

视译译文：

断　句	译　文
Thus, actions to be taken	因此，将要采取的行动，
by emerging economy authorities	也就是新兴经济体的行动，
to bolster confidence in the appropriateness of their policies,	是为了加强人们对其政策合理性的信心。
as well as efforts by the international community	国际社会也将做出努力，
to provide necessary financial support	提供必要的金融支持，
in this moment of crisis,	应对这一危机时刻。
will be critical	这些措施举足轻重，
in order to attain the hoped-for revival of global growth	关系到大家企盼的全球经济复苏
by 2010.	到 2010 年是否能够实现。

句 7： In the remainder of my presentation, I will review the undertakings of last weekend's Summit from the point of view of my IMF colleagues and myself regarding the near-term actions that we view as crucial to restoring growth and financial sector soundness, as well as those measures that we consider to be essential for improving the medium-term performance of the global financial system and for reducing the risk of future crises.

笔译译文： 在下面的讲话中，我将以我个人以及诸位国际货币基金组织同僚的角度谈谈上周末峰会的各项承诺，其中既包括我们视为对恢复经济增长和金融健康至关重要的近期行动，也包括我们认为对改善全球金融体系的中期表现以及对减少未来危机风险必不可少的那些措施。

视译译文：

断　句	译　文
In the remainder of my presentation,	在下面的讲话中，
I will review the undertakings of last weekend's Summit	我要谈谈上周末峰会的各项承诺，
from the point of view of my IMF colleagues and myself	这是国际货币基金组织的诸位同僚以及我本人的观点。
regarding the near-term actions	这些承诺包括近期行动，
that we view as crucial	我们认为这些行动非常重要，
to restoring growth and financial sector soundness,	关系到能否恢复经济增长和金融系统的健康。
as well as those measures	另外还包括一些举措，
that we consider to be essential	我们认为也十分关键，
for improving the medium-term performance	它们将决定能否改善中期表现，
of the global financial system	这是就全球金融体系而言，
and for reducing the risk of future crises.	它们还关系到能否降低未来危机的风险。

句 8： The IMF Executive Board recently approved a short-term liquidity facility (SLF) designed to provide substantial liquidity support to emerging countries with good policies and good track records that are experiencing liquidity shortages because of deteriorating external market conditions.

笔译译文：　国际货币基金组织执行委员会最近批准了一种"短期流动贷款工具"（SLF），旨在为政策得力、记录良好的新兴经济体提供充足的流动资金支持，这些经济体正因外部市场环境不断恶化而面临流动资金短缺的问题。

视译译文：

断　句	译　文
The IMF Executive Board	国际货币基金组织执行委员会
recently approved a short-term liquidity facility (SLF)	最近批准了一种"短期流动贷款工具"（SLF），
designed to provide substantial liquidity support	旨在提供充足的流动资金支持，
to emerging countries	帮助一些新兴经济体，
with good policies and good track records	它们政策得力、记录良好，
that are experiencing liquidity shortages	但却面临流动资金短缺问题，
because of deteriorating external market conditions.	这一问题是不断恶化外部市场环境造成的。

4 参考译文

后危机时代世界经济（节选 1）

国际货币基金组织第一副总裁　约翰·利普斯基
约翰·霍普金斯大学高等国际研究院
2008 年 11 月 17 日

引言

　　感谢高等国际研究院（SAIS）给予我这个机会，为在座的尊敬的听众就这样一个极具挑战，至关重要，又亟待解决的问题发表演讲。随着当前众多发达经济体已陷入衰退，或濒临衰退边缘，过去的几周内，各国已一致认识到近期全球经济面临的威胁已是何等严重。同时，尚未有迹象表明金融市场动荡和去杠杆化的局面已发生根本性转变。其中去杠杆化是不断加剧的全球经济困境的一种表象，同时也是其成因。与此相反，金融压力与发达经济体锐减的需求相互交织，对新兴经济体产生着巨大影响，并伴随有潜在的巨大负面影响。

上周末 20 国集团金融市场和世界经济峰会在华盛顿召开。这次峰会既是各国对当前的巨大挑战所作出的空前回应，也是世界经济秩序不断演变的有力证明。这次峰会证明各国最高政治领导层意识到在不遗余力地消除危机近期影响的同时，还必须立即着手认真处理造成当前危机的根本原因。值得注意的是，此次峰会的重要前提是只有通过国际合作，这些努力才能奏效，同时合作的范围无论在政策上还是在参与国家方面都应比此前更为宽泛。本次峰会的公报已经明确地体现了这一前提。

因此，就许多重要方面而言，未来的几个月对于全球经济、国际金融市场以及全球治理都既是一次考验，又是一个转折点。尽管上周末各国一致认同的努力可能并不足以被称作一种崭新的国际金融结构，但其涉及范围之广、意义之大却绝不容低估。为了大力推动改革，峰会决定成立工作组，并具体设定了工作组达成共识的期限，同时与会国还明确承诺于明年第二季度前再次聚首。

峰会还反映出各国从根本上形成了对于未来全球体系既定本质的共识。峰会公报中特别强调：各国提出的改革"只有建立在遵循自由市场原则的基础之上才能获得成功。这些原则包括法治、尊重私有财产、开放贸易及投资、市场竞争以及高效且监管到位的金融系统"。此外，峰会上各国对采取行动的必要性认同程度之高，政治意愿之强，都使我们有理由满怀希望，甚至可以乐观地认为当前的金融危机为全球经济以及国际金融市场重大结构性变革创造了机遇，我们绝不会错失良机。

最后，20 国集团领导人承诺推动新一轮多哈多边贸易谈判，力争在今年内达成共识，尽管人们普遍对谈判能否在可预见的未来达成协议怀有质疑。

日益深化的挑战

来自占全球国民生产总值 85% 的各个经济体的政府领导人与财政部长仅在几星期前才得到通知，在此情况下能够同意聚首华盛顿，堪称史无前例。实际上，白宫消息源表示众多领导人共同参加一个工作会议尚属首次。然而各与会国的目的显而易见：在过去两个月中，全球经济前景明显恶化，并且全球金融危机已经急转直下，形势加剧恶化。在各发达经济体中，消费者与企业信心都已跌至几十年来的最低水平，商业活动大幅放缓，在一些国家甚至出现了经济萎缩。而最令人堪忧的是这次经济危机对新兴经济体造成了突如其来的严重损失。在这些国家中，去杠杆化与资产抛售已经导致资金流逆转、国家及企业债务激增以及货币大幅贬值。

因此，我们目前预计 2009 年世界经济增长率仅为 2.25%。仅数周之隔，这一数字比《世界经济展望》十月刊中公布的预测又降低了 0.75 个百分点。最新的预测显示，2009 年发达经济体的年衰退速度将是 0.25 个百分点。这标志着这些国家在战后的首次集体年度衰退。

新兴经济体的增长前景同样因近期的经济形势而受挫。但据国际货币基金组织的最新预测，尽管地区间存在着巨大差异，新兴经济体 2009 年的活动将有 5% 的增长。由此不难预见，明年的全球增长将全部来源于新兴经济体。但是，目前威胁经济增长的不利因素即便对于新兴经济体而言仍十分巨大。实际上，这一进一步调低的预测仍不能一锤定音。因此，各新兴经济体为增强人们对于政府政策的合理性的信心采取何种行动，国际社会在此危机时刻给予何种必要的金融支持，对于到 2010 年实现普遍企盼的全球经济复苏显得尤为重要。

在下面的讲话中，我将以我个人以及诸位国际货币基金组织同僚的角度谈谈上周末峰会的各项承诺，其中既包括我们视为对恢复经济增长和金融健康至关重要的近期行动，也包括我们认为对改善全球金融体系的中期表现以及对减少未来危机风险必不可少的那些措施。最后，我将概述峰会公报为国际货币基金组织设计的角色，并简单介绍本组织为协助成员国战胜危机所展开的行动。

维持全球需求

由于增长形势急剧恶化，上周末的峰会上各国一致同意出台新的货币及财政政策以保证全球需求便不足为奇了。近期发达国家纷纷采取政策行动，利用公共资产负债表为金融机构注入资金、全面提供政府担保，以及增加流动资金供给。毫无疑问，上述举措不仅重要而且十分必要。迅速有效地将这些政策落到实处对于重树信心将起到至关重要的作用。但是仅有这些措施仍不足以扭转全球生产的颓势。

随着通货膨胀得到缓解，众多发达经济体与新兴经济体都得以进一步放松其货币政策。

——多家中央银行已就此采取决定性措施，例如美联储大幅降低政策利率，英格兰银行近期大幅降息，欧洲央行与澳大利亚、瑞士等多个发达经济体明确转向宽松政策。许多主要新兴经济体的央行也纷纷降低利率，放宽准备金要求。

但是总体而言，若金融环境仍然混乱无序，货币放松也很难收到刺激需求的效果。具体地说，调查数据显示，自今年初金融危机爆发以来，各国银行已大幅提高了贷款标准。此举对于贷款总量的影响通常不会立即显现。因此，目前提高贷款标准所产生的消极影响将会在一段时间后波及大众。换言之，去杠杆化过程很可能会从扩大风险波及范围转向信贷总量减少。对于一向依赖资金流入扩大银行信贷的新兴经济体而言，货币政策恐怕只是杯水车薪。

因此，财政扩张对于维持内需将起到至关重要的作用也便顺理成章了。这一观点在峰会公报中也得到了充分认可。

——美、中等国以及众多欧洲经济体已经宣布了财政刺激方案。在信心受挫的整体环境下，各国对其各项财政措施将会产生的影响都要深思熟虑，既要斟酌政策出台的时机又要考虑其促进生产的力度。由于缓冲需求锐减的形势刻不容缓，所有财政刺激政策都应该立竿见影。因此，创新性的措施便大有裨益。例如，扶助低收入家庭的举措将有利于拉动需求，还会使最迫切需要救助的家庭受益。同理，美国等联邦制国家向各州一次性注资将可以避免在州一级出现顺景气循环财政紧缩，不失为一计良策。

我们的研究显示，全球财政刺激在国民生产总值中的比重只要不超过2%都属合理范围。此外，主要贸易伙伴国若能够几乎同时采取财政政策行动，将更为行之有效。尽管如此，对于经济相对薄弱，或是债务可持续性尚成问题的国家，财政行动并不可取。因此，财政政策框架坚实、有能力支持新的财政举措、以及债务可持续性良好的国家在此方面应当身先士卒。

防止流动性冲击演化为清偿能力危机

尽管宏观经济政策对于维持需求至关重要，新兴经济体面临着防止流动性紧缩演化为清偿能力危机的重大挑战。继一段时间的经济高速增长后，去杠杆化对于这些经济体的影响已经初露端倪，并与日俱增。经济尤为薄弱的国家自然首当其冲，即便是一些经济基础坚实的国家也未能幸免。这一问题在国内金融市场流动性强的国家尤为突出。这些国家此前获得了可观的资金流，现在却面临着外部资金骤然流出的局面。以往的经验表明，应对这些挑战需要发达经济体与新兴经济体齐心协力。就受到波及的新兴经济体而言，当务之急是处理由资金流逆转造成的流动性与汇率双重压力。目前看来，新兴经济体旨在提高流动性的政策对于重铸信心效果十分有限，即使是一些外汇储备充裕的国家也不例外。

在采用浮动汇率制的新兴经济体中，汇率调整有助于缓解资金外流带来的压力。不言而喻，实行固定汇率制的国家缺乏此类政策自由度，因而面临着一系列截然不同的挑战。

与此同时，拥有坚实外汇储备的新兴经济体有可能根据自身需求保证外汇的流动性。

尽管如此，即便是处在可以实现的最理想经济环境中，新兴经济体在未来一段时间内仍将面临来自全球金融去杠杆化的压力。因此，流动资金供应仍将是新兴经济体抵御经济风暴的重要法宝。

国际货币基金组织执行委员会最近批准了一种"短期流动性贷款工具"（SLF），旨在为政策得力、记录良好的新兴经济体提供充足的流动资金支持，这些经济体正因外部市场环境不断恶化而面临流动资金短缺的问题。这一创新举措的目的是使各国能够立刻获得紧急贷款，并且不附带任何事后贷款条件。如果此举被证明有效，将会固定为货币基金组织的一项长期政策工具。美联储也与巴西、韩国、墨西哥及新加坡等国的中央银行签署了货币互换协议，以期缓解当前美元资金短缺的局面。此协议将延续到 2009 年 4 月。

地区性措施同样可以发挥作用。各国致力于建立区域性国际储备库，进一步为面临强大外部资金压力的国家提供后盾。在亚洲，这一目标是通过双边货币互换实现的。这些措施尚有扩展的空间，例如可将其与新出台的短期流动性贷款工具挂钩。

四、自主训练

请在 15 分钟之内迅速阅读下面的讲话，了解大意。学生可组成对子练习，互相监控对视译技巧的掌握情况、视译质量和现场表现，或以边视译边录音的形式进行个人练习。视译时要保持正常语速，译文要顺畅达意。如遇难句，可在首次视译后参照"实战练习"中难句分析与视译处理的方法进行练习，找出解决方法。

Toward a Post-Crisis World Economy (Excerpt 2)

John Lipsky

November 17, 2008

Improving the Global Financial System

Looking beyond the immediate challenges, the crisis has made clear that new thinking and action are needed in at least three areas related to the global financial architecture. First, the design of financial regulation needs to be improved. Second, a better way of assessing systemic risk must be found. Third, mechanisms for more effective, coordinated actions are needed to reduce the risk of crises and to address them when they occur.

This crisis has shown the limits of the current regulatory and supervisory frameworks at both domestic and international levels. Open financial markets can provide tremendous benefits by lowering the cost of capital, but more effective regulation is needed to realize this potential. As has been demonstrated all too graphically, financial innovation and integration have increased the speed and extent to which shocks are being transmitted across asset classes and economies. However, regulation and supervision remain geared at individual financial institutions and do not adequately consider the systemic and international implications of domestic institutions' actions. Moreover, macro-prudential tools do not sufficiently take into account business and financial cycles, which has led to an excessive buildup of leverage.

The challenge, therefore, is to design new rules and institutions that reduce systemic risks, improve financial intermediation, and properly adjust the perimeter of regulation and supervision, without imposing unnecessary burdens.

—More effective capital and liquidity requirements would make financial institutions—especially those that are highly interconnected—more resilient to risk. Counter-cyclical macro-prudential rules appear to be a promising way to reduce the buildup of systemic risks. Greater use of centralized clearing houses and organized exchanges would help to improve the robustness of the financial infrastructure to counterparty failures.

—Supervisory and regulatory frameworks should be more globally coordinated to ensure that the perimeter of regulation and supervision is appropriate. The crisis has underscored the tension between globally active financial institutions and nationally bounded regulators and supervisors. The tension exists with regard to both crisis prevention and resolution and is most evident when dealing with the resolution of global banks headquartered in relatively small countries.

—More information—and also better information—would help market participants and authorities improve their assessments of systemic risks. This requires reviewing transparency, disclosure and reporting rules. Information requirements also could cover a much larger set of institutions, including insurance companies and off-balance sheet entities.

This crisis has made clear the enormous costs of not identifying risks early enough. A more effective approach to detecting risks will require close cooperation among key policymakers to bring together the scatter of international and national macro-financial information and expertise.

—The starting point for any early warning system—as it is for better regulation and supervision—must be better information on global financial and economic developments. Better risk assessment will also mean strengthening macro-financial analysis and enhancing work on early warning systems.

—Early warning and surveillance work will also require finding the right incentive balance between countries voluntarily engaging in vulnerability assessments and making assessments mandatory. In doing so, decisions will need to be made about the usefulness of models relying on "name and shame", "comply or explain", and binding commitments to act.

—The private sector clearly needs to improve its risk management systems, as the real world has proved to be even riskier than reflected in conventional models. But accomplishing this may require the creation of new business forms, and not just new systems. The reformed regulatory framework should create the correct incentives to encourage this to take place.

The G-20's Action Plan

In fact, the Summit addressed all these issues in a concrete fashion. Looking beyond the short-term need to support global demand, the Summit participants adopted a sweeping Action Plan to Implement Principles for Reform. Working Groups will be formed to pursue policy reforms in five broad areas: Strengthening Transparency and Accountability; Enhancing Sound Regulation; Promoting Integrity in Financial Markets; Reinforcing International Cooperation; and Reforming International Financial Institutions.

In each of these areas, the Summit participants agreed on a set of short-term issues, with specific reform proposals expected to be ready for consideration by the end of March 2009. They also agreed on a set of medium-term actions to be pursued by the Working Groups. The Plan comprises some 50 concrete steps to be taken by G-20 members and various international entities, of which over half are to be delivered by the end of next year's first quarter.

The Summit's Action Plan responds directly to the key challenges. Specifically, the Summit Communiqué's Action Plan calls for new agreement on the valuation of complex securities, a review of the role of credit rating agencies, and an improvement of the infrastructure for the credit default swap market and other over-the-counter derivative markets. Additionally, the Action Plan calls for a review of standards for risk management practices and improved standards for managing liquidity risk.

The Action Plan also calls for the IMF, working together with an expanded Financial Stability Forum (FSF) and with standard-setting bodies to develop recommendations for mitigating the current system's apparent pro-cyclicality, as well as to help improve the scope of existing regulations. Moreover, the IMF is tasked with helping to improve the cross-border consistency of regulations and to enhance international regulatory cooperation. To this end, supervisors are instructed to establish supervisory "colleges" for all major cross-border financial institutions. The Summit Communiqué also commits G-20 members to undertake a Financial Sector Assessment Program (FSAP) report, conducted jointly with by the IMF and the World Bank. To date, all but two of the countries that attended the Summit have either already had FSAPs or have initiated them.

Of course, the exact outcomes of the G-20 efforts cannot be taken for granted. Among other things, it goes without saying that the near-term deadline will fall due after a new US Administration takes office. But it is notable that the most significant specific challenges have been identified, and a clear politically-endorsed mandate has been established with a defined deadline for concrete proposals. Rather than dismissing this effort as just a collection of good intentions, international stake-holders in this area hopefully will keep up the pressure for decisive action along the lines specified in the Action Plan.

The Role of the Fund

Before concluding, I would like to address the role of the IMF in these very challenging times.

—First, the Fund continues to conduct its regular multilateral and bilateral surveillance and to provide policy advice and technical assistance to members.

—Second, the Fund has moved quickly to help emerging economies battered by the crisis and the sharp slowdown in advanced economies. As the crisis deepens and spreads, the Fund can disburse more than $200 billion in liquid resources to support member countries facing financing shortfalls. Indeed, several countries already have sought financial support from the Fund in recent weeks, including Hungary, Iceland, and Ukraine, and more arrangements are under negotiation.

—Third, as it became clear that innovative policy tools were needed, the Fund responded by acting to deploy its resources in new ways. Recently, the Exogenous Shock Facility has been made easier for low income members to access, while the new SLF I mentioned earlier provides those members with strong macroeconomic positions and records of consistent policy implementation large upfront access to Fund resources to help address short-term, self-correcting external liquidity pressures that give rise to balance of payments needs.

—Fourth, while the Fund can draw on additional resources through standing borrowing arrangements with members, there remains a serious question as to whether the cumulative pool of resources will be sufficient to meet the needs of members as the crisis continues to spread. A more systematic approach to international liquidity provision should be a high priority—be it through the co-financing of IMF-supported programs (as was done in the case of Hungary) or increasing the Fund's loanable resources. In the first instance, it would seem prudent to aim for a doubling of the resources available for Fund lending, even if the resources appear adequate in the current situation.

With respect to improving the financial architecture, the Fund already is taking several steps. Consistent with the core mandate of the Fund to promote global financial stability, we already have begun strengthening our early warning capabilities. However, better understanding is needed regarding the linkages between financial sector developments and macroeconomic performance (for instance, on the relationship between monetary policy and risk taking). In response, we are taking the lead in research in this area. New and better operational tools also need to be developed for macro-financial surveillance. We at the IMF therefore are eager to strengthen our collaboration with others involved in this area.

Of course, the role of the Fund was an important topic for last weekend's Summit. During the Summit sessions, in bilateral discussions, and in the Summit Declaration, G-20 leaders made it clear that they look to the Fund to play a critical role in the period ahead in crisis management, in drawing lessons from the crisis, in strengthening surveillance, and in rebuilding the international architecture. Specifically, they:

—Strongly supported the Fund's role in crisis management and response, including its new short-term liquidity facility, while also calling for continued review and adaptation of its lending instruments.

—Agreed to insure that the Fund's resources are sufficient to play its role. In that regard, the Japanese authorities announced their commitment to provide an additional $100 billion to augment the Fund's loanable resources, and called on others to help to double the Fund existing liquid reserves.

—Asked the Fund to conduct vigorous and even-handed surveillance of all its members, with greater attention to their financial sectors and stronger macro-financial policy advice; as part of this, they committed all G-20 members to undertake an FSAP.

—Asked the Fund, in collaboration with an expanded FSF, to better integrate regulatory and supervisory responses into our macro-prudential analysis and to develop our early warning capability.

—Asked the Fund to take a lead role in drawing lessons from the current crisis; and more generally to strengthen collaboration with the FSF, along the lines of last week's agreement between the heads of the two institutions.

—Called for the Fund to be involved in the development of recommendations to mitigate pro-cyclicality of the financial system.

—Called on the Fund to provide capacity-building for the formulation and implementation of new regulations, consistent with international standards.

The leaders also emphasized that they want to see reform of the Bretton Woods institutions themselves. In particular, they emphasized the need to insure that emerging and developing economies have greater voice and representation in the institutions, and in the international system as a whole.

Conclusion

The broad picture that I have sought to develop here today is one where it has been recognized at the highest level of political authority that action across a range of areas is needed urgently to help the global economy and the financial system regain their footing. There is no need to make exaggerated claims about requiring a new system. Already, an impressive consensus has emerged about the reforms required to correct the flaws of the existing system, and they are substantial. Macroeconomic policy action—especially fiscal policy—is becoming increasingly relevant and necessary for a broad swath of countries. Financial sector policy reforms also must continue to be implemented and fine tuned as needed. And collectively, we must work together to strengthen the global financial architecture in a way that reduces future risks by re-examining regulatory weaknesses, forging ahead with new tools for detecting and warning about vulnerabilities, and recognizing the importance of financial integration and cross-border financing in designing regulations and new mechanisms for crisis prevention and resolution.

The G-20 Summit on Financial Markets and the World Economy represented an unprecedented political messaging of the increasingly powerful agreement in favor of broad action in order to confront the daunting and in many ways unprecedented challenges of the current crisis. By any standards, the Summit laid out an ambitious agenda. My Fund colleagues and I stand ready to assist the G-20 leaders as they develop a detailed implementation plan to turn today's concerns and challenges into specific actions. First and foremost, the IMF stands ready to use its financial resources and expertise to help pave the way toward a more resilient post-crisis global economy.

第**3**单元

视译单位之间的衔接

基本技巧：

- 在类意群间加入名词或代词作为连接成分；
- 明确译出原文的暗含内容作为连接成分。

一、技巧讲解：类意群之间的衔接

我们在前两单元中讲解了视译的基本原则和断句方法。视译最重要的原则是依序顺译，也就是基本上按照原文句子的顺序翻译下来。由于汉英两种语言高度的灵活性和丰富的语言元素，依序顺译是完全可能的。依序顺译的重要环节是合理断句。使用类意群作为断句的基本单位方便了依序顺译，也使得视译更加符合汉语习惯。

在学习了断句的基本技巧之后，我们会发现，由于汉语意合的特点，许多类意群是可以不用任何连接词就能顺译下来的。比如句子 The old man, who was walking slowly along the riverside, looked around and stopped from time to time. 我们将它视译为："那位老人慢慢地沿着河边走，向四周张望，并不时地停下脚步。"在视译这个句子的时候，我们依照断句的顺序，译出汉语短句，没有必要加任何连接词，句子很通顺，意思也很清楚。在视译中，许多句子都可以这样处理。

但是有的时候，在使用类意群断句之后，在两个类意群之间如果不加进一个连接成分，整个句子就会很不通顺，听起来不连贯，甚至是支离破碎，不成句子。在这种情况下，我们就需要使用汉语的连接成分来连接两个类意群，让视译出来的句子通顺连贯。下面我们举例说明这个问题。

例 1： That those young people who had been so energetic died so suddenly in the earthquake was a real shock to everybody.

首先按照类意群断句：That those young people // who had been so energetic // died so suddenly in the earthquake // was a real shock to everyone. 然后做视译："那些年轻人 // 曾经是那样地充满活力 // 突然在地震中死去，// 这的确是令人震惊的事情。"

可以看出，在这个句子里，前面的三个类意群都可以很顺妥地直接翻译下来，但是原来句子的主语是一个以 that 引导的很长的从句，原来的谓语部分 was a real shock 是很难在不加任何连接成分的情况下与整个句子译成一体的。所以，我们必须加一个代词"这"来连接第三和第四个类意群。"这"指代前面的整个主语从句。

视译的连接成分不是语法中的连接词，而是连接两个类意群之间的一种句子成分，它可以是代词、名词，也可以是词组等，目的是使整个句子通顺。在视译中，有两种情况尤其需要使用这种连接成分：一是需要增加名词或代词作连接成分的句子和需要增加同位语作连接成分的句子（比如"亦即"、"或者说"等）；二是有些介词引导的句子成分。下面我们分别讲解这两种情况。

1 需要增加名词或代词作连接成分的句子

在不少情况下，英文句子属于复合句，而在视译中要拆句顺译。为了使前后句子成分连贯通顺，需要在句子中的连接部位增加名词或代词作为连接成分。比如句子 An old friend came to our university to visit us last night. 在笔译中，可以把它译为："一个老朋友昨晚到我们学校来看望我们。"这样做要将原来在句末的时间状语提到前面。在视译中，遇到较长的句子，这样调整顺序就比较困难了。一般来说，我们可以将这个句子分为三个类意群：An old friend came to our university // to visit us // last night. 按照顺序依次译出："一个老朋友到学校 // 来看望我们 // 这是昨晚的事情。"在这个句子里，我们加入了指示代词"这"，并将原来的时间状语变成一个短句，听起来就顺妥了。

这类句子在视译中会经常遇到，我们再举几个例子加以说明。

例 2： In this small town, almost everyone knew Mr. Smith, the onetime boss of a prestigious company called Smith & Sons.

译文 1：在这个小城里，几乎每个人都认识史密斯先生，他曾经是一家叫做史密斯父子的大公司的老板。

译文 2：在这个小城里，几乎每个人都认识史密斯先生，他曾经是一家大公司的老板，<u>这家公司叫做史密斯父子公司</u>。

【讲解】　视译的时候，比较自然的断句是将 called Smith & Sons 作为一个视译单位，整个句子的类意群划分为：In this small town, // almost everyone knew Mr. Smith, // the onetime boss of a prestigious company // called Smith & Sons. 如果将最后一部分分开来作为一个类意群，翻译时就必须加进连接成分。在这里，我们加入了一个指示代词"这家"并重复名词"公司"，使最后的部分与前面自然衔接。

例 3：　The method was largely developed by physicists, chemists and biologists; it was later adopted by people working in such areas as education, psychology and sociology, where the subjects of research were often people.

译文 1：这种（科学）方法在很大程度上先是由物理学家、化学家和生物学家使用，后来为在教育学、心理学和社会学等领域内（其研究对象是人）工作的研究人员所采纳而发展起来的。（宋天锡，2003：278-279）

译文 2：这种方法的发明者主要是物理学家、化学家和生物学家，后来采纳这种方法的是另外一些领域的研究人员，<u>这些领域</u>包括教育学、心理学和社会学，研究对象多是人本身。

【讲解】　这是一个长句，包含两个并列分句，在第二个分句中，又有一个非限定性的地点状语从句，另外还有被动语态等成分，所以视译起来有一定难度。我们首先来断句：The method was largely developed // by physicists, chemists and biologists; // it was later adopted // by people working in such areas // as education, psychology and sociology, // where the subjects of research were often people. 然后依次译成中文："这种方法的发明者主要是 // 物理学家、化学家和生物学家，// 后来采纳这种方法的是 // 另外一些领域的研究人员，// <u>这些领域</u>包括教育学、心理学和社会学，// 研究对象多是人本身。"

可以看出，在视译中，为了使第四个和第五个类意群之间能够顺利衔接，我们加入了"这些领域"作为连接成分。

2　介词引导的句子成分

在英语中，我们往往遇到以介词引导的英语短语，比如 Finally he succeeded in inventing the new product through repeated consultation and experiments. 在这个句子中，以介词 through 引导的句子成分是作为方式状语出现的。这类句子还有不少，属于常见句之列。比如 She tried to pronounce every sound correctly by reading the poem aloud every morning. 这个句子常见的笔译形式是：“她每天早上都在朗读这首诗歌，为的是将每一个音都发准。”

从上面的笔译译文来看，需要较大幅度地调整原文语序，并且要将介词引导的句子成分放到句首。在视译中，对于这种以介词引导的句子成分，只要合理加进连接成分，就可以不必调整原文语序。我们先以上面的两个句子为例，说明如何加进连接成分。

例 4： Finally he succeeded in inventing the new product through repeated consultation and experiments.

译文 1： 他通过无数次咨询和试验终于发明这一新产品。

译文 2： 他终于发明了这一新产品，因为他做了无数次的咨询和试验。

【讲解】 这个句子可以分为三个类意群：Finally he succeeded // in inventing the new product // through repeated consultation and experiments. 视译难点在第二和第三个类意群的连接上面。如果没有恰当的连接成分，又不调整语序，译出的句子会不通顺。在这种情况下，我们通过分析句子成分发现以 through 引导的状语部分可以归于原因状语之列，那么，我们就可以将原因状语的暗含关系以增益的方式明译出来，于是，在译文的连接部分加进了“因为”，然后再添上主语“他”，这就使得两个类意群比较自然地连接在一起了。

例 5： She tried to pronounce every sound correctly by reading the poem aloud every morning.

译文 1： 她每天早上都大声朗读这首诗歌，为的是将每一个音都发准。

译文 2： 她试图将每一个音都发准，方法是每天早上大声朗读这首诗歌。

【讲解】 这个句子的视译方法与例 4 是一样的。先用类意群将句子断为两个部分：She tried to pronounce every sound correctly // by reading the poem aloud every morning. 然后依次译出成中文，而关键是将 by 引导的方式状语明译出来。所以加进“方法是”这一连接成分，就保证了视译人员能够在基本不调整原文语序的情况下将句子比较顺妥地翻译出来了。另外，其他一些介词短语成分也可以使用类似的方法加以处理。

例 6： Despite the heavy rain, they managed to arrive at the summer camp in good time.

译文 1： 虽然天下大雨，但他们还是及时到达了夏令营地。

译文 2： 虽然天下大雨，但他们还是到达了夏令营地，<u>并且是及时到达</u>。

【讲解】 这个句子的难点是 in good time 的处理。根据一目可及的原则，介词短语 in good time 往往在习惯上会被分为一个独立的类意群，整个句子可以被断开成：Despite the heavy rain, // they managed to arrive at the summer camp // in good time. 如果视译时不在这个表示时间的介词短语之前加连接成分，句子就会支离破碎。所以加进"并且是"作为连接成分，译出的句子就通顺了。

从第一单元到第三单元，我们讲解了视译的主要原则和基本技巧。视译的主要原则是顺译，基本技巧是合理断句。在合理断句之后，还必须注意视译单位类意群之间的自然衔接，否则，视译质量就会降低，甚至使句子不能流畅地表达出来。所以，顺译、断句和衔接成为视译的三条基本要求。

二、语段视译

1 词汇与表达

在进行语段视译前，请先预习以下词汇与表达。

Asian American	亚裔美国人
family grocery	家庭经营的杂货店
legacy	遗产
endemic	某地（或某些人中）流行的
identity crisis	认同危机
accommodationist	倾向白人思想观点的

2 视译语段

请在 3 分钟之内迅速阅读下面的语段，了解大意，然后结合所学要点进行视译练习。视译时要保持正常语速，译文要顺畅达意。

It is often said that Asian Americans are a "model minority", with parents who work 18 hours a day in the family grocery and children who work with equal amazing perseverance in the classroom. At a glance, the evidence seems clear: while the first Asians to come to America lived poorly as farmers, miners and railway workers, we now enjoy one of the highest average incomes in the country. Here at Harvard, 18% of the class of 1996 are Asian Americans, compared to 3% of the total US population. By focusing on the "positive stereotype", however, one neglects the other side of our lives. For many of us—the second generation—there is something uncomfortable about being Asian in America. Although many of us appreciate the great sacrifices our parents have made, their economic success somehow represents for us an unsatisfying legacy. We suffer in particular from an endemic identity crisis. We have begun to question the accommodationist ways of our forebears, our quietly studious manner, our narrow priorities, and our previous notions of success.[1]（陈文伯，1998：320-303）

原译文：美国亚裔人经常被称为"模范少数民族"。他们的父母每天在家庭经营的杂货店干 18 个小时，而其子女也以同样令人惊异的坚韧精神在课堂里努力学习。粗略一看，赢得这一称号的证据似乎明摆着：第一批亚洲人来到美国时，他们当农民，当矿工，当铁路工人，生活贫困；而现在我们亚裔美国人的收入属于这个国家最高的平均收入。在哈佛大学，1996 届学生 18% 是亚裔美国人，而亚裔美国人的人口却只占美国人口的 3%。但是，人们注意力都集中在这一"固定形象的积极方面"，往往忽略了我们生活的另一面。我们第二代的许多人都觉得生活在美国而身为亚裔不怎么舒服。我们很感激父母做出的巨大牺牲，不知怎地尽管他们经济上很有成就，但给我们留下的却是一种不令人满意的处境。尤其折磨我们的是我们这类人特有的身份危机感。我们开始对祖辈那种文化归化白人的生活方式产生怀疑，对我们自己埋头读书、狭隘的生活追求以及先前对成功的理解都产生了怀疑。（陈文伯，1998：498-499）

3 视译译文

	断　句	译　文
1	It is often said	人们常说，
2	that Asian Americans are a "model minority",	亚裔美国人是"模范少数民族"，

（待续）

---

1 较原文略有删减。

（续上表）

	断　句	译　文
3	with parents who work 18 hours a day	父母每天工作 18 小时，
4	in the family grocery	在家庭经营的杂货店辛劳。
5	and children who work with equal amazing perseverance	子女也以同样惊人的坚韧精神，
6	in the classroom.	在学校里刻苦学习。
7	At a glance,	粗略一看，
8	the evidence seems clear:	成功的证据十分清楚：
9	while the first Asians to come to America	第一批亚洲人来到美国，
10	lived poorly	他们生活贫困，
11	as farmers, miners and railway workers,	当农民、当矿工、当铁路工人，
12	we now enjoy one of the highest average incomes in the country.	而我们现在却是美国平均收入最高的群体之一。
13	Here at Harvard,	就在哈佛大学，
14	18% of the class of 1996	18% 的 1996 届学生
15	are Asian Americans,	是亚裔美国人，
16	compared to 3% of the total US population.	而亚裔美国人只占美国总人口的 3%。
17	By focusing on the "positive stereotype",	如果只看到这种"积极形象"的方面，
18	however, one neglects the other side of our lives.	那就会忽视了我们生活的另一面。
19	For many of us—	对于我们中许多人来说，
20	the second generation—	也就是对第二代移民来说，
21	there is something uncomfortable	总有不舒服的感觉，
22	about being Asian in America.	这就是作为亚裔美国人的感觉。

（待续）

（续上表）

	断　句	译　文
23	Although many of us	虽然我们许多人
24	appreciate the great sacrifices	感激那种巨大的牺牲，
25	our parents have made,	即我们父辈做出的牺牲，
26	their economic success somehow	但他们在经济上的成功，
27	represents for us an unsatisfying legacy.	却给我们留下了并不令人满意的处境。
28	We suffer in particular	我们尤其感到难受的是
29	from an endemic identity crisis.	一种特有的认同危机。
30	We have begun to question	于是我们开始质疑，
31	the accommodationist ways of our forebears,	质疑我们父辈归顺的生活方式，
32	our quietly studious manner,	质疑我们埋头读书的态度，
33	our narrow priorities,	质疑我们狭隘的目标，
34	and our previous notions of success.	质疑我们以前对成功的理解。

4 视译点评

1. 原文第一句：It is often said // that Asian Americans are a "model minority", // with parents who work 18 hours a day // in the family grocery // and children who work with equal amazing perseverance // in the classroom.

　　这个句子是一个复合句，带有一个主语从句和一个以介词引导的状语，而这个状语中又包含两个定语从句。如果我们合理断句并使用视译技巧，这个句子仍然可以译得很通顺。难点是两个定语从句中的地点状语 in the family grocery 和 in the classroom。这两个状语被视为单独的视译单位，在处理上，我们也就加进动词，将其译为独立的句子"在家庭经营的杂货店辛劳"和"在学校里刻苦学习"。

2. 原文第五句：For many of us— // the second generation— // there is something uncomfortable // about being Asian in America.

　　这个句子虽然是一个简单句，但插入和修饰的成分较多，也造成了视译的困难。视译时，有两个地方需要特别注意：第一，插入部分是一个名词词组作同位语，我们加入连接成分"也就是"，以便于上下衔接；第二，about being Asian in America 这个介词短语，根据视译单位断句的原则被单列为一个视译单位。在视译时，我们先把前面的部分译出"……总有不舒服的感觉"，然后另起一句，并加入连接成分"这就是"，译出介词短语："这就是作为亚裔美国人的感觉"。

3. 原文第六句：Although many of us // appreciate the great sacrifices // our parents have made, // their economic success somehow // represents for us an unsatisfying legacy.

这也是一个复合长句，在让步状语从句中包含了一个定语从句，主句也比较长。我们将句子分为五个视译单位，依次译出。难点是让步状语从句中的定语从句，我们先译出"感激那种巨大的牺牲"，然后加连接成分"即"，引出定语从句"我们父辈做出的牺牲"，使句子上下自然衔接。

三、实战练习

1　词汇与表达

请先熟悉以下词汇与表达，并适当地运用在视译中。

FAO (Food and Agriculture Organization)	联合国粮农组织
de jure	法律上的
de facto	实际的，事实上的
loan portfolio	投资比例
Bankable Investment Project Profiles (BIPPs)	可由银行担保的投资项目概览
UEMOA (Union Economique et Monétaire Ouest Africaine)	西非国家经济货币联盟
ECOWAS (Economic Community of West African States)	西非国家经济共同体
SADC (Southern African Development Community)	南部非洲发展共同体
COMESA (Common Market for Eastern and Southern Africa)	东部和南部非洲共同市场

IGAD (InterGovernmental Authority on Development)	政府间发展管理局
UMA (Union of the Arab Maghreb)	阿拉伯马格里布联盟
phytosanitary	植物检疫
Codex Alimentarius	食品法典
CARICOM (Caribbean Community)	加勒比共同体
Montevideo	蒙得维的亚（乌拉圭首都）
the Ibero-American Summit	伊比利亚美洲国家首脑会议
task force	特别工作组
the Bretton Woods institutions	布雷顿森林体系机构
WFP (World Food Program)	联合国世界粮食计划署
IFAD (International Fund for Agricultural Development)	国际农业发展基金
United Nations Chief Executive Board	联合国系统行政首长协调委员会，缩写为 CEB
whim	反复无常
OECD (Organization for Economic Cooperation and Development)	经济合作与发展组织，简称经合组织
avian influenza	禽流感
Newcastle disease	新城疫
foot-and-mouth disease	口蹄疫
Rift Valley fever	里夫特裂谷热
contagious	传染性
bovine pleuropneumonia	牛胸膜肺炎
pest of small ruminant	小反刍动物疫病
bluetongue disease	蓝舌病
African swine fever	非洲猪瘟
tropical bont tick	热带花蜱
screwworm	旋丽蝇幼虫
wheat stem rust	小麦锈病
locust	蝗虫
Pharaoh	法老
order of magnitude	数量级

2 实战课文

请在 15 分钟之内迅速阅读下面的讲话，了解大意。视译时要保持正常语速，译文要顺畅达意。

High-Level Conference on World Food Security: the Challenges of Climate Change and Bioenergy[1]

Director-General of the FAO   Jacques Diouf

Rome, 2008

We are gathered here in the eternal city of Rome for a *de jure* High-Level Conference that has become a *de facto* summit. We have before us a world food crisis that has recently had tragic social and political consequences in different continents, with riots and deaths that can endanger world peace and security.

Those sad events are however but the chronicle of disaster foretold. In 1996, in this very chamber, 112 heads of state and government and the representatives of 186 members of the Organization solemnly pledged to reduce by half the number of hunger in the world by the year 2015 and adopted a program to achieve that target. But already in 2002, we had to convene a second world summit to draw the international community's attention to the fact that resources to finance agricultural programs in developing countries were decreasing, instead of rising. With such a trend, the summit target would not be reached in 2015, but in 2150. An Anti-Hunger Program, with financial requirements estimated at 24 billion dollars per year, had been prepared for that meeting.

Today, the facts speak for themselves: from 1980 to 2005, aid to agriculture fell from 8 billion dollars (2004 basis) in 1984 to 3.4 billion dollars in 2004, representing a reduction in real terms of 58%. Agriculture's share of Official Development Assistance fell from 17% in 1980 to 3% in 2006. **The international and regional financial institutions saw a drastic reduction in resources allocated to the activity that constitutes the principal livelihood of 70% of the world's poor.（句 1）** In one telling case, the loan portfolio to agriculture of one institution plummeted from 33% in 1979 to 1% in 2007.

In cooperation with FAO, the developing countries did in fact prepare policies,

---

1 原文参见 http://www.fao.org/fileadmin/user_upload/foodclimate/statements/fao_diouf_e.pdf。

strategies and programs that, if they had received appropriate funding, would have assured world food security.

Global food production must be doubled to feed a world population currently standing at 6 billion and expected to rise to 9 billion by 2050.

Thus, following a meeting of African experts in December 2001 in Rome, the Ministers for Agriculture met at the FAO Regional Conference for Africa in Cairo in February 2002, and again in Maputo just before the July 2003 African Union Summit. On that occasion, the heads of state and government adopted the Comprehensive Africa Agriculture Development Program (CAADP) and its companion documents prepared with the support of FAO. The Program requires an investment of 25 billion dollars per year for water control, rural infrastructure, trade capacity, increased crop production and reduced hunger, agricultural research and the dissemination of technology, animal production, forestry, fisheries and aquaculture.

In this context, 51 African countries, with the support of FAO, prepared National Medium-Term Investment Programs (NMTIPs) and Bankable Investment Project Profiles (BIPPs).

The Regional Economic Communities—UEMOA, ECOWAS, SADC, COMESA, IGAD and UMA—have, with FAO's support, also prepared regional food security programs which focus on intra-regional trade and WTO sanitary and phytosanitary standards, based on the rules established by WHO and FAO for consumer protection in the framework of the Codex Alimentarius and the International Plant Protection Convention.

Following implementation of the pilot phases of national and regional food security programs in the countries of CARICOM, Central and South America, the Ibero-American Summit approved in November 2006 in Montevideo, Uruguay, the Initiative Hunger-Free Latin America and the Caribbean by 2025. （句2）

Similar regional programs were prepared, in cooperation with FAO, in Central Europe and Central Asia for the Organization of the Black Sea Economic Cooperation and the Economic Cooperation Organization.

Plans, programs and projects—well and good—therefore exist to address food security, even though they may require further refinement and updating.

But sadly the international community only reacts when the media beams the painful spectacle of world suffering into the homes of the wealthy countries.

（句 3 ）

Based on world agricultural statistics and the projections that FAO is responsible for preparing, already last September, I alerted public opinion to the risks of social and political unrest due to hunger. On 17 December, 2007, to avoid jeopardizing the 2008 agricultural season, I launched an appeal for the mobilization of 1.7 billion dollars in grants to enable the farmers of poor countries to have access to the fertilizer, seeds and animal feed that had risen in price by 98, 72 and 60%, respectively. All in vain, despite broad press coverage and correspondence to the member nations and the financial institutions. Some few countries such as Spain did offer their immediate support to agricultural production. I should like to pay tribute to those countries.

It was only when the destitute and those excluded from the banquets of the rich took to the streets to voice their discontent and despair that the first reactions in support of food aid began to emerge.

The causes and consequences of the present crisis have been explained at length so I shall not return to them. What is important today is to realize that the time for talking is long past. Now is the time for action.

The UN Secretary-General has set up and chairs the Task Force of the United Nations system, the Bretton Woods Institutions and other international organizations to bring a coordinated response to the food crisis. He saw fit to appoint the Director-General of FAO as Vice Chair of that Task Force. I should like to take this solemn opportunity to thank him profoundly for that expression of confidence.

The Comprehensive Framework for Action prepared by the Task Force provides guidelines on the needs that will be specified, country by country, with the assistance of the local representatives of FAO, WFP, IFAD and the World Bank, in cooperation with the governments. （句 4 ） In this connection, on 29 April in Berne, the Secretary-General of the United Nations presented to the press the communiqué approved by the United Nations Chief Executives Board (CEB) for coordination on the immediate needs to deal with the food crisis. We must therefore mobilize the necessary resources now.

Of course, there was a pressing need, despite escalating prices, to maintain the volume of food aid for 88 million people. We must thank those countries that contributed so generously to meet the required 755 million dollars in this regard.

But there are 862 million people in the world who do not have adequate access to food. They need to enhance their living conditions in dignity, working with the means of their generation. They need high-yield seeds, fertilizer, animal feed and other modern inputs. They cannot continue to toil as in the Middle Ages under conditions of uncertainty and exposure to the whims of the weather. Investments are therefore needed: in rural infrastructure, especially for water control with irrigation and drainage, considering for example that 96% of arable land in sub-Saharan Africa depends on rainfall. They need storage facilities to avoid harvest losses that can amount to 40 to 60% for certain crops. Rural roads are essential to bring in modern factors of production and enable harvests to reach domestic and regional markets at competitive prices.

The current food crisis goes beyond the traditional humanitarian dimension, which has an eminently ethical foundation. This time it also affects the developed countries. Rising inflation is 40 to 50% the result of higher food prices. In a context of high and accelerated growth of gross domestic product of the emerging countries, we must seek sustainable and viable global solutions that will narrow the gap between global food supply and demand. If we do not urgently take the courageous decisions that are required in the present circumstances, the restrictive measures taken by producer countries to meet the needs of their populations, the impact of climate change and speculation on futures markets will place the world in a dangerous situation. Whatever the extent of their financial reserves, some countries might not find food to buy.

The structural solution to the problem of food security in the world lies in increasing production and productivity in the low-income food-deficit countries. That calls for innovative and imaginative solutions, besides official development assistance. Partnership agreements are needed between countries that have financial resources, management capabilities and technologies and countries that have land, water and human resources. Only in this way will it be possible to assure balanced international relationships for sustainable agricultural development.

The challenges of climate change, bioenergy, trans-boundary animal and plant diseases and agricultural commodity prices can only be met through frank dialog based on objective analysis devoid of partisan and short-term interests. In the coming days, the interactive roundtables on these issues and information from the preparatory technical meetings will provide an appropriate framework for dialog leading to consensus.

Yet, obligation to truth already compels me to note certain facts:

—Nobody understands how a carbon market of 64 billion dollars can be created in the developed countries to offset global warming but that no funds can be found to prevent the annual deforestation of 13 million hectares, especially in the developing countries whose tropical forest ecosystems act as carbon sinks for some 190 giga metric tons.

—Nobody understands how 11 to 12 billion dollars in subsidies in 2006 and protective tariff policies have had the effect of diverting 100 million metric tons of cereals from human consumption, mostly to satisfy a thirst for fuel for vehicles.

—Nobody understands how in a time of globalization of trade, with the notable exception of avian influenza that could lead us to human calamity, there has been no significant investment in the prevention of Newcastle disease, foot-and-mouth disease, Rift Valley fever, contagious bovine pleuropneumonia, the pest of small ruminants, bluetongue disease, African swine fever, tropical bont tick and the New World Screwworm, but also wheat stem rust that since 1999 has spread from Uganda to Iran and could reach India, Pakistan and China, the fruit fly and finally desert locusts, a scourge familiar since the time of the Pharaohs.

—But above all, nobody understands how: first, the OECD countries have created a distortion of world markets with the 372 billion dollars spent in 2006 on supporting their agriculture; next, that in a single country food wastage can amount to 100 billion dollars annually; that the excess consumption by the world's obese costs 20 billion dollars annually, to which must be added indirect costs of 100 billion dollars resulting from premature death and related diseases; and finally that in 2006 the world spent 1,200 billion dollars on the purchase of arms.

Against that backdrop, how can we explain to people of good sense and good faith that it is not possible to find 30 billion dollars a year to enable 862 million hungry people to enjoy the most fundamental of human rights: the right to food, and thus the right to life. **It is resources of this order of magnitude that would make it possible definitively to lay to rest the specter of conflicts over food that are looming on the horizon.** (句 5)

In fact, the problem of food insecurity is a political one. It is a question of priorities in the face of the most fundamental of human needs. And it is the choices made by governments that determine the allocation of resources.

I should like to thank most sincerely the heads of state and government and the other participants at this conference who have traveled thousands of kilometers so that, together and in a spirit of solidarity, appropriate solutions to the serious problems of world food security in a multilateral context may be found. I should like to conclude by expressing my infinite gratitude to the government and to the people of Italy for the generous hospitality that they have always displayed at these landmark moments in human history.

3 难句分析与视译处理

句1： The international and regional financial institutions saw a drastic reduction in resources allocated to the activity that constitutes the principal livelihood of 70% of the world's poor.

笔译译文： 国际和区域金融机构为农业活动分配的资源急剧减少，而农业是全世界 70% 穷人的主要生计。

视译译文：

断　句	译　文
The international and regional financial institutions	国际和区域金融机构
saw a drastic reduction in resources	急剧减少资源投入，
allocated to the activity	这些资源是投向农业活动的，
that constitutes the principal livelihood	而农业构成了主要的生计，
of 70% of the world's poor.	对世界上 70% 的穷人都是如此。

句2： Following implementation of the pilot phases of national and regional food security programs in the countries of CARICOM, Central and South America, the Ibero-American Summit approved in November 2006 in Montevideo, Uruguay, the Initiative Hunger-Free Latin America and the Caribbean by 2025.

笔译译文： 在加勒比共同体国家及中南美洲国家执行国家和区域粮食安全计划试点项目之后，2006 年 11 月，伊比利亚美洲国家首脑会议在乌拉圭蒙得维的亚批准了"2025 年拉丁美洲及加勒比无饥饿"计划。

视译译文：

断　句	译　文
Following implementation of the pilot phases	首先是执行试点项目阶段，
of national and regional food security programs	即实施国家和区域粮食安全项目，
in the countries of CARICOM, Central and South America,	这是在加勒比共同体国家及中南美洲国家进行的。
the Ibero-American Summit approved	之后，伊比利亚美洲国家举行首脑会议，
in November 2006	时间是 2006 年 11 月，
in Montevideo, Uruguay,	地点在乌拉圭的蒙得维的亚，
the Initiative Hunger-Free Latin America and the Caribbean by 2025.	会议批准了 "2025 年拉丁美洲及加勒比无饥饿" 计划。

句 3：　But sadly the international community only reacts when the media beams the painful spectacle of world suffering into the homes of the wealthy countries.

笔译译文：但遗憾的是，只有通过媒体报道，让富裕国家的人们坐在家中收看到世界遭受苦难的情境时，国际社会才做出反应。

视译译文：

断　句	译　文
But sadly the international community only reacts	但遗憾的是国际社会反应迟缓，
when the media beams	是媒体先行报道了
the painful spectacle of world suffering	世界遭受苦难的情况，
into the homes of the wealthy countries.	把消息传到了富国国民的家中。

句 4：　The Comprehensive Framework for Action prepared by the Task Force provides guidelines on the needs that will be specified, country by country, with the assistance of the local representatives of FAO, WFP, IFAD and the World Bank, in cooperation with the governments.

笔译译文： 工作组拟定的综合行动框架提供了关于如何确定需要的准则。这些需要将在粮农组织、粮食计划署、国际农业发展基金和世界银行这些国际组织当地代表的协助下，与各国政府合作按国家具体情况确定。

视译译文：

断　句	译　文
The Comprehensive Framework for Action	综合行动框架
prepared by the Task Force	是工作组拟定的，
provides guidelines on the needs	提供了关于如何确定需求的准则，
that will be specified, country by country,	这类需求要按国家逐一确定，
with the assistance of the local representatives	由国际组织的当地代表协助，
of FAO, WFP, IFAD and the World Bank,	这些组织包括粮农组织、粮食计划署、农发基金和世界银行，
in cooperation with the governments.	并且还要与各国政府合作完成。

句 5： It is resources of this order of magnitude that would make it possible definitively to lay to rest the specter of conflicts over food that are looming on the horizon.

笔译译文： 这笔数额就是我们驱除地平线上正在出现的粮食冲突这一幽灵所需的资金。

视译译文：

断　句	译　文
It is resources of this order of magnitude	只有这笔数额
that would make it possible	才有可能
definitively to lay to rest	彻底地平息
the specter of conflicts over food	争夺粮食的冲突，
that are looming on the horizon.	这类冲突像幽灵一样威胁着全球。

4　**参考译文**

世界粮食安全高级别会议：气候变化和生物能源的挑战
世界粮农组织总干事　雅克・迪乌夫
罗马，2008 年

我们在永恒之城罗马相聚，参加一次法律意义上的高级别会议，而实际上这已成为一次首脑会议。我们正面临着一次世界粮食危机，这次危机最近已在各大陆造成了悲惨的社会和政治后果，引发骚乱和死亡，这可能会危及世界和平与安全。

然而，这些悲惨的事件仅仅是记录了早就预测到了的灾难。1996 年，就在这个会议厅里，112 位国家元首和政府首脑及本组织 186 个成员国的代表庄严承诺，到 2015 年将世界饥饿人数减少一半，并为实现这一目标通过了一项计划。但到了 2002 年，我们就不得不举行第二次世界首脑会议来提请国际社会注意以下事实，即用于资助发展中国家农业计划的资源不但没有增长，反而是在减少。根据这种趋势，首脑会议的目标将无法在 2015 年实现，而是要推迟到 2150 年才能实现。那次会议还制定了一项"战胜饥饿计划"，估计每年需要的资金为 240 亿美元。

今天，事实不言自明：对农业的援助从 1984 年的 80 亿美元（2004 年基准）降至 2004 年的 34 亿美元，按实际值计算下降 58%。农业在官方发展援助中所占的比例从 1980 年的 17% 降至 2006 年的 3%。国际和区域金融机构为农业活动分配的资源急剧减少，而农业是全世界 70% 穷人的主要生计。有一个显著的例子，某机构给予农业的贷款比例从 1979 年的 33% 暴跌至 2007 年的 1%。

发展中国家与粮农组织合作，确实制定了有关政策、战略和计划，要是这些国家获得适当的资助，这些政策、战略和计划本将能够保障世界粮食安全。

全球粮食产量必须翻番才能供养目前 60 亿世界人口，而预计到 2050 年世界人口将增加到 90 亿。

因此，在非洲专家于 2001 年 12 月在罗马举行会议之后，它们的农业部长参加了 2002 年 2 月在开罗召开的粮农组织非洲区域会议，后又于 2003 年 7 月非洲联盟首脑会议之前在马普托举行了会议。在非洲联盟首脑会议上，国家元首和政府首脑通过了在粮农组织的支持下制定的非洲农业全面发展计划及其有关文件。该计划要求每年投资 250 亿美元，用于水控制、农村基础设施、贸易能力、提高作物产量及减少饥饿、农业研究和技术推广、畜牧生产、林业、渔业和水产养殖业。

在这种背景下，非洲 51 个国家在粮农组织的支持下拟定了国家中期投资计划和可由银行担保的投资项目概览。

　　西非国家经济货币联盟、西非国家经济共同体、南部非洲发展共同体、东部和南部非洲共同市场、政府间发展管理局及阿拉伯马格里布联盟等区域经济共同体还在粮农组织的支持下制定了区域粮食安全计划。它们根据世卫组织和粮农组织在食品法典和《国际植物保护公约》框架内为消费者保护确立的规则，注重区域内贸易及世贸组织卫生和植物检疫标准。

　　在加勒比共同体国家及中南美洲国家执行国家和区域粮食安全计划试点项目之后，2006 年 11 月，伊比利亚美洲国家首脑会议在乌拉圭蒙得维的亚批准了"2025 年拉丁美洲及加勒比无饥饿"计划。

　　与粮农组织合作，在中欧和中亚，也为黑海经济合作组织及经济合作组织制定了类似的区域计划。

　　因此，我们已有解决粮食安全问题的各类良好的计划和项目，尽管这些计划和项目可能需要进一步完善和更新。

　　但遗憾的是，只有通过媒体报道，让富裕国家的人们坐在家中收看到世界遭受苦难的情境时，国际社会才做出反应。

　　根据粮农组织负责编制的世界农业统计资料和预测，我早在去年 9 月就提醒公众舆论注意饥饿引起社会和政局动荡的风险。为了保障 2008 年农作季节，我于 2007 年 12 月 17 日呼吁筹集 17 亿美元赠款，以便使贫穷国家的农民能够获得化肥、种子和动物饲料，这些商品的价格分别上涨了 98%、72% 和 60%。然而，尽管进行了广泛的新闻报道并与成员国和金融机构进行了联系，却毫无结果，西班牙等少数几个国家确实为农业生产立即提供了支持。我向这些国家表示敬意。

　　只有当穷人和未能享受富人盛宴的人走上街头表达不满和绝望时，国际社会才开始做出最初的粮食援助反应。

　　关于本次危机的原因和后果已经说了很多，我就不再重复了。今天，重要的是认识到光说不做的时刻早已过去。现已到了该采取行动的时候了。

　　联合国秘书长设立并主持联合国系统、布雷顿森林机构和其他国际组织的工作组，以便协调一致地应对粮食危机。他认为粮农组织总干事适合担任该工作组副主席。我想借此庄严的场合深深感谢他的信任。

　　工作组拟定的综合行动框架提供了关于如何确定需要的准则。这些需要将在粮农组织、粮食计划署、国际农业发展基金和世界银行当地代表的协助下，与各国政府合作按国家具体情况确定。在这方面，联合国秘书长于 4 月 29 日在伯尔尼向媒体介绍了联合国系统行政首长协调委员会批准的关于协调立即应对粮食危机所需行动的公报。因此，我们现在必须筹集必要的资源。

　　当然，尽管价格上涨，我们仍然迫切需要维持对 8,800 万人民的粮食援助量。

我们必须感谢那些慷慨解囊，帮助我们筹集为此所需的 7.55 亿美元的国家。

　　然而，世界上有 8.62 亿人民得不到充足食物。他们需要有尊严，需要依靠现代手段来改善自己的生活条件。他们需要高产种子、化肥、动物饲料和其他现代投入。他们不能还像中世纪农民那样劳作，饱受不确定条件和无常天气的影响。因此，需要在农村基础设施方面投资，特别需要在水控制方面投资，以便进行灌溉和排水，例如撒哈拉以南非洲 96% 的耕地依赖降雨。他们需要储存设施以避免收获后的损失，某些作物的收获后损失可能高达 60%。必须修建农村道路以便带来现代生产资料，使他们的收获以有竞争力的价格进入国内和地区市场。

　　当前的粮食危机超出了传统人道主义范畴，具有显著的伦理基础。这次粮食危机也影响了发达国家。由于食品价格上涨，不断上升的通货膨胀率达到 40% 至 50%。在新兴国家国内生产总值大幅且快速增长的情况下，我们必须寻找可持续和可行的全球解决办法，以缩小全球粮食供求差距。如果我们不立即做出当前情况所急需的果敢决定，生产国为满足本国人民需要而采取的限制性措施、气候变化的影响及期货市场投机，将使世界处于危险境地。一些国家即便有财政储备可能也买不到粮食。

　　从结构上解决世界粮食安全问题的办法在于提高低收入缺粮国的产量和生产力。除了官方发展援助行动之外，还要采取新颖和富有想象力的办法。拥有财政资源、管理能力和技术的国家，与拥有土地、水和人力资源的国家之间需要建立伙伴关系。只有这样才能保证建立平衡的国际可持续农业发展关系。

　　气候变化、生物能源、跨界动植物疫病和农业商品价格的挑战，只有在客观分析的基础上，摒弃集团和短期利益，进行坦诚对话才能有效应对。这几天，关于这些问题的互动圆桌会议和技术筹备会议所提供的信息，将为对话提供适当框架，从而达成一致意见。

　　然而，实事求是起见，我必须指出某些实情：

　　——没有人明白为何能在发达国家建立一个 640 亿美元的碳市场以抵消全球变暖，但却找不到资金来防止每年 1,300 万公顷的森林砍伐，特别是在其热带森林生态系统提供 1,900 亿公吨的碳汇的发展中国家。

　　——没有人明白 2006 年的 110 亿至 120 亿美元的补贴和保护性关税政策为何可以将 1 亿公吨谷物从人类消费转向主要用于满足车辆燃料的需要。

　　——没有人明白，在贸易全球化的时代，除了可能引起人类灾难的禽流感之外，怎么没有提供大量投资来预防新城疫、口蹄疫、里夫特裂谷热、牛传染性胸膜肺炎、小反刍动物疫病、蓝舌病、非洲猪瘟、热带花蜱和新世界旋丽蝇幼虫，也没有提供大量投资来预防小麦锈病、果蝇和沙漠蝗虫，小麦锈病自 1999 年以来从乌干达传播到伊朗，可能传到印度、巴基斯坦和中国；而果蝇和沙漠蝗则是自法老时代以来就熟悉的灾害。

——最为重要的是，没有人明白：首先，经合组织国家是怎样创造了一个扭曲的世界市场，先在 2006 年用 3,720 亿美元来支持其农业；然后，仅一个国家一年如何可能浪费 1,000 亿美元的粮食；世界肥胖者每年过量消费为何花 200 亿美元，再加上因过早死亡和有关疾病而产生的 1,000 亿美元的间接费用；最后，世界在 2006 年为何可以花 12,000 亿美元购买军火。

在这种情况下，我们如何向善良的人民解释，我们每年无法找到 300 亿美元让 8.62 亿饥饿的人民能够享有最基本的人权，即食物权，也就是生命权？这笔数额就是我们驱除地平线上正在出现的粮食冲突这一幽灵所需的资金。

实际上，粮食不安全问题是一个政治问题。它是在面临人最基本的需要时的一个优先次序问题。这正是政府确定资源分配时作出的选择。

我谨向不远万里前来参加会议的国家元首、政府首脑及其他与会者表示最真挚的谢意，你们的到来使我们能够本着团结的精神，共同在一个多边场合找到解决世界严峻的粮食安全问题的适当办法。最后，我谨对意大利政府和人民在人类历史的这些里程碑式活动中始终保持的慷慨好客表示万分感谢。

四、自主训练

请在 15 分钟之内迅速阅读下面的讲话，了解大意。学生可组成对子练习，互相监控对视译技巧的掌握情况、视译质量和现场表现，或以边视译边录音的形式进行个人练习。视译时要保持正常语速，译文要顺畅达意。如遇难句，可在首次视译后参照"实战练习"中难句分析与视译处理的方法进行练习，找出解决方法。

Address at the UNESCO Education Leaders Forum[1]
US Secretary of Education   Margaret Spellings

Paris, 2008

Thank you, Ralph[2], for that kind introduction, and for your work at Microsoft to build partnerships that go well beyond technology. To my friend Gerri Elliott and everyone else from Microsoft, thank you for making this event happen. I know this

---

1 原文参见 http://www.ed.gov/news/speeches/2008/07/07072008.html。

2 Ralph Young, 微软全球公共事务部副总裁。

is a transitional time for you all. You're losing a great leader in Bill Gates. Microsoft's loss is education's gain. We're thrilled to have his intellect and commitment.

Director-General Matsuura, thank you for your leadership of UNESCO, which has made it one of the strongest voices for education in the world. You have done a terrific job. The United States is proud to be your partner in that effort.

Let me also say a word about our host city and country. Some people talk about "springtime in Paris". As a student of history, I prefer being here between the Fourth of July and Bastille Day! Your nation supported our revolution, taught our founding fathers, and gave us the "gift" of liberty, and you have our everlasting thanks.

There is a paradox to education. A quality education can open up worlds of opportunity and bring people together. And yet, much of it takes place alone, with quiet study within the four walls of a library or classroom. The same is true for technology, I would guess. Long days spent in isolation, writing code and perfecting software, have given us the ability to communicate with people anywhere in the world in a nanosecond.

The technology revolution has provided a golden opportunity to improve higher education and expand its reach. Now, we must make it more accessible, affordable, and accountable.

But we no longer have the luxury of being isolated, as we once did. We cannot learn from the past without a vision of a future—a vision both expansive and inclusive—a vision based on individual choice and need. That's why, in 2005, I convened a Commission on the Future of Higher Education to take advantage of this golden opportunity. We invited the best and brightest leaders from academia, the private sector, and government to develop a plan for the future—including Microsoft's Gerri Elliott.

The report, *A Test of Leadership*, called for universities and colleges to change from "a system primarily based on reputation to one based on performance". It got a lot of attention and commentary. Some said: "We've been doing this a lot longer than you"—and they were right! Some universities in America are more than three centuries old. Some said, we have "the best system of higher education in the world"—a boast we hear so often that we often forget how hard other nations are working to compete. And a few people said, "Please don't tell me how to do my job. I know how to do it."

I would agree that we have done a good job of educating society's elite. We've been good at advancing opportunity for people who were afforded it at birth. But that alone is no longer our only work. Now, we must do more, much more. I do not want to tell universities how to do their job. But, as Secretary of Education, I do want to let them know what we at the federal level expect as a one-third investor—a true partner—in American higher education.

We expect them:

To knock down barriers and change habits which inhibit progress;

To build human capital by educating more people from diverse economic and cultural backgrounds;

To use technology and innovation to advance change and empower students; and

To continue our emphasis on excellence in research and scholarship, as well as nurture and cultivate partnerships with private and philanthropic sectors.

Higher education must become more agile, informative, and student-centered. That is the only way to achieve sustainable success, as this conference contemplates.

And so I have urged our colleges and universities to adopt my Higher Education Commission's recommendations as soon as possible. These recommendations include greater collaboration and alignment of coursework between colleges and high schools. We need freshmen prepared to succeed, not saddled with expensive, time-consuming remedial classes.

Another recommendation is to focus on non-traditional learners, such as adults returning to school to gain an edge in the competitive global economy.

We also must place a greater emphasis on community college students. These are often students who work while attending school. Community colleges have pioneered flexible and agile learning opportunities, based on technology, and tailored to consumer demands and local workforce needs. That is why roughly half of our 14 million undergraduates are enrolled in them.

Above all, we need more information and transparency in higher education.

While helping my daughter choose a college a few years ago, I found plenty of guides on the best "party schools", but none on the "best prospects for opportunity after graduation", for example. We can shop for a car online, and find out price, gas mileage, even the number of cup-holders. But it is often difficult to find out the true cost of a four-year degree or the average length of time it takes to get one. I believe that a portion of ever-rising tuition costs should be invested in better data and information systems that can make choosing the right school a "point-and-click" exercise—easier and more accessible.

I know you feel the same way. UNESCO has launched a new portal that will provide comparative, up-to-date information on higher education in different countries.

It's time to get out of our comfort zone, to throw open the gates of academia and start collaborating with others to make things better. I am optimistic we can make it happen. Why? Because we are doing it now—by preparing our young students, in primary and secondary school, to succeed in college and in life.

Six years ago, President Bush signed the No Child Left Behind Act into law. It does not tell schools how to do their job. But it does let them know what is expected from them. First and foremost is to bring every child up to grade level or better in reading and math. And, like UNESCO's Education for All campaign, we finally gave ourselves a real deadline: 2014. Of course, I have yet to meet a mom or dad willing to wait that long!

The law was a response to a system that educated some students very well, but kept others in pockets of despair, isolated from their futures. They were mainly minority and low-income students, living mainly in the inner cities of America. The system was dysfunctional, a "rising tide of mediocrity", in the words of our famous 1983 A Nation at Risk report. So we pushed ahead, knocking down barriers, changing habits, rising above the tide.

We found that when we set the expectations bar higher, our children and teachers work harder to clear it. We found that when we measure and publish test scores and other information, schools and communities work harder to move children forward. Today, reading and math scores are rising, and our "achievement gap" between minority and white students is finally narrowing considerably. We've learnt that what gets measured, gets done. This is what it means to cultivate human capital.

That goes for adults, too. Remember, students are not the only ones who drop out of school. Half of our teachers leave the profession within five years. So we established a $100 million Teacher Incentive Fund to help reward teachers who get the best results. And we are empowering parents with better information and more choices, including after-school programs and free tutoring, even transportation to a better-performing public school.

Finally, we recognize that 90% of the fastest-growing jobs require post-secondary training or education—especially in science, math, and technology. Two years ago, we began awarding special grants to our college students who take a rigorous course of study and/or study in the science and math fields. More than $400 million in grants were awarded in just the first year, benefiting 360,000 students, many of modest means, who are getting good grades in these challenging fields and courses.

In short, we are shifting our educational center of gravity away from generic traditions and toward the needs of the individual—more mobile, more connected, and more familiar with technology than ever before.

In America, it took 18 years to go from "a nation at risk" to "a nation of results". Once again, we do not have that luxury today! Our world is moving too fast.

Higher education must follow the trends we've applied to primary and secondary systems, toward openness, transparency, and accountability. That is the only way to solve what Bill Gates calls "the problem of scale" and help as many people as possible.

Metcalfe's Law states that as the number of users on a network grows, the value of that network increases exponentially. Therefore, the best technology is that which benefits the most people, who then improve the technology just by using it.

Imagine Cup finalist Louis Sayers said it well: "There's no one telling us that we can't do something.... If we don't like (it), we change it, and at the end of the day we know that (it) was built by us." That is how we build a global platform for collaboration. It is the opposite of isolation. And it's exactly what we need right now!

Students care little for labels like public or private, for-profit or non-profit. They do care about convenience, affordability, quality, responsiveness—and results.

None of us can afford to leave our human capital untapped. Sixty years after the United Nations proclaimed education to be a fundamental human right, nearly 800 million people across the globe cannot read or write, two thirds of them women. About one in four children fails to complete just five years of basic education.

Let us commit to getting high-quality educational resources in their hands. Let us vow to make higher education the centerpiece of a new era of global change and cooperation. By working together, we can set both a course for the future and an example for today.

Thank you, Microsoft and UNESCO, for engaging all of us in this critical topic. Let's get to work. We have nothing to lose and a world to gain.

定语的视译（I）：定语短语

> **基本技巧：**
> • 依照译出语语序将定语短语顺译为
>   独立的短语或短句。

一、技巧讲解：定语短语的视译

　　定语在英语中的位置比较稳定。单词作定语一般放在被修饰语前面，定语短语放在被修饰语后面。放在修饰语前面的定语有形容词、代词、名词等，视译时依次译出即可。比如 We have a lot of hard work to do. 依次译出为："我们有许多艰苦的工作要做。"

　　我们需要处理的往往是定语短语，因为定语短语一般都放在被修饰语的后面，有些定语短语又比较长，造成了语序处理的困难。所以本单元讲解的重点是如何处理后置定语短语。定语短语虽然与被修饰语关系密切，并很可能同属一个意群，但由于不能一目可及，所以在视译中通常将其划为一个独立的类意群，再译成独立的汉语短语或短句，保持译出语语序。

　　作为定语短语的成分有：1）分词短语；2）不定式短语；3）介词短语；4）其他词组。下面我们举例说明在视译过程中，如何根据保持译出语语序的原则，处理这些不同的定语短语，请特别注意有下划线的部分。

例 1： The woman holding a baby in her arms is waiting to see the doctor.

译文 1：那个抱着婴儿的妇女正等着医生看病。

译文 2：那个妇女抱着个婴儿，正在等医生看病。

【讲解】 这是一个包含现在分词短语作定语的句子。译文 1 将定语短语 holding

a baby in her arms 前置，以"的"字连接，成为标准的汉语句式。译文 2 没有调整原来的语序，而是将 holding a baby in her arms 作为一个视译单位，顺译下来，译为一个分句，这是比较典型的视译方法。

例 2： That summer we launched a rocket designed by ourselves.

译文 1： 那年夏天我们发射了一枚自行研制的火箭。

译文 2： 那年夏天我们发射了一枚火箭，是我们自行研制的。

【讲解】 这是一个包含过去分词短语作定语的句子。译文 1 将定语短语前置。译文 2 将定语短语作为一个视译单位处理，并据此译为独立的分句。

例 3： Their aim is to find ways to satisfy the peasants' demand "to change low-yielding land to high-yielding land".

译文 1： 他们的目的是找寻途径来满足农民"变低产为高产"的要求。(张道真，1979：452)

译文 2： 他们的目的是寻找方法，满足农民的要求，也就是"变低产田为高产田"。

【讲解】 这个句子中有两个不定式短语。我们主要来看第二个作定语的不定式短语。译文 1 将这个定语短语 to change low-yielding land to high-yielding land 置于被修饰语 demand 前面，再用"的"字连接，即"满足农民'变低产为高产'的要求"。译文 2 将"满足农民要求"作为一个视译单位先行译出，然后将不定式短语也作为一个视译单位，译成一个相对独立的短句，并加上"也就是"来连接。这样，句子便保持了原来的语序，使译员能够顺序译出。即便不加"也就是"，这个句子也很清楚，可译为："他们的目的是寻找方法，满足农民的要求，'变低产田为高产田'。"

例 4： No rose without a thorn.

译文 1： 没有不带刺的玫瑰。(张道真，2007：525)

译文 2： 没有玫瑰不带刺。

【讲解】 这是一个包含介词短语作定语的省略句（原句为：There is no rose without a thorn）。译文 1 根据笔译原则将定语前置。译文 2 将 without a thorn 作为一个视译单位，并将这个定语短语后置，保持原语序。

定语短语在句中是经常出现的成分。如果视译或同传人员像做笔译一样去调整定语短语的位置，则要花费很多时间，一旦养成习惯，改起来也不容易。

所以，要从一些简单的句子开始练习，将后置定语短语依照原文顺序，译成独立短语或短句，并逐步养成习惯。这样就会大大加快翻译的速度。

二、语段视译

1 词汇与表达

在进行语段视译前，请先预习以下词汇与表达。

bass	贝司（低音乐器）
dalliance	一时的消遣
The Times	《泰晤士报》
click	进行顺利，成功

2 视译语段

请在 3 分钟之内迅速阅读下面的语段，了解大意，然后结合所学要点进行视译练习。视译时要保持正常语速，译文要顺畅达意。

Running the country is all well and good, but Tony Blair still wonders if he could have made it as a rock star. "I've always wondered, could I have actually ever done it," the onetime lead singer of a rock band called the Ugly Rumors, more recently prime minister, told his former bass player in an interview. "I was quite serious about it. It wasn't just a mere dalliance—it was a bit more than that for me." Blair told ex-bass player Mark Ellen. Excerpts of the interview were printed in *The Times*. "With politics, it all clicked into place for me somehow. Whereas with music you had to have a particular set of attributes that I didn't quite have, and it never happened for me even though I was desperately keen to carry on." Blair, 51, said that he still gets a thrill meeting rock icons of his youth like Paul McCartney or David Bowie. "They say: 'It must be so interesting what you do,' and I say: 'It's not as interesting as what you do.'" （摘自《英语学习》，2005 年第 5 期，第 8 页）

原译文：管理国家当然也是份不错的工作，但托尼·布莱尔还是想知道自己究竟有没有成为摇滚明星的资质。"我总是在想，我究竟行还是不行，"在一次采访中，这位曾经是"丑陋流言"摇滚乐队主唱、现在的英国首相对原乐队的

87

贝司手马克·埃伦说。"我对摇滚乐是非常认真的，决不只是玩票而已——对我来说，摇滚的意义不止于此。"《泰晤士报》刊载了这次采访的一些片段，布莱尔还说："我在政坛上打拼的时候，一切似乎都自然而然，进行得非常顺利。搞音乐的时候就不同了，你必须有一系列特殊的素质，而那正是我缺乏的东西。尽管我拼命想继续我的摇滚生涯，但我却从未拥有那样的素质。"现年51岁的布莱尔说，时到如今，在见到保罗·麦卡特尼和大卫·鲍伊等年轻时代的偶像时，他仍然会兴奋不已。"他们说：'你的工作肯定有意思极了，'而我说：'没有你们有意思。'"（冰尘译）

视译译文：

	断 句	译 文
1	Running the country is all well and good,	管理国家当然很不错，
2	but Tony Blair still wonders	但托尼·布莱尔还是想知道
3	if he could have made it as a rock star.	自己究竟能不能成为摇滚明星。
4	"I've always wondered,	"我总是在想，
5	could I have actually ever done it,"	我究竟行还是不行。"
6	the onetime lead singer of a rock band	布莱尔曾经是一个摇滚乐队主唱，
7	called the Ugly Rumors,	那个乐队叫"丑陋的流言"。
8	more recently prime minister,	现在他是英国首相，
9	told his former bass player in an interview.	在一次采访中就是这样对原乐队的贝司手说的：
10	"I was quite serious about it.	"我对摇滚乐是非常认真的，
11	It wasn't just a mere dalliance—	我不是玩票——
12	it was a bit more than that for me."	摇滚的意义不止于此。"
13	Blair told ex-bass player Mark Ellen.	这是布莱尔对原贝司手马克·埃伦说的话。
14	Excerpts of the interview were printed in *The Times*.	采访的片段登在《泰晤士报》上，
15	"With politics,	"在政坛上，
16	it all clicked into place for me somehow.	一切对我似乎都顺利自然。

（待续）

（续上表）

	断　句	译　文
17	Whereas with music	搞音乐就不同了，
18	you had to have a particular set of attributes	你必须有一系列特殊素质，
19	that I didn't quite have,	那是我比较缺乏的东西，
20	and it never happened for me	我从未拥有那样的素质，
21	even though I was desperately keen to carry on."	我曾想努力继续我的摇滚生涯。"
22	Blair, 51, said	现年 51 岁的布莱尔说，
23	that he still gets a thrill	他有时仍然会兴奋不已，
24	meeting rock icons of his youth	这就是见到他年轻时的摇滚偶像的时候，
25	like Paul McCartney or David Bowie.	比如保罗·麦卡特尼和大卫·鲍伊。
26	"They say: 'It must be so interesting what you do,'	"他们说：'你的工作肯定有意思极了，'
27	and I say: 'It's not as interesting as what you do.'"	而我说：'没有你们的有意思。'"

3　视译点评

1. 原文第二句：…, the onetime lead singer of a rock band // called the Ugly Rumors, // more　recently prime minister, // told his former bass player in an interview.

　　视译时，此句的并列主语 the onetime lead singer of a rock band called the Ugly Rumors 和 more recently prime minister 可依照类意群断句法分成三个视译单位：the onetime lead singer of a rock band // called the Ugly Rumors, // more recently prime minister，然后用增添主语和谓语的方法将每个单位译成分句："布莱尔曾经是一个摇滚乐队主唱"，"那个乐队叫'丑陋的流言'"，"现在他是英国首相"。

2. 原文第八句：… he still gets a thrill // meeting rock icons of his youth // like

Paul McCartney or David Bowie.

原译文按照汉语表达习惯调整了语序，将引发情感的原因置于情感之前："时到如今，在见到保罗·麦卡特尼和大卫·鲍伊等年轻时代的偶像时，他仍然会兴奋不已。"而视译时，为了顺序译出此句，又要听起来通畅，需要把这个句子断为三个视译单位：he still gets a thrill // meeting rock icons of his youth // like Paul McCartney or David Bowie，分别译为"他有时仍然会兴奋不已"，"这就是在见到他年轻时的摇滚偶像的时候"，"比如保罗·麦卡特尼和大卫·鲍伊"，其中第二个视译单位通过添加"这就是"使这个分句与前面的分句在意思上连接起来。

三、实战练习

1 词汇与表达

请先熟悉以下词汇与表达，并适当地运用在视译中。

subsidiary	子公司
mirror image	翻版
main frame	总体框架
allegiance	忠诚
government inducement	政府优惠政策
workforce	劳动力
maximize the competitiveness	最大化竞争力
a fair and competitive market place	公平竞争的市场
anti-trust legislation	反托拉斯法
fair trading	公平贸易
European Union	欧盟
multilateral agreement on investment	多边投资协议
cable system	有线（通讯）系统
balanced budget	平衡预算
a run on the US dollar	挤兑美元
Japanese yen	日元
central bank	中央银行
French franc	法国法郎
currency run	货币流失

peso	比索（菲律宾和一些拉丁美洲国家的货币）
the fixed rate	固定汇率
overvalue	估价太高
undervalue	估价太低
without merit	毫无是处
pound	英镑
monetary union	货币联盟
borrow short	短期借入
lend long	长期借出
World Bank	世界银行
outcast	被抛弃的人或物
floating exchange rate	浮动汇率
flexible system of floating rates	弹性浮动汇率体系
systemic breakdown	系统崩溃
be given free reign	完全自由，不受限制
IMF rules and practices	国际货币基金组织规则和做法
derivative	衍生品，衍生物
hedge fund	对冲基金
highly leveraged	高举债率的

2 实战课文

　　请在 15 分钟之内迅速阅读下面的讲话，了解大意。视译时要保持正常语速，译文要顺畅达意。

Economic Globalization (Excerpt 1)
Malcolm Fraser

2000

　　Globalization involves both the organization of industry and the structure of the financial markets.

　　We have had global corporations for decades. Once a global corporation has subsidiaries in a number of countries, it would have those subsidiaries organized as a mirror image of itself. **While many international companies are still organized in this traditional manner, change is under way and corporations who move too**

slowly will be left behind. （句 1 ） Now a globalized company will have quite a different structure. The products or services may be the same. But instead of separate national units in different countries, there will be only one selling unit—the world. **Some aspects of corporate activity will obviously be organized locally but the main frame of the corporation will be organized on a global basis, sourcing different production components from the best current source.** （句 2 ） The new outlook for corporations organized in such a way has no allegiance to any particular place of production. Such corporations pursue low wage cost opportunities and more favorable government inducements wherever they will, worldwide. Corporations are mobile to a much greater extent than ever before.

The new global organization of industry has consequences for social policy. Many governments would have conducted policies designed to see that workers gained a fair share of the returns of an enterprise. With the globalization of industry, such policies are much more difficult to sustain. **Governments now tend to argue for lower wages, for smaller workforces, to maximize the competitiveness of their particular country as a home for global investment.** （句 3 ） Accompanying these changes we find a growing disparity in wealth between rich and poor in many countries. This may not matter so much if the poor were also becoming better off compared to their own earlier standards but in many cases this is not so. Even in wealthy countries, some workers are paid a wage which could not support even the smallest of families. In this day, if that is what the market determines, then that is what must happen.

It has long been recognized that a fair and competitive market place is a rare thing—an equal number of suppliers, an equal number of buyers, all of the same financial strength. Such situations do not exist. That is why anti-trust legislation was born. It is why fair trading practices were put in place. With the internationalization of trade and commerce, with the globalization of corporations, such national rules to preserve fair trading are no longer effective. For the most part there are no international rules. Where there has been an attempt to establish such rules, they often have a rather different purpose. For example, the European Union sought to promote a multilateral agreement on investment. If it had been accepted, it probably would have reduced the authority of national governments even further and given global corporations an even more influential position.

In today's world, governments must fashion their policies to meet the wishes of the international marketplace. Peter Drucker pointed out that in 1995 when the United States Senate failed to pass a balanced budget amendment, the world's currency traders panicked and started a run on the US dollar which he believed was already undervalued at least 10% against the Japanese *yen*. At that time, the dollar fell from 106 *yen* to the dollar to less than 80 in two weeks. The central banks of the United States, England, Germany, Japan, Switzerland and France, tried to reverse the trend but failed, losing billions in the attempt. It took the dollar more than a year to climb back to its original undervalued rate. A similar run against the French franc forced President Mitterand to change his economic policies in 1981. Currency runs can have a recognized cause. In Mexico, fiscal irresponsibility led to a run on the peso which wiped out six years of economic gains. To avoid such dangers, countries need to run tight monetary and fiscal policies. This establishes a limitation on national authority but still only provides a very limited guarantee of security.

Despite good policy and best intentions, the market often does not produce a sensible result. **The dollar fell by 50% against the *yen* when President Reagan and the Japanese government both agreed to give up the fixed rate of 250 *yen* to \$1 in 1983. (句 4)** The dollar had certainly been overvalued but it went into free fall and did not stop until it had lost 60% of its value against the *yen*. That is until it hit 110 two years after the event. This is a significant example of the market behaving irrationally, without merit. But if it can happen to the United States, the most powerful economy, what of other countries? A run on the pound, together with other factors, caused Britain to leave the Monetary Union some years ago. More recently, Asian economies, which had suffered the old sin of borrowing short and lending long, have suffered the most severe economic recessions. Countries that were held by the World Bank as a prime example of how a developing country should behave, suddenly became outcasts. Everyone was wise after the event and enumerated reasons why the collapse was not only the fault of the countries concerned but also inevitable because poor economic practices and inadequate supervision were so obvious, even though these factors had not been pointed out before the collapse.

The IMF's insistence on immediately floating exchange rates can often exacerbate the crisis. The flexible system of floating rates, largely in place since the early 1970s, which was meant to make life easier for governments, has made the financial conditions for capitalism far more volatile and far more unstable. We all know enough of markets to know that they favor the powerful and that markets can overwhelm and destroy smaller players. Sometimes smaller players are entire nations. **Perhaps we can understand the consequences of establishing such market dominance when we realize that these changes dramatically effect the capacity of governments to exercise their judgment.** （句 5） Instead, whatever exercise of judgment is involved is made by the tens of thousands of players in the market place themselves. This is one of the reasons why the proponents in many places favor the market. They distrust the judgment of governments. But we have seen enough of the market, in moving the United States currency, in moving other currencies without logic, in the collapse in Asia, to know that the market itself can be unpredictable and dramatic in its consequences.

For the world as a whole, the most serious problem is volatility, possibly leading to systemic breakdown. There is much to reflect on since the Asian economic problems of 1997. There has been a great deal of discussion about the present system and about changes that need to be made. We need also to note that Malaysia, which refused to follow IMF restrictions, seems to have recovered quite well. **This raises a significant question mark about the universality of rules currently accepted as inviolate by the International Monetary Fund.** （句 6） The fact that China maintained the value of its currency throughout the crisis also provided a great sense of stability. By maintaining its currency China calmed financial markets and defined the limits of the Asian crisis. It is a clear case of a government judgment being superior to that which would have been imposed if the markets had been given free reign. Perhaps more than anything else, this should lead us to question the universal application of IMF rules and practices.

For a while it appeared that the reform process would move forward but the tendency seems to be "it's all right, we have escaped, leave well enough alone". We need to understand that the problems in Thailand, Republic of Korea, Malaysia and Indonesia were not just problems within the countries involving inadequate financial institutions or prudential supervision. The world's financial markets were also very much at fault. The whole crisis demonstrated the instability and volatility of financial structures. It also demonstrated that the major contributor to recovery was the stability of the Chinese currency itself. In the case of the Asian crisis, it was the lender that was the wild card.

There remains an urgent need to reform the system, to establish much tougher international rules for prudential supervision and control. The International Monetary Fund has demonstrated time and time again that it acts principally after crises have occurred. It seeks to pick up the pieces. It has been ineffective in avoiding crises. If this is as a consequence of its charter, it certainly needs reviewing. The IMF's present operations are inadequate. The task is international and global. Whether it is a reformed International Monetary Fund or a new institution is a matter for debate.

The non-bank financial sector, the derivative and hedging markets are huge in their operations and unpredictable in their impacts. Very often corporations operating in these markets totally escape the normal network of supervision which is applied to the official banking sector, yet the risks undertaken in these areas are substantial and capable of leading us into systemic breakdown if we don't establish structures to deal with them. It is not as though we have not had significant warning of serious problems. When we woke up one morning and found that Alan Greenspan had organized the bail-out of for Long Term Capital Management, we knew that he did so because he had no option. If Long Term Capital Management, operating with highly leveraged hedge funds had been allowed to go bust, it could have led to systemic breakdown in the entire financial system.

3 难句分析与视译处理

句 1：　 While many international companies are still organized in this traditional manner, change is under way and corporations who move too slowly will be left behind.

笔译译文：现在，许多国际性公司仍然按照这一传统模式组成，但变化正在产生，行动缓慢的公司将被甩在后面。

视译译文：

断　句	译　文
While many international companies	现在，许多国际性公司
are still organized in this traditional manner,	其组织结构仍然遵循传统方式，
change is under way	但是它们正在发生变化，
and corporations who move too slowly	一些公司行动缓慢，
will be left behind.	就会被甩在后面。

句2： Some aspects of corporate activity will obviously be organized locally, but the main frame of the corporation will be organized on a global basis, sourcing different production components from the best current source.

笔译译文： 公司活动中的某些方面显然还是要由当地组织安排，但公司的总体框架将以全球为组织基础，并在全球范围内，从现有最佳资源中获取不同的生产要素。

视译译文：

断　句	译　文
Some aspects of corporate activity	公司的某些活动，
will obviously be organized locally,	显然是在地方上安排，
but the main frame of the corporation	但公司的总体框架，
will be organized on a global basis,	将有着全球性的基础，
sourcing different production components	不同的生产要素，
from the best current source.	会取自全球的最佳来源。

句3： Governments now tend to argue for lower wages, for smaller workforces, to maximize the competitiveness of their particular country as a home for global investment.

笔译译文： 现在，为了在最大程度上提高本国作为全球投资目的地的竞争力，各国政府都倾向于较低工资和较小的劳动力规模。

视译译文：

断　句	译　文
Governments now tend to argue	各国政府现在往往希望
for lower wages,	降低工资、
for smaller workforces,	压缩人力，
to maximize the competitiveness	以便最大程度地提高竞争力，
of their particular country	使它们的国家，
as a home for global investment.	成为全球投资的场所。

句 4： The dollar fell by 50% against the *yen* when President Reagan and the Japanese government both agreed to give up the fixed rate of 250 yen to $1 in 1983.

笔译译文： 1983 年，里根总统和日本政府同意取消日元对美元 250 比 1 的固定汇率，随后，美元对日元的汇率下跌了 50%。

视译译文：

断　句	译　文
The dollar fell by 50% against the *yen*	美元对日元下跌了 50%，
when President Reagan and the Japanese government both agreed	因为里根总统和日本政府都同意，
to give up the fixed rate	取消固定汇率，
of 250 *yen* to $1	也就是 250 日元对 1 美元，
in 1983.	那是 1983 年的事情。

句 5： Perhaps we can understand the consequences of establishing such market dominance when we realize that these changes dramatically effect the capacity of governments to exercise their judgment.

笔译译文： 也许，只有意识到这些变化对政府的判断能力的影响有多么巨大，我们才能了解建立这种市场统治地位的种种后果。

视译译文：

断　句	译　文
Perhaps we can understand	也许我们能够明白，
the consequences of establishing such market dominance	建立这种市场主导地位的种种后果，
when we realize	条件是我们先要认识到，
that these changes dramatically effect	这些变化严重地影响到，
the capacity of governments	政府的能力，
to exercise their judgment.	也就是政府的判断力。

句 6： This raises a significant question mark about the universality of rules currently accepted as inviolate by the International Monetary Fund.

笔译译文： 这就提出了一个重要的问题：现在被国际货币基金组织奉为金科玉律的规则是否具有普遍适用性呢?

视译译文：

断　句	译　文
This raises a significant question mark	这就提出了一个重要的问题,
about the universality of rules	那就是规则是否具有普遍适用性,
currently accepted as inviolate	现在这些规则被奉为金科玉律,
by the International Monetary Fund.	国际货币基金组织就是这样认为的。

4 参考译文

经济全球化（节选1）
马尔科姆・弗雷泽
2000 年

全球化浪潮不仅影响了产业的组织形式，而且也深入到了金融市场结构之中。

全球性公司的产生已有几十年的历史了。当一家全球性的公司在许多国家设立子公司时，这些子公司肯定是其母公司的翻版。现在，许多国际性公司仍然按照这一传统模式组成，但变化正在产生，行动缓慢的公司将被甩在后面。现在的全球性公司将具有完全不同的结构。其产品和服务也同样如此。全球性公司不再分别在各个国家建立全国性的经销单位，而是只有一个统一的经销单位——全世界。公司活动中的某些方面显然还是要由当地组织安排，但公司的总体框架将以全球为组织基础，并在全球的范围内，从现有最佳资源获取不同的生产要素。这是一种全新的观念，以这种形式组织的公司不再局限于任何生产地点。这些公司会在世界范围内的任何地方寻找低工资成本的机会和更加优惠的政府鼓励措施。公司的移动能力大大超过了以往任何时候。

新的全球性产业组织形式对社会政策也产生了影响。许多政府过去实行的政策都旨在使员工从企业的收益中获得公正的分配。但是，随着产业的全球化，这种政策越来越难以继续了。现在，为了在最大程度上提高本国作为全球投资目的地的竞争力，各国政府都倾向于较低工资和较小的劳动力规模。伴随着这些变化，我们发现，在许多国家中，贫富差距日趋扩大。如果贫穷者与其以前的状况相比，生活水平有所改善，情况还不至于这么糟，但实际情况却往往不是这样。即使在富裕国家，许多劳动者得到的工资连一个最小规模家庭的生活都难以维持。在今天，如果一切都要由市场来决定，那么，这就是必然的结果。

　　长久以来，人们早已达成了共识，即：一个完全公平竞争的市场是不可能存在的。同等数量的供应商，同等数量的购买商，相同的经济实力，这种情况不可能存在。这正是反托拉斯法之所以产生的原因，也是需要推进公平贸易行为的原因。但随着贸易和商业的国际化、公司的全球化，这些保证公平贸易的国家规则已不再适用了。在多数情况下，国际规则并不存在。建立国际规则的努力往往另有所图。例如，欧盟曾力求达成一项多边投资协议。如果这一多边协议被接受，就可能进一步削弱国家政府的权威，并使全球性的公司获得更大的影响力。

　　在当今世界，政府政策的制定必须满足国际市场的愿望。彼德·德鲁克指出，1995 年，由于美国参议院没有批准通过一项平衡预算修正案，全世界的外汇交易商们惊恐万分，纷纷挤兑美元。而他认为那时美元兑日元已贬值了至少10%。当时，在两个星期之内，日元与美元的比价从 106 比 1 降到了不到 80 比 1。美国、英国、德国、日本、瑞士和法国的中央银行想扭转这种不良趋势，但没有成功，而且还损失了几十亿美元。一年多以后，美元才恢复到原先那个与日元的偏低汇率。1981 年，法国法郎也经受过相似的经历，密特朗总统被迫因此调整了他的经济政策。还有一个公认的原因也可能造成挤兑货币。在墨西哥，由于不负责任的财政政策，导致了挤兑比索，使墨西哥六年的经济成果付之东流。为了避免这类金融风险，各国需要实行紧缩的金融和财政政策。这使得国家的权威受到限制，但即便如此，国家金融安全的保证还是非常有限。

　　尽管有好的政策和意愿，市场往往产生不了好的结果。1983 年，里根总统和日本政府同意取消日元对美元 250 比 1 的固定汇率，随后，美元对日元的汇率下跌了 50%。此前，美元相对于日元肯定是定值过高了，但是，美元兑日元的汇率开始一路狂跌，一直下降了 60% 多，两年后，在日元与美元的比价跌到了 110 比 1 时，这场风暴才算停止。这是市场行为何其缺乏理智、何其狂暴不羁的一个典型例子。美国是世界上最强的经济体，既然它也会发生这种情况，其他国家就更不用说了。几年前，由于挤兑英镑，再加上其他一些因素，英国被迫脱离了货币联盟组织。最近，由于受旧有的短期借进、长期借出的经济模式之害，亚洲经济遭受了最为严重的衰退。被世界银行树立为发展中国家重要榜样的各个国家瞬间被打入了万劫不复的深渊。这场风暴过去后，大家似乎都成了事后诸葛亮，头头是道地说明出现这场大崩溃并不仅仅是由于这些国家的错误，而是有其必然性的，因为在这些国家，糟糕的经济惯例和监督不力的情况显而易见。然而，在此危机之前，谁也没有指出过这些问题。

国际货币基金组织坚持要实行即时浮动汇率，这往往只会进一步加深这种危机。弹性浮动汇率体系大体于 70 年代初期普遍实行，其本意是为各国政府创造一个较为宽松的经济环境，但却使得资本主义制度的金融环境更加不稳定，更加不安全。我们都了解市场，知道市场推崇强手，市场可以操纵和摧毁较小的参与者。有时，较小的市场参与者就是整个国家。也许，只有意识到这些变化对政府的判断能力的影响有多么巨大，我们才能了解建立这种市场统治地位的种种后果。然而，无论如何判断，这些判断都是由成千上万的市场参与者自己作出的。这就是在许多地方市场主导地位的支持者推崇市场的原因。他们不信任政府的判断。但对于市场的方方面面，我们看到的已经不少了，我们看到了变换不定的美元汇率，我们看到了变换不定的其他货币汇率，我们还看到了亚洲经济的崩溃，我们了解到，市场本身是不可预测的，其后果令人震惊。

从全世界范围来看，最严重的问题是市场的变幻无常，这可能导致系统性的崩溃。1997 年开始的亚洲经济危机为我们提供了许多反思的机会。关于现有体系存在的问题和需要进行的变化，已经进行了很多的讨论。我们还需要特别指出，拒绝接受国际货币基金组织限制条件的马来西亚看来恢复得很好。这就提出了一个重要的问题：现在被国际货币基金组织奉为金科玉律的规则是否具有普遍适用性呢？中国在整个亚洲金融风暴的过程中一直保持其货币不贬值，这也为如何保持经济稳定提供了一个重要的例子。通过保持其货币价值，中国稳定了金融市场，阻止了亚洲金融风暴进一步蔓延。它为我们提供了一个典型的例子：政府的判断不为自由放任的市场的影响所左右。这一事例比其他任何事例都更清晰地促使我们质疑国际货币基金组织的规则和做法的普遍适用性。

有一段时间，看起来好像改革进程正在推进，但其趋势似乎在表明"没问题，我们已经躲过了这场风暴，现在不是好好的吗？"但我们应该知道，泰国、韩国、马来西亚和印度尼西亚出现的问题并不仅仅是由于这些国家本身金融体系不完善或缺乏审慎的监督制度，世界金融市场也存在很大问题。整个危机过程表明世界金融结构是如何的不稳定和变幻不定。它也表明，亚洲经济复苏的重要促成因素是中国货币的稳定性。至于亚洲金融危机，破坏游戏规则的恰恰是贷方。

现在的国际经济体系仍迫切需要进行改革，制定更加严格的国际规则，实行审慎的监督和控制。过去的事例一再表明，国际货币基金组织主要是在危机出现后作出反应。它所做的只是收拾残局，并不能有效地避免危机。如果这种情况的发生是其宪章规定所致，我们就肯定需要重新审阅宪章。目前国际货币基金组织的运作方式确实存在问题。这是一项国际性和全球性的任务，是对国际货币基金组织进行改革，还是建立一个新的机构代替它，这个问题需要讨论。

非银行金融领域、金融衍生品与对冲基金市场的操作规模极为庞大，其影响也根本无法预知。在这个市场中运作的公司常常可以完全逃脱正常监督系统的监督，因为这些系统只是针对官方的银行领域的。然而，这些领域承受的风险极大，如果我们没有应对机制，可能会引起系统性的崩溃。我们也不是没有得到过严厉的警告。某天早上，我们一觉睡醒，发现艾伦·格林斯潘已组织对美国长期资本管理公司进行紧急援助，我们知道，他也是迫不得已而为之。这家美国公司从事高举债率对冲基金交易，如果任其破产，就会导致整个金融系统的系统性崩溃。

四、自主训练

请在 15 分钟之内迅速阅读下面的讲话，了解大意。学生可组成对子练习，互相监控对视译技巧的掌握情况、视译质量和现场表现，或以边视译边录音的形式进行个人练习。视译时要保持正常语速，译文要顺畅达意。如遇难句，可在首次视译后参照"实战练习"中难句分析与视译处理的方法进行练习，找出解决方法。

Economic Globalization (Excerpt 2)

Malcolm Fraser

2000

We have been warned by George Sorrows. He wrote: "Although I have made a fortune in the financial markets, I now fear that untrammeled intensification of *laissez-faire* capitalism and the spread of market values to all areas of life is endangering our open and democratic society.... Too much competition and too little cooperation can cause intolerable inequities and instability. The doctrine of *laissez-faire* capitalism holds that the common good is best served by the uninhibited pursuit of self interest. Unless it is tempered by a recognition of a common interest that ought to take precedence over particular interests, our present system ... is liable to breakdown." Sorrows' own record suggests we should listen to his warnings. The increasing volatility in financial markets, especially in currency and stock markets, the unpredictability of hedge funds operations all suggest that the challenges they involve should be taken up with some energy. There are two specific challenges: how to preserve some form of equity and reasonable competition in a globalized market place and how to establish stability within the financial markets themselves.

There is an urgent need to establish an international body to establish rules for fair trading in a globalized environment. Middle ranking and small countries would have most to gain from such an innovation. National institutions that may exist to achieve such an objective are now largely irrelevant if a country is to maintain its competitive place as an attractive home for international investments. Even more important, we need to establish a more stable exchange rate regime. That may require different approaches for emerging markets and the currencies of developed industrialized countries. There is a real need to reduce short-term volatility and uncertainty in financial markets. This has to be compatible, with sufficient flexibility for adjustment in the medium term.

The US dollar and the euro together will cover the great majority of world financial markets. The stability of the trans-Atlantic exchange rate therefore is crucial for world stability but, in view of the importance of the yen and the *yuan* in the Asian region, the stability of these currencies against the dollar and the euro is also a prime objective. Representatives of major world currencies should consult about and coordinate their fundamental policy objectives and their implications for achieving greater exchange rate stability. If greater stability is established between major countries, other countries, especially those with small open economies should be permitted to choose their own exchange rate regime. No one system is appropriate at all times and in all places. However, whatever regime is chosen should be designed to reduce volatility, to encourage investment and allow for the flexibility necessary to adapt to changing circumstances.

The current financial system is fragile. It needs greater strength and depth.

This requires more effective supervision of international financial transactions. An international framework is needed for prudential supervision. That is essential for the creation of sufficient international liquidity while discouraging reckless risk-taking on the parts of lenders and borrowers. In establishing such supervision, countries other than the G7, particularly developing countries and countries whose economies are in transition, should be involved. An international regulatory authority should be established. Such an authority should establish standards of best practice in all forms of financial regulation, monitor compliance with those standards and coordinate mechanisms for limiting the risks posed by non-compliance. In addition to prudential supervision, there is a need for international standards of disclosure, market control and cross-border mergers. Achieving best practice in prudential regulation involves not only a political commitment but also technical expertise. Many countries need assistance in this regard.

Order in international financial markets requires a certain balance between short-and long-term capital flows. Equally important is consistency between a country's state of financial development and the speed with which capital can enter and exit its markets. The IMF[1] has been mistaken in requiring full capital account convertibility for all member states. In certain situations it will be appropriate for some emerging markets to restrict short-term capital inflows and to impede the movement of flight capital belonging to national citizens. Chile has set an example in this regard. Such practices would have modified the severity of the recent Asian crisis.

The IMF should continue with adequate conditions to provide assistance to states experiencing financial crisis. But in responding to such a situation, the IMF should pay more attention to a country's history and its individual economic situation. It should not intrude on the World Bank's responsibility for long-term development issues, as it sought to do in Indonesia.

The IMF's financial resources should be strengthened as a means of averting crises through the provision of contingency funds. Immediate access to adequate funding can be essential for this purpose if crises are to be avoided. Finding a way to encourage the IMF to help avert crises instead of just reacting to crises after they have occurred is a most important requirement. In any liquidity arrangement,

---

1 International Monetary Fund.

assisting a country in distress, the IMF should take care not to absolve lenders of their responsibility. In some cases IMF bail-outs have done more to help the lenders than the countries themselves. The lenders need to carry their own risk.

As a footnote to these comments, I want to make two specific suggestions concerning the Asian Pacific region. In some ways this region is less structured and less organized than other parts of the world. In North and South America there is NAFTA[1], which presumably will ultimately cover the whole region. There is also the organization of American States. Europe has its European Union, which grows larger. In our region, APEC has been established to promote and advance freer trade. Its original intention was that it would move faster than the World Trade Organization. Those who promoted APEC in the first instance sought to confine its impact to the countries of East and Southeast Asia. The United States wished to be involved and so countries on the Pacific Rim, with widely diverging interests, are now part of APEC. This expansion has mitigated against APEC being a pace-setter in the search for freer trade. The membership is so large and diverse that it is difficult to advance the specific interests of East and Southeast Asia adequately or effectively.

Our own region needs to give greater attention to regional interests and regional concerns. In the first instance this could be best promoted by a political conference of leaders of all East and Southeast Asian countries, which of course should include countries like Australia and new Zealand, which would meet annually. It would have its own secretariat. It would have a number of serious questions to address: Is APEC meeting its objectives? Should East and Southeast Asia seek to move faster and more effectively? While it is not a subject for discussion at this forum, such a meeting could also address security concerns. The interests of the countries within the region do not necessarily coincide with the interests of countries external to the region. In some instances, such forces divert countries from paying adequate attention to their own security. In the longer term, the relationship between countries of a region provides the only security that is viable and which can sustain itself.

On economic matters, such a forum could also examine in practical ways, a suggestion originally derived from Japan. At the beginning of the Asian crisis, Japan suggested that a fund should be established for the region, by the region, perhaps called an Asian monetary fund. The purpose of such fund would clearly be

---

1 North American Free Trade Agreement.

to promote stability in regional financial markets, to advance transparency and to encourage all governments to maintain adequate prudential supervision or regulation of those operating in the capital markets. With the resources of Japan and of China and of other countries within the region, the establishment of such a fund is within the capacity of the region.

The idea was never seriously examined because the United States wished to preserve the dominance of the International Monetary Fund. When one examines the relationship between the International Monetary Fund and the United States Congress, and the manner in which that Congress seeks to impose its will on the policies of the Fund, the attraction of a more independent body becomes attractive. In short compass, while globalization of corporations and of the financial markets is indeed a global phenomenon, whose longer term consequences are not yet well understood, there is much that China and Asia could do to advance the region's interests in a highly competitive world.

定语的视译（Ⅱ）：定语从句

基本技巧：
* 将定语从句作为其先行词后面的一个独立部分单独译出。

一、技巧讲解：定语从句的视译

　　这一单元的重点是如何对定语从句进行视译。"英语的定语既可前置，也可后置，但汉语的则只能前置"。（华先发，2004：110）英语定语从句是英语定语的一个常用形式，其位置是在中心词之后。定语从句可以是限定性的，也可以是非限定性的，而汉语中没有类似英语定语从句的成分，只有限定性定语，其位置总是在中心词之前。笔译时，英语定语从句的这种特定的后置位置往往要求译者作较大的调整，将其按照汉语的表达习惯置于中心词之前。

　　在同传或视译中，时间不允许口译员进行这样的调整，所以，一般来说，置于先行词之后的定语从句应该另分一句翻译。定语从句较长时，尤其需要如此。

例 1： Congress made public a survey of human rights in 105 countries that receive US aid.

译文 1： 国会公布了接受美国援助的 105 个国家的人权情况调查报告。

译文 2： 国会公布了 105 个国家的人权状况，这些国家接受美国的援助。

【讲解】 按照汉语表达习惯，译文 1 将定语从句 that receive US aid 移到先行词之前，作定语短语，这是笔译时常用的方法。而在视译时译员为了节省时间以跟上讲话者，往往顺着译出语中定语从句在句中的位置，将其单独译成一句："这些国家接受美国的援助"。

例2： That those who had learnt from us now excelled us was a real challenge.

译文1：向我们学习的人反倒超过了我们，这确实对我们是一个促进。

译文2：那些人曾向我们学习，但却超过了我们，这确实是一个挑战。

【讲解】 译文1按照笔译的习惯调整了原句中定语从句的位置，将其置于先行词those之前，译作定语短语。视译时，要保持定语从句who had learnt from us在句中的位置，不作任何调整，可以先译出先行词those，将其作为定语从句的主语，然后依序译出定语从句，先行词和定语从句构成译入语句中的一个分句："那些人曾向我们学习"。将定语从句单独译出，将先行词作为该句主语，这是视译中常用的翻译定语从句的技巧。

例3： My brother-in-law's laugh, which was very infectious, broke the silence.

译文1：我姐夫富有感染力的笑声打破了沉默。（浩瀚&马光，2001：395）

译文2：我姐夫的笑声富有感染力，它打破了沉默。

【讲解】 原句中非限定性定语从句which was very infectious在译文1中被译作laugh的定语短语，置于句中主语部分的中心词之前，成为限定性定语。而视译时，译员要跟上讲话人的语速，需要尽量保持原句各个部分的语序，因此，可以将先行词laugh译作定语从句which was very infectious的主语，使先行词和定语从句合并成一个分句——"我姐夫的笑声富有感染力"，然后通过添加主语将原句中的谓语和宾语单独译成另一分句"它打破了沉默"。

例4： A spirited discussion springs up between a young girl who insists that women have outgrown the jumping-on-the-chair at-the-sight-of-a-mouse era, and a colonel who says that they haven't.

译文1：一位年轻女士和一位上校展开了热烈的争论，女士坚持妇女已经不再看见老鼠就吓得跳上椅子，那种时代早过去了；上校则认为没有过去。（陈文伯，1998：81-82）

译文2：一场热烈的争论开始了。一方是一位年轻的女士，她坚持认为，妇女已经不再一见到老鼠就跳到椅子上去，那个时代已经过去了；另一方是一位上校，他认为那种时代没有过去。

【讲解】　原句是一个带有两个定语从句的典型的英语长句，在视译中属于是很难处理的句子。视译时，时间不允许译员像译文 1 那样调整全句语序，可以根据前面讲过的视译单位，将长句断成类意群，依序译出。给其中修饰 a young girl 的定语从句 who insists that women have outgrown the jumping-on-the-chair at-the-sight-of-a-mouse era 添加主语"她"后，依次译成三个分句："她坚持认为"，"妇女已经不再见到老鼠就跳到椅子上去"和"那个时代已经过去了"。这样就比较符合口语的表达习惯。

例 5：　Thousands of red, beautiful roses that blossom almost at the same time make the park the great resort of people in spring.

译文 1：差不多同时开放的几千朵美丽红玫瑰，在春季里吸引了许多人常到公园来。（陈定安，1998：186）

译文 2：几千朵美丽的红玫瑰，差不多同时开放，使公园成为春季吸引游人的好地方。

【讲解】　译文 2 将以 that 引导的定语从句顺译为独立的短句"差不多同时开放"，翻译时保持了原句的语序。

　　定语从句是视译中的一个难点，尤其是长定语从句，往往会消耗视译人员大量的时间。但如果在思维上将长定语从句考虑为一个独立的成分，不改变这个从句的后置位置，基本上都可以将它处理得比较得当。具体的做法就是：先将先行词译出；然后依照原语序将定语从句作为独立句子译出；先行词在许多情况下可以作为独立句子的主语；必要时加连接类词语使译出的句子更加通顺。

二、语段视译

1　词汇与表达

在进行语段视译前，请先预习以下词汇与表达。

antipathy	反感，厌恶
plank road	木板路

2 视译语段

请在 3 分钟之内迅速阅读下面的语段，了解大意，然后结合所学要点进行视译练习。视译时要保持正常语速，译文要顺畅达意。

Despite the clear-cut technological advantages, the railroad didn't become the primary means of transportation for nearly 20 years after first pioneering American railroads were introduced in the early 1830s. Besides the stiff competition of water transportation, an important hindrance to railroad development was public antipathy, which had its roots in ignorance, conservatism, and vested interest. People thought that speeds of 20 to 30 miles per hour would be physically harmful to passengers. Many honestly believed that the railroad would prove to be impractical and uneconomical and would not provide services as dependent as that of the waterways. Unsurprisingly, the most vigorous opposition to railroads came from groups whose economic interests suffered from the competition of the new industry. Millions of dollars had been spent on canals, rivers, highways, and plank roads, and thousands of people depended on the transportation enterprises for their livelihood. （摘自《英语学习》，2003 年第 6 期，第 68 页）

原译文：尽管铁路运输在技术上有明显的优势，但是美国的铁路在 19 世纪 30 年代早期闪亮登场后的近 20 年中却没有成为首要的交通运输手段。除了水上运输的激烈竞争之外，阻碍铁路运输发展的主要因素是公众的反感，它根源于愚昧无知、守旧和既得利益。人们以为 20 至 30 英里的时速会对旅客的身体造成损害。许多人深信铁路运输不切实际、浪费资源，也不会提供像水路运输那样可靠的服务。对铁路最强烈的反对来自那些经济利益受到这个新行业竞争冲击的集团，这不足为怪。上百万的美元被用于建造运河、水道、公路和木板路，成千上万的人依靠这些运输企业谋生。（付美榕译）

3 视译译文

	断 句	译 文
1	Despite the clear-cut technological advantages,	虽然具有明显的技术优势，
2	the railroad didn't become the primary means of transportation	铁路并没有成为当时主要的运输工具。

（待续）

（续上表）

	断　句	译　文
3	for nearly 20 years	最初近 20 年都是如此，
4	after first pioneering American railroads were introduced	而美国初次建设铁路，
5	in the early 1830s.	是在 19 世纪 30 年代初。
6	Besides the stiff competition of water transportation,	除了水路运输的激烈竞争，
7	an important hindrance to railroad development	有一个重要因素阻碍了铁路的发展，
8	was public antipathy,	这就是公众的反感，
9	which had its roots in ignorance, conservatism, and vested interest.	其根源在于愚昧、保守和既得利益。
10	People thought that	人们认为，
11	speeds of 20 to 30 miles per hour	时速 20 至 30 英里，
12	would be physically harmful to passengers.	会损害旅客的身体。
13	Many honestly believed	许多人深信，
14	that the railroad would prove to be impractical and uneconomical	铁路既不实用也不经济，
15	and would not provide services	提供的服务
16	as dependent as that of the waterways.	也不会像水路那样可靠。
17	Unsurprisingly,	毫不奇怪，
18	the most vigorous opposition to railroads	最强烈反对铁路的，
19	came from groups	是这样一些集团，
20	whose economic interests suffered	它们的经济利益受到损害，
21	from the competition of the new industry.	冲击就来自这一新兴行业。
22	Millions of dollars had been spent on	上百万的美元已投入到

（待续）

（续上表）

	断　句	译　文
23	canals, rivers, highways, and plank roads,	修筑运河、河道、公路和木板路，
24	and thousands of people	成千上万的人
25	depended on the transportation enterprises for their livelihood.	依靠这些传统运输业谋生。

4　视译点评

1. 原文第一句：Despite the clear-cut technological advantages, // the railroad didn't become the primary means of transportation // for nearly 20 years // after first pioneering American railroads // were introduced in the early 1830s.

　　视译时按照前述顺译和划定视译单位的基本原则，把 despite the clear-cut technological advantages 这个介词短语通过增加"具有"译成汉语分句："虽然具有明显的技术优势"，再将主句进行划分：the railroad didn't become the primary means of transportation // for nearly 20 years // after first pioneering American railroads were introduced // in the early 1830s. 由此把它分别译成三个汉语分句："铁路并没有成为当时主要的运输工具"，"最初近 20 年都是如此"，"而美国初次建设铁路"，"是在 19 世纪 30 年代初"。在这个句子里，特别难处理的是其中的介词词组 for nearly 20 years，我们将这个短语作为一个独立的成分处理，译为："最初近 20 年都是如此"，这样就顺利译出了似乎无法顺译的句子成分。

2. 原文第二句：Besides the stiff competition of water transportation, // an important hindrance to railroad development // was public antipathy, // which had its roots in ignorance, conservatism, and vested interest.

　　此句主语 an important hindrance to railroad development 被译成一个"有"字句分句，其中的名词 hindrance 在译入语中被转译成动词"阻碍"，即："有一个重要因素<u>阻碍了</u>铁路的发展"，而句中谓语部分 was public antipathy 通过添加"这"译成又一个分句："<u>这</u>就是公众的反感"，最后的非限定性定语从句被另外译成一个分句："<u>其根源</u>在于愚昧、保守和既得利益"。译出语中定语从句的谓语 had its roots 被转译成名词"根源"作主语，介词 in 转译成动词"在于"。

3. 原文第五句：Unsurprisingly, // the most vigorous opposition to railroads // came from groups // whose economic interests suffered // from the competition of the new industry.

我们现根据类意群将这个句子分为五个视译单位，依次译出："毫不奇怪"，"最强烈反对铁路的"，"是这样一些集团"，"它们的经济利益受到损害"，"冲击就来自这一新兴工业"。其中定语从句 whose economic interests suffered from the competition of the new industry 根据本单元所讲的原则译成独立的分句，把其中的关系代词译为"它们的"，使句子更加清楚易懂。另外，定语从句本身的断句方法与任何句子的断句方法是一样的，这个定语从句较长，要再分出一个视译单位 from the competition of the new industry，通过添加"冲击"并把介词 from 转译成动词"来自"形成另一个分句。

三、实战练习

1　词汇与表达

请先熟悉以下词汇与表达，并适当地运用在视译中。

Lee Kuan Yew	李光耀（新加坡前总理）
plug its economy into the global grid	将经济纳入全球网格
GATT（the General Agreement on Trade and Tariffs）	关贸总协定
economic autarchy	经济上的闭关自守
in US dollar term	以美元计
foreign direct investment	直接外来投资，缩写为 FDI
FDI inflow	直接外来投资的流入
percentage point	百分点
cost-benefit equation	成本效益衡量
knowledge economy	知识经济
Obuchi Commission	小渊委员会
ethnocentric	种族中心主义
homogenous	单一种族的，同质性的
gold card	金卡
R&D（research and development）	研发（研究与发展）

Goh Chok Tong	吴作栋（新加坡前总理）
returned brains flow	人才回流
tax concession	税务优惠
volatile capital flow	资金流动大幅波动

2 实战课文

请在 15 分钟之内迅速阅读下面的讲话，了解大意。视译时要保持正常语速，译文要顺畅达意。

Economic Globalization—China and Asia (Excerpt 1)

Lee Kuan Yew

Beijing, 2000

Globalization and the New Economy

Since Deng Xiaoping announced the reform and the new open policy in 1978, the economy of China has changed dramatically. Foreign trade, then about 12%, has trebled to 36% of China's GDP, and is still growing. When China decided to join the WTO and reached agreement with the United States in November 1999, China signaled to the world that it was taking a major step to plug its economy into the global grid—although this system is at present still dominated by America, Western Europe and Japan. This dominance is because even before the end of World War II, the Americans and their main ally, the British, had prepared the blueprints for the IMF, the World Bank and GATT.

Before World War II, international trade was most free within the boundaries of each of the empires, the American, British, various European, and Japanese. There were trade barriers between these imperial blocs. The Americans were determined to dissolve these empires after World War II. The General Agreement on Trade and Tariffs (GATT) was designed to facilitate cross-border trade in goods and services without the unifying control of the opposing system of economic autarchy led by the Soviet Union. **But no one foresaw that technological advances in communications and transportation would lead to the growth and proliferation of multinational corporations that are able to expand the production and sale of goods followed by services, across national boundaries, and market them to all parts of the world.** (句 1)

Driving Force of Globalization

Technology has been the driving force of globalization. **It (technology) enabled producers to maximize profits by moving capital, machinery and management expertise to countries where raw materials or labor and infrastructure gave them comparative advantage.** （句 2） This made for unprecedented economic growth and prosperity worldwide, …

The impact of free trade and investments on the world's progress was enormous. Between 1965 and 1999, world GDP in US dollar terms grew 15 times, but world trade increased twice as fast, 30 times. The growth rate of foreign direct investments (FDI) has outstripped that of domestic investments. In 1998 the sum total of FDI, worldwide, was over US $4.1trillion.

In the past 20 years, China's trade in goods expanded double the rate of world trade. China is now the 9th largest trading nation in the world. FDI inflows, near zero in 1978, reached US $45.5 billion in 1998, about 5% of GDP. In 1998 the cumulative total amount of FDI in China was US $261 billion. China is the world's 3rd largest destination for FDI inflows, after the US and the UK. Since 1978, China's per-capita income grew at an annual average rate of 8.3%. China's share of global GDP increased from 2.4% in 1978 to 3.2% in 1999.

International trade liberlization spurs economic growth. **A one percentage point increase in the share of imports and exports in a country's GDP raises its per-capita income by more than two percentage points. Countries have improved their industrial and management capabilities through the transfer of resources, and the spread of technology.** （句 3）

Cost / Benefit Equation of Globalization

Globalization, especially after the developments in the IT sector, has led to developed countries needing more of talent. They have relaxed immigration rules and increased the mobility of talent in the developing world. The number of immigrants into the US from 1971 to 1997 was about 19 million, nearly 3 times the number in the preceeding period. Human talent is at present the most scarce and valuable resource for creating wealth in the knowledge economy. The US is considering an increase in their limit for foreign professionals from 115,000 to 200,000 a year. Germany has announced it wants to attract 20,000 IT professionals from outside the European Union. The British are changing their laws to make it easy for their companies to recruit IT experts from Asia. Even for Japan, its Obuchi Commission has recommended that the ethnocentric and homogenous Japanese should encourage foreigners to live and work in Japan, and that foreign students who have graduated from Japanese schools and colleges be given the right to stay and work. The Repubic of Korea wants to attract 200,000 workers in high-tech industries by offering "gold cards" to foreign engineers and computer programmers, allowing them to stay 10 years in the country.

China has the largest pool of talent, but its trained talent is a fraction of its total potential. Rough estimates put China's R&D scientists at half a million, compared to 1 million in the US and 0.8 million in Japan. Even so, Premier Zhu Rongji recently told Singapore's Prime Minister Goh Chok Tong that two thirds of China's top graduates leave China. However, if the pattern of flow in Taiwan region is a guide, many of these graduates will return in the next 10 to 30 years to bring back their profit-making skills in technology, management and marketing and, most important, their networks of contacts with scientists and businessmen in the US and EU.

Taiwan region built its computer industry through such a returned brains flow. They came back to Taiwan to use the large reservoir of engineers and technicians who could make computer chips and peripherals at a fraction of costs in the US. It will not be practical to prevent young talents from leaving China. Many will find ways to leave... The longer they work in the US or EU the deeper their knowledge and the wider their networks, vital support for new industries.

A negative result of globalization is the widening of the inequality between the highly educated and the less educated, between urban and rural incomes, and between coastal and inland provinces. The highly educated can move between countries, especially in sectors like IT and the Internet. The less educated are not mobile and cannot get into the developed countries where wages are higher. This is unavoidable in a world driven by market forces. In 1998, China's coastal regions absorbed 84% of FDI and produced 90% of its 1999 exports. This year the Chinese government has forced economic development on the inland regions by giving special tax concessions and spending 70% of its infrastructure development budget for the year 2000 in these provinces. Globalization has also made China more vulnerable to volatile capital flows. This can be minimized by China restructuring and strengthening its financial system before opening up its capital accounts.

3 难句分析与视译处理

句 1：　But no one foresaw that technological advances in communications and transportation would lead to the growth and proliferation of multinational corporations that are able to expand the production and sale of goods followed by services, across national boundaries, and market them to all parts of the world.

笔译译文：　但是没有人预见到，通讯和交通领域里的科技发展将促使跨国公司的兴起和激增，这些跨国公司可以跨越国界，将货物的生产、销售及其后的服务扩展到世界各地。

视译译文：

断　句	译　文
But no one foresaw	但是没有人预见到，
that technological advances in communications and transportation	通讯和交通领域里的技术发展
would lead to the growth and proliferation of multinational corporations	会促成跨国公司的发展和迅速增长。
that are able to expand	这些公司可以扩展
the production and sale of goods	生产和货物销售，
followed by services,	以及其后的服务，
across national boundaries,	使其跨越国界，
and market them to all parts of the world.	销往世界各地。

句 2：　It (technology) enabled producers to maximize profits by moving capital, machinery and management expertise to countries where raw materials or labor and infrastructure gave them comparative advantage.

笔译译文：　科技能让制造商把资金、机器和管理专业知识转移到在原料、劳工及基础设施方面能给予他们相对优势的国家去，从而赚取最大的利润。

视译译文:

断　句	译　文
It (technology) enabled producers to maximize profits,	科技能让制造商获取最大利润,
by moving capital, machinery and management expertise to countries	方法是将资本、设备和管理专业知识转移到一些国家,
where raw materials or labor and infrastructure	那里的原料或劳工和基础设施,
gave them comparative advantage.	能够给他们相对优势。

句 3:　　A one percentage point increase in the share of imports and exports in a country's GDP raises its per-capita income by more than two percentage points. Countries have improved their industrial and management capabilities through the transfer of resources and the spread of technology.

笔译译文:　一个国家的进出口在其国内生产总值所占的比例增加一个百分点,其人均收入就会提高超过两个百分点。各国也通过资源的转移和科技的传播,提升了它们的工业及管理能力。

视译译文:

断　句	译　文
A one percentage point increase	每一个百分点的增长,
in the share of imports and exports in a country's GDP	亦即国家进出口占 GDP 的份额的增长,
raises its per-capita income	就会增加其人均收入,
by more than two percentage points.	增加幅度超过两个百分点。
Countries have improved	国家提高了
their industrial and management capabilities	工业和管理能力,
through the transfer of resources and the spread of technology.	方法是转让资源和传播技术。

4　参考译文

经济全球化——中国与亚洲（节选 1）
李光耀
北京，2000 年

全球化与新经济

自从邓小平先生于 1978 年宣布改革开放政策至今，中国的经济已经起了巨大的变化。当时，中国的外贸只占国内生产总值的近 12%，如今已达 36%，是当时的三倍，而且还在不断增长。当中国决定加入世贸组织，并于去年 11 月同美国达成协议时，便已向世人预示，它正采取重大举措，要把中国的经济纳入全球网格，虽然目前这个网格仍然由美国、西欧及日本所支配。这种支配地位的产生，是由于早在第二次世界大战结束之前，美国和它的主要盟国——英国，就已经拟好了国际货币基金组织、世界银行以及关贸总协定等组织的蓝图。

在第二次世界大战之前，国际贸易在美国、英国、欧洲其他各国和日本等帝国的境内都很自由，但在帝国集团之间却存在着贸易壁垒。大战结束后，美国决意要解除这些帝国集团。关贸总协定设立的目的就是要促进跨边界货物与服务贸易，而非苏联领导的经济闭关体系下的统一控制。但是没有人预见到，通讯和交通领域里的科技发展将促成跨国公司的发展和激增，这些跨国企业可以跨越国界，将货物的生产、销售及其后的服务扩展到世界各地。

全球化的推动力

科技是全球化的推动力，它能让制造商把资金、机器和管理专业知识转移到在原料、劳工及基础设施方面能给予他们相对优势的国家去，从而赚取最大的利润。这就使得全球各地取得了前所未有的经济增长与繁荣，……

自由贸易与投资对世界的发展起着重大的作用。从 1965 年到 1999 年，全球的国内生产总值以美元计增长了 15 倍，但全球贸易却以双倍的速度增长，达到 30 倍。外来直接投资的增长率超过了国内投资。1998 年，全球的外来直接投资总额超过 41,000 亿美元。

过去 20 年，中国的货物贸易增长率是世界贸易增长率的两倍。目前，中国是世界第九大贸易国。流入中国的外来直接投资在 1978 年时几乎为零，到了 1998 年却达到 455 亿美元，约占国内生产总值的 5%。1998 年，中国的外来直接投资累计总额达 2,610 亿美元。中国的外来直接投资在世界上排行第三，只落在美国和英国之后。自 1978 年以来，中国的人均收入平均每年增加8.3%。中国在全球国内生产总值所占的比例也从 1978 年的 2.4% 增加到 1999 年的 3.2%。

国际贸易自由化刺激了经济增长。一个国家的进出口在其国内生产总值所占的比例增加一个百分点，其人均收入就会提高超过两个百分点。各国也通过资源的转移和科技的传播，提升了它们的工业及管理能力。

全球化的成本效益衡量

全球化增加了发达国家对人才的需求，尤其是在信息技术领域取得了显著的发展之后。这些国家都放宽了移民条例，提高了发展中国家的人才流动性。1971 年到 1997 年之间，移居美国的移民约有 1,900 万，几乎是之前那段时期的三倍。目前，在知识经济里，人才是创造财富的最稀缺的资源。美国正考虑把引进外国专业人员的限制人数，从每年的 11.5 万人增加到 20 万人。德国也宣布，它要从欧盟以外吸引两万名信息技术专业人员。英国正在修改法律，以便让英国公司能更容易地从亚洲招聘信息技术专才。在日本，小渊委员会甚至已建议，具有强烈民族中心主义的、由单一民族构成的日本应该鼓励外国人到日本生活和工作，并建议让毕业自日本学府的外国学生有权在日本居住和工作。韩国则发给"金卡"，允许外国工程师和电脑程序员在该国居留 10 年，希望借此吸引 20 万高科技人员。

中国拥有最多的人才，但受过训练的人才却只是占总潜在人才的一小部分。粗略估计，在中国从事研究与发展的科学家只有 50 万名，美国和日本则分别有 100 万和 80 万名。即便如此，朱镕基总理最近告诉新加坡吴作栋总理，中国有三分之二的顶尖大学毕业生在毕业后去了国外。不过，如果台湾地区的人才流动可以作为一个样板的话，这些大学毕业生当中，有许多会在以后的 10 年到 30 年内回流，并带回他们在科技、管理和销售等方面的盈利技能。更重要的是，他们也会把他们同美国和欧盟科学家及商人建立的联络网带回中国。

台湾地区就是通过这样的人才回流建立起它的电脑业的。这些人才回到台湾后利用当地大批的工程师和技术人员生产电脑晶片和辅助材料，所需的成本只是美国生产成本的一小部分。要阻止年轻人才离开中国是不切实际的。很多人都会找寻门路离开，……这些年轻人在美国或欧盟国家工作的时间越长，知识就会越深，联络网就会越广，这些都是发展新兴产业不可或缺的重要支柱。

全球化的一个不良后果是，它扩大了受过高等教育和受教育不多的人之间的不平等，加剧了城市和乡村收入的不平均，以及沿海和内陆省份发展的不平衡现象。受过高等教育的人士可以在发达国家之间自由流动，寻求高报酬，特别是在信息技术和互联网的领域里。受教育不多的人却缺乏流动性，无法到工资较高的发达国家去工作。在一个由市场力量所推动的世界里，这种现象是无法避免的。1998年，中国的沿海地区吸收了84%的外来直接投资，并生产了中国1999年90%的出口产品。今年，中国政府把经济发展的焦点放在内陆地区，给予这些地区特别的税务优惠，并把2000年基础设施发展预算的70%用在这些省份。全球化也使中国更容易受到资金流波动的影响。但是，只要中国在开放资本账户之前重组并加强其金融体系，就能减少这种影响。

四、自主训练

请在15分钟之内迅速阅读下面的讲话，了解大意。学生可组成对子练习，互相监控对视译技巧的掌握情况、视译质量和现场表现，或以边视译边录音的形式进行个人练习。视译时要保持正常语速，译文要顺畅达意。如遇难句，可在首次视译后参照"实战练习"中难句分析与视译处理的方法进行练习，找出解决方法。

Economic Globalization—China and Asia (Excerpt 2)

Lee Kuan Yew

Beijing, 2000

Internet and the New Economy

The digital revolution has swept the developed world. Computers have developed the Internet. With the convergence of communications, computers and the media, the Internet will be one powerful multi-media network. All these have spawned the "New Economy" in America. Computers and the Internet have increased GDP growth in America by 0.4 to 0.6 percentage points per annum. IT and the Internet have also given companies of the Old Economy a powerful tool to increase productivity and profits. They now can have direct access to their multiple suppliers; they can check current sales and inventories, and reach their consumers directly making for lower costs and high productivity. The Europeans, the Japanese and Newly Industrialized Economies are several years behind.

Other countries like China have noted this development and are building up the necessary infrastructure for this New Economy as rapidly as possible. Internet users in China have more than quadrupled to 9 million in 1999, placing it now among the top 10 countries in Internet use. Growing at 100% per annum, it will reach 60 million by 2003, according to China's Academy of Social Sciences. However at present, China lags behind most East Asian economies in the penetration rate of Internet hosts, telephone lines and personal computers.

The digital revolution can raise China's long-term growth rate by one to three percentage points per annum. Therefore China should rapidly expand the use of computers and the Internet. China's government has been developing the information infrastructure and broadening and deepening its capital markets. Already there are several high-tech and Internet parks in Beijing, Shanghai, Guangdong, Shenzhen and Tianjin. However, to maximize the value of digital technology the government has to deregulate the telecoms market. China has undertaken to liberalize this sector on joining the WTO, allow up to 50% foreign ownership within two years after that, and lift all restrictions on telecoms service providers within 6 years of WTO membership.

Capital Markets

To enable entrepreneurs to flourish, a country has to develop its capital market. Although China has a high savings rate (42% of GDP in 1998), little of this was channeled to the private sector, and even less to the high-tech start-ups. The banking system is dominated by the state-owned banks that have rarely been funding the private sector, especially the high-tech start-ups. China's stock market capitalization at the end of 1999 was only 33% of GDP, one of the lowest in the world, lagging behind the ASEAN[1] countries and India. Most of the companies listed in the Shanghai and Shenzhen stock exchanges in February 2000 are state-owned enterprises. The China Securities Regulatory Commission gave priority in listing to state-owned enterprises. This has made it difficult for new start-ups.

Education to Master Technology

A key factor for success in the high-tech sector is the education system. The low educational levels of China's workforce is a handicap. Twelve percent of its workforce is illiterate, 35% have only primary school education and only 3.5% have tertiary education. Only 6% of each year's cohort of students reached tertiary

---

1 Association of Southeast Asian Nations.

institutions. Hence the "211 Project" (under which China will establish 100 world-class universities for the 21st century to meet high-tech manpower needs).

It is important to remember that it is not officials of government or state-owned corporations but private individuals who will spawn the high-tech start-ups. They need to be facilitated by regulators who come from the generation that grew up with the new technology, regulators who are knowledgeable about what is happening in Silicon Valley and beyond. Government officials in their 50s do not have that understanding of the potentials of this digital revolution.

The Internet Generation Should Lead the Way

In Singapore, political leaders are men in their 50s and 40s, but they are not as digital savvy as those who are in their creative and productive years, the 20s and 30s. Dotcom start-ups are by and large formed by people in their 20s. To help create a conducive environment and facilitate the growth of Internet start-ups in dotcom companies, Singapore has chosen regulators who have themselves grown up in the Internet era, people in their 30s. They have a better grasp of the potential of this technology and are closer to the thinking of the generation younger than themselves, in their 20s. They can regulate with a lighter hand and allow creative talent to flower.

China has the people who know how to make full use of globalization and the New Economy. It has been educating able graduate students in economics, management and computers. Its most valuable assets are the many thousands of its brightest and best in their 20s and 30s who have studied and worked abroad, especially in America. Many are now in lower or middle rank positions in China or still overseas. In 20 to 30 years, they will rise to the top layers of government and business, fully conversant with the latest developments in the contemporary world. They will bring China abreast of the US, Japan and EU in government and business practices.

China has made a strategic decision that has profound economic and geo-political implications for itself and the world. Chinese enterprises will learn from, work with and compete against the advanced nations. Global competition will increase the efficiency and productivity of domestic enterprises. But there will be creative destruction of outdated industrial plants which will lead to unemployment and its social consequences. The result, however, will be a China that is one of the most important players in the global exchange of goods, services, capital, talent and ideas in the 21st century.

第6单元

同位语的视译

> **基本技巧：**
> - 将同位语短语译成独立语或短句；
> - 将同位语从句译为独立句子；
> - 在必要的时候加入适当连接成分。

一、技巧讲解：同位语的视译

　　英语中的同位语是一个常见的句子成分。有些语法学家将同位语视为定语的一种，有些则将其单列出来。在视译中，同位语的翻译技巧有时与定语的相似，但总体上讲，同位语有着自己的一些明显的特征，在视译中可以归为一类，便于在训练中熟练掌握，在实战中积极应用。

　　同位语可以由三种成分构成：1) 单词。名词、代词、形容词等都可以作同位语。比如：We ourselves wanted to see such a result. 2) 词组。比如：This is Mr. Smith, former American Ambassador to Russia. 3) 从句。比如：The news that he was seriously ill was false, fabricated by someone with an ulterior motive. 为了说明同位语在视译中的处理方式，我们将这几个典型的同位语按照一般笔译的方法译成汉语：1) 我们自己想要看到这样的结果。2) 这是前美国驻俄罗斯大使史密斯先生。3) 他得重病的消息是假的，是有些别有用心的人编造出来的。

　　从这几个句子的翻译中我们可以发现，如果换做是视译，一个单词作同位语的情况是很容易处理的，许多情况可以保持英文词序，如：I myself（我自己）、they both（他们两人）、his brother Bob（他哥哥鲍勃）等。有些即便颠倒一下顺序，由于同位语只有一个单词，也是在一目可及的长度之内，调整起来是容易的。但如果是词组作同位语，按一般的笔译处理，很可能需要颠

125

倒语序，上面的第二个例子就是这种情况，比较长的词组更是如此。再举一个例子：We are visiting Athens, the site of the glorious ancient Greek civilization. 它的笔译译文是："我们正在参观伟大的古希腊文明圣地雅典。"由于这个句子中的同位语较长，在视译的时候，要像笔译这样调整语序难以做到。所以，我们一般将其视译为："我们正在参观雅典，这是伟大的古希腊文明圣地。"

下面讲解的是涉及三类同位语的视译技巧。由于视译时，处理单词构成的同位语很容易，所以重点将放在较长的同位语短语和同位语从句的处理上。

1 同位语短语的视译

对于由较长的短语构成的同位语，视译的基本技巧是先将同位语前面的部分作为一个短句译出，然后加入适当的连接成分，最后将同位语作为另外一个短句译出。

例 1： As for the story behind the painting, we need to ask Ms. Jones, head of the National Museum of Fine Arts.

译文 1： 说到这幅画背后的故事，我们需要问问国家美术博物馆馆长琼斯女士。

译文 2： 说到这幅画背后的故事，我们需要问问琼斯女士，她是国家美术博物馆馆长。

【讲解】 译文 1 是比较严谨的笔译译文，将同位语置于它所说明的名词之前。由于同位语短语比较长，这样做势必要较大幅度地调整原句语序，这不是视译提倡的方法。视译的基本技巧是将同位语作为一个单独的短句译出，中间加入适当的连接成分，在本句中，就加进了"她是"，使两个短句之间有一个自然的衔接。

例 2： All people, old and young, had expressed their hope to invest more in education.

译文 1： 所有老老少少的人们都表达了他们对增加教育投入的希望。

译文 2： 所有的人，无论老少，都表达了他们的希望，这就是增加教育投入。

【讲解】 这是一个用形容词短语作同位语的句子，译文 1 将 old and young 置于名词之前。在视译中，我们将其单独译为一个短语，并加入"无论"前后连接，以便于顺译。另外，在这个句子里，还有一个不定式短语 to invest more in education，在原译文中也是处理为前置的。译文 2 将其处理为另外一个句子，并加入"这就是"（也可以加入"即"）前后连接。

126

例 3：　Qinghai Lake, the largest inland body of salt water in China, lies 3,198 meters above sea level.

译文 1：我国最大的内陆咸水湖青海湖海拔 3,198 米。（张道真，2007：534）

译文 2：青海湖是中国最大的内陆咸水湖，海拔 3,198 米。

【讲解】　这个句子中间插进一个较长的同位语。在视译断句时，一般是这样做的：Qinghai Lake, // the largest inland body of salt water in China, // lies 3,198 meters above sea level. 具体视译的时候，先将主语及其同位语作为一个短句译出，然后将原文的谓语部分另起一句翻译出来。原来只有一句话的译文在视译中成为两个短句。由于前后逻辑关系明确，所以在两个短句之间不必加连接成分。

2　同位语从句的视译

同位语从句一般是置于它所说明的名词之后。在笔译中，可以置于被说明的名词之前或是之后。比如 He expressed the hope that he would come to Beijing again. 可以译为："他表达了再访北京的希望。"也可以译为："他表示希望再访北京。"在视译中，我们一般采取第二种方式，即先将同位语之前的部分译为一个短句，再将同位语从句单独译成一句，必要时中间加入连接成分。

例 4：　The fact that movable-type printing was invented by the Chinese is often forgotten.

译文 1：中国人发明活字印刷术的事实往往被遗忘了。

译文 2：活字印刷术是中国人发明的，这一事实往往被遗忘了。

【讲解】　这个句子中有一个说明 fact 的同位语从句，在笔译中，可以将它置于被说明的名词之前，译为"中国人发明活字印刷术的事实"。但在视译中，我们首先把 fact 连同后面的同位语从句译为一个独立的句子，然后将原句谓语部分单独译出，中间加入连接成分"这一事实"，使句子顺畅。

例 5：　Everybody understands that the possibility always exists that the world champion may be defeated by an unknown athlete.

译文 1：每个人都明白，世界冠军被无名运动员打败的可能性总是存在的。

译文 2：每个人都明白，总是存在这种可能，这就是世界冠军会被打败，被无名运动员打败。

【讲解】　在这个句子中，possibility 后有一个较长的同位语从句。在视译中，我们将这个句子断为五个类意群：Everybody understands // that the possibility always exists // that the world champion may be defeated // by an unknown athlete. 然后依次译出。在单独译出同位语从句的时候，前面加上连接成分"这就是"。

例6： We have to agree with his conclusion that the price of oil products will continue to rise at least for another decade.

译文1： 我们不得不同意他关于石油产品价格至少在未来十年里会继续攀升的结论。

译文2： 我们不得不同意他的结论，即石油产品价格会持续攀升，至少在未来十年是这样。

【讲解】 首先断句：We have to agree with his conclusion // that the price of oil products // will continue to rise // at least for another decade. 然后依次译出。在这里，我们加入"即"，连接名词conclusion和同位语从句。从上面几个例句可以看出，在翻译同位语从句的时候，很重要的一点是加入一个连接成分，使同位语跟被同位语说明的名词能够自然地衔接起来。常用的连接成分有"这就是"、"那就是"、"也就是"、"即"等。需要特别注意的是，在翻译这类句子的时候，如果能够恰当、灵活地使用连接成分，视译质量就会提高，译出来的句子也会顺畅妥贴。

3 其他同位语的视译技巧

还有另外一些同位语的表示方法，其基本技巧与上面所讲解的基本原理是一样的，这里再举几个例子加以说明。

例7： Energetic, enthusiastic, and healthy, these young men and women demonstrated to the world that the future would be theirs.

译文1： 这些年轻的男男女女充满活力、满腔热情、体魄健康，向世界表明未来属于他们。

译文2： 充满活力、满腔热情、体魄健康，就是这样一些年轻的男男女女，向世界表明未来属于他们。

【讲解】 这是一个形容词前置作同位语的句子。由于有三个并列的形容词出现，同位语部分较长，如果将主语先行译出，就要调整语序。我们不妨将这三个形容词先翻译出来，然后加进"就是这样一些"作为连接部分，使整个句子仍然能够自然地顺译下来。

例 8： All the people there had some doubt whether they were able to complete the work on schedule.

译文 1： 那里所有的人对他们是否能够按时完成任务心存怀疑。

译文 2： 那里所有的人都心存怀疑，<u>不知</u>他们是否能够按时完成任务。

【讲解】 这是一个由连接副词 whether 引导的同位语从句，视译方法与上面的例子是一样的，先将主句译出，然后再翻译同位语从句，使用"不知"作连接成分。需要注意的是，在翻译以连接副词或是连接代词（比如 when, where, what, how 等）引导的同位语从句时，要根据具体情况，使用相应的连接词语。

二、语段视译

1 词汇与表达

在进行语段视译前，请先预习以下词汇与表达。

a bundle of	一沓；一捆
civic building	政府办公楼
janitor	守门人
aluminum can	易拉罐
a wad of	一沓；一卷
split with…	与……均分
tempting	诱人的

2 视译语段

请在 3 分钟之内迅速阅读下面的语段，了解大意，然后结合所学要点进行视译练习。视译时要保持正常语速，译文要顺畅达意。

When Kim Bogue accidentally threw her wallet away with her lunch, she had little hope that she'd recover the $900 and bundle of credit cards inside. With a team of co-workers, she twice searched the Santa Ana civic buildings where she works as a janitor, but found nothing. "I was sick all weekend," said Bogue, who was saving the money for a trip to Thailand, her home country. The same weekend, a homeless man who roams the building also was searching for something. He made his routine visit to the trash bins nearby to look for aluminum cans. Instead, he found Bogue's wallet. That Monday, the man, who declined to be identified, gave the money to Sherry Wesley who works in one of the buildings. "He came to me with the wad of money and said: 'This probably belongs to someone that you work with. Can you return it?'" Grateful, Bogue gave the man a $100 reward, which he split with Wesley. She gave the money to her church. While the money would serve as a tempting find, especially for a homeless man, Wesley said the man's action did not surprise her. "I know he has got the biggest heart," she said. "Somebody like that who is so down on their luck and willing to help someone out is a rare thing." (节选自 《英语学习》，2006 年第 10 期，第 4 页)

原译文： 金·博格不小心把自己的钱包连同吃剩的午餐一起扔掉了，完全没有指望能够把里面装着的 900 美元和一沓子信用卡找回来。博格在圣安娜的政府办公区里当看门人，她和几个同事一起在楼里找了两遍，但却一无所获。"整个周末我心情都非常糟糕，"博格说，那笔钱是她攒下来作回泰国老家的旅费用的。同一个周末，一名长年在圣安娜政府办公区周围游荡的无家可归者也在寻找着什么东西。他照例去翻检办公楼附近的垃圾箱，希望能找到些易拉罐，但却意外地发现了博格的钱包。到了星期一，这位不愿公开姓名的男子把钱交到也在政府办公区工作的谢莉·韦斯利。韦斯利说："他拿着这卷钱来找我，对我说：'这可能是你哪个同事的东西，你能帮我还回去吗？'"感激不已的博格给了这人 100 美元谢礼，而他把一半分给了韦斯利，后者又把分到的钱捐给了教堂。这笔钱是个不小的诱惑，对一个无家可归的人来说更是如此。但韦斯利说她并不为这人的行为感到惊讶。"我知道他拥有最高贵的心灵，"她说，"像他那样背运透顶却仍然乐于助人的人实在是非常难得。"（冰尘编译）

3 视译译文

断 句	译 文
When Kim Bogue accidentally threw her wallet away	金·博格不小心扔掉了钱包，
with her lunch,	这是跟吃剩的午餐一起扔掉的，
she had little hope	她根本不指望

（待续）

（续上表）

断 句	译 文
that she'd recover the $900	能够找回里面的 900 美元，
and bundle of credit cards inside.	还有一沓子信用卡。
With a team of co-workers,	她和同事们一起，
she twice searched the Santa Ana civic buildings	在圣安娜政府办公楼里找了两遍，
where she works as a janitor,	她就是在这里当看门人，
but found nothing.	但寻找一无所获。
"I was sick all weekend," said Bogue,	"我整个周末心情都很糟糕，"博格说，
who was saving the money	她攒这笔钱，
for a trip to Thailand, her home country.	是为了回泰国老家的。
The same weekend,	同一个周末，
a homeless man who roams the building	一个无家可归者在楼周围游荡，
also was searching for something.	他也在找什么东西。
He made his routine visit to the trash bins nearby	他照例去附近的垃圾箱
to look for aluminum cans.	翻找易拉罐。
Instead, he found Bogue's wallet.	但却发现了博格的钱包。
That Monday,	到了周一，
the man, who declined to be identified,	这个人不愿公开自己的姓名，
gave the money to Sherry Wesley	他把钱给了谢莉·韦斯利，
who works in one of the buildings.	韦斯利也在这个办公区工作。
"He came to me	"他找到我，
with the wad of money	手里拿着那一沓钱，
and said:	他说：
'This probably belongs to someone	'这钱可能是什么人的，
that you work with.	大概是你的同事。
Can you return it?'"	你可以还回去吗？'"

（待续）

（续上表）

断　句	译　文
Grateful, Bogue gave the man a $100 reward,	感激不已的博格给了这人 100 美元谢礼，
which he split with Wesley.	他分了一半给韦斯利。
She gave the money to her church.	韦斯利把钱捐给了教堂。
While the money would serve as a tempting find,	这笔钱是个不小的诱惑，
especially for a homeless man,	尤其是对于一个无家可归的人来说。
Wesley said	但韦斯利说
the man's action did not surprise her.	这人的行为并没有使她感到惊奇。
"I know he has got the biggest heart," she said.	"我知道他有一颗美丽的心,"她说。
"Somebody like that	"像他这样的人
who is so down on their luck	虽然命运不济，
and willing to help someone out	但却乐于助人，
is a rare thing."	实在难能可贵。"

4　视译点评

1. 原文第一句：… she had little hope // that she'd recover the $900 // and bundle of credit cards inside.

这是一个含有同位语从句的复合句，我们先将原句断为三个类意群。然后，第一步将同位语从句之前的部分翻译出来："她根本不指望"，第二步将同位语从句译出："能够找回里面的 900 美元，还有一沓子信用卡。"这类句子还有 He has no idea at all what has been going on.（他根本不知道发生了什么事情。）

2. 原文第三句："I was sick all weekend," said Bogue, // who was saving the money // for a trip to Thailand, her home country.

这是一个比较复杂的句子，包含一个非限定性定语从句，从句中还有一个同位语短语。在视译的时候，我们将定语从句单独译出："她攒这笔钱，是为了回泰国老家的。"注意，从习惯上说，who was saving the money 会被自然地断为一个类意群，而它后面是介词短语引导的目的状语，我们将其单独译为"是为了回泰国老家的"，其中的同位语短语也顺势翻译为"泰国老家"。

3. 原文第九句：Grateful, Bogue gave the man a \$100 reward, // which he split with Wesley.

　　这里有一个以形容词作同位语的成分，句子中还包含一个非限定性定语从句。我们将同位语和它后面的人名直接处理为"感激不已的博格"，非限定性定语从句则分句另译，再加进一个人称代词"他"作为连接，使整个句子通顺流畅。

4. 原文最后一句：Somebody like that // who is so down on their luck // and willing to help someone out // is a rare thing.

　　这是一个比较复杂的句子。首先看一下这个句子的成分。句子之中有一个定语从句 who is so down on their luck and willing to help someone out 来说明 that，而介词短语 like that 又是作定语修饰 somebody。我们先把句子断好，然后逐个译出："像他这样的人，// 虽然命运不济，// 但却乐于助人，// 实在难能可贵。"

三、实战练习

1　词汇与表达

　　请先熟悉以下词汇与表达，并适当地运用在视译中。

negate	取消，使无效
step change	明显的改进
biodiversity	生物多样化
organic waste	有机废物
European Council	欧洲理事会
feedstock	（送入机器或加工厂的）给料，原料
set-aside	储备
European Committee on Standardization	欧洲标准化委员会

2 实战课文

请在 15 分钟之内迅速阅读下面的讲话，了解大意。视译时要保持正常语速，译文要顺畅达意。

Biofuels—the Green Alternative for Transport[1]

Energy Commissioner   Andris Piebalgs

Brussels, July 2007

It is a great pleasure for me to be speaking at this significant event. In my address today, I would like to cover three key questions:

—Why are biofuels important?

—What is the European Union doing to promote them? And

—Why do we need to work together at international level in this policy area?

The Importance of Biofuels

Biofuels are important because they tackle two of the most difficult challenges we face in energy policy.

The first challenge is security of energy supply. Transport depends on oil for 98% of its fuel. That degree of dependence would be a worry, whatever the fuel. It is of double concern given that oil is the fossil fuel of which global supplies are lowest, and of which the EU has least. We need to pursue many solutions to this problem; but today, biofuels are just about the only large-scale option available to diversify fuel sources in the transport sector. We must ensure that we take advantage of the opportunities they offer.

The second challenge is climate change. Greenhouse gas emissions in transport are growing fast. This growth is negating the savings being made elsewhere. **On present trends, transport will account for more than 60% of the EU's increase in carbon dioxide emissions between 2005 and 2020.** （句 1）it is essential for these trends to be reversed. At EU level, there are just two policies with the capacity to do this on a significant scale: vehicle efficiency improvements and biofuels. We must promote them both strongly.

---

1 原文参见 http://europa.eu/rapid/pressReleasesAction.do?reference=SPEECH/07/466&format=
HTML&aged=0&language=EN&guiLanguage=en。

Biofuels offer other opportunities too—notably their potential contribution to employment in rural areas, both in the EU and in developing countries—as well as the scope for technological development, for example in second-generation biofuels. For all these reasons, biofuels are a key part of our energy policy.

The EU's Policy for Promoting Biofuels

The European Union's promotion of biofuels took its first big step forward in 2003, with the adoption of our biofuels directive—a piece of legislation that each EU member state must translate into national law. At that time, biofuels only had half a percent of the transport fuel market. The directive set two "indicative" targets—a 2% share of the EU fuel market in 2005 and a 5.75% share in 2010. Disappointingly, we did not achieve this first indicative target. Even last year, biofuels' share only reached 1.5%. But the pace of implementation is picking up. I am glad to say that nearly all the 27 EU member states have now put measures in place to support biofuels—a big contrast from the situation in 2003, when only 5 were doing so. Some are using tax exemptions, others are using "biofuel obligations" under which fuel suppliers must include a given proportion of biofuel in the fuel they sell. Many are using both these tools. With this major increase in member states' efforts, we expect to see biofuels' share reach 4 to 4.5 percent in 2010. Still, though, it does not look as if the full 2010 target will be achieved.

Given the increasing urgency of the problems we aim to address—insecure energy supplies and climate change—we therefore reviewed our policy, aiming both to improve our ability to achieve the targets we have set and to look forward beyond 2010. I am glad to say that this review has found its place in a clear and supportive overall policy framework: the Action Plan for launching a "new energy policy for Europe", set out in March by the EU member states. This plan reaffirms the importance of greenhouse gas reduction and security of supply as key objectives of energy policy. For renewable energy in general, we now propose a binding European target of a 20% share in 2020—three times higher than its contribution today. For biofuels, we propose a 10% share of the transport market in 2020. But this time this target will no longer be indicative—it, too, will be binding.

This strategy represents a step change in the ambition of our policies on renewable energy, and in the introduction of a strong European policy framework to support their achievement. (句 2) For biofuels, it will mean nearly a sevenfold increase in consumption. It is, of course, essential to ensure that this increase is fulfilled in a sustainable way. We cannot just sit back and assume that this will happen automatically.

Most biofuels deliver solid greenhouse gas savings—but there exist inefficient production techniques that do not. The use of these production techniques must be avoided.

Most biofuels will be produced on land that has been cultivated for generations. But some will come from land that is newly brought into cultivation. Here, there is a risk of causing big greenhouse gas losses through the release of carbon stored in the soil and in plants. There is also a risk of disturbing biodiversity and disrupting natural habitats. These risks, too, need to be avoided.

Furthermore, in order to achieve the 10% biofuel share as efficiently as possible, we must aim at the earliest possible entry into the market of "second-generation" biofuels. These can be made from a wider range of raw materials such as straw, organic wastes and woody material. This will increase the security of supply benefits of the policy, as well as its environmental performance.

The EU's Action Plan underlined the need for such a strong push for "second-generation" biofuels and for an effective sustainability scheme. Now the European Parliament will give its view in September. We hope that it will also support this approach. Meanwhile we are working out how to translate our ideas into a solid proposal for legislation. **We plan to incorporate our biofuel measures, alongside other measures needed to push the share of renewable energy up to 20%, in a single directive.** (句 3) This should be ready before the end of the year. It will then be up to the European Council and Parliament to consider the proposal and reach a final view. The directive will give legal backing to the 10% target for biofuels.

Alongside this, it will contain a sustainability scheme. The details of this are still being worked out. Our initial ideas are as follows:

—First, we need to set minimum sustainability standards for biofuels;

—Second, only biofuels that meet these standards will count toward the 10% target; and

—Third, only these biofuels will be eligible for tax exemptions; only they will count toward biofuel obligations.

These rules will, of course, apply equally to domestically produced biofuels and to imports. There is, of course, a great deal of debate about what exactly the minimum sustainability standards should be. The European Commission recently held a consultation exercise in which stakeholders from within and outside the EU expressed many different ideas on this point. We are studying the results closely, and we also look forward to hearing the views that will be expressed during this conference. It is crucial to get this part of our policy right, and to devise measures that are simple yet effective.

International Cooperation for Promoting Biofuels

This brings me to the last point I would like to cover: why do we need to work together at international level as we develop our biofuel policies?

One important reason is that we expect and hope to see an increase in global trade in biofuels and in biofuel feedstocks. Now, as far as the EU is concerned, **I should point out that we could—if we had to—fulfil our 10% target for 2020 entirely through domestically produced biofuels—notably, by using "set-aside" agricultural land and by reducing the rate at which arable land is being abandoned in the EU.（句 4）** This approach would imply only a small increase in agricultural commodity prices—a matter of a few percentage points.

However, even if this approach is technically possible, it is not the one that we want to follow. We think that this purely domestic sourcing of biofuels is neither likely—given current trade rules, and the increased trade liberalization we hope to see in future—nor desirable. Instead, we aim at a "balanced approach" under which domestically produced biofuels and imports will both contribute to meeting the EU's growing needs.

We are keen to work constructively with other countries, regions and international organizations to create the necessary framework for this increased trade in biofuels. We need to ensure that our biofuel standards, and those of our main trading partners, create no unnecessary obstacles. With the European Committee on Standardization, we convened an international conference on this topic in February. This set out a roadmap for our future work on internationally compatible biofuel standards. We will continue to work vigorously to implement this. We also need to work for convergence on biofuel sustainability—both on the minimum standards that will be set for biofuel use in each country or region, and for the procedures to be used to verify these.

But trade issues are not the only reason for working together. A wider principle of solidarity is also at play, because when one country or region adopts a sustainable policy of biofuel development, everyone gains.

We all gain from the consequent reduction in greenhouse gas emissions.

We all gain as biofuels become an increasingly credible alternative to oil-based fuels in the transport market.

We all gain from the emergence of new opportunities for economic development in rural areas.

And we all gain because each country's experience offers lessons that others can draw on. At EU level we have learnt a lot from the pioneering efforts of certain member states, from Brazil and from others internationally. We must, and we will, plan our biofuels policies to take advantage of these benefits from international cooperation.

For all these reasons, the European Commission is committed to giving a strong international dimension to its work on biofuels. This conference is a signal of this commitment and an important step in taking it forward.

Biofuels are not the panacea for all our energy problems. But they are an essential component of our future approach to energy policy, and a way to make sure that the transport sector plays its full part in our efforts to tackle global warming and to diversify fuel sources. It is exciting to see so many people gathered here today. I look forward with great interest to the lessons that we will be able to learn over the next day and a half of discussions.

3 难句分析与视译处理

句 1： On present trends, transport will account for more than 60% of the EU's increase in carbon dioxide emissions between 2005 and 2020.

笔译译文： 根据现在的趋势，欧盟在 2005 到 2020 年间增加的二氧化碳排放量中，由交通运输产生的将占到 60% 以上。

视译译文：

断　句	译　文
On present trends,	根据现在的趋势，
transport will account for more than 60%	交通运输将占到 60% 以上，
of the EU's increase in carbon dioxide emissions	这是指占欧盟新增二氧化碳排放量的比重，
between 2005 and 2020.	时间是 2005 到 2020 年之间。

句 2：　　 This strategy represents a step change in the ambition of our policies on renewable energy, and in the introduction of a strong European policy framework to support their achievement.

笔译译文：这一战略代表我们在实现可再生能源政策上的雄心壮志以及在出台一个支持实现政策目标的坚实的欧洲政策框架方面取得的显著进展。

视译译文：

断　句	译　文
This strategy represents a step change	这一战略表示了显著的进展，
in the ambition of our policies on renewable energy,	是向实施可再生能源政策宏大目标的迈进，
and in the introduction of a strong European policy framework	同时还将出台一个坚实的欧洲政策框架，
to support their achievement.	以便支持政策目标的实现。

句 3：　　 We plan to incorporate our biofuel measures, alongside other measures needed to push the share of renewable energy up to 20%, in a single directive.

笔译译文：我们计划将我们的生物燃料措施与为把可再生能源的份额增加到 20% 所需的其他措施一并写入同一项规定。

视译译文：

断　句	译　文
We plan to incorporate our biofuel measures,	我们计划提出生物燃料措施，
alongside other measures	连同其他必要措施，
needed to push the share of renewable energy up to 20%,	这些措施可把再生能源的份额增加到 20%，
in a single directive.	我们会将这些一并写入同一项规定。

句 4：　　 I should point out that we could—if we had to—fulfil our 10% target for 2020 entirely through domestically produced biofuels—notably, by using "set-aside" agricultural land and by reducing the rate at which arable land is being abandoned in the EU.

笔译译文： 我要指出的是我们能够完全依靠我们自己生产的生物燃料实现2020 年 10% 的目标——如果这是必要的——显然，这要通过使用"储备"农业用地以及通过在欧盟减少可耕地的废弃率来实现。

视译译文：

断　句	译　文
I should point out that	我要指出的是
we could—if we had to—	我们能够——如果这是必要的——
fulfil our 10% target for 2020	实现 2020 年 10% 的目标，
entirely through domestically produced biofuels—	并且是完全依靠自己生产的生物燃料，
notably, by using "set-aside" agricultural land	显然，我们要使用"储备"农业用地，
and by reducing the rate	同时要减缓速度，
at which arable land is being abandoned in the EU.	也就是欧盟可耕地的废弃速度。

4　参考译文

生物燃料——交通运输燃料的绿色替代品

欧盟能源事务委员　安德里斯·皮耶巴尔格斯
布鲁塞尔，2007 年 7 月

非常高兴能够在这一重要场合发表演讲。我今天将谈三个主要问题：
——生物燃料为什么重要？
——欧盟为促进生物燃料正在开展哪些工作？
——我们为什么需要在相关政策领域开展国际合作？

生物燃料的重要性

生物燃料之所以重要是因为这些燃料能应对我们的能源政策所面临的最严峻挑战中的两个。

第一个挑战是能源供给的安全问题。交通运输 98% 的燃料依赖石油。无论是何种燃料，如此高的依赖程度都会令人不安。由于石油这种矿物燃料的全球供给量最低，而欧盟又最缺乏石油，这种情况就更加令人担忧。对于这个问题，我们需要寻求多种解决方案，但是今天，生物燃料恰恰是使交通运输业燃料来源多样化的唯一可获得的、规模又较大的选择。我们必须确保生物燃料为我们提供的机遇能够得到利用。

第二个挑战是气候变化。交通运输过程中温室气体的排放增加很快。这方面的增长抵消了在其他方面排放的减少。根据现在的趋势，欧盟在 2005 到 2020 年间增加的二氧化碳排放量中，由交通运输产生的将占到 60% 以上。因此，扭转这种趋势十分必要。在欧盟，只有两种政策能够在相当的程度上做到这一点：一是提高机动车的效率；二是采用生物燃料。我们必须大力推行这两项政策。

生物燃料还提供了其他机遇——十分明显，这些燃料在欧盟和其他发展中国家的农村地区的就业方面有做出贡献的潜能，在扩大技术发展的范围方面也是如此，比如，在第二代生物燃料方面。因此，生物燃料是我们能源政策的重要部分。

欧盟促进生物燃料发展的政策

2003 年，欧盟生物燃料的促进工作向前迈出了第一大步，通过了生物燃料法规，每个欧盟成员国必须将这条规定纳入本国法律。那时，生物燃料仅占交通运输燃料市场的 0.5%。这项法规制定了两个“象征性”目标——生物燃料在 2005 年取得欧盟燃料市场 2% 的份额，在 2010 年取得 5.75% 的份额。令人失望的是我们未能实现第一个象征性目标。即便是到去年，生物燃料的份额也仅达到 1.5%。但是，这项法规的实施速度正在加快。我高兴地告诉大家，几乎所有的 27 个欧盟成员国都已经为支持生物燃料制定了措施——这与 2003 年的情况形成了鲜明的对照，那时，只有五个国家制定了措施。现在，一些国家采取了免税政策，另一些国家规定了“生物燃料义务”，这种义务要求燃料供应商必须在他们销售的燃料中包括一定比例的生物燃料。许多国家则是两项并用。由于成员国努力力度的加大，我们期望看到生物燃料在 2010 年能够占到 4% 到 4.5% 的市场份额。当然，全面实现 2010 年目标的前景并不乐观。

由于我们打算要解决的问题越来越紧迫——能源供应的不安全和气候变化——我们复审了我们的政策，为的是增强实现我们制定的目标的能力，并且还要着眼于 2010 年之后。我高兴地告诉大家，复审是在一个明确的、有利的全面政策框架中进行的：即推行“欧洲新能源政策”的行动计划，这是欧盟成员国在今年三月制定的。这个计划重申了将减少温室气体和供应安全作为能源政策目标的重要性。对于一般的可再生能源，我们现在提出一个具有约束力的欧洲目标，要求其市场份额在 2020 年占到 20%，也就是说其作用应是现在的三倍。对于生物燃料，我们提出到 2020 年其份额要占到交通运输市场的 10%，但是，这次这个目标将不再是象征性的——它也将成为具有约束力的目标。

这一战略体现了我们在实现可再生能源政策的雄心壮志以及在出台一个支持实现政策目标的坚实的欧洲政策框架方面取得的显著进展。对于生物燃料，这一战略将意味着增加近七倍的消费量。当然，必须确保以可持续的方式实现以上增长。我们不能只是坐等其成，等着目标自动实现。

多数生物燃料能够切实储存温室气体，但却仍存在着一些无法做到减排的低效能生产技术。必须避免使用此类生产技术。

多数生物燃料源于经过几代人耕作的土地。但是也有一些来自新近开垦的土地。这就会有风险，因为释放贮藏在土壤和植物中的碳会导致大量温室气体的丢失。此外，还会有另一种风险，即生产生物燃料可能破坏生物的多样性，破坏动植物自然的生存环境。我们也要避免这些风险。

再者，为了尽可能有效地实现 10% 的生物燃料份额，我们必须尽可能早地进入"第二代"生物燃料市场。麦秆、有机废物、木本材料等多种原材料都可以用以制造生物燃料。这样，就能加强这种政策带来的供应安全性，也能增加政策在环境方面的成效。

欧盟的行动计划强调大力推动利用"第二代"生物燃料的需要，强调有效的可持续能力规划的需要。欧洲议会将在九月发表意见。我们希望议会也支持这种态度。同时，我们正在想办法把我们的想法变成论据充足的立法提议。我们计划将我们的生物燃料措施与为把可再生能源的份额增加到 20% 所需的其他措施一起写入同一项规定。这一工作应该在年底前完成。那时，将由欧洲理事会和欧洲议会来考虑我们的提议，并达成最终的意见。这个规定将使生物燃料达到 10% 的目标有法可依。

同时，规定还会包括一个可持续能力规划。具体的内容还在制定之中。以下是我们的初衷：

首先，我们需要制定最基本的生物燃料可持续能力标准；

第二，只有符合这些标准的生物燃料才能计入实现 10% 的目标内；

第三，只有这些生物燃料有资格享受免税；只有使用这些生物燃料才能算作履行生物燃料义务。

当然，这些规定会对国内生产的生物燃料和进口的生物燃料一视同仁。对于最基本可持续能力标准究竟应该包括什么有很多争论。因此，欧洲委员会最近开展了咨询，欧盟内部以及欧盟之外的各利益攸关方发表了很多不同的看法。我们正在认真地研究各方意见，我们也期待听取本次大会上发表的看法。关键是要把我们政策的这一部分制定正确，要制定出简单有效的措施。

开展国际合作，促进生物燃料

最后，我想谈谈为什么我们在发展生物燃料政策之时需要国际合作。

一个重要的原因是我们期待并希望看到生物燃料和生物燃料原料的国际贸易有所增加。现在就欧盟而言，我要指出的是我们能够完全依靠我们自己生产的生物燃料实现 2020 年 10% 的目标——如果这是必要的——显然，这要通过使用"储备"农业用地以及通过在欧盟减少可耕地的废弃率来实现。这种方法只会使农业商品价格小幅增长——只会涨几个百分点。

然而，即便这一做法在技术上是可能的，这也并不是我们想采用的方法。我们认为这种纯粹依靠从国内获取生物燃料的方法既是不可能的——考虑到现行的贸易规定和我们希望在未来看到的贸易自由化程度的提高——也是不会令人满意的。我们的目标是采取"平衡的方法"，同时利用国内和进口的生物燃料来满足欧盟不断增长的需求。

我们非常愿意与其他国家、地区以及国际组织开展建设性的合作，共同为业已增大的生物燃料贸易创立必要的框架。我们需要保证我们的生物燃料标准和我们主要贸易伙伴的相关标准不会造成不必要的障碍。今年 2 月，我们与欧洲标准化委员会一起召开了一个有关生物燃料标准的国际会议。此会为我们未来制定国际适用的生物燃料标准确定了路线图。我们将继续大力实施这个路线图。我们还要努力整合生物燃料的可持续能力——一方面是制定每个国家或地区使用生物燃料的基本标准，另一方面是确定批准这些标准的程序。

但是，贸易问题并不是需要合作的唯一原因。更为广泛的团结原则也在发挥作用，因为任何一个国家或地区采取发展生物燃料的可持续政策都会使大家从中受益。

我们受益于温室气体排放的减少。

我们受益于生物燃料在交通运输市场上日益成为石油类燃料的可靠替代品。

我们受益于农村经济发展的新机遇。

我们还受益于各国经验教训的相互交流。就欧盟来说，我们从一些成员国、从巴西以及其他国家的开拓经历中取得了很多经验。我们必须，也将利用国际合作带来的收获制定我们的生物燃料政策。

为此，欧洲委员会将致力于生物燃料方面的国际合作。本次大会标志着我们的决心，也标志着我们向前迈出的重要一步。

生物燃料并不是解决我们所有能源问题的万能药。但是，生物燃料是我们能源政策未来考虑的必要组成部分，是确保交通运输业在我们努力应对全球变暖问题和使燃料原料多样化时充分发挥其作用的方法。看到这么多人今天在此相聚，真令人激动。我以极大的兴趣期待着明天及（后天）半天的讨论，希望听到我们可以借鉴的经验。

四、自主训练

请在 15 分钟之内迅速阅读下面的讲话，了解大意。学生可组成对子练习，互相监控对视译技巧的掌握情况、视译质量和现场表现，或以边视译边录音的形式进行个人练习。视译时要保持正常语速，译文要顺畅达意。如遇难句，可在首次视译后参照"实战练习"中难句分析与视译处理的方法进行练习，找出解决方法。

Remarks at the China-US Innovation Conference[1] (Excerpt)

US Secretary of Commerce　Carlos M. Gutierrez

Beijing, 2007

I am pleased to be in Beijing this week. Each time I visit there is change, from construction for the Olympics to the building cranes remaking the landscape. These changes are symbolic of the dramatic transformation taking place not only within China, but also with China's relationship to the world.

Later this week I will participate in the Joint Commission on Commerce and Trade as well as the Strategic Economic Dialog (SED). Both are important bilateral conversations between our two governments. As our relationship grows, so do the challenges and opportunities. This week we hope to address issues of importance to both countries. This conference is part of that process—in fact it is an outcome of the May SED meeting in Washington, D.C. It is an acknowledgment of the importance of innovation in creating robust, healthy and growing economies worldwide.

1　原文参见 http://www.commerce.gov/NewsRoom/SecretarySpeeches/PROD01_004893。

The world is more competitive than ever before. As China, along with India and Russia have become full participants in the global economy over the past 20 years or so, three billion consumers have joined the world's economy. By changing China's economic approach, you've generated a flood of new ideas, consumers and competitors that has revolutionized the global marketplace.

Twenty years ago, trade accounted for 17% of the world's economy—today it's roughly 30% growing.

Twenty years ago, the world economy was worth about $15 trillion—today it's estimated to be $48 trillion.

As barriers to trade fall and countries embrace new people and ideas, innovative societies emerge. In the United States, our market-based economy has helped promote a culture of entrepreneurship and innovation. Advances in nanotechnology, biofuels and information technology move our economy forward, giving us a competitive edge. In fact, the World Economic Forum recently ranked us the number one competitive economy in the world, in large part due to our ability to encourage innovation. The ideas and the ingenious products that have been developed as a result have enriched America's social and economic life, creating wealth and a high standard of living.

Discoverers, inventors, creators and risk-takers play an integral role in our economic progress. Companies like Google, Dell, Cisco and eBay didn't exist 30 years ago. But they were founded in America—a place where creativity and ingenuity are encouraged and rewarded. Americans file millions of patents every year—more than any other nation. US innovation industries account for over half of all US exports. They represent 40% of US economic growth and employ 18 million Americans who earn 40% more than the average US wage.

We in government are not generating growth, creating jobs, allocating capital and launching new products. That's being done by the innovators and entrepreneurs in the private sector. We believe that government's role is to create the environment for continued success. A study by INSEAD, one of Europe's premier business schools, ranked the US as the world's first innovator. They pointed to our "environment for innovation" comprised of our technological sophistication, business markets and capital, and our topnotch academic and research institutions. But that same study pointed out factors that threaten our position—one of the largest ones being education and our need to "produce more scientists and engineers from within". That's why we are working to promote more research, incentivize innovation, and strengthen our education system:

We have doubled the funding for innovation-enabling federal research;

We have proposed to make permanent a research and development tax credit which will encourage private sector research; and

We are strengthening our public education system, particularly in the areas of math and science.

While we work on these areas in our own society, there are a number of key principles that we have embraced and continue to promote in order to keep the momentum going. The question to ask today is, "What does it take to sustain an environment for innovation?"

First, we have to continue opening global markets. Both of our economies have benefited from increased international engagement. America and China must work together to stem the rising tide of protectionist sentiment in our nations. We must demonstrate to our citizens the benefits that free and fair trade can bring to our economies. We must show that we will hold our trading partners accountable for their commitments to open their markets. And we must also show them the dangers of over-regulation that burdens the economy and costs jobs. This is not only important for the US, but also for China's global partnerships.

We believe respect for intellectual property rights (IPR) is critical to an innovative economy—ours as well as our trading partners'. That is why it has been an important part of our bilateral and multilateral negotiations and agreements. Consistent, transparent and equitably-enforced rules regulating intellectual property increases incentives for innovation. Without clear rules and strong enforcement, no country can fully develop the economy it wants, nor build the strong, recognizable and respected brands that are hallmarks of developed economies.

Societies can't aspire to innovation-driven growth while not enforcing intellectual property rights. This is one of the major challenges we face in our relationship with China. While some progress has been made recently, such as new rules requiring legal operating software to be pre-loaded on computers, and a commitment to join the World Intellectual Property Organization, more needs to be done. We believe it is a hurdle that China still must overcome to truly become an open, innovation-driven society. Last year, more Chinese patents were filed in China than foreign patents. Clearly, Chinese innovators have a great stake in effective IPR protection. Importantly, a lack of intellectual property enforcement has an impact beyond economics. For example, counterfeit drugs impact the health and safety of those who think they're getting the real deal. And sometimes, sadly, they kill.

Ensuring the safety of products is essential for the growth of an innovative society. Consumers will not buy what they fear. We've found that managing the challenges we face in a science-based, transparent and open way is the right approach. We also recognize that product safety doesn't begin and end with inspections at the border—it must be built-in from the start. This is a watershed moment for China. Each country makes a choice as to how they will ensure the safety of the products their companies produce. China—and all of our trading partners—must do their part to ensure their products are safe.

Transparency and predictability in regulations and laws governing business and investment are also critical. They send positive signals to potential partners in both our countries. Capital allocators look for secure, predictable markets, and they watch with concern where uncertainty exists. Open societies are open to foreign investment and competition from foreign firms. Economies benefit when true competition is welcomed. Allowing foreign firms to bring in new products and services gives consumers more choices, and strengthens the domestic market. Building in predictability, transparency and reliability for investors will make China a more attractive market for US firms, particularly US exports.

Open societies benefit when standards are market-driven, consensus-based and voluntary. Strong, innovative economies require a flexible regulatory system that supports market-driven technical standards. These standards should allow all stakeholders, including the private sector, to participate in the standards-setting process. No country has benefited more from global standards than China. China has been able to develop products based on global standards and sell them around the world. Global standards create a common language through which innovators can collaborate.

We are increasingly concerned about the implementation of government-mandated proprietary technology standards. While this approach may appear to provide a competitive advantage in the short term, it in fact inhibits cooperation and limits collaboration. These regulations will not only limit product development, they also reduce consumer choice. In open, market-driven societies, consumers have the real power. Let them make the choices that best suit their needs. In the US, the government does not pick winners and losers. Picking which products or technologies will succeed and which will fail is left up to the consumers, not government.

The government has an important role to play in creating an environment for innovation. We educate children, keep taxes low, open new markets, fund basic research, make federal regulations reasonable and protect intellectual property. This environment then allows the private sector to create jobs, allocate capital and launch new products and services that benefit consumers, economies and countries.

These principles are foundations of innovation-driven societies. Fully embracing them will help China continue to move from an advanced developing economy to an advanced developed economy. They will also help us create a sustainable, mutually beneficial relationship. China's leaders signal that they understand this. Last month Premier Wen Jiabao gave a speech entitled "Only an Open and Inclusive Nation Can Be Strong". He said that, "China's development history over the past 30 years tells us that today's world is open and it is impossible for a country to develop by isolating itself." We want this to be reflected in the discussions we are having this week. Openness is at the core of the future of our relationship. Maintaining openness is not easy, but necessary. Innovation begets change, and change is difficult—we must resist forces that want to take us backwards.

It's up to us to find ways to work together to create an environment that results in sustainable, open and mutually beneficial relationships—and that will only happen when innovators can thrive. History has shown that countries that have followed aggressive industrial policies by trying to pick winners and losers have ended up eroding their competitiveness and weakening the marketplace, not strengthening it.

China must demonstrate that it is a responsible stakeholder in the global economy. The eyes of the world are on China. Its growing importance places great responsibility on the shoulders of the Chinese government and its business leaders. A prosperous China is in America's interests, and a prosperous America is in China's best interests. By working together we both can win and turn our creativity into products that benefit everyone.

第7单元

状语的视译（I）：状语短语

> 基本技巧：
> - 视译时，使状语在译入语和译出语中所处的位置保持一致。

一、技巧讲解：状语短语的视译

状语的位置在英语和汉语中都是比较灵活的。根据不同的需要，状语可以前置、后置或置于句中。英语语法书通常告诉我们，由于汉英两种语言的不同，英语中状语的位置往往与汉语中状语的位置十分不同或是恰恰相反。（张道真，1979：521-522）所以，在笔译中，状语的位置较原文会有很大的调整。

但是，在视译中，我们遵循的基本原则是保持译出语语序不变，所以，英语中状语的位置在什么地方，汉语中基本也要保持在什么地方。由于汉语是高度灵活的语言，这是可以做到的。比如 I shall go rain and shine. 这个句子比较通常的译法是："不管天晴还是下雨，我都要去。"（张道真，1979：521）这个句子译文与原文的状语位置完全颠倒。但在视译中，这样的句子可以译为："我一定要去，不管天晴还是下雨。"

即便是一些大家熟知的规则，在视译中也要根据情况加以改变。比如，英语中如果时间和地点状语都出现，一般地点状语在前，时间状语在后。但是译成汉语的时候，则一般是时间状语在前，地点状语在后。例如句子 We are going to hold a meeting in the auditorium tomorrow evening. 通常我们将其译为："我们明天晚上在大礼堂召开会议。"但是，在视译中，我们还是要坚持保持英语原来的语序。这样，这个句子的视译译文就是："我们要召开会议，地点是大礼堂，时间是明天晚上。"

一般来说，状语短语仍可译为一个汉语短语，或译为一个汉语的短句。比如，The commander has told his men that they must finish the task as soon as possible. 这个句子的笔译译文是："指挥员告诉战士们他们必须尽快完成任务。"而在视译中，最后的 as soon as possible 往往被分列为一个类意群，作为一个独立的视译单位，因为一般译员看到这里会习惯地停顿。所以，我们将它单独译为一个短语。视译译文为："指挥员告诉战士们 // 他们必须完成任务 // 越快越好。"

词类转换或是其他转换方式也是保持原语序的一种基本技巧。比如，Are you to go home or stay at the college during the vacation? 这个句子的笔译译文是："你假期里回家还是留在学校？"而相应的视译译文则是："你回家还是留在学校过假期？"视译中将原来的状语"假期里"转化为一个动宾结构的短语"过假期"，这样处理起来就方便多了。由于汉语是使用动词很多的语言，所以将其他词类转换为动词是视译中常用的技巧。

有些英语状语在译成汉语的时候，可以前置，也可以后置。无论在什么位置，句子的意义没有任何变化。比如，Steel parts are usually covered with grease for fear that they should rust. 这句话可以译为："钢制零件通常涂上润滑油，以防生锈。"也可以译为："为了防锈，钢制零件通常涂上润滑油。"在视译中，我们使用第一种译法，以便保持译出语的语序。

下面我们举一些例子来说明如何翻译状语短语。

例1： I got to know her while studying in a provincial college.

译文1： 我是在一所省里的大学读书的时候认识她的。

译文2： 我认识她的时候正在一所省里的大学读书。

【讲解】 while studying in a provincial college 是这个句子中的时间状语，译文 1 将整个状语短语置于句子中间，将原句语序完全打乱。这样做必须首先读完或听完整个句子才能进行翻译。译文 2 先把主句译出，然后将以 while 引导的状语短语译为一个相对独立的短句，使整个句子可以按照原语序译出。

例2： We decided to stay at home rather than to see a movie because of the rain.

译文1： 由于下雨，我们决定呆在家里而不是去看电影。

译文2： 我们决定呆在家里而不是去看电影，因为天下雨了。

【讲解】 译文 1 根据原句句法，调整了汉译语序，将状语置于句首。译文 2 的关键是将状语短语视译为一个相对独立的短句"因为天下雨了"，这样不仅可以按照原语序依次译出，而且听起来也很顺畅。

例 3：　Now we have understood that the world is not rich <u>in natural resources</u>.

译文 1：我们现在明白了，世界的<u>自然资源</u>并不丰富。

译文 2：我们现在明白了，世界并不是<u>富有自然资源</u>。

例 4：　They started pumping water to the fields, <u>working from dawn to dark</u>.

译文 1：他们开始<u>起早贪黑地</u>抽水浇地。（张道真，1979：271）

译文 2：他们开始抽水浇地，<u>从早干到晚</u>。

【讲解】　例 3 和例 4 跟上面的例子在翻译技巧的运用上是相同的。笔译的译文一般是调整语序，而视译的方法是不调整语序。当然，我们需要知道，当一个句子短的时候，熟练的译员即使调整语序，也可以比较流利的完成翻译。但是，视译和同传的训练要求译员养成良好的视译习惯，所以，即便是短句，也要根据视译的要求来做。我们为了说明问题，所举例子都比较简单，实战中，很长的状语短语是常常出现的。即便是再熟练的译员，遇到这种情况，也必须按照原文顺序，依次翻译。

二、语段视译

1　词汇与表达

在进行语段视译前，请先预习以下词汇与表达。

sounding board	传声筒
weather vane	风向标

2　视译语段

请在 3 分钟之内迅速阅读下面的语段，了解大意，然后结合所学要点进行视译练习。视译时要保持正常语速，译文要顺畅达意。

Three big uncertainties loom over the Rice State Department. The first concerns the new secretary herself. For four years, Ms. Rice has been a sounding board, tutor, and weather vane. She will now have to articulate a clearer view of the post-al-

Qeada world. For example, she has a lot of expertise in Russia. But should America's attitude to Vladimir Putin's centralization of power be determined by the need to keep good relations with a partner in the war on terror? Or should it be influenced more by Mr. Bush's view that the best way to starve global terrorism is to encourage democracy? The second uncertainty concerns her department. Does she spend time shaping it, replacing the diplomats in charge of the DPRK and the Middle East, while risking the sort of hostility and disruption? The third uncertainty is how much appetite there is on both sides of the Atlantic for real diplomatic engagement. Even before the election, Mr. Bush and Ms. Rice privately indicated that, three years after September 11th, it was time to patch things up in Europe and the Middle East.[1] （摘自《英语文摘》，2005 年第 1 期，第 9 至 10 页）

原译文：赖斯的国务院面临三大不确定因素。一是赖斯本人。四年来，赖斯是传声筒，是辅导老师，也是风向标。现在，赖斯要在后基地组织的世界中更为明确地表达自己的观点。举个例子：赖斯是俄罗斯问题专家，那么，对于一个弗拉基米尔·普京高度集权的俄罗斯，美国在制定对俄政策时是应该出于反恐需要与其保持伙伴关系，抑或更多地接受布什的观点？因为在布什看来，战胜国际恐怖主义的最有效途径，是推广民主。第二大不确定因素来自国务院。如果赖斯花时间改造国务院，比如说调整主管朝鲜和中东事务的官员，可能会招致敌意和干扰。第三个不确定因素在于大西洋两岸对进行实质性的外交接触有多大的兴趣。还在大选之前，布什和赖斯就曾私下表示，经历了 9·11 事件三年之后，现在是在欧洲和中东修补关系的时候了。（曾志宏译）

3 视译译文

	断 句	译 文
1	Three big uncertainties	三大不确定因素，
2	loom over the Rice State Department.	笼罩着赖斯的国务院。
3	The first concerns the new secretary herself.	第一个是新任国务卿本人。
4	For four years,	四年来，

（待续）

---

1 较原文有删节。

（续上表）

	断 句	译 文
5	Ms. Rice has been a sounding board, tutor, and weather vane.	赖斯女士是传声筒，是辅导老师，是风向标，
6	She will now have to articulate a clearer view	她现在却需要表达更加清晰的观点，
7	of the post-al-Qeada world.	说明如何看待后基地组织时期的世界。
8	For example,	比如，
9	she has a lot of expertise in Russia.	她专门研究俄罗斯，
10	But should America's attitude to	但美国的态度应该是什么呢？
11	Vladimir Putin's centralization of power	面对普京的集权政策，
12	be determined by the need to keep good relations	美国要维持俄美良好关系，
13	with a partner in the war on terror?	继续成为反恐战争中的伙伴吗？
14	Or should it be influenced more by Mr. Bush's view	还是更多地受到布什观念的影响，
15	that the best way to starve global terrorism	而布什认为战胜全球恐怖主义的最好方式，
16	is to encourage democracy?	就是推行民主。
17	The second uncertainty concerns her department.	第二个不确定因素涉及国务院。
18	Does she spend time shaping it,	她是否会花费时间改造国务院，
19	replacing the diplomats in charge of the DPRK and the Middle East,	调整主管朝鲜和中东事务的外交官，
20	while risking the sort of hostility and disruption?	并因此招致敌意和干扰吗？
21	The third uncertainty is	第三个不确定因素是

（待续）

（续上表）

	断 句	译 文
22	how much appetite there is	到底存在多大的可能，
23	on both sides of the Atlantic	使大西洋两岸
24	for real diplomatic engagement.	能够开展真正的外交接触？
25	Even before the election,	还是在大选之前，
26	Mr. Bush and Ms. Rice privately indicated	布什和赖斯就私下表示，
27	that, three years after September 11th,	9·11过去三年了，
28	it was time to patch things up	现在应该修补关系了，
29	in Europe and the Middle East.	这当然说的是在欧洲和中东。

4 视译点评

1. 原文第四句： She will now have to articulate a clearer view // of the post-al-Qeada world.

虽然此句是个简单句，并不很长，但是介词短语 of the post-al-Qeada world 在汉译时，作为定语，习惯置于其所修饰的中心词 view 之前，所以译为："她现在需要更加清楚地表明对后基地组织的世界的看法。"做视译时，为了避免调整语序，可以将 articulate a clearer view of the post-al-Qeada world 断成两部分，其中第一个类意群是 articulate a clearer view，第二个是 of the post-al-Qeada world, 分别译作"表示更加清晰的观点"和"说明如何看待后基地组织时期的世界"。

2. 原文第六句： But should America's attitude to // Vladimir Putin's centralization of power // be determined by the need to keep good relations // with a partner in the war on terror?

此句是个疑问长句，又是被动句式，笔译时需要读完长句，然后在语序、主语等方面进行调整。所以，笔译译文是："那么，对于一个弗拉基米尔·普京高度集权的俄罗斯，美国在制定对俄政策时是应该出于反恐需要与其保持伙伴关系吗？"此外，原译文将此疑问句与原文第七句疑问句的主句部分合并译成一个结构紧凑的句子："美国……是应该……抑或……？"这些调整在时间允许的情况下是可取的。但是，视译时为了节省时间，要尽量坚持顺译的原则，所以，此疑问句依照视译单位被断为四个类意群，并将其中的第一部分先译成一个疑问短句："但美国的态度应该是什么呢？"然后运用增词、增加主语、改变词性等方法依次译出后面三个相互衔接自然的视译单位，构成一个疑问句："面对普京的集权政策，美国要维持俄美良好关系，继续成为反恐战争中的伙伴吗？"这样，视译译文既保持了原文语序，又在有限的时间内顺畅地传达了原文的信息。

3. 原文第七句：Or should it be influenced more by Mr. Bush's view // that the best way to starve global terrorism // is to encourage democracy?

　　同第六句一样，这也是一个较长的疑问句，其中主句也是被动句式并带有一个作同位语的从句。视译时，依视译单位断句，可断为三个类意群，承接前一句的意思，分别译成："还是更多地受到布什观念的影响，// 而布什认为战胜全球恐怖主义的最好方式，// 就是推行民主。"其中，在视译第二个类意群时重复了同位语从句所修饰的 Mr. Bush's view，并将这个词组处理成主谓语结构的视译单位，自然连接后面的类意群 that the best way to starve global terrorism，这样有利于听众理解传达的信息。the best way to starve global terrorism 译成："反对全球恐怖主义的最好方式"，虽然略调整语序，但是由于调整是在一目可及的范围之内，加上 the best way to do sth. 的表达在汉语中一般可较为方便固定地译为"……的最好方式"，所以，不会影响视译速度。

4. 原文第九句：Does she spend time shaping it, // replacing the diplomats in charge of the DPRK and the Middle East, // while risking the sort of hostility and disruption?

　　对于这个很长的一般疑问句，由于 while risking the sort of hostility and disruption 表示主句可能造成的后果，所以，原译文将此疑问句译作条件句："如果赖斯花时间改造国务院，比如说调整主管朝鲜和中东事务的官员，可能会招致敌意和干扰。"视译时，在一目可及的范围无法读完整个疑问句，更无暇推敲，最便捷的译法是将句子断成三个类意群，分别译作三个分句，并保持疑问句式："她是否会花费时间改造国务院，// 调整主管朝鲜和中东事务的官员，// 并因此招致敌意和干扰吗？"

5. 原文第十句：The third uncertainty is // how much appetite there is // on both sides of the Atlantic // for real diplomatic engagement.

由于句中表语从句实际上是一个疑问句，原译文按汉语表达习惯调整了语序，将表语中的疑问部分 how much appetite there is 置于句末，全句译为："第三个不确定因素在于大西洋两岸对进行实质性的外交接触<u>有多大的兴趣</u>。"视译时，保持原句中表语部分的疑问句的语序，将这部分断为三个类意群，分别译作："<u>到底存在多大的可能</u>，// 使大西洋两岸 // 能够开展真正的外交接触？"原文中介词 on 和 for 在汉语中分别译作动词"使"和"能够开展"，以连接上下文。这样一来，译出语听起来就更加通顺达意了。

三、实战练习

1 词汇与表达

请先熟悉以下词汇与表达，并适当地运用在视译中。

term for normalization	正常化条件
envision	预见
bulwark	保障，支柱
unwarranted aspersion	毫无根据的中伤
head of state	国家元首
constructive relation	建设性关系
complementary	互补的
international trade regime	国际贸易机制
communicable diseases	传染病
trade in narcotics	贩运毒品
approach	态度；方式，方法
racial segregation	种族隔离
civil right	民权
right injustice	匡正非正义行为
acquire a stake in	与……相关
enlightened self-interest	开明的自我利益
security alliance	安全同盟
security framework	安全框架

2　实战课文

请在 15 分钟之内迅速阅读下面的讲话，了解大意。视译时要保持正常语速，译文要顺畅达意。

The Challenges of Governance in the 21st Century (Excerpt 1)
Jimmy Carter

Exactly 20 years ago, I informed my principal advisors that during my Presidency, I wanted to establish full diplomatic relations between the United States and China on terms that would protect American interests, maintain American credibility, and meet legitimate Chinese concerns. （句 1） By the summer of 1978, the setting was propitious, and in December, 1978 China's preeminent leader Deng Xiaoping and I agreed upon the terms for normalization. That agreement was one of the major accomplishments of my administration. Vice Premier Deng Xiaoping and I envisioned normalization to be much more than a tactic. We recognized its historic significance. **We envisioned a multipolar world of increasing openness in which Sino-American cooperation would be a bulwark for world peace and prosperity.** （句 2）

Based upon the firm but long postponed opportunity provided by the Shanghai Communiqué of 1972, we committed our government and citizens to work together on behalf of future generations of Americans and Chinese. （句 3） We knew each side bore responsibilities in a mutual effort. We began to forge a partnership that we hoped would survive inevitable stresses. We harbored no illusion about the enormity and difficulty of the task before us. Setbacks would be inevitable. Decades of patience and persistence would be required before the bonds between our two countries became firm and predictable. But we know that future generations would condemn us if we did not start the process.

In recent years, for reasons that are known to all, both Americans and Chinese have lost sight of the original vision that brought us together. The relationship seems to have lost a sense of the common purpose. In both countries, all too many commentators are casting unwarranted aspersions on the intent of the other side. Some even forecast inevitable rivalry and conflict between our two countries. I disagree. Through mutual efforts, we can forge a bright future.

On the eve of President Jiang Zemin's important trip to the United States—the first by a Chinese head of state after an excessive lapse of 10 years—perhaps it would be helpful to remind ourselves of the original aspirations for Sino-American relations. That is the main purpose of this fifth trip of mine to China: as a private citizen, to use my limited influence to help both sides seize the many opportunities that exist for constructive relations between the Chinese and American people. The rationale for extensive, deep, enduring, and mutually beneficial relations between our peoples is as persuasive as ever:

We share common strategic interests in preventing the proliferation of weapons of mass destruction and creating stable post-cold war security arrangements, so that no country feels impelled to embark upon an expansionist path.

We have a common desire to promote stability on the Korean Peninsula, to prevent the reappearance of age-old Asian rivalries, and to consolidate the good relations among all major powers in the Asia-Pacific region. Everyone would suffer if an arms race were to erupt in this part of the world.

Our economies are complementary, and a genuinely open international trade regime benefits us both. Both sides profit from increased trade, investment, and access to each other's markets.

All humankind looks to our two countries to address such issues as global climatic change, the spread of communicable diseases, trade in narcotics, or the dangers of terrorism. Constructive relations between our two countries will not guarantee solution to these problems. Without our active cooperation, however, the efforts will surely fail.

These realistic considerations demand constructive Sino-American relations. But my approach to China has also reflected other influences. I first visited China as a young American naval officer in 1949. My submarine called at the harbors of Hong Kong, Shanghai, and Qingdao, and I witnessed the poverty and suffering of a nation struggling to recover from foreign invasion, civil war, and chaos. Moreover, before, during, and after my Presidency, **I have believed that the gaps between the privileged and the downtrodden, between the oppressed and the oppressor, between the rich and the poor, between the developed and the developing worlds are the greatest sources of tension, conflict and violence both within and among nations.** (句 4)

That belief inspired me, before my Presidency, to condemn racial segregation and to support the civil rights of African-Americans in my native land. That belief explains the attention my administration devoted to Latin America, Africa, the Middle East, and Asia: returning the Panama Canal Zone to Panama; helping to bring an end to the racist governments in southern Africa; achieving peace with hope for both Israelis and Palestinians alike; firmly resisting the Soviet invasion of Afghanistan; and returning human rights, broadly defined, to the agenda of American foreign policy. In all these instances, the United States sought to right previous injustices and to promote a more stable and equitable world. Since my Presidency, at the Carter Center, we similarly have devoted ourselves to the problems of the impoverished, the weak, and the oppressed, seeking to enable the less fortunate among us to overcome their afflictions and to have greater control over their own destiny. One of the most successful projects of the Carter Center, of course, was to assist China in its efforts to aid the physically handicapped.

From this perspective, China's rapid economic development and the resulting improved quality of life for most Chinese—nearly a quarter of humanity—significantly reduces global inequality. China's economic development and its increasing involvement in the international economic system mean that the Chinese people are acquiring an increased stake in world peace and stability.

Put it simply, as President, I felt that a prosperous China, integrated into the international economy, would become a more positive and constructive force in world affairs than the China of the 1960s and early 1970s. （句 5） The record since 1977 largely demonstrates the wisdom of that policy. That process should continue to go forward rapidly, before rather than after China acquires major military might.

4　难句分析与视译处理

句 1：　Exactly 20 years ago, I informed my principal advisors that during my Presidency, I wanted to establish full diplomatic relations between the United States and China on terms that would protect American interests, maintain American credibility, and meet legitimate Chinese concerns.

笔译译文：　整整 20 年前，我告诉我的主要顾问：在担任总统期间，我要在既能维护美国利益、保持美国信誉，又能兼顾中国正当关注的问题的情况下，建立美中两国间全面的外交关系。

视译译文：

断 句	译 文
Exactly 20 years ago,	整整 20 年前，
I informed my principal advisors	我告诉主要顾问：
that during my Presidency,	在担任总统期间，
I wanted to establish full diplomatic relations	我要建立正式的外交关系，
between the United States and China	就是与中国正式建交，
on terms that would protect American interests,	条件是能维护美国利益、
maintain American credibility,	保持美国信誉，
and meet legitimate Chinese concerns.	也能照顾到中国正当关注的问题。

句 2：　We envisioned a multipolar world of increasing openness in which Sino-American cooperation would be a bulwark for world peace and prosperity.

笔译译文：我们预见，未来的世界是一个持续开放的多极世界，中美合作将是世界和平、繁荣的砥柱。

视译译文：

断 句	译 文
We envisioned a multipolar world	我们预见到的是一个多极世界，
of increasing openness	它会越来越开放，
in which	在这个世界里，
Sino-American cooperation	中美合作，
would be a bulwark for world peace and prosperity.	就能够保障世界的和平与繁荣。

句 3：　Based upon the firm but long delayed opportunity provided by the Shanghai Communiqué of 1972, we committed our government and citizens to work together on behalf of future generations of American and Chinese.

笔译译文：1972 年的《上海公报》所提供的机遇被拖延得太久了。然而，就

是在这种机遇的坚实基础上，我们承诺我国政府和人民致力于共
建美中关系的明天。

视译译文：

断　句	译　文
Based upon the firm but long delayed opportunity	基于坚实的、但又被延误太久的机遇，
provided by the Shanghai Communiqué of 1972,	也就是 1972 年《上海公报》提供的机遇，
we committed	我们承诺，
our government and citizens	我国政府和人民，
to work together	一定共同努力，
on behalf of future generations of Americans and Chinese.	共建美中关系的明天。

句 4：　　I have believed that the gaps between the privileged and the
downtrodden, between the oppressed and the oppressor, between
the rich and the poor, between the developed and the developing
worlds are the greatest sources of tension, conflict and violence
both within and among nations.

笔译译文：　我一直认为：各国之间和国际间紧张、冲突和暴力的根源在于高
贵者和卑贱者之间、压迫者和被压迫者之间、富人和穷人之间、
发达国家和发展中国家之间存在着鸿沟。

视译译文：

断　句	译　文
I have believed	我一直认为，
that the gaps	有一条鸿沟，
between the privileged and the downtrodden,	横挡在高贵者和卑贱者之间、
between the oppressed and the oppressor,	压迫者和被压迫者之间、
between the rich and the poor,	富人和穷人之间、

（待续）

161

（续上表）

断　句	译　文
between the developed and the developing worlds	发达国家和发展中国家之间。
are the greatest sources of tension, conflict and violence	这就是紧张、冲突和暴力的根源所在，
both within and among nations.	无论在国内还是国际上都是如此。

句 5： Put it simply, as President, I felt that a prosperous China, integrated into the international economy, would become a more positive and constructive force in world affairs than the China of the 1960s and early 1970s.

笔译译文： 简而言之，作为总统，我认为：较之于 20 世纪 60 年代和 70 年代早期的中国而言，一个充分参与国际经济的、繁荣的中国，将成为世界事务中更积极的、更具建设性的力量。

视译译文：

断　句	译　文
Put it simply,	简言之，
as President,	作为总统，
I felt	我当时就认为，
that a prosperous China,	一个繁荣昌盛的中国，
integrated into the international economy,	融入国际经济之后，
would become a more positive and constructive force	会成为更积极、更具建设性的力量，
in world affairs	在世界事务中发挥作用，
than the China of the 1960s and early 1970s.	这是 20 世纪 60 年代和 70 年代早期的中国所无法做到的。

4 **参考译文**

21 世纪对领导者的挑战（节选 1）

吉米·卡特

整整 20 年前，我告诉我的主要顾问：在担任总统期间，我要在既能维护美国利益、保持美国信誉，又能兼顾中国正当关注的情况下，建立起美中两国间全面的外交关系。1978 年夏，情况比较有利。同年 12 月，我与中国杰出的领袖邓小平就关系正常化的条件达成协议。这是我任内的一项重大成就。我和邓小平副总理都认为：关系正常化绝非策略性的举措。我们认识到它具有历史意义。我们预见，未来的世界是一个持续开放的多极世界，中美合作将是世界和平、繁荣的砥柱。

1972 年的《上海公报》所提供的机遇被拖延得太久了。然而，就是在这种机遇坚实的基础上，我们承诺我国政府和人民致力于共建美中关系的明天。我们知道，合作就意味着双方都要承担责任。我们开始建立伙伴关系，希望这一关系能够经受住不可避免的压力。我们非常清楚我们所从事的工作是巨大的、极为困难的，难免会遇到挫折。需要耐心、坚定地努力数十载，才能在两国间建立起牢固、可靠的关系。但我们知道，如果现在不启动这一进程，后人将不会饶恕我们。

出于众所周知的原因，近年来，美国人和中国人都不再具有双方当初接触时所具有的远见卓识。两国关系中似乎已找不到具有共同目标的感觉。两国的评论家们对对方的意图妄加评论，这样的人太多了。有人甚至预测，两国间的对抗乃至冲突在所难免。对此，我并不苟同，我们共同努力能够创造一个光明的未来。

江泽民主席即将对美国进行的重要访问，是长达十年以来中国国家元首第一次访美。在江主席访问的前夕，回顾一下建立中美关系的初衷也许是有帮助的。我此番第五次访华主要目的正在于此：作为普通公民，利用自己有限的影响力来帮助双方抓住众多的机遇，促进中美人民之间建设性的关系。两国人民需要发展广泛、深入、持久和互利的关系，这个道理历来令人信服：

我们拥有共同的战略利益，要防止大规模杀伤性武器的扩散及做出冷战后稳固的安全安排，以免各国被迫走上扩张主义的道路。

我们双方都想促成朝鲜半岛的稳定，阻止年代久远的亚洲敌对关系重现，巩固亚太区域所有大国之间的关系。世界上这一区域如果出现军备竞赛，大家都会遭殃。

我们两国的经济具有互补性，真正开放的国际贸易制度对双方都有利。双方都得益于贸易和投资的增长以及能够进入对方的市场。

全人类指望我们两国来处理全球气候变暖、传染病的传播、贩运毒品以及恐怖主义带来的危险等诸多问题。即使我们两国间有了建设性的关系，也不能保证这些问题得到解决。可是如果我们不积极合作，这方面的努力必定付诸东流。

这些现实的考虑要求中美两国建立起建设性的关系。但是我对中国的态度也反应出其他因素的影响。我第一次访问中国是在1949年，那时我还是美国海军一名年轻的军官。我所在的潜水艇访问了香港、上海和青岛的港口，亲眼目睹了正在和外来侵略、内战以及混乱作斗争的中国所经历的贫困和痛苦。而且，不论在我担任总统之前、在任期间，还是卸任之后，我一直以为：各国内部和国际间紧张、冲突和暴力的根源在于高贵者和卑贱者之间、压迫者和被压迫者之间、富人和穷人之间、发达国家和发展中国家之间存在着鸿沟。

在我担任总统之前，这样的信念激励我对我国的种族隔离现象进行了谴责，支持非洲裔美国人享有公民权。这一信念说明了卡特政府何以对拉丁美洲、非洲、中东和亚洲较为重视：把巴拿马运河区归还给巴拿马；推动南部非洲各国种族主义政府下台；在给以色列人和巴勒斯坦人都带来希望的情况下实现和平；坚决抗击苏联入侵阿富汗；将广义上的人权重新列入美国外交政策的日程。美国通过所有这些事件，力图匡正以前的非正义行为，使世界更趋稳定和公正。同样，卸任之后，我们通过卡特中心，致力于解决贫困者、弱者和被压迫者的问题，努力帮助我们当中的不幸者提高能力，克服困苦，更好地掌握自己的命运。当然，卡特中心最成功的项目之一就是帮助中国做好残疾人工作。

从这一观点来看，中国经济的迅速发展、以及由此带来的中国大多数人生活质量的提高，大大地减少了全球不平等的现象，因为中国人口几乎占全人类的四分之一。中国的经济在发展，中国越来越多地参与国际经济体系，这意味着世界的和平稳定与中国人民更加密切相关。

简而言之，作为总统，我认为：较之于20世纪60年代和70年代早期的中国而言，一个充分参与国际经济的、繁荣的中国，将成为世界事务中更积极、更具建设性的力量。1977年以来的情况基本表明，该政策是明智之举。在中国尚未成为军事大国之前，而不是在其获得军事实力之后，我们就应当将此进程高速保持下去。

四、自主训练

请在 15 分钟之内迅速阅读下面的讲话，了解大意。学生可组成对子练习，互相监控对视译技巧的掌握情况、视译质量和现场表现，或以边视译边录音的形式进行个人练习。视译时要保持正常语速，译文要顺畅达意。如遇难句，可在首次视译后参照"实战练习"中难句分析与视译处理的方法进行练习，找出解决方法。

The Challenges of Governance in the 21st Century (Excerpt 2)
Jimmy Carter

Each of my successors and the American public have accepted this viewpoint. Enlightened self-interest has prevailed, and both the public and private sectors of the United States have done much to facilitate China's economic development.

Beginning in 1979, the American people have welcomed over 100,000 Chinese visiting scholars and students to our colleges and universities, with the overwhelming number having been funded by the United States. Many have now returned to China to contribute to their motherland and countless thousands of others will do so in the future. I am very proud of this exchange, and hope that it can be expanded in the future.

The United States accepted the entry of the People's Republic of China into the World Bank and the IMF before its non-market economy fully merited membership.

The United States has opened its markets to Chinese goods. Americans consume nearly 40% of all Chinese exports. American corporations and financial institutions are investing heavily in China, and American firms are particularly generous in facilitating technology transfers to China.

Some ill-advised Americans condemn the policy of welcoming China's growing participation in world affairs. They seek to constrain American trade and diplomatic contact with China. They fear China's economic development and the likely gradual growth in military power that will come with it. To such voices, I say: It is far better to anticipate the challenges and opportunities posed by a prosperous and friendly China than to confront the dangers of an alienated China or attempt the worthless task of keeping China weak and isolated.

In short, every American administration since 1972 has recognized that the

American interests are served by a secure, modernizing, humane and well governed China that contributes to global and regional stability and prosperity. And such a China corresponds to the yearnings of the Chinese government and its people. Similarly, in my view, China's interests are served by a United States that is secure, economically sound, well governed, and constructive in its foreign policy. And I am sure the American people would welcome a statement from China's leaders along these lines. What does this formulation really mean? To answer this question, we must look not to the past but to the future. We must not dwell excessively on the road we have traversed since the Shanghai Communiqué, the normalization of diplomatic relations, and the 1982 agreement on arms sales to Taiwan, although those documents remain binding. Rather we must explore the terrain ahead.

All humanity and all governments are confronting a similar set of unprecedented but poorly understood challenges resulting from demographic and technological change. For example, throughout the world, people's aspiration and expectations are being transformed through the ease of communication and transportation: the spread of television, satellite dishes, fax machines, personal computers, and electronic communications. Governments cannot halt these technological changes. To the contrary, they must learn to utilize the opportunities that new technologies offer.

These developments also mean that pursuit of national security, economic growth, and effective governance will be conceptually different in the years ahead than they were in the 20th century. These changes are already evident. In the realm of security, for example, technological changes are transforming weaponry and military strategy. No nation can effectively attain its security by intimidating its neighbors and making them feel insecure. Those who feel insecure have increasing access to weapons of mass destruction. In the economic realm, individual countries find it difficult to design an independent growth strategy in an integrated global economy. Political and economic leaders are increasingly subject to the discipline of external forces and institutions. Should they seek to exempt themselves from the constraints of international financial and commercial forces, their economies will stagnate.

And rulers everywhere are increasingly judged by their adherence to international standards of conduct. Permit me to cite several examples:

Nations are criticized when they do not fulfill their financial obligations to international organizations, such as the United States for its failure to meet its payments to the United Nations.

Nations find themselves isolated when they depart from accepted international commercial practices, such as the United States is learning in the controversy over the Helms-Burton Act.

Nations come under special scrutiny when they violate internationally accepted standards of human rights or when it appears they are denying basic freedoms to ethnic and religious minorities.

In light of these changes, what will be required for the United States and China—indeed for any country—to be effectively and humanely governed in the 21st century? Clearly, the fundamental nature of human beings will not change. All people will still share common yearnings: to have adequate food, shelter, and clothing; to live without fear of random violence, arbitrary arrest and torture; to worship as they choose; to enjoy freedom of speech and assembly and to participate in their own governance. Responding to these yearnings is the essence of promoting human rights. And our Constitutions, laws, and our voluntary accession to many international charters and covenants obligate both of our countries to meet these yearnings.

But effective governance in the 21st century will entail more than government protecting the human rights of its citizens against abuses. Positive actions will also be required:

Providing for the welfare of increasing numbers of elderly citizens;

Providing humane solutions to the consequences of unprecedented population migration within and among nations；

Strengthening the rule of law;

Improving techniques for resolving civil conflicts;

Enabling citizens to participate in the major political decisions that will affect their lives;

Developing effective means for securing adequate governmental revenue；

Preventing vast inequities in income distribution even as the global economy seems to be exacerbating inequalities among and within countries;

Striking the appropriate balance between regulation of the market and permitting it to flourish；and

Appropriately allocating authority among the central, provincial, and local governments.

These are some of the issues that demographic and technological challenges are bringing to the fore. Neither of our countries will enjoy stability and prosperity if these challenges of governance go unmet. These are the challenges that both China and the United States must solve if our countries are to be effectively and humanely governed in the 21st century. In recognition of our inadequacies, both of our countries are experimenting in many areas of governance, in the light of our own traditions and international commitments. For example, the United States is decentralizing its welfare system, increasing competition in the market place and adjusting the responsibilities of the national and state governments. China is conducting village elections, expanding the rule of law, enlivening parliamentary bodies, developing a market economy, and improving urban governance. In both countries, these reforms are just beginning. Creative thinking is needed concerning how governments and societies everywhere can best benefit from the implications of technological change, economic integration, and multipolarity in the 21st century. The best answers are likely to be conceived not by national governments but at the local levels, not only by government but also in the private sector.

In different ways, both of our countries fall short of our aspirations and commitments, and it is beneficial for each of us to evaluate ourselves and one another. Each of us should welcome reminders of our deficiencies—as long as the comments are constructive rather than arrogant or self-righteous. And when one of us makes improvements, the other should acknowledge it. Both China and the United States have neglected these simple points in our human rights discussions in recent years.

I offer the Carter Center as one location where influential people from our two countries, on the basis of equality and mutual respect, can share ideas on the challenges of the 21st century. We have much to learn from each other as we separately seek solutions suited to our distinctive conditions and historical experiences. Extensive dialog and cooperation on issues of human rights and governance can foster mutual trust and help us surmount the strategic, economic, and cultural differences that could divide us. Let us join hands to build a better future for our two peoples and all humanity. Let us resume the journey Deng Xiaoping and I started 20 years ago.

第8单元

状语的视译（II）：状语从句

> **基本技巧：**
> - 保持状语从句在译出语中的语序不变，并将其译为与译入语中其他成分并列的分句。

一、技巧讲解：状语从句的视译

在视译中，状语从句的翻译基本技巧与定语从句相似，即状语从句一般要译成单独的一个分句，状语从句的位置也要保持其在译出语中的位置。

状语从句在英语中有前置和后置两种。有的状语从句可以前置或是后置，比如，If you go there, I will go with you. 这是一个前置的条件状语从句，这个句子也可以写成：I will go with you if you go there. 这两个句子的意思没有什么变化，语序却是大不一样。也有的状语从句只能后置，比如，Those countries have made greater progress than we expected. 其中以 than 引导的比较状语从句只能放在句子的后面，不能随便调整。还有些状语从句在习惯上总是置于句子的开始，比如：Small as it is, that country is rich in natural resources.

我们在做笔译的时候，往往会调整状语的语序。但在视译中，无论是上面的哪一种状语从句，我们都要按照原来的语序翻译。比如：Pure iron is not used in industry because it is too soft. 这个句子典型的笔译译文为："纯铁太软，所以不能用在工业上。"（张培基，1980：148）但典型的视译译文为："纯铁不能用在工业上，因为它太软。"再如：They stepped into a helicopter and flew high in the sky in order that they might have a bird's-eye view of the city. 笔译译文是："为了对这个城市作鸟瞰，他们跨进直升飞机，凌空飞行。"（张培基，1980：152） 视译译文则是："他们跨进直升飞机，凌空飞行，为的是能够鸟瞰这个城市。"

笔译中状语从句位置需要颠倒的多是一些让步状语从句，比较常见的有以 if 或 although 引导的让步状语从句。比如上面的句子 If you go there, I will go with you. 以及 I will go with you if you go there. 无论是状语从句在句首还是句尾，在笔译中我们都会译成："如果你去那里，我会跟你一起去。"但是，我们在做视译的时候，原则上是不调整句子的语序的。所以，我们在做第一句的时候，可以译为："如果你去那里，我会跟你一起去。"在做第二句的时候，仍然不要调整译出语的语序，可以译为："我会跟你一起去，如果你到那里去的话。"因为这里把条件状语后置，所以听起来有些欧化的味道，不是典型的汉语句式，不过在现代汉语中已经被接受，并经常出现。

下面我们根据状语从句的不同类型举一些例子，说明如何视译英语中的状语从句。

例 1：　He stole, not because he wanted the money but because he liked stealing.

译文 1：他偷窃的目的不是钱，他就是喜欢偷。（叶子南，2001：91）

译文 2：他偷窃，不是因为需要钱，而是因为喜欢偷。

【讲解】　原句中的状语从句表示原因。译文 1 按照汉语的表达习惯，经调整顺序和改变词性，被译成两个分句。原句中的主句和原因状语的一部分 He stole, not because he wanted the money 构成第一个分句，其中主句 He stole 在笔译时成为定语，修饰由 because 改译成的主语"目的"，而把 he wanted the money 这个部分译为系表结构"不是钱"，这个分句就被译为"他偷窃的目的不是钱"。原因状语 but because he liked stealing 译为另一个分句"他就是喜欢偷"。但是，在视译时，为了尽量保持译出语的语序，做到顺视译单位依次译出，就可以将此句译成三个分句：主句单独译作一个分句"他偷窃"，然后在译出语中用"不是……，而是……"的汉语表达结构将两个原因状语分别译成第二和第三个分句"不是因为需要钱"，"而是因为喜欢偷"。

例 2：　How can you expect your children to be truthful when you yourself tell lies? （叶子南，2001：92）

译文 1：如果你自己说假话，怎么能够期待你的孩子说真话呢？

译文 2：你怎么能够期待孩子说真话，如果你自己说假话的话。

译文 3[1]：*你怎么能够期待孩子说真话呢？因为你自己就在说假话。*

【讲解】　原句中的状语从句形式上是一个时间状语从句，实际上表示条件。译文 1 将状语从句提前，并将表示条件的含义译出。原文中的状语从句在译文中仍作状语，但是语序按照汉语表达习惯调整到主句之前。然而，在视译中，这种颠倒原语序的做法是不符合要求的。所以，我们需要按照以下的方法来做：依照原句中的视译单位，利用汉语句法的灵活性，特别是视译的口译特点，将状语从句仍保留在原位作条件状语，即像译文 2 那样。当然，我们还可以将原句的主语在译文中译成疑问句，将条件状语从句译成表原因的答语，即像译文 3 的样子，这样听起来更加符合汉语习惯。

例 3：　The materials are excellent for use where the value of parts is not high. (许建平，2000：146)

译文 1：*如果零件价值不高，使用这些材料是最好不过的了。*

译文 2：*这些材料用起来很好，当然，条件是零件价值不要很高。*

【讲解】　原句中的状语从句是一个形式上的地点状语从句，实际上表示条件。它在译文 1 中被译成条件状语并按汉语的表达习惯调整到主句之前。视译时，原句中的状语从句仍保持在原位，并通过增添表示语气的词"当然"适当过渡，译作一个分句"当然，条件是如果零件价值不高的话"。

　　另外，如果保持原语序做出的译文不太符合汉语的习惯，也可以通过一些补救和变通的办法改善句子的质量。下面举两个例子予以说明。

例 4：　The crop failed because the season was dry.

译文 1：*因为气候干旱，作物歉收。*（张培基，1980：147）

译文 2：*收成不好，因为气候干旱。*

译文 3：*收成不好，原因是气候干旱。*

例 5：　I still think that you made a mistake while I admit what you say. (许建平，2000：148)

译文 1：*就算我承认你说的没错，我还是认为你犯了个错误。*

译文 2：*我仍然认为你犯了个错误，尽管我承认你说的不错。*

1　译文 3 为视译译文。

译文 3：我还是认为你犯了个错误，*当然，我也承认你说的没错*。

通过这几个例子可以看出，如果我们不拘泥于原文的句法和词语，就能够做出比较地道的翻译。比如汉语中的"当然"、"不过"等都是可以灵活使用的连接性词语。另外，还可以通过将状语从句的实际意义明确译出的方式，使译文更加通顺地道。比如将 because 译为"原因是"，将 if 译为"条件是"等。

综合上述的技巧，我们在做状语从句的视译时，可以按照原语序将其译为译入语中一个独立的分句，并在必要时使用连接成分或过渡词语使译出的句子更加通顺。

二、语段视译

1 词汇与表达

在进行语段视译前，请先预习以下词汇与表达。

subservience	俯首帖耳
moan	抱怨
be condemned to	注定
ulcer	溃疡

2 视译语段

请在 3 分钟之内迅速阅读下面的语段，了解大意，然后结合所学要点进行视译练习。视译时要保持正常语速，译文要顺畅达意。

Life for almost everybody is a long competitive struggle where very few can win the race, and those who do not win are unhappy. When I try to understand what it is that prevents so many Americans from being as happy as one might expect, it seems to me that there are two causes, of which one goes much deeper than the other. The one that goes least deep is the necessity for subservience in some large organization. If you are an energetic man with a strong view as to the right way of doing the job with which you are concerned, you find yourself invariably under the orders of some big man at the top who is elderly, weary and cynical. Whenever you have a bright idea the boss puts a stopper on it. The more energetic you are and more vision you have, the more you will suffer from the impossibility of doing any of the things that you feel ought to be done. When you go home and moan to your wife, she tells you that you are a silly fellow and that if you become the proper sort of yes-man, your income would soon be doubled. If you try divorce and remarriage it is very unlikely that there will be any change in this respect. And so you are condemned to great ulcers and premature old age. [1]（许建平，2000：345-346）

原译文：几乎对每个人而言，生活是一场持久的竞争，很少人能成为赢家，而赢不了的人便要垂头丧气。我弄不清为什么那么多美国人不像人们料想的那样欢乐，觉得似乎有两个原因，其中一个比另一个深刻得多。那个浅显的原因是，在大机构里供职必须俯首帖耳。如果你是个精力充沛的人，对于如何恰当地完成你的工作有着独到的见解，你发现自己总是听命于上面的某个大人物，他上了年纪，精力不支，还爱吹毛求疵。你有一个好主意，老板就把你一棍子打死。你越是积极，越有见地，你就越苦于无法完成你觉得自己应该完成的工作。你回家向妻子抱怨时，妻子会说你是个蠢货，还说你若是个唯唯诺诺的人，你的收入很快就会翻一番。如果你想离婚再娶一个女人，这种情况不会发生任何改变。因此，你注定要得胃溃疡，未老先衰。（孙致礼译）

3　视译译文

	断　句	译　文
1	Life for almost everybody	生活对几乎每个人来说，
2	is a long competitive struggle	都是漫长的竞争，
3	where very few can win the race,	很少有人能够成为赢家，
4	and those who do not win are unhappy.	赢不了的人就垂头丧气。
5	When I try to understand	我试图弄明白
6	what it is	到底是什么
7	that prevents so many Americans from being as happy	使得那么多美国人不快活。
8	as one might expect,	而人们原以为他们是快活的。
9	it seems to me	我觉得，

（待续）

1　较原文略有删减。

（续上表）

	断 句	译 文
10	that there are two causes,	有两个原因，
11	of which one goes much deeper than the other.	一个比另外一个更加深刻。
12	The one that goes least deep is	比较浅显的一个原因是，
13	the necessity for subservience in some large organization.	必须以卑谦的态度在大公司任职。
14	If you are an energetic man	如果你是一个精力充沛的人，
15	with a strong view as to the right way of doing the job	坚信自己知道如何做好工作，
16	with which you are concerned,	也就是做好自己的本职工作，
17	you find yourself invariably under the orders	那你就会发现自己只能被迫服从命令，
18	of some big man at the top	某个大人物高高在上，
19	who is elderly, weary and cynical.	年老疲惫，吹毛求疵。
20	Whenever you have a bright idea	只要你有个好主意，
21	the boss puts a stopper on it.	他一定把它枪毙。
22	The more energetic you are	你越是充满精力，
23	and more vision you have,	越是卓有见地，
24	the more you will suffer	就越是要受罪，
25	from the impossibility of doing any of the things	因为你根本没有办法做事情，
26	that you feel ought to be done.	你认为应该做的事都做不成。
27	When you go home and moan to your wife,	你回家向妻子抱怨，
28	she tells you	她会说
29	that you are a silly fellow and	你是个蠢货，
30	that if you become the proper sort of yes-man,	如果你是一个唯唯诺诺的员工，

（待续）

（续上表）

	断　句	译　文
31	your income would soon be doubled.	收入很快就会翻一番。
32	If you try divorce and remarriage	即便你离婚再娶，
33	it is very unlikely	很可能
34	that there will be any change in this respect.	这种情况也不会好转。
35	And so you are condemned to	于是你注定要
36	great ulcers and premature old age.	疾病缠身，未老先衰。

4　视译点评

1. 原文第一句：Life for almost everybody // is a long competitive struggle // where very few can win the race, // and those who do not win are unhappy.

此句分为四个类意群，依次顺译，句中的定语从句 where very few can win the race 和 who do not win are unhappy 分别被译成分句"很少有人能够成为赢家"和"赢不了的人就垂头丧气"。

2. 原文第二句：When I try to understand // what it is // that prevents so many Americans from being as happy // as one might expect, // it seems to me // that there are two causes, // of which one goes much deeper than the other.

此句是个典型的英语长句，主句和从句中又都分别带有从句，视译时依照类意群顺序分为六个类意群。其中，从句中的宾语从句 what it is that prevents so many Americans from being as happy as one might expect 被分成三个类意群，依次译成三个分句"到底是什么"，"使得那么多美国人不快活"和"而人们原以为他们是快活的"。第二个分句把英语 prevent sb. from doing sth. 译为"使得那么多美国人不快活"，自然与前一个视译单位的意思连接，而第三个分句在 expect 后面按汉语习惯补上了"他们是快活的"。

3. 原文第三句：The one that goes least deep is // the necessity for subservience in some large organization.

这句话的英文原文其实有点问题，因为两个事物做比较，一般不用最高级形容词。但原句的意思是明白的。视译时，将其中名词 necessity 译为动词

"必须"连接后面的内容。同样，原文第六句"… the more you will suffer from the impossibility of doing any of the things"中的名词 impossibility 也译为动词"没有办法"。

4. 原文第四句：If you are an energetic man // with a strong view as to the right way of doing the job // with which you are concerned, // you find yourself invariably under the orders // of some big man at the top // who is elderly, weary and cynical.

此长句可顺序分为六个类意群。从句中的介词短语 with a strong view as to the right way of doing the job 是第二个类意群，译成动词词组构成的分句："坚信自己知道如何做好工作"，第三个类意群是定语从句 with which you are concerned，也译成分句："也就是做好自己的本职工作"，第四个类意群 you find yourself invariably under the orders 中的副词 invariably 译成动词词组"只能被迫"，而介词短语 under the orders 也译成动词词组"服从命令"，这样一来，六个汉语分句连接流畅，达意清楚。

5. 原文第八句：If you try divorce and remarriage // it is very unlikely // that there will be any change in this respect.

此句可分为三个类意群，其中第二个类意群按照汉语表达习惯，将否定意思 unlikely 改译为肯定意思"可能"。遇到这类情况一般都是这样处理，比如 I don't think that… 等句式。然后在第三个类意群处表达原文的否定意思："这种情况也不会发生任何变化"。

6. 原文最后一句：And so you are condemned to // great ulcers and premature old age.

句中介词宾语 great ulcers 和 premature old age，分别译成两个分句"疾病缠身"和"未老先衰"。

三、实战练习

1 词汇与表达

请先熟悉以下词汇与表达，并适当地运用在视译中。

| Millennium Development Goals (MDGs) | （联合国）千年发展目标 |
| underpin | 支持 |

spiral	不断急剧地上升
imperil	使陷入危险，危及
deplorable	悲惨的，可叹的
pandemic	大流行病
devastation	毁坏，破坏
unravel	拆散
dengue fever	登革热
Copenhagen	哥本哈根
Hokkaido	北海道
stand tall	显示出自信
trilateral	三边的
augur	预示

2 **实战课文**

请在 15 分钟之内迅速阅读下面的讲话，了解大意。视译时要保持正常语速，译文要顺畅达意。

Address at China Foreign Affairs University[1] (Excerpt)

Ban Ki-moon

Beijing, 2008

It is always a pleasure for me to come to China and to see first-hand its ongoing transformation. Today, I am especially honored by this opportunity to speak to all of you—the current and future faces of China in the world.

There is a common saying that this will be the Asia-Pacific century. It is certainly true that what China does, and how China fares, is profoundly and increasingly significant to the world at large. Your country's economic progress, its growing leadership on global issues, and its dynamic engagement with the United Nations all give us true cause for optimism.

As this great nation grows in stature and prominence on the world stage, it will turn ever more to the graduates of this university to serve the needs of the country and

---

1　原文参见 http://www.un.org.cn/local/zh/cms/p/news/82/659/speech_content.html。

increase its engagement in the outside world. This is a task that I know you will all be well prepared for. Your academy is the cradle of Chinese diplomacy; **this is an institution that has firmly established itself as an authoritative forum in active and inter-active dialogs on the issues concerning China and its expanding role in the international community.** (句 1) Indeed, it is in these great halls that some of China's finest minds first get together to discuss and dissect the global challenges of our time—challenges where the role of China will be critical in the next few years.

It is about those global challenges I want to speak to you this afternoon—issues that might affect not only China's peaceful development, but also the international order underpinning our collective drive toward global prosperity.

The ties that bind our international order are stretched to breaking point by three linked challenges—food and fuel prices, climate change, and the quest to reach the Millennium Development Goals by the deadline of 2015. (句 2)

Spiraling fuel costs threaten global growth and therefore our continued ability to lift the world's poor out of poverty. Each day, spiraling energy prices further accentuate divisions between the world's "haves" and "have-nots". Similarly, climate change hurts us all, but it endangers the world's poor and vulnerable regions the most. The very people who have contributed the least to this problem are being shouldered with the greatest burden.

The rising cost of food represents an even more immediate danger. Food scarcity has already resulted in worldwide riots. Unaddressed, it imperils civic order, community harmony and the most basic social contract between state and citizen. At the same time, rising malnutrition also exacerbates growing disparities in global healthcare systems which divide not only the rich from the poor, but also the healthy from the chronically sick.

In another age, it is possible that some of these trends—however deplorable— could have been contained. But our global age is different—it does not permit such separation. At a time of international travel and global pandemics, of integrated commodities markets and worldwide refugee flows, what happens in one part of the world affects all parts of the world.

China is no exception. You have all seen how climate change can lead to extreme and unpredictable weather events. Last year, you battled unprecedented rains and floods that washed away homes and took hundreds of lives. This year, floodwaters again threaten millions of people even as the nation mourns earthquake devastation in Sichuan. Earlier this year, an exceptional freeze paralyzed road and rail traffic just as millions of Chinese were trying to get home for the Lunar New Year celebrations.

The climate events reflect humanity's interconnectedness. They are also a warning. Because today's triple threat of energy, climate and food challenges affects us all. It represents the proverbial loose thread that could unravel our entire international order.

Every country stands to lose from such an unraveling. But leading nations, like China, that have most at stake in the international system stand to lose the most. A global economic slowdown would affect this country's manufacturing base. Continued climate change could deprive millions more of their homes. The global food crisis could result in grain shortages and social unrest. And the confluence of all three of these trends could destabilize the very international order that has facilitated China's progress.

And yet, I strongly believe that we are not fated to watch our world fall into permanent crises. We can renew the ties that bind our international order. We can do so by asserting our common interests, our common ideals and—above all—our common humanity.

We have always seen how the greatest challenges bring forth humanity's most ennobling responses. Most recently, in Sichuan, I saw for myself the Chinese nation rise to face a tragedy of unimaginable magnitude. With the assistance of the entire international community, the Chinese government mounted a remarkable rescue and recovery effort that stands as an example of how united efforts can address extraordinary situations. In Sichuan, I saw the world come together in solidarity with China. Now, I look to all of you to remain united with the international community as we face even greater global challenges.

How do we do this? Through the one international organization that is truly universal, and universally legitimate—the United Nations. The UN already gives us the tools to tackle today's challenges, linking country to country, region to region, neighbor to neighbor, rich to poor, public to private, person to person. But it needs the support and engagement of its member states, particularly leading powers such as China, to deliver on an ambitious agenda. We need dedicated, bold, and sustained leadership from governments working together in a common, universal framework.

China is already leading national efforts on several of these fronts. Despite its large population, this nation remains a net exporter of cereals. As Premier Wen Jiabao has noted, China's self-reliance in feeding its people is indeed a great contribution to the world. Similarly, China's economic success has lifted many millions out of poverty and set a shining example of progress toward the Millennium Development Goals.

These domestic successes are undeniable. But China also has an important role to play as a global power working with the rest of the international community to address challenges that can only be met through our collective efforts. That is why I have called for world leaders, including China, to take urgent steps to address the global food crisis.

Earlier this month, world leaders gathered in Rome pledged six billion dollars to supply emergency aid to feed the poorest and to develop long-term solutions to the food crisis. **These pledges must now be reflected in immediate food assistance, as well as seeds, fertilizer and irrigation for smallholder farmers in countries worst affected by the food crisis.** (句 3) At a time of high energy and transportation costs, food production needs to be boosted where the hungry live.

We must also support the world's farmers by removing export restrictions and levies on food commodities, in particular those procured for humanitarian purposes; and cut agricultural subsidies in developed countries to free new resources for agricultural investment in low income, food insecure countries. (句 4)

Increased food production also requires enhanced efforts to combat climate change. Rising temperatures are changing weather patterns, eroding soils and drying up water systems. Global warming is also expanding the habitat of mosquitoes, widening the transmission of tropical diseases such as malaria and dengue fever. If farmers are confined to sick beds, agricultural yields will continue to stagnate.

Climate change has the potential to impact nearly all aspects of human activity. By now it is clear that we will all, rich and poor, suffer from extreme weather events, rising sea levels, the collapse of ecosystems and amplified health risks.

Much was achieved at the UN Climate Change Conference in Bali last December. We must press forward to achieve the agreement that the world expects and needs. Developed countries must lead the way in the negotiations. Major emitters from the developing world must also increase their contribution to reduce carbon emissions. They must act together in light of the agreed principle of common but differentiated responsibilities. With the Climate Change Conference in Copenhagen less than 18 months away, the future of the planet is literally at stake.

Equally, Chinese business has a key role to play in developing and providing solutions for clean technology, renewable energy, efficient products, and sustainable goods. Today, Chinese enterprises are developing exciting and innovative approaches. Already, your country ranks among the leaders in wind generation and solar panel production. By investing and planning today for a future that protects our planet, Chinese business has an opportunity to be a true front-runner.

The perfect storm of climate change and the food crisis underscore that the international community is in the midst of a development emergency. Despite the strides made by countries like China in recent years, the world as a whole is not on track to achieve the Millennium Development Goals by the target date of 2015. **Failure to meet these Goals would prove a devastating blow to the commitments made and trust forged between the developed and developing world at the start of the millennium. （句 5 ）** It would also strain the relationship between governments and the governed. We are already past the midpoint in the MDG race. But we are not yet past the point of no return. There is still time to make up for lost ground, if the international community acts together.

In a few days time, the world's leading industrialized nations will meet in Hokkaido. I will use the occasion to once again urge donor nations to deliver on their pledges to more than double aid to Africa—the continent farthest from the finish line in the MDG race. We need to organize on a war footing to fight malaria, tuberculosis, HIV/AIDS and other infectious diseases across Africa. This effort can be jumpstarted by providing insecticide treated bed nets to every African who requires one. At the same time, we must also increase our focus on maternal health, which influences so many other development indicators yet remains the slowest moving development goal. Finally, we must strengthen primary healthcare systems. In particular, we need to increase and sustain investment in training and supporting health workers with a focus on community-level efforts.

Given the strong and growing ties to Africa, China has a leading role to play in this effort. You are well on your way to becoming Africa's largest trading partner. And you are lending support to African nations in areas as diverse as infrastructure development, agriculture, commercial exchanges and education and training. If this spirit of China-Africa cooperation is brought to bear on other challenges—such as food security and fighting HIV/AIDS—China can help propel Africa toward meeting the Millennium Development Goals, in full and on time.

This global agenda may appear ambitious, but it remains wholly achievable. What it requires is collective and sustained effort. As I noted earlier, the food crisis, climate change and the world's development emergency are not concerns for any one country or any particular region. They represent a complex global challenge that demands a comprehensive international response.

The United Nations is the natural forum for mounting this response. Our organization provides a multilateral platform for implementing concrete actions on all fronts. But the UN cannot act alone—we require the leadership and guidance of our member states.

This is an area where China stands tall. You are leading activities of the UN as one of the five permanent members of the Security Council and your financial and peacekeeping contribution is growing. China will need to rise even higher in both rankings if we are to meet growing global challenges. Today, the entire United Nations system expects China to help lead on the international agenda. For my part, I look to China not simply because of its prominent position in the United Nations and within the broader world community; I do so because the responsibility of this nation is growing day by day.

China has achieved economic growth that is the envy of countries around the world. You have made progress in reducing poverty on a scale unprecedented in human history. And through trade and investment, you are already helping others replicate your success.

China's constructive engagement is particularly evident in Northeast Asia— a region that is beginning to work together in many areas of common interest and concern. I am particularly heartened at the trilateral dynamics of Japan, the Republic of Korea and China. These three countries are increasingly looking to their common future as friendly neighbors with global interests and responsibilities. I wholeheartedly welcome their agreement to hold their first trilateral summit, and also to cooperate on climate change, the food and energy crisis, and assistance to Africa. All three are working together as part of the multilateral six-party talks on denuclearization of the Korean Peninsula, a process that carries the most realistic promise to defuse one of the gravest security threats in the region. Increasing trilateral cooperation matters a lot in addressing environmental and other challenges, all these issues are central to the United Nations. It is only natural and indeed necessary that this trilateral partnership and the UN work together.

As Secretary-General of the United Nations, I look forward to working closely with the people and government of China to advance our shared goals, and to meet the great challenges of our day.

China's remarkable and peaceful development augurs well for the coming Asia-Pacific century. Through continued and constructive engagement in the world and in the work of the United Nations, China can help ensure that this is also everyone's era.

As you all know, in just a few weeks the world's leading athletes will arrive in Beijing to compete for Olympic glory. A select few will make it to the medals platform, many will not. But if, as I expect, they all compete in the true spirit of the Olympics—challenging each other to be stronger, to reach higher, and to go faster—then it is the Olympic movement that will emerge as the true winner in Beijing.

As in the Olympics, there is no doubt in anyone's mind that China is a medal contender in race for development and prosperity. But if China's rise can help and guide others along the way, then all humanity can collectively reach for gold medals together.

This, dear students, is your challenge. For you inherit not just China's future, but the task of helping to build the well-being of the whole world. I know you are all ready to take on this challenge. And I, as Secretary-General, am glad to welcome you, and the great nation of China, on board.

3 难句分析与视译处理

句 1：　　… this is an institution that has firmly established itself as an authoritative forum in active and inter-active dialogs on the issues concerning China and its expanding role in the international community.

笔译译文：……（贵校）已经建立了牢固的地位，成为了就中国有关的各项议题及其在国际社会发挥着日益广泛的作用、开展积极的互动性讨论的权威论坛。

视译译文：

断　句	译　文
… this is an institution	贵校
that has firmly established itself	已经牢固地确立了自己的地位，

（待续）

(续上表)

断　句	译　文
as an authoritative forum	成为了一个权威论坛，
in active and inter-active dialogs	积极开展互动式对话，
on the issues concerning China	讨论有关中国的各项议题，
and its expanding role in the international community.	以及中国在国际社会日益加大的作用。

句2：　　The ties that bind our international order are stretched to breaking point by three linked challenges—food and fuel prices, climate change, and the quest to reach the Millennium Development Goals by the deadline of 2015.

笔译译文：　维系着我们的国际秩序的纽带正被三种相互关联的挑战绷得很紧，快要断裂了——这些挑战就是粮价和燃料价、气候变化、以及努力争取在2015年最后限期之前实现各项千年发展目标。

视译译文：

断　句	译　文
The ties that bind our international order	这些纽带维系着我们的国际秩序，
are stretched to breaking point	已经绷得就要断了，
by three linked challenges—	原因是存在三种相互关联的挑战，
food and fuel prices,	这就是粮价和燃料价、
climate change,	气候变化、
and the quest to reach the Millennium Development Goals	以及实现千年发展目标，
by the deadline of 2015.	并且实现目标的最后期限是2015年。

句3：　　These pledges must now be reflected in immediate food assistance, as well as seeds, fertilizer and irrigation for smallholder farmers in countries worst affected by the food crisis.

笔译译文：　这些认捐现在必须化为即时的粮食援助，必须为受粮食危机影响最大的国家的小农场主提供种子、肥料和灌溉援助。

视译译文：

断 句	译 文
These pledges must now be reflected	这些认捐必须
in immediate food assistance,	立即用于粮食援助，
as well as seeds, fertilizer and irrigation	也要用来提供种子、化肥和灌溉，
for smallholder farmers	帮助那些小农场主，
in countries worst affected by the food crisis.	他们的国家正深陷粮食危机之中。

句 4： We must also support the world's farmers by removing export restrictions and levies on food commodities, in particular those procured for humanitarian purposes; and cut agricultural subsidies in developed countries to free new resources for agricultural investment in low income, food insecure countries.

笔译译文： 我们必须用种种方法支持全世界的农民，要消除出口限制，取消对粮食商品，特别是对以人道主义为目的而采购的粮食商品的课税；发达国家要削减农业补贴，释放新的资源，在低收入、粮食不安全的国家进行农业投资。

视译译文：

断 句	译 文
We must also support the world's farmers	我们也必须支持全世界的农民，
by removing export restrictions	方法是消除出口限制，
and levies on food commodities,	取消对粮食商品的课税，
in particular those procured for humanitarian purposes;	特别是用于人道主义援助的商品；
and cut agricultural subsidies in developed countries	还要削减发达国家的农业补贴，
to free new resources	争取释放新的资源，
for agricultural investment	促进农业投资，
in low income, food insecure countries.	投向那些收入低、粮食不安全的国家。

185

句5： Failure to meet these Goals would prove a devastating blow to the commitments made and trust forged between the developed and developing world at the start of the millennium.

笔译译文： 如果这些目标无法实现，发达国家和发展中国家在千年之初作出的承诺和建立的信任就会遭受灾难性的打击。

视译译文：

断 句	译 文
Failure to meet these Goals	如果不能实现这些目标
would prove a devastating blow	就会严重地打击
to the commitments made	我们作出的承诺
and trust forged	和建立的信任，
between the developed and developing world	这些承诺和信任是在发达国家和发展中国家之间形成的，
at the start of the millennium.	是千年之初双方取得的成果。

4 参考译文

在中国外交学院的讲话（节选）
潘基文
北京，2008 年

对我来说，到中国来，亲眼看看中国正在发生的变化，总是一件乐事。今天，我有机会跟你们大家——当今中国向世界展示的面孔，以及中国将来向世界展示的面孔——讲讲话，感到特别荣幸。

人们都在说这个世纪是亚太世纪。这一点也不假，中国在干什么，中国国情如何，都对全世界有深远的影响，意义越来越重大。贵国的经济进步，在处理全球议题方面日益增长的领导力，对联合国活动的大力参与，都是让我们感到乐观的真正理由。

随着这个伟大的国家在国际舞台上的身影越来越强大，角色越来越重要，中国一定会日益重用贵学院的毕业生，为本国需要服务，扩大同外面的世界的接触。我知道，为完成这项任务，你们大家都已做好了准备。贵学院是中国外交的摇篮，已经建立了牢固的地位，成为了就中国有关的各项议题以及其在国际社会发挥日益广泛的作用、开展积极的互动性讨论的权威论坛。的确，就是在这些大堂里，中国的一些精英首次聚集一起，讨论和分析我们这个时代所面临的全球性挑战——在今后几年，中国在这方面所起的作用将是至关重要的。

今天下午，我就是想同大家讲讲这些全球性挑战——这些议题不仅可以影响到中国的和平发展，还可以影响到我们集体努力争取全球繁荣所依赖的国际秩序。

维系着我们的国际秩序的纽带正被三种相互关联的挑战绷得很紧，快要断裂了。这些挑战就是粮价和燃料价、气候变化以及努力争取在 2015 年最后限期之前实现各项千年发展目标。

不断急剧上升的燃料价格威胁到全球增长，从而影响到我们有没有能力继续协助世界上的穷人脱贫。能源价格天天在急剧上升，使世界上"有"与"没有"的人分野日益扩大。气候变化同样对我们大家造成伤害，但对世界上的贫穷和弱势区域危害最大。对于这个问题，责任最小的人却要挑起最重的担子。

粮价上涨造成的危险更为直接。粮荒已在世界各地酿成暴乱。如果不予以处理，就会危及公共秩序、社会和谐，就会伤害到国家与公民之间最基本的社会契约。与此同时，营养不良日益严重，进一步加大了全球卫生保健系统之间日益悬殊的差别，这不仅造成了贫富差别，还把健康的人和长期患病的人划分开来。

在另一个年代里，这些趋势中的有些趋势——不管多么糟糕——或许都可能得到抑制。但是我们所处的全球性年代是不一样的——它不容许我们将这些趋势分隔处理。在我们这个国际旅行风行、全球流行病肆虐、商品市场一体化以及难民在全世界流动的时代里，世界上一个地方发生的事都会影响到世界上所有其他地方。

中国也不例外。大家都看到，气候变化可以带来极端和无法预测的气候事件。去年，你们与突然而来的暴雨和洪水作斗争，这些暴雨和洪水冲毁了不少家园，夺去了许多生命。今年，就在中国全国都在为四川震灾伤心难过的时候，洪水又再次威胁着数百万的人们。今年早些时候，正当无数中国人在设法回家庆祝农历新年时，就出现过一次格外严重的、造成公路和铁路交通瘫痪的冰冻事件。

这些气候事件反映出我们人类是息息相关的。这些事件也是一种警告。因为今天能源、气候和粮食挑战这三重威胁影响到了我们大家。这就是人们常说的那种松线头，足以拆散我们整个国际秩序。

如果国际秩序就这样垮了，每个国家都会受损。不过，像中国这样居于领导地位、对国际体系利害最为攸关的国家，可能会损失最大。如果全球经济发展减速，就会影响这个国家的制造业基础。如果气候变化持续不断，就会使更多数不尽的人流离失所。全球粮食危机会造成缺粮和社会动荡不安。所有这三个趋势合在一起，就会破坏一直在推动中国进步的国际秩序。

可是，我坚信，我们并不是注定会要看到我们的世界陷入永久的危机。我们可以更新维系我们国际秩序的纽带。我们可以通过表明我们的共同利益和共同理想，尤其是申明我们的人类共性来实现这个目标。

我们总是可以看到最大的挑战如何激发人类作出最崇高的反应。最近，在四川，我亲眼看到中华民族振奋起来，直面一个规模无法想象的悲剧。在整个国际社会的支持下，中国政府展开了举世瞩目的救援和善后工作，足可成为齐心合力应付非常情况的典范。在四川，我看到全世界团结在一起支援中国。现在，我希望你们大家继续同国际社会团结在一起，共同面对更大的全球性挑战。

怎样才能做到这一点呢？要通过一个真正全球参与的、全球公认的正当合法的国际组织——联合国去进行。联合国已经把应对当今各种挑战的工具交与我们，将国与国、区域与区域、近邻与近邻、穷与富、公与私、人与人联系起来。但这需要各会员国的支持与参与，将联合国伟大的议程付诸实践，尤其是中国这样的大国。我们需要各国政府尽心尽力、勇敢果断、坚持不懈地担当起领导责任，在一个共同的全球框架下携手合作。

中国已经在这些方面的许多领域领导各国开展合作。中国虽然人口众多，但仍然是个谷物净出口国。正如温家宝总理所指出的，中国自力更生养活了本国人民，这的确对世界作出了伟大贡献。同样，中国在经济方面取得的成就已经帮助无数人脱了贫，为逐步实现千年发展目标树立了光辉的典范。

这些国内成就都是无法否认的。但中国也要发挥世界大国的重要作用，要同国际社会其他国家一同努力，应对只有通过我们集体努力才能应付得了的各项挑战。这就是我呼吁世界领导者，包括中国领导者，采取紧急措施，处理全球粮食危机的原因。

这个月早些时候，世界领导人齐集罗马，认捐了 60 亿美元，以提供紧急援助，让最贫穷的人不再挨饿，同时，他们还承诺制定长期处理粮食危机的解决办法。这些认捐现在必须化为即时的粮食援助，必须为受粮食危机影响最大的国家的小农场主提供种子、肥料和灌溉援助。在能源和交通费用上涨的时候，我们需要在有人挨饿的地方增加粮食生产。

我们必须用种种方法支持全世界的农民，要消除出口限制，取消对粮食商品，特别是对以人道主义为目的而采购的粮食商品的课税；发达国家要削减农业补贴；释放新的资源，在低收入、粮食不安全的国家进行农业投资。

在增加粮食生产的同时，也需要进一步努力控制气候变化。气温上升正在改变天气状况，造成土壤侵蚀，水系统干枯。全球变暖亦扩大了蚊虫繁殖的环境，扩大了疟疾和登革热等热带病的传染范围。如果农民都卧病在床，农业生产就会继续停滞不前。

气候变化有可能影响到人类活动的几乎所有方面。现在我们都清楚，我们所有人，不论贫富，都会因为极端气候事件、海平面上升、生态系统毁坏、健康危险增多而受到危害。

去年 12 月在巴厘岛举行的联合国气候变化会议取得了不少成就。我们必须进一步要求达成全世界都期盼和需要的协议。发达国家必须带头开展谈判，发展中国家中的排放大国也要为减少排放做出更大贡献。他们必须按照共同但有区别的责任这个商定原则来一起采取行动。再过不到 18 个月，气候变化会议又要在哥本哈根举行，这切实关系到地球的未来。

同样，中国企业也可以发挥关键作用，帮助发展和提供解决办法，促进清洁技术、可再生能源、高能效产品和可持续商品。今天，中国企业正在提出各种令人振奋的创新思路。你们国家在风力发电和太阳能板生产方面已经名列前茅。如果中国企业今天为保护地球的将来作出投资和规划，他们就有机会成为真正的领先者。

气候变化和粮食危机这个完美风暴向我们强调指出，国际社会正处在一个发展的紧急情况之中。虽然像中国这样的国家近年来大步向前，但是对于在2015 年到来之时实现千年发展目标这一既定目标，全世界总的来说还未上轨道。如果这些目标无法实现，发达国家和发展中国家在千年之初做出的承诺和建立的信任就会遭受灾难性的打击，也会造成政府与民众之间关系紧张。在千年发展目标的竞赛中，我们已经跑过中点。但我们还没有跑过不可逆转的那一点。如果国际社会共同行动起来，现在还有时间可以迎头赶上去。

再过几天，世界上的工业大国将齐聚北海道。我将利用这次机会再次敦促捐助国落实他们的承诺，将提供给非洲的援助翻上一番以上。非洲是距离千年发展目标竞赛终点最远的一个地区。我们必须组织起来，做好战斗准备，向肆虐整个非洲的疟疾、结核病、艾滋病病毒与艾滋病、以及其他传染病开战。要开始这项工作，可以向有此需要的每一个非洲人提供经杀虫剂处理的蚊帐。与此同时，我们也必须将更多的注意力集中在产妇保健上。产妇保健影响到众多其他的发展指标，但却仍然是进展最慢的发展目标。最后，必须加强初级卫生保健系统。特别是，必须增加和持续投资于卫生工作人员的培训与支援，工作的重点在社区一级。

中国与非洲关系紧密，而且在日益加强，既然如此，中国在这方面就要起带头作用。你们正在一步一步地成为非洲最大的贸易伙伴。你们正在支援非洲各国，在基础设施的发展、农业、商务交往、以及教育和培训等各个方面提供援助。如果将这种中非合作精神用于应对其他的挑战——例如粮食安全和防治艾滋病病毒和艾滋病——中国可以协助推动非洲一把，让非洲全面并按时实现千年发展目标。

这个全球性议程虽然看起来雄心勃勃，但仍然是完全可以实现的。所需要的是集体作出持续不断的努力。我早些时候说过，粮食危机、气候变化以及世界发展的紧急局势都不仅仅是任何一个国家或任何某个区域所关注的问题。他们构成了一个复杂的全球性挑战，需要有一种综合全面的国际对策。

联合国自然是倡议这种对策的论坛。我们的组织提供了一个可以在全方位实施具体行动的多边平台，但联合国不能单独行动——我们需要我们的会员国提供领导和指引。

对此，中国充满自豪自信。作为联合国安理会五个常任理事国之一，你们领导着联合国的活动，在捐助各个基金和派遣维和部队方面，你们的作用正在不断增大。如果我们要迎接日益增长的全球性挑战，中国在上述两方面还要争取更高的名次。今天，整个联合国都盼望中国协助带头推动国际议程的工作。就我个人来说，我仰仗中国，不仅仅是因为中国在联合国以至在更广大的世界社会中占有举足轻重的地位，也是因为中国的责任在日益增大。

中国已经实现了令世界各国羡慕的经济增长。你们在减贫方面取得的成就，规模之大胜过人类历史的任何时期。你们又通过贸易与投资，协助他国走上与你们相似的成功之路。

中国的建设性参与活动在东北亚特别明显——这个区域正开始在许多大家共同关心和利害攸关的领域携手合作。我对日、韩、中三国的积极互动感到特别高兴。作为拥有全球利益和责任的友好邻邦，这三个国家正日益重视他们的共同未来。我真心诚意地欢迎三国商定举行第一次三边峰会，同时在气候变化、粮食和能源危机、援助非洲各方面进行合作。这三个国家都合作参与关于朝鲜半岛非核化的多边六方会谈。对于消除该区域最为严重的安全威胁而言，这个会谈是最为实事求是的保证。日益加强的三边合作对于应对环境及其他挑战十分必要，而所有这些议题对联合国来说都是至关重要的。这个不断发展的三边伙伴关系与联合国携手合作是再自然不过的，也的确是很有必要的。

作为联合国秘书长，我期盼与中国人民和政府密切合作，推进我们的共同目标，应对我们当代的各大挑战。

中国举世瞩目的和平发展告诉人们，这的确可能是亚太世纪的到来。不过，通过不断建设性地参与世界事务和联合国的工作，中国可以协助确保这也是我们大家的时代。

大家都知道，再过几个星期，世界上最顶尖的运动员将来到北京，为争取奥林匹克荣誉进行竞技。只有少数佼佼者会登上领奖台，很多运动员都不会获此殊荣。但如果他们，像我所期待的那样，个个本着奥林匹克的真正精神竞技——挑战彼此，争取更强、更高、更快——那么，奥林匹克运动就会在北京成为真正的胜利者。

无疑在每个人心中，中国在发展和繁荣的竞赛中都有夺牌的实力，就像在奥运会上一样。但如果中国在崛起途中能顺便提携和指引他国，那么全人类都能集体争取夺金。

亲爱的同学们，这就是你们要面对的挑战。因为你们不仅继承了中国的未来，也继承了协助为全世界谋幸福的任务。我知道，你们都已做好准备，接受这项挑战。就我个人而言，我欢迎大家，欢迎伟大的中华民族，加入我们。

四、自主训练

请在 15 分钟之内迅速阅读下面的讲话，了解大意。学生可组成对子练习，互相监控对视译技巧的掌握情况、视译质量和现场表现，或以边视译边录音的形式进行个人练习。视译时要保持正常语速，译文要顺畅达意。如遇难句，可在首次视译后参照"实战练习"中难句分析与视译处理的方法进行练习，找出解决方法。

Establishing New Habits of Cooperation in US-China Economic Relations[1] (Excerpt)

Ambassador Alan F. Holmer

Tsinghua University, 2007

Our Changing Economic Relationship

China's reemergence on the global stage is one of the most consequential geopolitical events of recent times. There is hardly an issue—from trade, to national security, to climate change—or a place—from the DPRK to Iran to Sudan—where American and Chinese interests do not increasingly overlap. Because China is so fully integrated into the global economy, what happens in China's economy affects the entire international community.

1　原文参见 http://www.ustreas.gov/press/releases/hp679.htm。

A cooperative, constructive and candid US-China relationship is central to understanding and responding to China's rise, in all its possible manifestations. As I look across the US-China economic relationship, it is clear to me that this relationship is entering a new phase.

First, US-China economic interdependence is deepening. We need each other more and on a broader number of economic and economically consequential issues. Over the past five years, according to US data, US exports to China have grown from $18 to $52 billion, while US imports from China have grown from $102 to $287 billion. Moreover, the United States and China are shaping, and being shaped by, global energy and environmental trends, which have strong economic consequences. For example, our countries are the world's largest energy consumers and the largest emitters of greenhouse gases.

Second, whereas trade and investment were once largely a source of stability in bilateral relations, they are now increasingly also a source of tension. Such tensions are straining the domestic consensus in both the United States and China on the benefits of economic engagement. When I first became deeply involved in international trade issues in the 1980s, we didn't have significant trade tensions with China—mainly because we didn't have much bilateral trade. In a sense, the fact that we have trade tensions reflects a maturing of our relationship and the rapid growth in bilateral trade and investment. We need to make sure we manage those tensions effectively in order to keep our bilateral economic relationship on an even keel.

Raising trade issues within the WTO is a normal mechanism for addressing disagreements among equal, sovereign trading nations. According to WTO statistics, the United States has had 99 cases filed against us since the WTO's founding in 1994; and the United States has filed 88 cases against 28 countries. In the case of China, five cases have been filed against China by the United States and two cases against the US by China. The EU has brought the most cases of any country against the United States (31), followed by Canada (14).

Anxieties about increasing trade manifest themselves in several ways, which leads me to the third dynamic confronting us: the rise of economic nationalism and protectionism in both our nations. These sentiments may constrain leaders from adopting policies that are in the long-term interests of the citizens and economies of the United States and China.

In responding to globalization, policymakers in both countries must resist the impulse to discard the hard-fought and long-term gains of open economies by pursuing short-term and misguided policy responses. For example, in the US, the Bush Administration continues to oppose congressional proposals, addressed at China's currency practices, which would be counter-productive and pose risks to the US economy. At the same time, Chinese barriers to US exports and investment, in the context of a large and rising Chinese current account surplus and protracted large-scale interventions in foreign currency markets, make it more difficult to keep the US economy open.

These three emerging dynamics to our economic relationship—deepening interdependence, a strained policy consensus, and the rise of economic protectionism—are mutual and require cooperative solutions.

Managing Complexity and Establishing New Habits of Cooperation

These dynamics informed the creation of the Strategic Economic Dialog (SED) by President Bush and President Hu Jintao in 2006. They envisioned a forum to allow both governments to communicate at the highest levels and with one voice on issues of long-term and strategic importance.

Managing our complex and increasingly interdependent relationship is daunting and requires speaking to the right people at the right time on the right issues and in the right way. I learnt a long time ago that if you are going to be successful in any kind of dialog, it is essential that you do everything you can to put yourself in the other person's shoes, to try to see the world the way he or she does. This is the way you achieve win-win agreements, ones that advance mutual interests, agreements that will withstand the tests of time. The Strategic Economic Dialog embraces this approach.

As a new and leading institution in US-China relations, the SED has created useful channels among policymakers in Washington and Beijing. In doing so, we are resetting the foundation for stable and prosperous economic interactions. The United States has three core objectives for the SED.

Establishing New Habits of Cooperation

First, through this framework, we are advancing the US-China economic relationship by establishing new habits of bilateral cooperation. We have embraced a broad agenda that covers cross-cutting economic and economically consequential issues, including regulatory transparency, energy conservation, environmental protection, innovation, food and product safety, as well as the important economic issues of exchange rate and macroeconomic policies, market access, and financial sector development and liberalization.

Our approach engages multiple and diverse government officials in both countries to facilitate more inclusive interactions. It breaks down classic bureaucratic stove-pipes that hinder effective communication and impede results. At the same time, we have continual, high-level interactions to set priorities and ensure their full implementation.

Having said that, good process does not ensure good results. Dialog among senior Chinese and American officials, while useful, needs to be more than talking for the sake of talking and can not give leaders "a pass" on issues of disagreement. It is about setting priorities, specifying consequences and fashioning practical solutions.

And that's what direct engagement does: it keeps the relationship on an even keel by lessening miscommunication and dispelling misperceptions so common in the history of the US-China relationship. It helps us signal to China that we welcome the rise of a confident, peaceful and prosperous China. A weak and insecure China is not in America's economic or security interests.

Accelerating China's Economic Transition

Second, it is vitally important that our policies accelerate the next wave of China's "reform and opening" process. The pace of China's growth has clearly been remarkable, but continued effort is needed.

China's top leaders now realize that a key challenge they face is taking the bold policy steps necessary for an economy that is no longer in the first stages of economic growth. We applaud the leadership's current efforts to transit to an economy that is more market-oriented, less reliant on low-value added manufacturing exports, one that depends more on the skills and resourcefulness of the Chinese people and less on material inputs and natural resource consumption.

A major risk China faces is that its government won't act quickly enough to take the policy steps necessary to deal with the economic and social imbalances created by its growth model. Without strong policy adjustments, China's economic growth path becomes unsustainable, as Chinese top leaders have publicly stated. We are encouraging key reforms that will help China manage the blistering pace of its economic growth; these include financial market liberalization and a plan for rebalancing growth. China has proven to the world that it can grow fast, but can it grow differently and, ultimately, sustainably, where the quality of growth is as important as the quantity.

Bold structural policies are needed to shift China's growth away from heavy industry, high energy use, capital intensiveness, and dependence on exports—toward greater reliance on domestic demand, production of services, and a greater share of China's national income accruing to China's households. To enable market forces to efficiently rebalance the economy and spread prosperity to all the Chinese, China needs more flexible prices, including a much more flexible, market-driven exchange rate. Exchange rate flexibility is also key to allowing monetary policy—the most potent instrument for guiding an economy—to focus on assuring price and financial stability.

Also, the RMB's exchange rate is increasingly being viewed by many countries as a source of unfair competition. A growing number of national leaders and multilateral institutions are calling for currency appreciation. The IMF's annual meeting held in Washington last month concluded with a communiqué that called for greater flexibility of the RMB.

The IMF communiqué acknowledged that an orderly unwinding of global imbalances while sustaining global growth is a shared responsibility. For America, it requires, among other things, steps to boost national saving in the United States, including continued fiscal consolidation. I'm pleased to report that we are making progress, though our work is not done. According to the latest data, the US federal budget deficit fell by about half, from 2% of GDP to 1% between 2005 and 2007.

A key to China's future success will be its willingness to accelerate the pace of its market-based economic reforms. Meeting and going beyond its WTO commitments, resisting protectionist sentiment, and opening up its economy to greater international competition for goods, and particularly, services, will help rebalance the Chinese economy and spread prosperity more broadly among the Chinese people. These reforms are—and will continue to be—resisted by increasingly influential Chinese businesses. In my judgment, the greatest risk to China's long-term economic security is not that China opens too fast, but, rather, that protectionists prevail, and Chinese reforms proceed too slowly.

Encouraging China's Responsibility in Global Engagement

Third, and finally, we are also encouraging China to act responsibly as a global economic power. We welcome China into key international financial institutions and are giving China a greater voice in them as well. Since the initiation of the SED in September 2006, we have supported China's efforts to join the Inter-American Development Bank (IADB) and the Paris-based Financial Action Task Force (FATF). We also strongly support a greater voting share for China in the IMF and World Bank. Increased participation will allow China to advance its interests in those institutions, but it is also important that Beijing recognize the responsibilities of greater participation.

China has become a major source of foreign aid for many of the poorest countries. We look forward to working with China, as a new and welcome participant, in multilateral efforts to assure that foreign aid and lending practices promote sustainable development.

This new era in US-China economic relations requires new and dynamic ways of doing business. We are meeting these challenges through the creation of the political space and the institutional capacity for long-term stability in our bilateral economic relations.

第9单元

句子成分的转换

> **基本技巧：**
> - 将包含动作意义的名词或名词词组译为动词或动宾结构。
> - 有些介词短语可译为动宾结构或独立句子。

一、技巧讲解：句子成分的转换

　　翻译最大的难处在于两种语言之间的差异，这种差异也表现在句子成分上面，包括单词和词组。由于汉英两种语言的不同，无论在口译还是笔译中，都会涉及句子成分的转换问题，所以在许多翻译教材中都会将词类和句子成分的转化作为重要的技巧介绍。（许建平，2000：62-75；宋天锡，2003：60-99）

　　视译的基本原则是顺译，所以，对句子成分的转换主要也是为了能够达到顺译的目的。比如，这样一个句子：This book is a careful study of the power struggle between the warring states. 在笔译中，我们可以将它译为："这本著作对交战各国之间的权力斗争做了认真的研究。"在译文中，我们没有改变原句名词 study 的词类，仍然译为名词。这个句子中以 of 引导的介词短语太长，在视译中，如果按照笔译的方法处理，则必须将句子顺序做较大的调整。但如果我们将 study 这个有动词意义的名词译为动词，句子就可以顺译下来。我们先将原句断句：This book is a careful study // of the power struggle between the warring states. 然后依序译出："这本著作认真研究了 // 交战各国之间的权力斗争。"由于将原句中名词 study 译为动词，原句中的形容词 careful 也随之转换为副词，译文不必做语序上的大幅度调整，便利了视译人员的依序顺译。

　　在这一单元里，我们重点讨论句子成分的转换。名词转换为动词是英译汉中最常见的一种方式。不少人说英语是名词性语言，汉语是动词性语言，这是有道理的。所以，无论是在笔译还是在视译中，在不少情况下这种转换都是必要的。但在视译中，关键的一点是要使句子能够顺译下去，所以，转换之后的动词一般应该是及物动词。如果不是及物动词，也要是能够加上"于"、"在"、"是"等词就可以与后面成分连接的词或词组，这样就很容易顺译了。另外，介词短语也常常转化为动词结构。下面我们讲解四种视译常用的转换技巧：第一，将动作性名词转换为动词；第二，将包含动宾关系的名词词组转换为动词；第三，将名词词组转换为包含动词的独立短句；第四，将介词短语转化为动词结构。

1 动作性名词转换为动词

英语中，常常见到包含动作意义的名词，比如 application、improvement、building 等，不一而足。这类词往往可以在译文中转换为动词，尤其是在它们后面跟着较长修饰语的时候。请看下面的例子，注意下划线部分的处理。

例1： His theory has found application for improving ecological conditions in this poor rural country.

译文1： 他的理论在改善这个贫穷的农业国家的生态条件方面得到了应用。

译文2： 他的理论已经用来改善这个贫穷的农业国家的生态条件。

【讲解】 这个句子里面的一个翻译难点是 application 这个动词性的名词。按照第一种翻译方法，将 application 仍译作名词"应用"，就必须将其置于句尾，语序也就需要做出较大幅度的调整。如果我们将 application 译为动词"用来"（也可以译为"应用于"），成为译文 2 的样子，就可以保持原文语序。实际上，凡是包含动作意义的名词几乎都可以用这种方式处理，而这类词在英语中出现的频率是很高的。

例2： We have conducted interviews with people of all walks of life in order to find their attitudes toward the new government policy.

译文1： 我们对各行各业的人做了采访，试图发现他们对政府新政策的态度。

译文2： 我们采访了各行各业的人，试图发现他们怎样看待政府的新政策。

【讲解】 这个句子里 interviews 和 attitudes 这两个名词在转换为动词之后更加利于顺译。如果不转化词类，就需要按照译文 1 的方法，译为"对"字句式，这样必然将一个较长的句子成分夹在"对"与后面的主要名词之间，因而必须颠倒语序。视译时，我们将 interviews 译

为动词 "采访"，将 attitude 也译为动词结构 "怎样对待"。这样一来，就不必大幅度调整语序。

2　包含动宾关系的名词词组转换为动词

在英语中，包含动宾关系的名词词组是很常见的（主要是指 "名词＋介词＋介词宾语" 的形式），以偏正结构的形式译出是笔译中常用的方法。比如，the translation of the book 译作 "这本书的翻译"，the examination of the samples 译作 "对样本的检验"，the proofreading of the manuscript 译作 "手稿的校对" 等等。对于较短的这类名词词组来说，只要可以划入同一个视译单位，这样做对视译也不会造成很大困难。但有的时候，这种名词词组里面又加入了很多修饰语，这样就可能需要较大幅度地调整语序，造成视译困难。下面我们举例说明这一问题。

例 3：　Through the face-to-face exchange, the two delegations had a better understanding of each other's intentions and capabilities.

译文 1：通过面对面的沟通，两个代表团对相互的意图和实力有了更好的了解。

译文 2：通过面对面的沟通，两个代表团更好地了解了相互的意图和实力。

【讲解】句子中需要词类转换的是名词 understanding。如果仍然将它译成名词，就是译文 1 的样子，即在较大幅度调整语序之后，将 "了解" 置于句尾。如果将 understanding 译为动词，则可基本按照原句顺序译出。同时，我们也发现，在名词转换为动词之后，原来修饰名词的形容词也相应地转换为副词。

类似这样的名词在英语中比比皆是，比如 work、research、study、love、hatred 等，都可以加 of 或其他介词构成一个包括动宾关系的名词词组。这些名词有着一个共同的特点，就是形式上是名词，实际上则表示动作。对于这类名词，几乎都可以用将其转换为动词的方法加以处理。

例 4：　The translation of the work of the great master on Greek mythology has made all of us realize his heartfelt love for life and humankind.

译文 1：对这位大师的希腊神话研究著作的翻译使我们都认识到他对生活和人类全心全意的热爱。

译文 2：翻译这位大师研究希腊神话的著作，使我们都认识到他全心全意地热爱生活、热爱人类。

【讲解】这个句子里面的两个动词性名词 translation 和 love，分别与两个句子成分相关：the translation of the work... 和 love for life and humankind。在视译中，我们分别将这两个成分译为"动词＋宾语"的形式，即："翻译这位大师研究希腊神话的著作"和"热爱生活、热爱人类"。这样就使句子能够按照原来的语序顺译出来了。

3 名词词组转换为动宾短句

还有一种名词可以转换为动词的情况。有些名词词组中包含一种动作意义，本身又比较长，遇到这类名词词组的时候就可以将其译为汉语中包含动词的独立短句。比如 the sight of the long river 可译为"看见那条大河"，the failure in the battlefield 可译为"在战场上打了败仗"等。一般来说，如果这种词组中有很多修饰成分和附加成分的时候，视译人员尤其需要将其作为短句先行译出。下面我们举例说明。

例 5： Careful forethought about the possible consequences would have helped them avoid all the trouble, which almost destroyed their plan completely.

译文 1： 事先对可能产生后果的认真考虑本来能够使他们避免所有这些差点毁了整个计划的麻烦。

译文 2： 事先若是认真考虑到可能产生的后果，本来是能够避免所有这些麻烦的，就是这些麻烦差点毁了整个计划。

【讲解】 Careful forethought about the possible consequences 这个名词词组很长，如果不做转换，就要将较长的修饰成分置于主要名词之前，造成视译困难（即便在笔译中也会比较拗口）。我们将这个长的名词词组转换为一个汉语的短句"事先若是认真考虑到可能产生的后果"，这样符合顺译的要求，先把原句作为主语的部分处理完，然后再接着译下面的部分，其中定语从句也作一个单独的句子加以处理。

例 6： The prospect of the collapse of the bipolar international system encouraged the nations all over to work together for a better world of peace and prosperity.

译文 1： 对两极国际体系解体的期望激励所有国家为建设一个和平与繁荣的世界而共同努力。

译文 2： 人们期望两极国际体系解体，这激励所有国家齐心协力，共同建设一个和平与繁荣的世界。

【讲解】 这个句子之中有一个长名词词组 The prospect of the collapse of the bipolar international system，如果按照原来句式翻译就必须较大幅度地调整语序。我们将这个名词词组译为一个短句"人们期望两极国际体系解体"，这就为下面视译的顺利进行做出了铺垫。

4　介词短语转化为动词结构

　　在英汉翻译中，不少介词短语可以转换为动词结构。当年，张培基等举过一个经典的例子："Coming!" Away she skimmed over the lawn, up the path, up the stairs, across the veranda, and into the porch. 这个句子译为："'来啦！'她转身蹦着跳着地跑了，越过草地，跑上小径，跨上台阶，穿过凉台，进了门廊。"（张培基，1980：49）其中的五个介词 over、up、up、across、into 分别被译为"越过"、"跑上"、"跨上"、"穿过"、"进了"五个动词。这个句子后来被多次引用，用来说明介词转化为动词的翻译技巧。

　　在视译中，我们更多地使用类似的方法，因为一旦将介词短语转换为动宾结构，就可以独立成句。上面的例子也说明了这个问题，即一经转化，就可以成为并列短句，顺译出来。我们再举两个例子加以说明。

例 7： The villagers spent a lot of human and material resources on a 10-year drive to make such a glorious achievement.

译文 1： 村民们在 10 年的奋斗中花费了大量人力物力才取得了如此辉煌的成就。

译文 2： 村民们花费了大量人力物力，经历了 10 年的奋斗，才取得了如此辉煌的成就。

【讲解】 这个句子中有一个介词短语 on a 10-year drive，如果将其仍旧译成状语，则需要调整语序，如译文 1。若是将这个介词短语转换为动宾结构，则可以单独译成一句，整个句子也就能够顺译下来。所以，译文 2 将其译为："经历了 10 年的奋斗"。

例 8： They had numerous meetings of various kinds to discuss and debate over important political, economic, and social issues during the turbulent years of the French Revolution.

译文 1： 在法国大革命的动荡岁月里，他们召开过无数各种各样的会议，讨论、辩论重要的政治、经济和社会问题。

译文 2： 他们召开过无数会议，各种各样的都有，讨论、辩论重要的政治、经济和社会问题，那是法国大革命动荡岁月里的事情了。

【讲解】 这个句子之中有一个时间状语 during the turbulent years of the French Revolution，它是修饰全句的。如果依旧译成状语，则需要调整语序，比如在译文 1 中，就将其置于全句之首，完全颠倒了原文语序。在视译中常用的处理方式是加进动词，将这个介词短语译为一个独立的句子："那是法国大革命动荡岁月里的事情了。"实际上，这类句子在视译中经常遇到，一般都可以按照这个原则处理。

综上所述，视译中将名词转换为动词是有一些技巧的。最简单的是，可以将包含动作意义的名词译为动词，也可以将具有动宾含义的名词词组中的名词译为动词。还可以将带有修饰语的名词词组译为独立短句，其中名词译为动词。另外，有些介词短语可以译为动宾结构或独立的句子。

二、语段视译

1 词汇与表达

在进行语段视译前，请先预习以下词汇与表达。

International Olympic Committee	国际奥委会
Barcelona	巴塞罗那（西班牙城市）
in style	有气派地，隆重地
impromptu	即兴的
fiesta	节日
Seoul	首尔（韩国首都，1988年奥运会时称为汉城）
put in a bid	提出申办（奥运会）
Munich	慕尼黑
Olympic facilities	奥运场馆
Los Angeles	洛杉矶
extravaganza	铺张华丽的演出或赛事
Montjuich Stadium	蒙特胡伊体育场

2 视译语段

请在 3 分钟之内迅速阅读下面的语段，了解大意，然后结合所学要点进行视译练习。视译时要保持正常语速，译文要顺畅达意。

October, 1986 when the International Olympic Committee awarded the 1992 Games to Barcelona, the city celebrated in style: jubilant inhabitants threw an impromptu fiesta and danced in the streets while fireworks screeched, zoomed and banged in the inky night sky. But the Games officials, competitors and spectators also have much cause to cheer because their next host after Seoul, the Republic of Korea, is one of the most handsome, civilized and pulsating cities in Europe. Barcelona is the first Spanish city to get the Olympics and has battled for 66 years to win the honor of staging them. In 1924 it put in a bid, but the Games went to Paris; in 1936 Barcelona tried again and lost and 1972 turned out not to be third time lucky when Munich was picked instead. This time Barcelona spent ￡8 million on a five-year campaign and was the favorite, so victory seemed reasonably assured. Barcelona plans to keep all the Olympic facilities within an eight-mile radius of the city, which should save everyone the raveling involved in Los Angeles. The athletes should approve of its site of their village: it's on the beach. The eye of the world will watch extravaganzas like the opening and closing ceremonies in the 70,000 seat Montjuich Stadium, sited on a 700-foot-high hill overlooking Barcelona and built originally for an International Exhibition in 1929. There are five museums on its grassy slopes, including the Museum of Art of Catalan, which has been one of the most fabulous collections of medieval art in the world. (方梦之，2005：234)

原译文：1986 年 10 月，国际奥委会选定巴塞罗那主办 1992 年奥运会，该城隆重庆祝。喜气洋洋的居民举行了即兴的欢庆盛会，在街上载歌载舞；在漆黑的夜空，烟火刺耳地尖叫着，腾空直上，砰然作响。但是奥运会组委会官员、参赛运动员和观众也颇有理由为此欢呼，因为这个继韩国首尔奥运会之后的主办城市是欧洲最有气派、最文明、最有节奏的城市之一。巴塞罗那是第一个承办奥运会的西班牙城市，它为了获得主办奥运会的殊荣，已奋斗了 66 年。1924 年，它便提出了承办申请，但奥运会的承办权落入了巴黎手中；1936 年，它又一次争取，还是没有成功；1972 年，它第三次不走运，慕尼黑被选中。这次，巴塞罗那在经历了 5 年奋战，耗资 800 万英镑之后，终于呼声最高，所以这次中选似乎是有一定把握的。巴塞罗那计划把所有的奥运会运动设施都安排在城市周围的 8 英里范围内，好让每个人都能避免像在洛杉矶那样的跋涉之苦。运动员一定会满意奥林匹克村修建在海滨。全世界都将注目那拥有 7 万座位的蒙特胡伊体育场内举行的开幕式和闭幕式一类铺张豪华的演出。这个原为1929 年国际博览会建造的体育场，坐落在俯瞰巴塞罗那的 700 英尺高的小山上。小山的草坡上有 5 所博物馆，其中包括藏有数量名列世界前茅的中世纪艺术精品的卡塔卢纳艺术博物馆。(钟平译，转引自方梦之，2005：253)

3 视译译文

	断　句	译　文
1	October, 1986	1986 年 10 月，
2	when the International Olympic Committee	国际奥委会
3	awarded the 1992 Games to Barcelona,	决定 1992 年奥运会在巴塞罗那举行。
4	the city celebrated in style:	巴塞罗那热烈庆祝：
5	jubilant inhabitants threw an impromptu fiesta	喜气洋洋的居民举行了即兴欢庆盛会，
6	and danced in the streets	他们在大街上载歌载舞，
7	while fireworks screeched, zoomed and banged	礼花烟火尖叫着腾空直上、砰然作响，
8	in the inky night sky.	划破了漆黑的夜空。
9	But the Games officials, competitors and spectators	奥委会官员、运动员和观众
10	also have much cause to cheer	也很有理由为此欢庆，
11	because their next host after Seoul, the Republic of Korea,	因为巴塞罗那是在韩国首尔之后承办奥运会的，
12	is one of the most handsome, civilized and pulsating cities in Europe.	它是一个最气派、最文明、最富活力的欧洲城市。
13	Barcelona is the first Spanish city to get the Olympics	巴塞罗那是第一个西班牙城市来承办奥运会，
14	and has battled for 66 years	它奋斗了 66 年
15	to win the honor of staging them.	为的就是获得承办殊荣。

（待续）

（续上表）

	断　句	译　文
16	In 1924	1924 年，
17	it put in a bid,	巴塞罗那提出承办申请，
18	but the Games went to Paris;	但奥运会定在巴黎举行。
19	in 1936	1936 年，
20	Barcelona tried again and lost	巴塞罗那再次申请并再次失败，
21	and 1972 turned out not to be third time lucky	1972 年第三次失败，
22	when Munich was picked instead.	而慕尼黑被选中。
23	This time Barcelona spent £8 million	这一次巴塞罗那耗资 800 万英镑，
24	on a five-year campaign	历经五年奋战，
25	and was the favorite,	呼声最高，
26	so victory seemed reasonably assured.	看来是胜券在握。
27	Barcelona plans to keep all the Olympic facilities	巴塞罗那计划把所有奥运场馆，
28	within an eight-mile radius of the city,	建造在城区 8 英里范围之内，
29	which should save everyone the traveling	以免去大家的奔波之苦，
30	involved in Los Angeles.	而洛杉矶奥运会时大家饱受此苦。
31	The athletes should approve of its site of their village:	运动员也会满意奥运村，
32	it's on the beach.	因为它就建在海边上。
33	The eye of the world will watch extravaganzas	全世界都将观看华丽壮观的演出，

（待续）

(续上表)

	断　句	译　文
34	like the opening and closing ceremonies	比如开幕式和闭幕式，
35	in the 70,000 seat Montjuich Stadium,	这将在有 7 万座位的蒙特胡伊体育场进行。
36	sited on a 700-foot-high hill	体育场建在 700 英尺高的山上，
37	overlooking Barcelona	俯瞰巴塞罗那，
38	and built originally for an International Exhibition in 1929.	原来是为 1929 年世博会建造的。
39	There are five museums on its grassy slopes,	有 5 个博物馆矗立在山的草坡上，
40	including the Museum of Art of Catalan,	其中就有卡塔卢纳博物馆，
41	which has been one of the most fabulous collections of medieval art	它拥有最精湛的中世纪艺术收藏，
42	in the world.	在全世界名列前茅。

4 视译点评

1. 原文第一句：October, 1986 // when the International Olympic Committee // awarded the 1992 Games to Barcelona, // the city celebrated in style: // jubilant inhabitants threw an impromptu fiesta // and danced in the streets // while fireworks screeched, zoomed and banged // in the inky night sky.

这是一个长句，我们先把带有定语从句的时间状语部分译成一个单独的句子："1986 年 10 月，国际奥委会决定 1992 年奥运会在巴塞罗那举行。"然后，再翻译句子后面的部分。视译难点是在较长的谓语之后有一个地点状语 in the inky night sky。因为在断句的时候，这个地点状语只能单独列为一个视译单位。视译的技巧是将这个介词引导的地点状语短语转换为一个动词短语"划破了漆黑的夜空"，这样就与上面的部分自然衔接起来了。

2. 原文第五句：This time Barcelona spent ￡8 million // on a five-year campaign // and was the favorite, // so victory seemed reasonably assured.

这个句子的视译难点是介词短语 on a five-year campaign，这个介词短语原来是 spend ... on ... 结构中的一部分，我们将这个介词短语转换为动词，译为"历经五年奋战"，这样就可以顺译下来了。 *介词—动词*

3. 原文第八句：The eye of the world will watch extravaganzas // like the opening and closing ceremonies // in the 70,000 seat Montjuich Stadium, // sited on a 700-foot-high hill // overlooking Barcelona // and built originally for an International Exhibition in 1929.

这是一个很长的句子，其中修饰语很多，包括表示地点的介词短语 in the 70,000 seat Montjuich Stadium，过去分词引导的定语 sited on a 700-foot-high hill，现在分词引导的短语 overlooking Barcelona 和过去分词引导的定语 and built originally for an International Exhibition in 1929。我们将第一个地点状语译为单独的句子"这将在有七万座位的蒙特胡伊体育场进行"，将第二个作定语的过去分词短语也译为一个独立的句子"体育场建在 700 英尺高的山上"，并顺势译出第三个现在分词短语"俯瞰巴塞罗那"。最后一个过去分词短语也译为一个包含动词结构的成分"原来是为 1929 年世博会建造的"。在这个句子的视译中，我们分别将介词短语、过去分词短语、现在分词短语等转换为包含有动词的结构，译成独立的短句或独立的句子成分。

三、实战练习

1　词汇与表达

请先熟悉以下词汇与表达，并适当地运用在视译中。

AERC（African Economic Research Consortium）	非洲经济研究联合会
ECA（Economic Commission for Africa）	联合国非洲经济委员会
dissemination	传播
annum	年
fixated	偏爱
endogenous	自发的，自生的
PRSP（Poverty Reduction Strategy Papers）	减贫战略文件
back-to-back with	与……同时举行

| plenary | 全会 |
| Damascene conversion | 彻底的转变 |

2 实战课文

请在 15 分钟之内迅速阅读下面的讲话，了解大意。视译时要保持正常语速，译文要顺畅达意。

"Using Knowledge and Peer Learning to Improve Policies to Reduce Poverty in Africa"[1]

UN Under Secretary-General   Abdoulie Janneh

Addis Ababa, 2006

I would like to welcome you all to this joint the AERC/ECA Conference on "Poverty, Inequality, and Labor Markets" organized to disseminate the results of an AERC research program on that theme. The ECA thanks AERC for inviting us to partner with them. For us, this partnership is consistent with our goal of advancing the frontiers of knowledge on issues that are of critical importance to our region and making that knowledge readily available to policymakers for improved decision-making. ECA is committed to partnering with African research institutions to accompany our countries in their search for durable answers to the challenges of development that they face.

Three days ago, I had the pleasure of welcoming a group of distinguished African experts and policymakers to the AERC/ECA Workshop on Asian Drivers. Although that workshop focused on the impact of Asia's two new emerging global economic giants, China and India, on Africa, its objective was to explore how best to leverage the growing economic engagement of those two countries to improve the human condition of our people. This is an objective that I believe is shared by this conference.

This conference is important for reasons that we all know—poverty remains a major development challenge in our region, a problem that bars our access to the club of developed countries. But the conference is important for another reason:

---

1   原文参见 www.uneca.org/eca_resources/speeches/janneh/2006/111006_speech_janneh.htm。

because it is a dissemination conference, it underscores our faith, our confidence that knowledge about the determinants of poverty can help us abolish it. Gareth Stedman Jones, in his 2004 book, *An End to Poverty?* which traces the history of ideas on poverty eradication not only reminds us that there once was a time when it was believed that the intellectual progress of humankind would be accompanied by a material transformation of the human condition but also shows that those ideas did indeed contribute to the near abolition of poverty in Western Europe.

More often than not, into stories on Africa and African countries is woven the word "impoverished". Evidence to support this characterization abounds: worsening social indicators, conflicts, bottom ranking in all leagues of human development. But things are changing. Strong growth has resumed and many of our countries have grown at more than 5% per annum consistently over six years now. This impressive performance as reported in ECA's 2006 Economic Report on Africa is not only due to strong commodity prices, but also due to much more prudent and knowledge-driven macroeconomic policies. And people are beginning to take notice. About two weeks ago, I read one of those investment advice columns in the *Financial Times* and I was pleasantly surprised to read the column advising that UK pension and hedge funds should consider investing in Nigerian banks because the country is poised for higher growth and returns would be high!

Notwithstanding these developments and initiatives, it is clear that despite impressive country-level performances and overall improvements in macroeconomic performance, poverty remains high. **It is difficult for me as a development practitioner to understand why this is so since Demery and his co-authors some time ago showed that growth was associated with poverty reduction in sub-Saharan Africa. （句 1）** Anyway, what the current evidence does suggest is that at current rates of growth, our region is performing rather poorly with respect to meeting the targets of the Millennium Development Goals (MDGs). The overall progress toward the achievement of the MDGs has not been very promising particularly in sub-Saharan Africa. Inequalities in access to social services and jobs as well as the poor employment growth remain a problem. The growth process remains too narrow and is generally said to be without jobs.

Without doubt the studies whose main findings you have come here to disseminate will confirm the current evidence and also propose some policy options. But I also hope that your conference will also address the much more critical question: what should Africa do to secure the positive gains of the recent past? A very commonplace answer to this is:

"More emphases need to be placed on improving the productive base of African countries and in parallel expanding market access. In this respect, both African leaders and development partners have a shared responsibility. African leaders must continue to be supportive of the private sector through the pursuit of prudent policies that nurture domestic price stability, minimize the cost of doing business, promote export competitiveness and facilitate market access."

But there is perhaps another answer, not opposed to the ones above, but perhaps the unseen superstructure on which the above are built. It is knowledge. Knowledge production (which you do); knowledge sharing (which is what this conference is about) and; knowledge use (which is what you hope to get out of this conference).

The importance of knowledge—in the three dimensions mentioned above—for economic growth is pretty well known. Francis Bacon long ago said "knowledge itself is power". The 1998 World Bank Development Report "Knowledge and Information for Development" made the point that successful development entails not just the closure of the physical or indeed human capital gaps but also close the knowledge gap—a point also made in ECA's publication *Harnessing Technologies for Development*. The economic journalist David Warsh notes in his new book *Knowledge and the Wealth of Nations*, that "new ideas, more than savings or investment or even education, are the keys to prosperity, both to private fortunes, large and small, and to the wealth of nations—to economic growth". **Your profession was fixated on knowledge in the 1990s as you engaged with the "New Growth Theory" following the publication of Paul Romer's very influential paper— "Endogenous Technological Change" in 1990—a paper you refer to as "Romer 90".** (句 2) This paper for the first time explicitly incorporated knowledge in your very fanciful and abstract growth models.

One key lesson that we at ECA have learnt from our work in the nearly 50 years of our existence is that knowledge about pathways to improve economic management holds the key to development. (句 3) We need to generate new knowledge as well as know how to use them. Knowledge use is critical for our region's progress toward the targets of the MDGs. It is therefore for that reason that knowledge is acutely emphasized in our current efforts to reposition this institution. Our current efforts are strongly geared toward conveying to our member states the view that improvements in the use of economic knowledge is critical for securing the progress recorded recently across the swathe of our continent and for moving forward.

We are redoubling our analytical work on poverty analysis and the Millennium Development Goals. For this reason, we have created a new section, MDGs/Poverty Analysis and Monitoring Section, to underscore the centrality of and the seriousness that we attach to Africa making progress in these areas. A key and very important component of our work in this area is peer learning (on poverty reduction strategies and the Millennium Development Goals) and knowledge management. Permit me to illustrate what we have done and are doing in this area with our flagship peer learning initiative, the African Learning Group on Poverty Reduction Strategy Papers (PRSP-LG). Some of you may have heard of this initiative and participated in one of its meetings.

Shortly after the introduction of the PRSP in 1999 by the World Bank and the International Monetary Fund as a prerequisite for access to debt relief, ECA hosted a workshop for African countries for dialog on the PRSP content and process and on its implications for the region.（句 4）In July 2000, ECA launched a high-level mission to several African countries at different stages of the PRSP process to learn first-hand how they were adjusting to the PRSP process and addressing the practical challenges that the process was raising.

One key message that came out of the workshop and the consultations with member states was that the Structural Adjustment Policies of the 1980s would have been better managed had there been a mechanism for the systematic sharing of experience and peer learning among countries, which could also have provided a platform for the articulation of a strong African voice in the international community on the continent's experience with the challenges of adjustment and poverty reduction.（句 5）

Given the context and in recognition of the operational challenges associated with the PRSP approach, the member states urged ECA to establish an African-owned forum that would facilitate African peer learning and serve as a mechanism through which Africans could ensure the relevance of the PRSP approach to Africa's development challenges.

In response to the request from member states, ECA established the African Learning Group on Poverty Reduction Strategy Papers (PRSP-LG) 2001. The LG has facilitated information sharing among diverse stakeholder groups in African countries (including civil society) on their experience with the PRSPs, and helped identify best practices and outstanding implementation challenges, while in addition promoting peer learning and African ownership of poverty reduction strategies.

Information distilled from meetings of the LG has enabled ECA to provide targeted advisory and policy support to member states, broker support from other development institutions and partners, and network expertise to assist countries. The LG was able to convey to Africa's development partners the region's concerns about the PRSP and thus contribute to influencing their policies toward the continent by organizing its meetings back-to-back with the plenary meeting of the Strategic Partnership with Africa (SPA), a grouping of major donors to Africa.

The crucial role that the LG has played was recognized by the African (Ministerial) Plenary on the PRS and MDGs in Cairo in March. The Plenary urged the ECA to revive the Learning Group (whose activities had been suspended while awaiting the results of a knowledge audit) and to broaden its mandate to include learning on the Millennium Development Goals. My colleagues will tell you more about the LG and what we have been doing to promote peer learning on the PRS and MDGs since Cairo.

So, broadly, the LG does what your conference seeks to do—disseminate knowledge on best practices on the PRS and MDGs. In many cases, there is a deep aversion for imagining the new, a reluctance to believe that new things can happen. A new idea—and there are many in the area of economics and economic policy—triumphs not because those opposed to it are brought around (or undergo a Damascene conversion) but because it is embraced by a new generation. Through our Peer Learning and Knowledge Sharing initiatives, we hope to encourage new generations of African policymakers to embrace new ideas and thus steer our member states to the new, to innovate. Through this process we aim to help our member states build appropriate knowledge assets to secure and carry forward their impressive performances of the recent past.

In their book, *Plowing the Sea: Nurturing the Hidden Sources of Growth in the Developing World,* Fairbanks and Lindsay advised that "leaders need to think about developing more sophisticated knowledge assets". It is my view that our leaders are already doing that as evidenced by the set of policies and management techniques that they have introduced over the recent past, policies and management techniques that in part explain the recent improvements in economic performance. **Your** conference will be a resounding success if it contributes in important ways to assisting countries in our region to develop the sophisticated knowledge assets needed to combat poverty, reduce inequality and improve labor market outcomes for our people.（句 6）

3　难句分析与视译处理

句 1：　It is difficult for me as a development practitioner to understand why this is so since Demery and his co-authors some time ago showed that growth was associated with poverty reduction in sub-Saharan Africa.

笔译译文：　作为发展专家，我很难理解为什么会是这样，因为迪米力与其著作合作者以前就表明经济增长与减少撒哈拉以南非洲地区的贫困相关联。

视译译文：

断　句	译　文
It is difficult	困难的是，
for me as a development practitioner	我身为发展专家，
to understand why this is so	无法理解为什么情况会是这样，
since Demery and his co-authors some time ago showed	因为迪米力及其共同作者此前已经表明，
that growth was associated with	经济增长会关系到
poverty reduction in sub-Saharan Africa.	撒哈拉以南非洲的减贫问题。

句 2：　Your profession was fixated on knowledge in the 1990s as you engaged with the "New Growth Theory" following the publication of Paul Romer's very influential paper—"Endogenous Technological Change" in 1990—a paper you refer to as "Romer 90".

笔译译文：　在 20 世纪 90 年代，你们这些专家都对知识偏爱有加，因为你们在保罗·罗默 1990 年发表了影响颇深的论文《自发的技术变化》之后对"新增长理论"非常感兴趣——你们把该论文称为"罗默 90"。

视译译文：

断　句	译　文
Your profession was fixated on knowledge	你们这些专家当时都偏爱知识，
in the 1990s	因为在 20 世纪 90 年代
as you engaged with the "New Growth Theory"	你们感兴趣的是"新增长理论"，
following the publication of Paul Romer's very influential paper—	此前保罗·罗默发表了很有影响的论文，
"Endogenous Technological Change" in 1990—	也就是 1990 年的《自发的技术变化》一文，
a paper you refer to as "Romer 90".	你们称该论文为"罗默 90"。

句 3：　　One key lesson that we at ECA have learnt from our work in the nearly 50 years of our existence is that knowledge about pathways to improve economic management holds the key to development.

笔译译文：　我们从 ECA 近 50 年的历史中得到的一个重要经验是掌握如何改进经济管理的知识是发展的关键。

视译译文：

断　句	译　文
One key lesson	有一条重要经验
that we at ECA have learnt	是我们从 ECA 学到的，
from our work in the nearly 50 years of our existence	近 50 年的历程告诉我们，
is that knowledge about pathways to improve economic management	知晓如何改进经济管理
holds the key to development.	是促进发展的关键。

句 4：　　Shortly after the introduction of the PRSP in 1999 by the World Bank and the International Monetary Fund as a prerequisite for access to debt relief, ECA hosted a workshop for African countries for dialog on the PRSP content and process and on its implications for the region.

笔译译文： 作为世界银行和国际货币基金组织对非洲实行债务免除的前提条件，1999 年世界银行和国际货币基金组织启动了减贫战略文件计划，之后不久，ECA 主办了旨在就有关减贫战略文件内容、进展以及对该地区的影响展开对话的研讨会。

视译译文：

断　句	译　文
Shortly after the introduction of the PRSP in 1999	1999 减贫战略文件出台，
by the World Bank and the International Monetary Fund	这是世行和国际货币组织撰写的，
as a prerequisite for access to debt relief,	提出了免除债务的先决条件。
ECA hosted a workshop	随后 ECA 主办了研讨会，
for African countries for dialog	促进非洲国家展开对话，
on the PRSP content and process and	讨论减贫战略文件的内容和进程
on its implications for the region.	以及对非洲地区的影响。

句 5： One key message that came out of the workshop and the consultations with member states was that the Structural Adjustment Policies of the 1980s would have been better managed had there been a mechanism for the systematic sharing of experience and peer learning among countries, which could also have provided a platform for the articulation of a strong African voice in the international community on the continent's experience with the challenges of adjustment and poverty reduction.

笔译译文： 从该研讨会和通过与成员国探讨得到的一个主要信息是如果 20 世纪 80 年代有国家间系统的经验交流和同伴互学机制，当时的结构调整政策就能够得到更好的管理，也还有可能在国际社会为宣传非洲大陆如何应对调整和减少贫困的挑战的经验提供一个发出强大的非洲之声的舞台。

视译译文:

断　句	译　文
One key message	有一个重要的信息,
that came out of the workshop and	既来自这次研讨会,
the consultations with member states	也来自成员国之间的磋商,
was that the Structural Adjustment Policies of the 1980s	这就是 20 世纪 80 年代的结构调整政策
would have been better managed	原本可以得到更好的实施,
had there been a mechanism	条件是当时要有一个机制,
for the systematic sharing of experience	保证大家系统地交流经验,
and peer learning among countries,	促使各国相互学习。
which could also have provided a platform	这种机制还可以提供一个舞台,
for the articulation of a strong African voice	清晰地发出强大的非洲之声,
in the international community	让国际社会
on the continent's experience	了解非洲大陆的经验,
with the challenges of adjustment and poverty reduction.	知道非洲如何应对调整和减贫引发的挑战。

句 6: Your conference will be a resounding success if it contributes in important ways to assisting countries in our region to develop the sophisticated knowledge assets needed to combat poverty, reduce inequality and improve labor market outcomes for our people.

笔译译文: 本次大会如果能够做出重要贡献,帮助我们地区的国家发展有助于他们战胜贫困,减少不平等现象的,能为我们的人民增加劳动力市场出路的尖端知识财富,就将是一个巨大的成功。

视译译文：

断　　句　　。	译　文
Your conference will be a resounding success	本次大会将取得巨大成功，
if it contributes in important ways	如果它能做出重要贡献，
to assisting countries in our region	帮助我们这一地区的国家
to develop the sophisticated knowledge assets needed	发展必要的尖端知识财富，
to combat poverty,	用来战胜贫困，
reduce inequality and	减少不平等现象，
improve labor market outcomes for our people.	并为我们的人民拓展劳动力市场。

4　参考译文

"用知识和同伴互学的方法改进政策，减少非洲贫困"
联合国副秘书长　阿卜杜利·詹纳
亚的斯亚贝巴，2006 年

欢迎各位出席非洲经济研究联合会与联合国非洲经济委员会（AERC/ECA）联合召开的本次"贫困、不平等、劳动市场"大会。大会的目的是传播有关这个议题的一项 AERC 研究项目结果。ECA 感谢 AERC 邀请我们与他们合作。对于我们而言，这种伙伴关系与我们的目标是一致的，一是要拓展对我们地区至关重要的问题的知识前沿，二是要使政策制定者能够方便地获得知识，从而提高决策水平。ECA 承诺与非洲研究机构建立伙伴关系，与我们的国家一起寻求应对我们面临的发展挑战的永久答案。

三天前，我有幸欢迎一些杰出的非洲专家和政策制定者出席 AERC/ECA 举办的亚洲推动者研讨会。虽然这个研讨会主要讨论亚洲两个新兴世界经济巨人，中国和印度对非洲的影响，会议的目的是探讨如何充分利用与这两个国家不断增加的经济接触来改善我们人民的人文条件。我相信大会也赞同这个目标。

　　我们都很清楚本次大会的重要性——贫困一直是我们地区主要的发展挑战，阻碍着我们进入发达国家俱乐部。但是，大会之所以重要还有另一个原因：因为这是一个传播大会，它强调我们的信仰和信心，我们相信了解造成贫穷的原因有助于消灭贫穷。加雷思·斯特德曼·琼斯在他 2004 年写的《终结贫穷?》一书中回顾了历史上对如何根除贫穷的各种想法，他不仅提醒我们曾经有一个时期人们相信人类的思想发展会带来人文方面物质条件的变化，他还表明这些想法的确为西欧基本消除贫穷做出了贡献。

　　关于非洲和非洲国家的报道通常总和"贫困"一词交织在一起，而反映这个特点的现象比比皆是：不断恶化的各项社会指标、冲突、处于所有人类发展的最底层。但是，情况正在发生变化。强劲的增长已经恢复，许多非洲国家已经连续六年保持年增长率超过 5%。ECA 2006 年非洲经济报告中描述的令人印象深刻的经济表现不仅是商品价格大幅上扬的结果，也是更加谨慎的、以知识为动力的宏观经济政策的成果。人们开始对此加以关注。大约两周前，我阅读了《金融时报》投资建议专栏中的一篇文章，我很高兴，因为我惊奇地读到该专栏建议英国养老金和对冲基金应该考虑对尼日利亚银行投资，理由是该国已为更高的增长做好了准备，投资者将会得到高回报！

　　尽管我们采取了重要行动并取得了发展，尽管国家层面取得的成绩和宏观经济表现出的全面改观令人激动，但是，贫困现象显然仍旧十分严重。作为发展专家，我很难理解为什么会是这样，因为迪米力与其著作合作者以前就表明经济增长与减少撒哈拉以南非洲地区的贫困相关联。无论怎样，现有的证据的确暗示按照目前的增长率，我们地区的发展与实现联合国千年发展目标提出的具体目标还相差甚远。要取得向实现千年发展目标迈进的全面进步，情况不容乐观，特别是在撒哈拉以南的非洲地区。社会服务和就业方面的不平等现象仍然存在，糟糕的就业增长率仍是问题。经济增长仍然十分有限，一般都无法创造就业岗位。

　　毫无疑问，你们在此传播的主要研究结果将证实我们的现状，并且就一些政策选择提出建议。但是，我还希望大会能处理更为严重的问题：非洲怎样才能保住近年来取得的积极成果？

　　老生常谈的答案是："需要大力改进非洲国家的生产基础，同时拓宽市场准入。对此，非洲领导人和发展伙伴担负着共同的责任。非洲领导人必须继续通过采取帮助稳定国内价格、尽量减少经商成本、提高出口竞争力和便利市场准入的谨慎政策对私营部门给予支持。"

　　但是，也许还有另一种答案，与上述答案并不矛盾，但也许是为上述答案提供一个无形的超级基础结构。这个答案就是知识。生产知识（这是你们的工作）；分享知识（这是本次大会的目的）；运用知识（这是各位希望取得的大会成果）。

知识的重要性——在上面谈的三个方面——对于经济增长来说是世人皆知的。弗朗西斯·培根很早以前就说过"知识就是力量"。1998 年世界银行发展报告《知识和信息对于发展的作用》提出成功的发展带来的不仅是缩小了人们在距离上和人文财富方面的差距，也缩小了知识方面的差距——ECA 出版的《掌握技术，实现发展》中也提出了这一点。经济记者大卫·沃施在其新书《知识与国家财富》中指出："新思想比积蓄、投资、甚至教育更为重要，是繁荣的关键。新思想对于个人财富，无论多少，非常关键，对于国家财富，对于其经济增长也是关键。"在 20 世纪 90 年代，你们这些专家都对知识偏爱有加，因为你们在保罗·罗默 1990 年发表了影响颇深的论文《自发的技术变化》之后对"新增长理论"非常感兴趣——你们把该论文称为"罗默 90"。这篇论文首次明确将知识纳入了你们富有想象力且抽象的增长模式之中。

我们从 ECA 近 50 年的历史中得到的一个重要经验是掌握如何改进经济管理的知识是发展的关键。我们需要发展新知识，也需要懂得如何运用这些知识。知识的运用对于在我们地区朝着千年发展目标进步至关重要。因此，我们在当前工作中大力强调知识的重要性，以便对体制进行调整。我们现在的努力是要明确地向我们的成员国传递这样一种观点，即改进经济知识的运用对保护我们宽广的大陆近年来取得的进步，对于我们的继续发展具有决定性的意义。

我们正再接再厉地做好贫困与千年发展目标的分析工作。为此，我们已经创立了一个新部门，千年发展目标与贫困分析监测处，以显示我们对非洲在这些领域取得进步的高度重视和严肃态度。我们在这个地区工作的重点是同伴互学（学习减少贫困的战略和千年发展目标）以及知识管理。请允许我用我们的同伴互学旗舰行动非洲减少贫困战略文件学习小组 (PRSP-LG) 说明我们已经完成的工作和正在开展的工作。你们有的人也许听说过这个行动并参加了相关的会议。

作为世界银行和国际货币基金组织对非洲实行债务免除的前提条件，1999年世界银行和国际货币基金组织启动了战略减贫文件计划，之后不久，ECA主办了旨在推进有关战略减贫文件内容、进展以及对该地区的影响展开对话的研讨会。2000 年 7 月，ECA 在开展战略减贫文件计划的不同阶段向几个非洲国家派遣了一个高级别代表团，为的是掌握他们如何适应战略减贫文件计划以及如何应对学习中遇到的具体挑战的第一手情况。

从该研讨会和通过与成员国探讨得到的一个主要信息是如果 20 世纪 80 年代有国家间系统的经验交流和同伴互学机制，当时的结构调整政策就能够得到更好的实施，也还有可能在国际社会为非洲大陆提供一个发出强大的非洲之声的舞台，宣传非洲应对调整和减少贫困的经验。

基于这样的背景，也由于认识到战略减贫文件运作方面的挑战，成员国敦促 ECA 建立一个非洲自己的论坛，既为非洲的同伴互学提供方便，又可以是一个使非洲人民能够确保战略减贫文件的学习与解决非洲发展所面临的挑战紧密结合的机制。

作为对成员国要求的回应，ECA 建立了 2001 非洲减少贫困战略文件学习小组。学习小组促进了非洲国家（包括公民社会）中不同的利益攸关组织之间有关开展非洲减少贫困战略文件学习小组的经验交流，帮助宣传优秀的做法并指出尚待解决的实施方面的挑战，同时还推动同伴互学和非洲自主的减少贫困战略。

学习小组会议上获取的信息使 ECA 能够向成员国提供有针对性的建议和政策支持，提供来自其他发展机构和伙伴的代理人支持，并为各国提供网络专业技术。学习小组能够向非洲的发展伙伴转达该地区对非洲减少贫困战略文件学习小组的关心，并通过不断组织学习小组与非洲的战略伙伴关系全会 (SPA)会谈，为影响他们的对非政策做出贡献。后者是对非的主要捐助者。

三月在开罗，学习小组的关键作用已经得到非洲（部长级）减贫战略与千年发展目标全会的赞扬。全会要求 ECA 重新启动学习小组（其活动在等待一项知识评估结果时临时中断），将其学习内容扩展到学习千年发展目标。我的同事将告诉你们更多有关学习小组的事宜以及我们自开罗会议之后为促进有关减少贫困和千年发展目标的同伴互学所作的努力。

因此，总的来说，学习小组所作的工作正是本次大会希望开展的工作——传播有关实现减贫战略和千年发展目标的先进做法的知识。但是，在许多情况下，还存在着对想象新鲜事物的深恶痛绝，不愿意相信出现新事情的可能性。新的思想——在经济学和经济政策方面有许多新思想——最终取得胜利，不是因为反对意见都被说服（或发生了彻底的转变），而是因为新思想受到了新一代的欢迎。通过我们的同伴互学和分享知识的计划，我们希望鼓励非洲新一代的政策制定者欢迎新思想，带领我们的成员国走向新天地，带领大家去创新。在此过程中，我们的目的是帮助我们的成员国积累适用的知识财富，从而保护他们过去的骄人成果，并继续向前迈进。

费尔班克斯和林赛在《耕耘大海：发掘发展中世界里蕴藏的增长源泉》一书中提出"领导者需要考虑发展更加先进的知识财富"。我的看法是领导者已经行动起来了。近年来他们引进了一整套政策和管理技术就是例证，这些政策和管理技术在一定程度上说明了近期在经济方面的改进。本次大会如果能够做出重要贡献，帮助我们地区的国家发展有助于他们战胜贫困，减少不平等现象的，能为我们的人民增加劳动力市场出路的尖端知识财富，就将是一个巨大的成功。

四、自主训练

请在 15 分钟之内迅速阅读下面的讲话，了解大意。学生可组成对子练习，互相监控对视译技巧的掌握情况、视译质量和现场表现，或以边视译边录音的形式进行个人练习。视译时要保持正常语速，译文要顺畅达意。如遇难句，可在首次视译后参照"实战练习"中难句分析与视译处理的方法进行练习，找出解决方法。

The Role of Europe on Sport[1]
Minister for Europe   Jim Murphy
London, 2008

I am very pleased to be here this morning. This conference comes at the end of a number of weeks of meetings and discussions with various stakeholders, asking the question: how can we make the European Union as a regional body work to meet the challenges facing Europe and the world in the 21st century? We've looked at the role of Europe on issues such as faith, climate change and social affairs. I'm looking forward to our conversation today on the role of Europe on the issue of sport.

You might be asking: What has that got to do with sport?

Two things.

First, because we're looking at these issues in the context of the Lisbon Treaty and the Lisbon Treaty is significant for sport in a number of ways.

Second, because sport has a wider role to play, in Europe and beyond, as a force for unity and a means of creating healthy societies in the widest sense of the word.

Let's start by looking at what the Treaty will do for sport. The Treaty has been demonized by some sections of the media. In a sense fiction has been dressed up as fact. But while my role today is not to defend the Lisbon Treaty I should make clear

---

1 原文参见 http://ukinargentina-stage.fco.gov.uk/en/newsroom/?view=Speech&id=5371344。

for the benefit of any sporting euro-sceptics here that the Treaty will not allow the EU to harmonize sporting regulations. This means that sport is one of the many areas in the Treaty where EU input is strictly limited to complementing or adding to action taken at national level.

What the Treaty will do is allow EU institutions to recognize the special nature of sport far more systematically than they have been able to do so far. This means that sport in Europe should not fall victim to unintended consequences of wider EU legislation.

The issues of specificity and autonomy are subject to ongoing debate and I know that some would have liked to see more guarantees in the Treaty. It is good that people are talking about the issues and the debate will continue. This year, for example, the Council of Europe is conducting a full investigation into autonomy.

But beyond the complexities of specificity and autonomy, the Treaty will recognize, for the first time, the important role of sport in European societies. Ratification of the Treaty will allow for a specific EU funding stream for sport projects, due to be piloted in 2009. This should put an end to the slightly dubious practice of manipulating sporting projects to fit alternative sources of funding— the funding of the Austrian and Czech Republic Nordic skiing team as a "tourism" project for example—and recognize that sport deserves to be funded for sport's sake.

And I hope we'll see the development of an EU sports program and an increase in the links between sport and relevant policies like health and education. And this brings me onto the second reason why sport is relevant to me as Europe Minister— because of its wider role of sport in society.

The links between sport and policies like health and education are obvious to all of us here. In my Glasgow constituency, the role of sport is clearly evident in engaging youngsters, because sport is inspirational—whether you are a spectator or a participant. Young people need to be inspired and sport provides just the right framework—it's about teamwork, fair play and striving to do your best; and it's about gaining in confidence, learning new skills, becoming fitter and stronger, having your talent recognized and developed. And sport provides so many different opportunities to suit different talents and interests—we need look no further than this room where a whole spectrum of sporting activity is represented, from ice hockey to equestrian sports, weightlifting to gliding.

There is no doubt that supporting sport at grass-roots level is an effective way to bring communities together. Historically, many major European sports clubs have their roots in local churches and workplaces. Sport cuts across cultural political and economic divides with football as perhaps the best example—over 700 million people across the globe watched the 2006 World Cup final. As I said earlier, sport encompasses a huge variety of activity, with over 700,000 sports clubs and associations within the EU. No wonder the British Olympic Association has described sport as the biggest social movement in Europe.

This is important, because the divisions we're seeing within Europe now have little to do with the divisions between nations that we're more familiar with from history. I'm talking about internal rifts between haves and have-nots and between different cultural and religious groupings within communities. There is a lot to do to address these issues but there is no doubt that sport has a part to play as a unifying force. Sport is a common interest that can counter the limiting belief that individuals can be categorized by their cultural, religious or economic background. I recently visited Sarajevo and while I was there I got the chance to represent the British Embassy football team in a match against a side of Bosnian MPs[1]. This gave me two things—first, a great opportunity to demonstrate the unifying nature of sport and second, a serious knee injury.

At national level, people's sporting affiliations can be a powerful public statement of their identity. The image of Nelson Mandela in 1995, at the Rugby World Cup Final in South Africa, dressed in a "Springbok" shirt was a gesture every bit as powerful as any one of his speeches. It gave all South Africans permission to be proud of their national identity and signaled to the world that the new South Africa would be a nation where all of its citizens could feel they belonged.

But what is the impact on national sporting affiliations of a Europe that is more mobile and culturally diverse than ever? I stand to be corrected by the sporting experts in this room today, but I believe the Ryder Cup, Golf and 10 pin bowling are the only events in the sporting calendar where Europeans can unite behind one team.

We could revisit Norman Tebbit's cricket test. Most of us will remember Lord Tebbit's naïve and misguided suggestion that a shift of sporting allegiance was a measure of successful integration. I wonder how popular that would be with the 5.5 million Brits currently living abroad today!

1　Members of Parliament.

Or we could argue that, while it's true that there's nothing like a sporting victory to inspire a sense of national pride, sport offers an even greater prize. And that is to watch healthy competitions build bridges between communities and between societies.

Sport does not divide us. It unites us—even when we're not playing for the same side. And the same can be said of Europe. Twenty seven nations more united by their common goals than divided by their national interests.

The world has changed, and I would argue changed for the better: the ease of international travel and the communications revolution have made the world a smaller place. But so too has the fact that the issues that dominate the media effect us wherever in the world we live—whether it's rising food and oil prices, climate change or conflict. These are challenges we need to meet together. We need to look outwards, form alliances, identify common goals and develop inclusive societies where people feel that they are part of a wider global community. This is what I want the EU to help us to achieve and these are objectives that sport can help us deliver.

Let's not forget that international sport was one of the great opportunities of globalization before the term "globalization" was invented. The International Olympic Committee, formed in 1894, predates the United Nations by over five decades and FIFA has been in existence since before the First World War.

Giving recognition to the role of sport in European societies is one clear benefit of the Lisbon Treaty that I believe even the most hardened euro-sceptic can support. Thank you.

第10单元

被动语态的视译

基本技巧：

- 将被动语态改译为主动语态；
- 另起一句译出施事方并重复动词以便成句；
- 避免使用"把"、"使"、"由"等汉语句式。

一、技巧讲解：被动语态的视译

被动语态在英语中使用范围很广，有些较长的带有被动语态的句子会给视译译员造成困难。如果我们看一下笔译时对于被动语态的处理，就会发现，在不少情况下，含有被动语态的句子在译成汉语时，语序要作较大的调整。

张培基先生总结了被动语态的笔译技巧，简单扼要地提出了三类含被动语态的句子的翻译方法。（张培基，1980：120-124）第一，译成汉语主动句。比如，The whole country was armed in a few days. 这个句子可以译为："几天以内全国武装起来了。"第二，译成汉语被动句。比如，Any minute we would surely be spotted by enemy planes flying in and out of the airfield. 我们可以把它译成："我们随时都会被出入机场的敌机发现。"第三，译成 "把"、"使"和"由"字句。比如，The famous hotel had been practically destroyed by the big fire. 译成"使"字句就是："大火使这著名的旅馆几乎全部毁灭。"这三种形式反映了被动句的一般翻译方法，其他一些研究翻译的学者也提出过类似的技巧。（王恩冕，2004：100-111）

用视译的要求衡量，第一类句子将被动句译为主动句，并且在语序上不作大的调整，比较符合视译的需要。这类句子的特点是施事方没有出现在句子里面。第二类句子则是语序变动很大的句子。这类句子要把施事方译出来，而原文句子中施事方是以 by 引导出来，并置于动词的后面，所以译起来很可能要调整语序。如果句子很短，视译时还可以调整处理。比如，The silence was broken by the chairman. 这个句子就可以译为："主席打破了沉默。"整个句子在译员一目可及的范围之内，所以调整也是可行的。当然，这个句子还可以用别的方式来译，使之更符合视译要求。但如果句子较长，这样处理就会有困难，比如上面的例句 Any minute we would surely be spotted by enemy planes flying in and out of the airfield. 这个句子有状语，施事方又带有一个较长的定语修饰语。所以，在视译时对语序做很大的调整是来不及的，只能另想办法处理。第三类句子对于视译来说也是比较困难的句式。无论使用"把"、"使"还是"由"字句，必须对原句语序做较大调整，因为汉语"把"、"使"和"由"字句后面必然有一个插入成分，然后才是原来句子中的动词部分。这样一来，不调整语序就是不可能的事情了。比如之前的例句 The famous hotel had been practically destroyed by the big fire.（大火使这著名的旅馆几乎全部毁灭。）这个句子中在"使"字后面，插入了"这著名的旅馆几乎全部"这个较长的成分，这就使得顺译变得困难了。

在视译中如何处理这三类被动语态呢？下面我们分别讲解。

1 可以译成汉语主动语态的句子

第一类是可以译成汉语主动语态的句子。这类句子一般不写明施事方，可以按照句子原来的顺序译出，原句动词部分可以作为一个视译单位。我们举几个例子来说明这类句子的翻译技巧。

例 1： The sense of inferiority that he acquired in his youth has never been totally eradicated.

译文 1： 他在青少年时期留下的自卑感，还没有完全消除。（张培基，1980：120）

译文 2： 有一种自卑感，是他在青少年时期留下的，一直都没有完全消除。

【讲解】 译文 2 中对被动语态的视译方法和笔译是一样的，将原来的被动语态 has never been totally eradicated 译为主动语态"一直都没有完全消除"。当然，在句子的前半部分，我们根据以前讲过的定语从句处理方式，将其分为两个类意群，顺序译出。

例 2： This kind of bags is seen everywhere.

译文 1： 人们到处可以看到这类手袋。

译文 2： 这类手袋随处可见。

【讲解】 句子的两种翻译方式在笔译中都可以见到，实际上是一种选择问题。在视译的时候，由于第二种方式更符合视译的顺译要求，所以我们建议这类句子基本上按照第二种方式翻译。它和例 1 使用的是同样的视译技巧。

例 3： It is reported that the three candidates are all going to attend the opening ceremony.

译文： 据报，三位候选人都要参加开幕式。

【讲解】 这类句子很多，视译的方法和笔译相似。同类句式有 It is reported / hoped / said / believed... 等等。在笔译中，主要有两种译法，一是例 3 中使用的方法，如"据报"、"希望"、"据说"等；另外一种是在翻译 It is believed / considered 等时，可加上"有人"、"大家"等主语，译为"有人相信"、"大家认为"，使汉语句子更加通顺。对这类句子的处理，张培基先生有过专门总结。(1980：121-122)

2　带有施事方的被动语态句

带有施事方的被动句，在翻译成汉语的时候多处理为被动句，所以要做语序上的调整，因为以 by 引导的施事方需要调整到句子的其他位置。一般笔译的基本方法是"主语＋被＋施事方＋动词"，而英语的基本句式是"主语＋动词＋施事方"，比较汉英的基本句式，就会发现调整语序似乎是不可避免的事情。确实，这样的翻译方法也符合汉语的习惯。

但在视译的时候，大幅度调整句子顺序是难以做到的事情。这就要求我们考虑如何在不作大幅度语序调整的前提下，顺畅地翻译这类被动句。一般来说，是先将 by 前面的部分作为一个独立的部分译出，然后将 by 引导的施事方译出，并重复原句动词，使后面部分也单独成为一个短句。请看下面的例句。

例 4： Our foreign policy is supported by the people all over the world.

译文 1： 我们的对外政策受到全世界人民的支持。(张培基，1980：122-123)

译文 2： 我对外政策受到了支持，全世界人民都支持。

【讲解】 译文 2 是一种最常用的视译方法，就是先将主语和被动语态形式的动词谓语部分 our foreign policy is supported 译出，使之成为一个独立的分句"我对外政策受到了支持"，然后另起一句，将施事方加入，并重复一遍动词，使句子通顺。

例 5： Any minute we would surely be spotted by enemy planes flying in and out of the airfield.

译文 1： 我们随时都会被出入机场的敌机发现。

译文 2： 随时我们都会被发现，被敌机发现，因为这些敌机不时出入机场。

【讲解】 我们先根据视译被动语态的基本技巧，将主语和动词部分 any minute we would surely be spotted 译为独立的分句"随时我们都会被发现"，然后加入施事方并重复动词，译成"被敌机发现"，最后以"因为"做连接成分，将分词定语短语译出。另外，由于这个句子的动词和施事方连在一起，中间没有插入其他成分，所以也可做小的语序调整，即："随时我们都会被敌机发现，因为这些敌机不时出入机场。"这对视译译员也不是很难的事情。

例 6： Americans are cushioned against rising commodity prices by the strong dollar.

译文 1： 美元的坚挺减缓了价格上涨给美国人造成的压力。（王恩冕，2004：105）

译文 2： 美国人压力减轻了，价格上涨造成了压力，但是美元坚挺减缓了压力。

【讲解】 这个句子比较难，因为不仅包含一个被动语态，而且被动语态的动词和施事方之间又加上了一个较长的短语。在这种情况下，调整施事方语序是几乎不可能的事情。所以，我们将原句分为三个类意译，然后依次译出。注意：在译"by + 施事方"的时候，灵活地使用了"（虽然）……，但是……"这样一个连接成分，自然地导出施事方。

3 　笔译中一般译为"把"、"使"和"由"字句的被动句式

汉语中"把"、"使"和"由"字句的句式都是常用句式，但是这类句型用在翻译中都有一个特点，就是把原文中的动词部分拆开处理，形成"把 + 插入部分 + 动词"的句式。在视译中，这种拆分需要调整语序。插入部分越长，调整幅度难度越大。所以，在视译中，要少用"把"、"使"和"由"句型。

在笔译中译为"把"、"使"和"由"的句子，在很多情况下是可以使用其他方式翻译出来的。在视译中，我们就要尽量使用这些其他方式，以便达到顺译的目的。我们举几个典型的例子说明这类句子的视译技巧。

例 7： Since the wingspan of the twin-engine bombers was too wide for the ship's elevator, they couldn't be stored below.

译文 1：　由于这种双引擎轰炸机翼展超过了升降机的宽度，所以不能把它们放在甲板底下。（张培基，1980：124）

译文 2：　这种双引擎轰炸机机翼太长，军舰的升降机装不下，所以不能停放在甲板底下。

【讲解】　在译文 2 中，我们将"把"字句改为主动句，直接译出。实际上是使用了将被动句译为主动句的方法。

例 8：　Most of the letters from his wife are read to him by the nurse in the hospital.

译文 1：　他的妻子给他的信件，大多数是由医院里的护士念给他听的。（张培基，1980：124）

译文 2：　妻子给他的大多数信件是念给他听的，念信的人是医院里的那个护士。

【讲解】　实际上，我们将这个句子分为三个类意群：Most of the letters from his wife // are read to him // by the nurse in the hospital. 译文 1 中的"由"字句改译为译文 2 的"是"字句，另外加一个明确施事方的词组"念信的人"，使句子更加通顺。

例 9：　And the astonishing thing is that this most dangerous operation was organized by a young attractive twenty-three-year-old Belgian girl, Andree De Jongh by name.

译文 1：　令人惊奇的是，这个极其危险的作战行动是由一个年青美貌的比利时姑娘组织的，她名叫安德·岱荣，23 岁。（张培基，1980：124）

译文 2：　令人惊奇的是，这个极其危险的作战行动，其组织者竟是一个年青漂亮的 23 岁比利时姑娘，名字叫安德·岱荣。

【讲解】　这是一个较长的句子，其中又有一个被动语态。我们先来根据类意群断句：And the astonishing thing is // that this most dangerous operation // was organized // by a young attractive twenty-three-year-old Belgian girl, // Andree De Jongh by name. 这样句子就分成了四个视译单位，每一个视译单位都不长，在一目可及的范围之内。然后我们顺次译出："令人惊奇的是，// 这个极其危险的作战行动，// 其组织者 // 竟是一个年青漂亮的 23 岁比利时姑娘，// 名字叫安德·岱荣。"在译被动语态的时候，我们将动词转化成为名词"其组织者"。这个转换，使我们没有必要使用"由"字句，句子顺译也就成为可能。

　　带有被动语态的句子分为不同的情况，上面我们列出的是最常见的三种。一种是原文不带施事方的句子，可译为主动句或加"被"字译为被动句；一种是原文带有施事方的，可先译出原句主体部分，然后另起一句译出施事方并重复动词；还有一种在笔译时常使用"把"、"使"、"由"等汉语句式，在视译时则要尽量避免。

二、语段视译

1 词汇与表达

　　在进行语段视译前，请先预习以下词汇与表达。

cap	完成，结束
Papua New Guinea	巴布亚新几内亚
chastise	严厉批评，斥责
dub	把……称为
Bali Road Map	巴厘岛路线图
lead	领导的，首席的

2 视译语段

　　请在 3 分钟之内迅速阅读下面的语段，了解大意，然后结合所学要点进行视译练习。视译时要保持正常语速，译文要顺畅达意。

In the nearly a decade since the US rejected the landmark climate change agreement known as the Kyoto Protocol, the US has become accustomed to being attacked at UN environmental gatherings. But the pounding it took in the tortured all-night negotiations that capped the UN climate change conference in Bali was unprecedented. Not only did developing nations, big and small, from India to Papua New Guinea, openly chastise the US for its last-minute refusal to endorse the new agreement dubbed the Bali Road Map, but—with the exception of a confused statement from Japan—not one of the allies that had generally stood with the US the past two weeks—Australia, Russia, Canada—rose in its defense. In the end, the US's total isolation was too much for even it to bear. "We've listened very closely to many of our colleagues here during these two weeks, but especially to what has been said in this hall today," said lead American negotiator Paula Dobiansky. "We will go forward and join consensus." Boos turned to cheers, and the deal was essentially sealed. （摘自《英语文摘》，2008 年第 2 期，第 4 页）

原译文：自从美国近 10 年前拒绝签署《京都议定书》这项具有里程碑意义的气候变化协议以来，它已经习惯了在联合国环境大会上成为众矢之的。但是在为巴厘岛联合国气候变化大会画上句号的倍受煎熬的通宵谈判中，美国所受的抨击之强烈是前所未有的。从印度到巴布亚新几内亚，大大小小的发展中国家公开斥责美国在最后一刻拒绝签署被称为"巴厘岛路线图"的新协议。不仅如此，除了日本发表了一个内容含糊的声明外，两周来通常与美国站在一起的盟国——澳大利亚、俄罗斯、加拿大——没有一个站出来为美国说话。最终，美国被彻底孤立的局面难堪到连它自己也无法忍受。美国代表团团长葆拉·多布里扬斯基说："这两周来，我们非常认真地倾听了众多同事发表的看法，特别是大家今天在这个会议厅发表的看法。我们将向前迈进，加入这一共识。"嘘声变成了喝彩，协议基本敲定。（李凤芹译）

3　视译译文

断　句	译　文
1　In the nearly a decade	近 10 年之前，
2　since the US rejected	美国拒绝签署
3　the landmark climate change agreement	里程碑式的气候变化议定书，
4　known as the Kyoto Protocol,	即《京都议定书》。
5　the US has become accustomed to being attacked	此后，美国已经习惯遭受抨击，
6　at UN environmental gatherings.	屡屡成为联合国环境大会上的众矢之的。
7　But the pounding	但这一次的抨击，
8　it took in the tortured all-night negotiations	使美国倍受煎熬地度过了通宵的谈判，
9　that capped the UN climate change conference in Bali	当晚的谈判也为巴厘岛联合国气候变化大会画上句号，

（待续）

231

（续上表）

	断　句	译　文
10	was unprecedented.	其间对美国的抨击是前所未有的。
11	Not only did developing nations,	不仅发展中国家
12	big and small,	无论大小，
13	from India to Papua New Guinea,	从印度到巴布亚新几内亚，
14	openly chastise the US	都公开斥责美国，
15	for its last-minute refusal	批评美国在最后一刻拒绝
16	to endorse the new agreement	签署新的协议
17	dubbed the Bali Road Map,	即巴厘岛路线图，
18	but—with the exception of a confused statement from Japan	而且除日本发表一个内容含糊的声明之外，
19	—not one of the allies	没有一个盟国，
20	that had generally stood with the US	也就是那些通常与美国站在一起的国家，
21	the past two weeks—	那些两周来支持美国的国家，
22	Australia, Russia, Canada—	比如澳大利亚、俄罗斯、加拿大，
23	rose in its defense.	肯站出来为美国说话。
24	In the end,	最终，
25	the US's total isolation	美国陷入彻底的孤立，
26	was too much for even it to bear.	局面连它自己也无法忍受。
27	"We've listened very closely to	"我们非常认真地倾听了
28	many of our colleagues here	众多同事发表的看法，
29	during these two weeks,	两周以来都是如此，
30	but especially to what has been said	但特别倾听了刚刚发表的看法，

（待续）

（续上表）

	断　句	译　文
31	in this hall today,"	也就是今天在这个会议厅的发言。"
32	said lead American negotiator Paula Dobiansky.	美国代表团团长葆拉·多布里扬斯基说。
33	"We will go forward	"我们将向前迈进，
34	and join consensus."	加入这一共识。"
35	Boos turned to cheers,	嘘声变成喝彩，
36	and the deal was essentially sealed.	协议基本敲定。

4　视译点评

1. 原文第一句：In the nearly a decade // since the US rejected the landmark climate change agreement // known as the Kyoto Protocol, // the US has become accustomed to being attacked // at UN environmental gatherings.

这是个长句，包含一个 since 引导的较长从句，构成了这个句子的视译难点。笔译时将主语"美国"提到句首，将 In the nearly a decade 插到句子中间。视译时，可将这一状语短语作为一个短句处理，译为"近 10 年之前"，然后将从句断句后译出："美国拒绝签署 // 里程碑式的气候变化议定书，// 即《京都议定书》。"下半句的难点是地点状语较长，按照一目可及的标准，在 at UN environmental gatherings 之前，往往会停顿。所以，我们将前面部分先行译出："此后，美国已经习惯遭受抨击"，然后单独译出地点状语，但是为了句子的上下连贯通顺，我们将英语单纯的地点状语也译为一个主谓结构的句式："屡屡成为联合国环境大会上的众矢之的。"

2. 原文第二句：But the pounding // it took in the tortured all-night negotiations // that capped the UN climate change conference in Bali // was unprecedented.

这是一个很难处理的句子。首先是一个名词加上一个很长的定语从句，紧接着在这个定语从句中又有一个定语从句。这样，主语和表语之间就有着两个很长的定语从句。这种情况对笔译并非容易的事情，要对定语反复调整。我们来看笔译译文："但是在为巴厘岛联合国气候变化大会画上句号的倍受煎熬的通宵谈判中，美国所受的抨击之强烈是前所未有的。"笔译的做法是先将两个定语从句分离出来，基本上是放在先行词前面译出，然后用"的"字连接。这样做视译显然不行。我们还是根据定语从句的基本视译方法，即先把先行词译出，然后将其定语从句按照原来顺序一一译出，再使用必要的连接词连成通顺的句子。同时，我们在视译过程中使用了更加灵活的变通句子的方式，将先行词和后面的定语从句以汉语动宾句式译出："……（谈判）为巴厘岛联合国气候变化大会画上句号。"

三、实战练习

1 词汇与表达

请先熟悉以下词汇与表达，并适当地运用在视译中。

IAEA（International Atomic Energy Agency）	国际原子能机构
IAEA Director-General	国际原子能机构总干事
Nobel Peace Prize laureate	诺贝尔和平奖得主
World Food Program	世界粮食计划署
reserve fuel bank	燃料储藏库
bona fide	诚意，善意
nuclear-weapon state	有核国家
fuel cycle	燃料循环
moratorium	暂停，暂禁
enrichment	（核燃料的）浓缩
warhead	弹头
genocide	种族灭绝，种族灭绝的大屠杀
anomaly	异常，反常

2 实战课文

请在 15 分钟之内迅速阅读下面的讲话，了解大意。视译时要保持正常语速，译文要顺畅达意。

2005 Nobel Lecture[1] (Excerpt 1)

IAEA Director-General and Nobel Peace Prize Laureate

Dr. Mohamed ElBaradei

The International Atomic Energy Agency and I are humbled, proud, delighted and above all strengthened in our resolve by this most worthy of honors.

My sister-in-law works for a group that supports orphanages in Cairo. She and her colleagues take care of children left behind by circumstances beyond their control. They feed these children, clothe them and teach them to read. At the International Atomic Energy Agency, my colleagues and I work to keep nuclear materials out of the reach of extremist groups. We inspect nuclear facilities all over the world, to be sure that peaceful nuclear activities are not being used as a cloak for weapons programs. My sister-in-law and I are working toward the same goal, through different paths: the security of the human family.

But why has this security so far eluded us? I believe it is because our security strategies have not yet caught up with the risks we are facing. **The globalization that has swept away the barriers to the movement of goods, ideas and people has also swept with it barriers that confined and localized security threats.** （句 1） A recent United Nations High-Level Panel identified five categories of threats that we face:

1. Poverty, infectious disease, and environmental degradation;

2. Armed conflict—both within and among states;

3. Organized crime;

4. Terrorism; and

5. Weapons of mass destruction.

These are all "threats without borders"—where traditional notions of national security have become obsolete. We cannot respond to these threats by building more walls, developing bigger weapons, or dispatching more troops. Quite to the contrary, by their very nature, these security threats require primarily multinational cooperation. But what is more important is that these are not separate or distinct threats. When we scratch the surface, we find them closely connected and interrelated.

1　原文参见 http://nobelprize.org/nobel_prizes/peace/laureates/2005/elbaradei-lecture-en.html。

We are 1,000 people here today in this august hall. Imagine for a moment that we represent the world's population. These 200 people on my left would be the wealthy of the world, who consume 80% of the available resources. And these 400 people on my right would be living on an income of less than $2 per day. This underprivileged group of people on my right is no less intelligent or less worthy than their fellow human beings on the other side of the aisle. They were simply born into this fate.

In the real world, this imbalance in living conditions inevitably leads to inequality of opportunity, and in many cases loss of hope. And what is worse, all too often the plight of the poor is compounded by and results in human rights abuses, a lack of good governance, and a deep sense of injustice. This combination naturally creates a most fertile breeding ground for civil wars, organized crime, and extremism in its different forms. In regions where conflicts have been left to fester for decades, countries continue to look for ways to offset their insecurities or project their "power". In some cases, they may be tempted to seek their own weapons of mass destruction, like others who have preceded them.

Fifteen years ago, when the Cold War ended, many of us hoped for a new world order to emerge. A world order rooted in human solidarity—a world order that would be equitable, inclusive and effective. But today we are nowhere near that goal. We may have torn down the walls between East and West, but we have yet to build the bridges between North and South—the rich and the poor.

Consider our development aid record. Last year, the nations of the world spent over $1 trillion on armaments. **But we contributed less than 10% of that amount—a mere $80 billion—as official development assistance to the developing parts of the world, where 850 million people suffer from hunger.** （句2）My friend James Morris heads the World Food Program, whose task is to feed the hungry. He recently told me, "If I could have just 1% of the money spent on global armaments, no one in this world would go to bed hungry." It should not be a surprise then that poverty continues to breed conflict. Of the 13 million deaths due to armed conflict in the last 10 years, 9 million occurred in sub-Saharan Africa, where the poorest of the poor live.

Consider also our approach to the sanctity and value of human life. In the aftermath of the September 2001 terrorist attacks in the United States, we all grieved deeply, and expressed outrage at this heinous crime—and rightly so. But many people today are unaware that, as the result of civil war in the Democratic Republic of Congo, 3.8 million people have lost their lives since 1998. Are we to conclude that our priorities are skewed and our approaches uneven?

With this "big picture" in mind, we can better understand the changing landscape in nuclear non-proliferation and disarmament. There are three main features to this changing landscape: the emergence of an extensive black market in nuclear material and equipment, the proliferation of nuclear weapons and sensitive nuclear technology, and the stagnation in nuclear disarmament.

Today, with globalization bringing us ever closer together, if we choose to ignore the insecurities of some, they will soon become the insecurities of all. Equally, with the spread of advanced science and technology, as long as some of us choose to rely on nuclear weapons, we continue to risk that these same weapons will become increasingly attractive to others. I have no doubt that, if we hope to escape self-destruction, then nuclear weapons should have no place in our collective conscience, and no role in our security.

To that end, we must ensure—absolutely—that no more countries acquire these deadly weapons. We must see to it that nuclear-weapon states take concrete steps toward nuclear disarmament. And we must put in place a security system that does not rely on nuclear deterrence. Are these goals realistic and within reach? I do believe they are. But then three steps are urgently required.

First, keep nuclear and radiological material out of the hands of extremist groups. In 2001, the IAEA together with the international community launched a worldwide campaign to enhance the security of such material, protecting nuclear facilities, securing powerful radioactive sources, training law enforcement officials, monitoring border crossings. In four years, we have completed perhaps 50% of the work. But this is not fast enough, because we are in a race against time.

Second, tighten control over the operations for producing the nuclear material that could be used in weapons. Under the current system, any country has the right to master these operations for civilian uses. But in doing so, it also masters the most difficult steps in making a nuclear bomb. To overcome this, I am hoping that we can make these operations multinational—so that no one country can have exclusive control over any such operation. **My plan is to begin by setting up a reserve fuel bank, under IAEA control, so that every country will be assured that it will get the fuel needed for its bona fide peaceful nuclear activities.** (句 3) This assurance of supply will remove the incentive and the just-ification for each country to develop its own fuel cycle. We should then be able to agree on a moratorium on new national facilities, and to begin to work on multinational arrangements for enrichment, fuel production, waste disposal and reprocessing.

We must also strengthen the verification system. IAEA inspections are the heart and soul of the nuclear non-proliferation regime. To be effective, it is essential that we are provided with the necessary authority, information, advanced technology, and resources. And our inspections must be backed by the UN Security Council, to be called on in cases of non-compliance.

Third, accelerate disarmament efforts. We still have eight or nine countries who possess nuclear weapons. We still have 27,000 warheads in existence. I believe this 27,000 is too many. A good start would be if the nuclear-weapon states reduced the strategic role given to these weapons. **More than 15 years after the end of the Cold War, it is incomprehensible to many that the major nuclear-weapon states operate with their arsenals on hair-trigger alert—such that, in the case of a possible launch of a nuclear attack, their leaders could have only 30 minutes to decide whether to retaliate, risking the devastation of entire nations in a matter of minutes.** （句 4 ）

These are three concrete steps that, I believe, can readily be taken: protect the material and strengthen verification, control the fuel cycle, accelerate disarmament efforts. But that is not enough. The hard part is: how do we create an environment in which nuclear weapons—like slavery or genocide—are regarded as a taboo and a historical anomaly?

3 难句分析与视译处理

句 1： The globalization that has swept away the barriers to the movement of goods, ideas and people has also swept with it barriers that confined and localized security threats.

笔译译文： 全球化为物资、思想和人员的交流扫除了障碍，而它同时也释放了一度限定在某一特定地区的安全威胁。

视译译文：

断　句	译　文
The globalization that has swept away the barriers	全球化扫除了障碍，
to the movement of goods, ideas and people	推动了物资、思想和人员的交流，
has also swept with it barriers	它同时也消除了另一些障碍，
that confined and localized security threats.	释放出一度限定在某一特定地区的安全威胁。

句 2： But we contributed less than 10% of that amount—a mere $80 billion—as official development assistance to the developing parts of the world, where 850 million people suffer from hunger.

笔译译文： 但是对于有 8.5 亿人口挨饿的发展中世界，我们给予的援助却不及上述的十分之一——只有 800 亿美元。

视译译文：

断　句	译　文
But we contributed less than 10% of that amount—	但是我们的援助却不及上述的十分之一——
a mere $80 billion—	仅拿出了 800 亿美元，
as official development assistance to	用作官方发展援助资金，
the developing parts of the world,	帮助发展中世界，
where 850 million people suffer from hunger.	而那里有 8.5 亿人在挨饿。

句 3： My plan is to begin by setting up a reserve fuel bank, under IAEA control, so that every country will be assured that it will get the fuel needed for its bona fide peaceful nuclear activities.

笔译译文： 我的计划是先建立一个在国际原子能机构控制下的燃料储存库，这样，任何一个国家在真正开展以和平为目的的核活动时都保证可以得到所需的燃料。

视译译文：

断　句	译　文
My plan is to begin by setting up a reserve fuel bank,	我计划先建立一个燃料储藏库，
under IAEA control,	由国际原子能机构负责管理，
so that every country will be assured	这样，任何一个国家都可以保证
that it will get the fuel needed	得到自己所需的燃料，
for its bona fide peaceful nuclear activities.	开展真正的以和平为目的的核活动。

句 4： More than 15 years after the end of the Cold War, it is incomprehensible to many that the major nuclear-weapon states operate with their arsenals on hair-trigger alert—such that, in the case of a possible launch of a nuclear attack, their leaders could have only 30 minutes to decide whether to retaliate, risking the devastation of entire nations in a matter of minutes.

笔译译文： 冷战结束后已经超过 15 年了。很多人不明白，几个核大国为什么始终使他们的核武库处于一触即发的备战状态。这是因为在可能遭受核打击的情况下，这些国家的领导者要冒着在短短几分钟内使所有国家毁于一旦的风险，做出是否实施报复性打击的决定，而他们只有半小时的决策时间。

视译译文：

断　句	译　文
More than 15 years	超过 15 年来，
after the end of the Cold War,	在冷战结束后的日子里，
it is incomprehensible to many	很多人不明白，
that the major nuclear-weapon states operate with their arsenals	几个核大国为什么始终使它们的核武库
on hair-trigger alert	处于一触即发的备战状态。

（待续）

（续上表）

断　句	译　文
—such that,	——这是因为，
in the case of a possible launch of a nuclear attack,	在可能遭受核打击的情况下，
their leaders could have only 30 minutes	这些国家的领导者只有半小时的时间
to decide whether to retaliate,	决定是否要实施报复性打击，
risking the devastation of entire nations	其风险是可能使所有国家毁于一旦，
in a matter of minutes.	在顷刻之间化为乌有。

4　参考译文

2005 年诺贝尔奖演说辞（节选 1）
国际原子能机构总干事，诺贝尔和平奖获得者
穆罕默德·埃尔巴拉迪博士

　　获此殊荣，我和国际原子能机构都倍感荣幸，我们感到非常的自豪和高兴，特别是这一殊荣更加坚定了我们的决心。

　　我兄弟的妻子在开罗一家救助孤儿的机构工作。她和她的同事们照顾着在混乱的时局中不幸丧失父母的孩子们。他们为这些孩子提供食物、衣服，并且教他们读书认字。在国际原子能机构，我和同事们的工作就是防止极端主义者获得核材料。我们核查世界各地的核设施，确保没有人打着和平利用核设施的幌子开发核武器。我和我兄弟的妻子的工作其实是殊途同归，最终目标都是确保人类大家庭的安全。

　　但是，为什么安全一直在躲闪着我们？我认为，这是因为我们的安全战略没有跟上时代变化，无法应对我们今天所面临的危险。全球化为物资、思想和人员的交流扫除了障碍，而它同时也释放了一度限定在某一特定地区的安全威胁。最近的一次联合国高层会议明确了我们现在面临的五大类威胁：

　　1. 贫穷、传染病、环境恶化；
　　2. 武装冲突——包括国家内部和国家之间的此类冲突；
　　3. 有组织犯罪；

4. 恐怖主义；

5. 大规模杀伤性武器。

这些都是"无疆界威胁"，传统的国家安全观对于这样的威胁都已经过时。靠修建围墙、研发更大的武器或派出更多的士兵来对付这些威胁已经无济于事。恰恰相反，从本质上看，这些威胁要求我们必须进行多国合作。但更重要的一点是，这些威胁并不是互相独立、易于分辨的。如果我们认真研究就会发现它们彼此之间有着盘根错节的联系。

现在这座雄伟的大厅里坐着约 1,000 人。想象一下我们代表整个世界的人口。我左侧的 200 人是世界上富有人群，他们消耗世界上 80% 的可以获取的资源，而我右侧 400 人的日开销则不足两美元。我右侧的这些弱势人群在聪明才干方面绝不比另一侧的人逊色。他们只是命运不济。

在现实世界中，这种生活条件上的不平衡会不可避免地导致机会的不均等，甚至使很多人彻底失去希望。更糟糕的是，人权状况恶劣、缺乏良好的政治治理以及社会不公带来的深切感受，一方面使贫困人口的境遇雪上加霜，另一方面也成为他们悲惨生活的痛苦后果。这种环境自然为内战、有组织犯罪和不同形式的极端主义提供了最为肥沃的温床。一些地区的冲突几十年来不断激化，这些地区的国家一直在寻找途径抵消他们的不安全因素，或是投射他们的"力量"。在一些情况下，他们可能会禁不住诱惑，效仿已有大规模杀伤性武器的国家，开始寻求他们自己的大规模杀伤性武器。

当 15 年前冷战结束的时候，我们中很多人希望看到一个新的世界秩序，一个植根于人类团结的，平等包容的、富有成效的世界秩序。但是今天我们距离这个目标仍然十分遥远。我们虽然已经推倒了隔断东西方的围墙，但是我们仍需要在南方和北方，也就是穷国与富国之间架起桥梁。

请大家想一想我们的发展援助纪录。去年，全世界花费在武器装备上的资金高达 1 万亿美元。但是对于有 8.5 亿人口挨饿的发展中世界，我们给予的援助却不及上述的十分之一——只有 800 亿美元。我的朋友詹姆斯·莫里斯是世界粮食计划署的负责人，他的任务就是消除饥饿。最近他告诉我，"如果把全球军备开销的百分之一给我，我就不会让世界上任何一个人饿着肚子睡觉。"因此，贫困不断地滋生冲突也就不足为怪。在过去 10 年间，全球死于武装冲突的 1,300 万人口中有 900 万是在最贫困人口集中的撒哈拉沙漠以南的非洲地区丧生的。

再想想我们是如何对待神圣而且宝贵的生命的。2001 年 9 月美国发生恐怖袭击事件之后，我们都表示了极大的悲痛及对这种滔天罪行的义愤，这是应该的。但是现在还有很多人并不知道，1998 年以来，380 万人在刚果民主共和国的内战中失去生命。由此，我们能否得出这样的结论：我们的关注重点偏差太多，而我们的解决办法也并不公平？

了解了这个大背景，我们就能更好地理解核不扩散和裁军的不断变化的走势。它有三大主要特征：买卖核材料和核设备的庞大黑市的出现，核武器与敏感核技术的扩散，裁军的停滞状态。

今天，当全球化使我们更加靠近彼此的时候，如果我们选择对一部分人面临的威胁听之任之的话，那么这些危险问题将很快会威胁所有的人。同样，随着先进科学技术的不断普及，只要我们中有些人选择依靠核武器，那么就难保其他人不会对核武器越来越感兴趣。我坚信，如果我们想避免自我毁灭，核武器就不应该在我们的集体意识中占有一席之地，也不应该在我们的安全事务中起任何作用。

为实现这一目标，我们必须保证——百分之百地确保——不再有更多的国家获得这类致命武器。我们还应该监督有核国家采取具体措施解除核武器。同时，我们应该建立一个不依靠核威慑的安全体制。这些目标现实吗？我们有能力实现吗？我确信答案是肯定的。但是我们迫切需要采取三个步骤。

第一，保证极端主义团体无法获得核材料和放射性材料。2001 年，国际原子能机构同整个国际社会一起开展了一场保护这些核材料安全的运动。我们保护核设施，保护强大的放射性材料的来源，培训执法人员，监视非法越境。四年内我们完成了大约一半的任务，但这还不够快，因为我们在同时间赛跑。

第二，加强对可以用于制造核武器的核材料的生产过程的控制。在现行体制下，任何国家都有权进行民用性质的核材料生产，但是，这样也就使得各国都可以掌握制造核弹的最尖端的步骤。为解决这个问题，我希望这些生产过程可以由多国参与进行，从而使任何一个国家都不能独自掌控整个过程。我的计划是先建立一个由国际原子能机构负责管理的燃料储存库，这样，任何一个国家在真诚地开展以和平为目的的核活动时都保证可以得到所需的燃料。这种供应保障将使各国失去自行进行燃料循环的积极性和理由。我们还应该就暂停兴建新的国家核设施达成一致，并在浓缩、燃料制造、废料处理和再处理方面进行多国合作。

我们还要强化核查体系。国际原子能机构的核查是核不扩散体制的核心。要取得成效，我们就必须享有必要的权力、信息、先进技术和资源。联合国安理会必须支持我们的调查，并在发现违规时发挥作用。

第三，我们要加快裁军脚步。仍然有八九个国家拥有核武器，世界上仍然有 2.7 万枚弹头，我认为 2.7 万是一个过于庞大的数字。如果有核国家能够减少这些武器的战略作用，那将是一个很好的开端。冷战结束已经超过 15 年了。

很多人不明白，几个核大国为什么始终使他们的核武库处于一触即发的备战状态。这是因为在可能遭受核打击的情况下，这些国家的领导者要冒着在短短几分钟内使所有国家毁于一旦的风险，做出是否实施报复性打击的决定，而他们只有半小时的决策时间。

我认为有三项措施比较容易执行：保护材料强化核查、控制燃料循环、加速裁军。但是这些还不够。困难的是，我们应该怎样营造一个环境，使核武器就像奴隶制度和种族灭绝一样被视为禁忌和历史的反常。

四、自主训练

请在 15 分钟之内迅速阅读下面的讲话，了解大意。学生可组成对子练习，互相监控对视译技巧的掌握情况、视译质量和现场表现，或以边视译边录音的形式进行个人练习。视译时要保持正常语速，译文要顺畅达意。如遇难句，可在首次视译后参照"实战练习"中难句分析与视译处理的方法进行练习，找出解决方法。

2005 Nobel Lecture (Excerpt 2)
IAEA Director-General and Nobel Peace Prize Laureate
Dr. Mohamed ElBaradei

Whether one believes in evolution, intelligent design, or Divine Creation, one thing is certain. Since the beginning of history, human beings have been at war with each other, under the pretext of religion, ideology, ethnicity and other reasons. And no civilization has ever willingly given up its most powerful weapons. We seem to agree today that we can share modern technology, but we still refuse to acknowledge that our values—at their very core—are shared values.

I am an Egyptian Muslim, educated in Cairo and New York, and now living in Vienna. My wife and I have spent half our lives in the North, half in the South. And we have experienced first-hand the unique nature of the human family and the common values we all share. Shakespeare speaks of every single member of that family in *The Merchant of Venice*, when he asks: "If you prick us, do we not bleed? If you tickle us, do we not laugh? If you poison us, do we not die? And if you wrong us, shall we not revenge?" And lest we forget:

There is no religion that was founded on intolerance and no religion that does not value the sanctity of human life.

Judaism asks that we value the beauty and joy of human existence.

Christianity says we should treat our neighbors as we would be treated.

Islam declares that killing one person unjustly is the same as killing all of humanity.

Hinduism recognizes the entire universe as one family.

Buddhism calls on us to cherish the oneness of all creation.

Some would say that it is too idealistic to believe in a society based on tolerance and the sanctity of human life, where borders, nationalities and ideologies are of marginal importance. To those I say, this is not idealism, but rather realism, because history has taught us that war rarely resolves our differences. Force does not heal old wounds; it opens new ones.

I have talked about our efforts to combat the misuse of nuclear energy. Let me now tell you how this very same energy is used for the benefit of humankind.

At the IAEA, we work daily on every continent to put nuclear and radiation techniques in the service of humankind. In Vietnam, farmers plant rice with greater nutritional value that was developed with IAEA assistance. Throughout Latin America, nuclear technology is being used to map underground aquifers, so that water supplies can be managed sustainably. In Ghana, a new radiotherapy machine is offering cancer treatment to thousands of patients. In the South Pacific, Japanese scientists are using nuclear techniques to study climate change. In India, eight new nuclear plants are under construction, to provide clean electricity for a growing nation—a case in point of the rising expectation for a surge in the use of nuclear energy worldwide. These projects, and a thousand others, exemplify the IAEA ideal: Atoms for Peace.

But the expanding use of nuclear energy and technology also makes it crucial that nuclear safety and security are maintained at the highest level. Since the Chernobyl accident, we have worked all over the globe to raise nuclear safety performance. And since the September 2001 terrorist attacks, we have worked with even greater intensity on nuclear security. On both fronts, we have built an international network of legal norms and performance standards. But our most tangible impact has been on the ground, hundreds of missions, in every part of the world, with international experts making sure nuclear activities are safe and secure.

I am very proud of the 2,300 hard working men and women that make up the IAEA staff—the colleagues with whom I share this honor. Some of them are here with me today. We come from over 90 countries. We bring many different perspectives to our work. Our diversity is our strength. We are limited in our authority. We have a very modest budget. And we have no armies. But armed with the strength of our convictions, we will continue to speak truth to power. And we will continue to carry out our mandate with independence and objectivity. The Nobel Peace Prize is a powerful message for us—to endure in our efforts to work for security and development. A durable peace is not a single achievement, but an environment, a process and a commitment.

The picture I have painted today may have seemed somewhat grim. Let me conclude by telling you why I have hope. I have hope because the positive aspects of globalization are enabling nations and peoples to become politically, economically and socially interdependent, making war an increasingly unacceptable option. Among the 25 members of the European Union, the degree of economic and socio-political dependencies has made the prospect of the use of force to resolve differences almost absurd. The same is emerging with regard to the Organization for Security and Cooperation in Europe, with some 55 member countries from Europe, Central Asia and North America. Could these models be expanded to a world model, through the same creative multilateral engagement and active international cooperation, where the strong are just and the weak secure?

I have hope because civil society is becoming better informed and more engaged. They are pressing their governments for change—to create democratic societies based on diversity, tolerance and equality. They are proposing creative solutions. They are raising awareness, donating funds, working to transform civic spirit from the local to the global. Working to bring the human family closer together. We now have the opportunity, more than at any time before, to give an affirmative answer to one of the oldest questions of all time: "Am I my brother's keeper?" What is required is a new mindset and a change of heart, to be able to see the person across the ocean as our neighbor.

Finally, I have hope because of what I see in my children, and some of their generation. I took my first trip abroad at the age of 19. My children were even more fortunate than I. They had their first exposure to foreign culture as infants, and they were raised in a multicultural environment. And I can say absolutely that my son and daughter are oblivious to color and race and nationality. They see no difference between their friends Noriko, Ma Fupo, Justin, Saulo and Hussam; to them, they are only fellow human beings and good friends. Globalization, through travel, media and communication, can also help us—as it has with my children and many of their peers—to see each other simply as human beings.

Imagine what would happen if the nations of the world spent as much on development as on building the machines of war. Imagine a world where every human being would live in freedom and dignity. Imagine a world in which we would shed the same tears when a child dies in Darfur or Vancouver. Imagine a world where we would settle our differences through diplomacy and dialog and not through bombs or bullets. Imagine if the only nuclear weapons remaining were the relics in our museums. Imagine the legacy we could leave to our children.

Imagine that such a world is within our grasp.

形容词和副词比较级的视译

> 基本技巧：
> - 将比较级引导词后面的部分译成独立的短语或短句。

一、技巧讲解：形容词和副词比较级的视译

形容词和副词的比较级在英文中很常见。带有比较级的简单的句子可以直接译出，不用做任何调整。比如 Today is warmer. 我们视译时可以直接译为："今天比较暖和。"有些句子虽然不能这样顺妥地译出，但如果句子不长，比较内容在一目可及范围之内，可以对语序稍加调整，然后译出，也不困难。比如 This house is cheaper than that one. 也可以直接译为："这所房子比那一所便宜。"在这里，我们虽然调整了原来的语序，将 than that one 置于形容词"便宜"前边来翻译，但因为比较级从句很短，所以这样做也是行得通的。

不过，我们往往会碰上一些比较长的短语或是句子，作为视译译员，这类短语或是句子不可能在一目可及范围之内，作为同声传译译员，也不可能全部听完句子再做翻译。比如， Cotton output was 20% higher than the previous year. 这个句子在笔译中可以不加思索地译为："棉花产量比前一年高 20%。"（张道真，2007：398）但是，在视译中我们一般会将整个句子分成两个类意群，第一个是 cotton output was 20% higher，第二个是 than the previous year。这样一来，就不可能再像笔译中那样调整语序了。对这样的句子，可以译成"棉花产量提高了 20%"和"这是与去年相比"两个分句。按照原来语序顺次译出，是视译和同传的基本原则，所以，我们在训练的时候，即便是比较短的句子，也最好按照顺序译出，以便养成良好的翻译习惯。比如上面的句子：This house is cheaper than that one. 依照视译的顺译原则，我们也可以这样翻译："这所房子比较便宜，那一所要贵一些。"

比较级有很多种表示形式，我们在这一单元里重点讲解两种基本的。一种是以 than 连接的比较级句式，一种是以 as 连接的比较级句式。下面，我们分别用实例来说明比较级的视译。另外，我们也会简要地讨论一下包含比较级句子的一些灵活处理方法。

1 以 than 连接的比较级句式

例 1： She has more time than I do.

译文 1： 她的时间比我多。（张道真，2007：398）

译文 2： 她的时间比较多，我的少。

【讲解】 译文 2 是比较典型的视译方法，就是将以 than 引导的比较级从句分为单独的一句翻译。这个句子很短，使用译文 1 也可以，甚至还更加简洁，但译文 2 是视译的方法，在长句子中尤其能显示出它的顺译优势。

例 2： Shopping at a supermarket is cheaper than going to the local shops.

译文 1： 在超市购物比在邻近商店购物便宜。（张道真，2007：397）

译文 2： 在超市购物比较便宜，而在邻近商店购物比较贵。

【讲解】 这个带有比较级从句的句子就比较长，在视译中，大致可以分 shopping at a supermarket is cheaper 和 than going to the local shops 为两个类意群，然后依次译出。在笔译中，一般要使用"比"字来表示比较级，而在视译或是同传中，中文的"意合"可以让我们比较从容地使用两个并列的句子将比较级的两个部分分别译出，这样就可以遵循顺译的基本原则了。

例 3： It takes less time to go there by plane than by train.

译文 1： 坐飞机到那里比坐火车快。（张道真，2007：397）

译文 2： 比较快的方法到那里去是坐飞机，而不是坐火车。

【讲解】 这是个比较难视译的句子，包含一个比较级（less ... than ...），中间又夹杂了许多成分。我们在做视译的时候，首先将句子分为三个类意群，即：It takes less time // to go there by plane // than by train. 然后分别译出："比较快的方法 // 到那里去是坐飞机 // 而不是坐火车。"实际上，我们仍然使用了将比较级成分作为单独成分翻译的方法。

2　以 as 连接的比较级句式

英语比较级还有一种表达形式，这就是 as … as … 及其否定表示方法 not so … as …。典型的句式是：He looks as young as five years ago. 这种句子的笔译也往往需要调整语序。比如这个句子一般译为："他看上去像五年前一样年轻。"在做视译的时候，我们还是尽量不要调整语序，往往将这种句子分成两个类意群，即：He looks as young // as five years ago. 然后依照顺序译成两个独立的成分："他看上去挺年轻，// 像五年前一样。"一般来说，视译的时候，将第二个 as 连接的部分作为一个独立成分处理。我们举几个例子说明这类句型的视译方法。

例 4：　On this issue, the UN Security Council was as resolute as many people had expected.

译文 1：在这个问题上，联合国安理会像许多人预期的那样坚定。

译文 2：在这个问题上，联合国安理会很坚定，像许多人预期的一样。

例 5：　Food is many times as expensive as it was 10 years ago.

译文 1：食品比 10 年前贵了好几倍。

译文 2：食品贵了好几倍，这是与 10 年前相比。

【讲解】　这两个句子的基本视译方法是一样的，即将以第二个 as 连接的部分作为一个单独的成分处理，放在句尾。不过，例 5 增加了一个代词成分"这"，目的是使句子更加顺妥。

例 6：　Your coffee is not so good as the coffee my mother makes.

译文 1：你煮的咖啡没有我妈煮的好。（张道真，2007：401）

译文 2：你煮的咖啡不太好，没有我妈煮的好。

【讲解】　这是 as … as … 的否定句式。视译时我们也是将以 as 引导的被比较的部分分离出来，作为单独成分处理。前一部分还是按照原来句子的形式处理成否定式，译为"不太好"，以便与后面的部分顺妥连接。后面则另起一句，但也要译为否定式，即："没有我妈煮的好。" 这种句子的关键是要将原来句子中的一个否定形式译为中文的两个否定形式，否则就会出现意义上的差错。

在很多情况下，as 可以引导一些成语，比如 as obstinate as a mule、as sharp as a needle、as stupid as a donkey 等。在视译中，一般将这类成语的意思译出即可，不必非要将原来的成语字对字译出。比如上面的例子可以译为"非常固执"、"非常敏锐"、"非常愚蠢"。当然，如果希望达到一定的修辞效果，也可以将第二个 as 之后的成分译出，常用的视译结构是"……像……"。比如"固执得像头骡子"，"敏锐得像根针"，"愚蠢得像头驴"。但是，我们推荐使用第一种方式，即不译 as 后面的成分。这样做有两个好处。一是有些这类成语的第二部分翻译出来并不符合汉语习惯，反而使人听不明白。比如把 as tame as a cat 译为"非常听话"比译为"像猫一样听话"更明白一些。第二，视译时，在能够简洁的地方要尽量简洁，千万不要拉长句子。这类成语的第一个形容词或是副词已经说明了意思，除非为了特殊的修辞原因，一般没有必要再把后面的成分翻译出来。

3 比较级的灵活处理

以上我们讲解了形容词和副词比较级最常见的两种句式的处理方法，主要的一点就是将被比较的部分，亦即以 than 或 as 引导的部分分离开来，译为独立的成分。当然除了以上两类典型的比较级句子以外，有的时候，带有以 than 或是 as 引导的比较级的句子也可以比较灵活地处理以保持译出语顺序，保证视译的流畅。

例 7：　Than him no one could show a more genuine generosity to his friends.
译文 1：没有人比他更能够表现出对朋友真正慷慨的态度。（薄冰，2006：414）
译文 2：比起他来，没有人能够表现出更加真切的慷慨来对待朋友。

例 8：　There the tuberculosis rate is 10 times as high as in North Carolina.
译文 1：那里的肺结核发病率是北卡罗来纳州的 10 倍。（张道真，2007：401）
译文 2：在那里，肺结核的发病率 10 倍于北卡罗来纳州。

例 9：　This stone gets the harder, the longer it is exposed to the weather.
译文 1：这块石头风吹日晒越久，它越硬。（薄冰，2006：421）
译文 2：这块石头越硬，说明它风吹日晒得越久。

带有形容词或副词比较级的句子，在句子比较长的时候，往往会使顺译比较困难，因而造成视译译员的困难。对于处理这类句子的视译技巧，我们通常先将以 than 或是 as 引导的被比较部分分离出来，把这一部分译为一个单独的短语或短句，必要时加代词、名词或其他简短成分连接两个部分。

二、语段视译

1　词汇与表达

在进行语段视译前，请先预习以下词汇与表达。

G8 country	八国集团成员
tsunami	海啸
interdependence	相互依赖

2　视译语段

请在 3 分钟之内迅速阅读下面的语段，了解大意，然后结合所学要点进行视译练习。视译时要保持正常语速，译文要顺畅达意。

British trade with China has doubled with the last five years alone. This growth is faster than that of any of other G8 countries. Britain is the largest European investor here. Culturally our links are also strong. More students from China study in the UK than from any other countries, and partnerships between our schools are growing. We have just launched the UK-China Partners in Science 2005 campaign, to strengthen our scientific links across the board. The partnership between our two countries is important not just for what it brings both of us, but also from the common work which Britain and China can do together in the world. There is a wider message in the global response to the tragedy of the tsunami. It is that people around the world feel that the interdependence of nations, so long talked about by statesmen, is today more than ever a concrete reality. This reality is also a challenge to which governments must respond. The first part of the challenge is economic—finding the determination not to seek shelter from the global market, but to exploit the opportunities that it offers.[1]（崔长青，2007：41-42）

原译文：英中两国的贸易在过去五年里就翻了一番。这一增幅超过了其他任何一个八国集团成员。英国是目前欧洲在中国的最大的投资者。我们两国在文化方面的联系也十分密切。在英国的中国留学生数量超过了世界任何一个其他国

1　此语段为原文节选。

家的留英学生，双方教育机构的合作也在加强。前不久双方推出的2005科技伙伴计划将加强彼此之间的科技联系。中英两国伙伴关系的重要性并不仅在于能够为我们两国带来什么，更在于中英可以在世界上就共同的课题开展合作。全球对于不久前海啸灾难的反应传达了一条意义更为深刻的信息。这就是，全世界的人们感到，以前一直是政治家们谈论的国家间的相互依赖，今天比以往任何时候都更加现实地存在着。这一现实也是各国政府必须回应的一种挑战。挑战的第一部分是经济方面的——必须下决心不在全球市场中寻求保护，而是充分利用全球市场提供的机会。

3 视译译文

	断 句	译 文
1	British trade with China has doubled	英中贸易翻了一番，
2	with the last five years alone.	这仅仅是过去五年的事情。
3	This growth is faster	这一增长是很快的，
4	than that of any of other G8 countries.	超过任何一个八国集团成员。
5	Britain is the largest European investor here.	英国是欧洲在中国最大的投资国。
6	Culturally our links are also strong.	文化上我们的联系也十分密切。
7	More students from China study in the UK	许多中国学生在英国留学，
8	than from any other countries,	其数量超过任何其他国家，
9	and partnerships between our schools are growing.	双方学校之间的伙伴关系也在加强，
10	We have just launched	我们不久前启动了
11	the UK-China Partners in Science 2005 campaign,	英中科学伙伴2005计划，
12	to strengthen our scientific links across the board.	目的是加强双方全方位的科技联系。

（待续）

（续上表）

	断　句	译　文
13	The partnership between our two countries is important	英中两国之间的伙伴关系是重要的，
14	not just for what it brings both of us,	这不仅因为它给两国带来利益，
15	but also from the common work	而且还创造了合作的机会，
16	which Britain and China can do together in the world.	使英中两国可以在当今世界上共同努力。
17	There is a wider message	有一条更为深远的信息，
18	in the global response to the tragedy of the tsunami.	包含在全球应对海啸灾难的行动之中。
19	It is that people around the world feel	这就是全世界的人们意识到，
20	that the interdependence of nations,	国家之间是相互依赖的，
21	so long talked about by statesmen,	过去这只是政治家的话题，
22	is today more than ever a concrete reality.	现在却是比以往更加实在的现实。
23	This reality is also a challenge	这一现实也是一个挑战，
24	to which governments must respond.	各国政府必须予以回应。
25	The first part of the challenge is economic—	挑战的第一个内容是经济方面的，
26	finding the determination	我们必须有决心，
27	not to seek shelter	不去寻求保护，
28	from the global market,	以规避全球市场，
29	but to exploit the opportunities	而是利用机会，
30	that it offers.	利用全球市场提供的机会。

4 视译点评

1. 原文第二句：This growth is faster // than that of any of other G8 countries.

　　根据比较级视译的基本技巧，我们将比较词 than 前面的部分首先译出，即将 This growth is faster 译为"这一增长是很快的"，然后将比较词后面的部分 than that of any of other G8 countries 译为："超过任何一个八国集团成员"。原文第五句的上半句 More students from China study in the UK than from any other countries 也是一个比较级，视译技巧是一样的。先将比较词 than 之前的部分译出："许多中国学生在英国留学"，然后将比较词后面的部分另分一句译出："其数量超过任何国家"。另外，从这两个句子的视译可以看出，翻译比较级的句子，不一定非用"比"，其他一些词，如"超过"、"多于"、"少于"等更加能够引出宾语的词，使用起来也是十分便利的。

2. 原文第七句：The partnership between our two countries is important // not just for what it brings both of us, // but also from the common work // which Britain and China can do together in the world.

　　这是一个较长的复合句，包含两个从句，一个介词宾语从句，一个定语从句。原译文很自然地将其译为："中英两国伙伴关系的重要性并不仅在于能够为我们两国带来什么，更在于中英可以在世界上就共同的课题开展合作。"其中定语从句是按照置于先行词之前的方式翻译的。视译时，我们仍按照视译的基本技巧，将其依次顺译。具体分以下几步进行，先译出主句的主干部分："英中两国之间的伙伴关系是重要的"；其次译出第一个状语从句，并将表示因果关系的词 for 译出，即："这不仅因为它给两国带来利益"；再次译出后半部分定语从句之前的成分："而且还创造了合作的机会"；最后将定语从句译成"使中英两国可以在当今世界上共同努力"。

3. 原文第九句：It is that people around the world feel // that the interdependence of nations, // so long talked about by statesmen, // is today more than ever a concrete reality.

　　这个句子也比较长，包含一个强调语式，一个宾语从句，一个插入语成分，还有一个比较级。对于英语的强调语式，可用汉语的一般句式翻译，即把 it is ... that 省去不译，直接译为"这就是全世界的人们意识到"。其中"这就是"是指上面的"信息"，而不是强调。从句中 the interdependence of nations 这一部分，译为独立短句"国家之间是相互依赖的"。当然，这个短语也可以译为短语"国家之间的相互依赖",但我们主张能够译成短句的仍以译为短句为好,因为这样可以不用刻意考虑其后的成分,译员也就能够更灵活地处理后面的部分。插入语 so long talked about by statesmen 也可译成一个短句:"过去这只是政治家的话题"。最后带有比较级的系动词加表语部分 is today more than ever a concrete reality,译为:"现在却是比以往更加实在的现实"。这样顺译下来,难度并不是特别大。

三、实战练习

1 词汇与表达

请先熟悉以下词汇与表达,并适当地运用在视译中。

general debate	一般性辩论
General Assembly	联合国大会
Africa Steering Group	非洲指导小组
Secretariat	秘书处
accountable	负有责任的
Quartet Representative	四方代表
Myanmar	缅甸
debt relief	减免债务
Universal Declaration of Human Rights	《世界人权宣言》
tribunal	法庭
Rwanda	卢旺达
Sierra Leone	塞拉利昂
impunity	免除惩罚

2 实战课文

请在 15 分钟之内迅速阅读下面的讲话,了解大意。视译时要保持正常语速,译文要顺畅达意。

A Stronger UN for a Better World[1]

Ban Ki-moon

New York, 2007

It is a pleasure and an honor to be with you, at this opening of the general debate of our 62nd General Assembly. I expect the year ahead to be among the most challenging in our history. And I am sure that, together, we can make it one of the most successful.

We are off to a strong start. During the past week, we hosted a high-level meeting of the Africa Steering Group on our Millennium Development Goals—clear signal of an important priority. World leaders also met to discuss our way forward on the Middle East, Afghanistan, Darfur and Iraq. Yesterday we concluded a highly successful conference on climate change. Our goal was to galvanize our efforts, to coordinate our work under one roof—this roof of our United Nations—so that we fight global warming together, as one. This, in itself, is a signal accomplishment. It is a model of how I hope we can work together in the future.

Looking to the coming year, and beyond, we can foresee a daunting array of challenges to come. They are problems that respect no borders—that no country, big or small, rich or poor, can resolve on its own. More than ever, we live in an era of collective action. Often it seems as though everybody wants the UN to do everything. We cannot deliver everything, of course. But that cannot be an excuse for doing nothing. Hence the theme of these remarks: A Stronger United Nations for a Better World.

Our changing world needs a stronger UN. We all understand the importance of a strong, robust, empowered Secretariat. My vision is an administration focused on results—efficient, directed, pragmatic and accountable, an administration representing excellence, integrity and pride in serving the global good. To deliver on this vision, we must modernize ourselves. We need an internal climate change at the UN. We need to think freshly about how we do our work. Our main themes should be to simplify, rationalize and delegate. To deliver on the world's high expectations for us, we need to be faster, more flexible and mobile. We need to pay less attention to rhetoric, and more attention to results—to getting things done.

I place a very high priority on implementing the management reforms you have

---

1　原文参见 http://www.un.org/apps/news/infocus/sgspeeches/search_full.asp?statID=122。

previously approved to promote greater transparency, accountability and efficiency. **I welcome the progress we have made over the past nine months in streamlining our budget processes, crafting our Capital Master Plan and putting our financial house in order.** （句 1 ） I am especially grateful to the 102 governments that have paid their annual budget assessments in full.

Together, we successfully re-organized our peacekeeping operations, affecting more than 100,000 UN field personnel in 18 multinational missions. I plan to continue the effort by strengthening the Department of Political Affairs. We must become more proactive in responding to crises. Well-planned and executed preventive diplomacy can save many lives and forestall many tragedies—a core Charter responsibility of our UN.

I will leave no stone unturned to end the tragedy in Darfur. The government of Sudan must live up to its pledge to join comprehensive peace talks and implement a ceasefire. We must also move forward with the agreement that ended the long-running civil war between north and south and prepare for elections in 2009. The crisis in Darfur grew from many causes. Any enduring solution must address all of them—security, politics, resources, water, humanitarian and development issues. There, as elsewhere, we must deal with root causes of conflict, however complex and entangled.

Peace in the Middle East is vital to the stability of the region and the world. We know what is required: an end to violence, an end to occupation, the creation of a Palestinian State at peace with itself and Israel, and a comprehensive regional peace between Israel and the Arab world. With renewed leadership from the Arab world and the United States, coupled with the efforts of Quartet Representative Tony Blair, the elements for a renewed push for peace are being brought together.

We also sincerely hope that the Lebanese people through national reconciliation will be able to restore political and social stability by electing their new president in accordance with their constitutional process. （句 2 ）

Iraq has become the whole world's problem. With the new Security Council Resolution 1770, the UN has an important role in promoting political negotiation and national reconciliation, as well as in providing humanitarian assistance to the Iraqi people. But we recognize that the safety and security of UN staff is paramount.

In Afghanistan, we must work more effectively with our partners to deal with drug trafficking and the financing of terrorism.

We are closely following events in Myanmar. **We again urge the authorities in Myanmar to exercise utmost restraint, to engage without delay in dialog with all the relevant parties to the national reconciliation process on the issues of concern to the people of Myanmar.**（句 3） In this regard, my Special Advisor is expected to visit Myanmar very soon.

From my first day in office, I have stressed the importance of disarmament, as mandated most recently in the General Assembly's support for my proposal to establish an Office of Disarmament Affairs.（句 4） We must reinvigorate our efforts to stop the proliferation of weapons of mass destruction and related technology, and especially to prevent such material from falling into the hands of terrorists. I am encouraged by recent progress on the DPRK issue. I sincerely hope that forthcoming inter-Korean Summit meeting will create a historic momentum, to bring peace, security, and eventually a peaceful reunification of the Korean Peninsula. I am confident that we will reach a negotiated solution with the Islamic Republic of Iran. Our ultimate goal remains the complete elimination of weapons of mass destruction. If we fail, these weapons may one day eliminate us.

We at the UN must take the long view, in politics as in life. Even as we deal with the here and now, we must think about tomorrow. Yesterday, I spoke about climate change as a defining issue of our time. We all agreed. Now is the time for action. Let us go to Bali and make a breakthrough.

We also agreed that solutions to global warming cannot come at the expense of economic development—the second pillar of the UN's work. Issues of development and social equity cannot take a backseat to issues of peace and security. This year marks the midpoint for our Millennium Development Goals. We have had successes. Around the world, unprecedented numbers of people are lifting themselves out of poverty. Yet the rising tide of globalization has not lifted all boats. We see this most acutely in Africa, home to most of what one World Bank economist calls "the bottom billion" of the world's poor. We must pay careful attention to these nations with special needs. We must heed the voices of the world's poorest peoples, who too often go unheard. That is why I convened the MDG Africa Steering Group earlier this month, bringing together leaders of major multilateral development organizations.

Our MDGs remain achievable, so long as we help the poorest nations break free of the traps that ensnare them. Some of those traps relate to bad governance. Others to disease and poor health care. It is intolerable that HIV/AIDS continues as a modern-day scourge. It is intolerable that almost 10 million children die each year before their fifth birthday, mostly from such preventable diseases as malaria. It is a scar on the moral conscience of the world.

This is not to say we will do things that these countries should, and can, do for themselves. The "Asian Miracle" has shown that successful development owes much to smart choices and rigorous execution. For our part, we must try to make our multilateral development programs more effective and coherent, to better integrate our efforts in health, education, agriculture and infrastructure so as to deliver better results. For their part, donor nations must do more to deliver on their promises of aid, debt relief and market access. Open, fair and non-discriminatory trading and financial systems are critical to the future of every developing country, in Africa and elsewhere. That is why we must do our utmost to advance the Doha Development Agenda, with its emphasis on development and "aid for trade".

The third pillar of the UN, human rights, is codified in the *Universal Declaration of Human Rights*, which marks its 60th anniversary in 2008. The Human Rights Council must live up to its responsibilities as the torchbearer for human rights consistently and equitably around the world. I will strive to translate the concept of our responsibility to protect from words to deeds, to ensure timely action so that populations do not face genocide, ethnic cleansing and crimes against humanity. Our international tribunals continue their work, from Rwanda to Sierra Leone and, soon, Lebanon. The age of impunity is dead. Meanwhile, the UN's brave and exceptionally committed humanitarian aid workers do their best to save lives. They help protect civilian populations from the depredations of armed militias, children from starvation, women from shameful violence.

This year did not bring a natural disaster on the scale of the 2004 tsunami. But the intensity of floods, droughts and extreme weather, perhaps made worse by climate change, have brought pain and suffering to many millions. This, above all, is the UN's front line. We stand up to help those who cannot help themselves.

I am humbled, often, by the scale of the challenges before us. So much is expected of us. Delivering on those hopes, faithfully and effectively, will require great effort and discipline. Transforming the way the UN does business—shifting our focus to emphasize results rather than bureaucratic process—will take patience, perseverance and courage. The pendulum of history is swinging in our favor. Multilateralism is back. An increasingly interdependent world recognizes that the challenges of tomorrow are best dealt with through the UN. Indeed, they can only be dealt with through the UN. Thank you.

3 难句分析与视译处理

句1： I welcome the progress we have made over the past nine months in streamlining our budget processes, crafting our Capital Master Plan and putting our financial house in order.

笔译译文： 我高兴地看到，在过去九个月中，我们在精简预算程序、制定基本建设总计划和整治财务情况方面取得了进展。

视译译文：

断　　句	译　　文
I welcome the progress we have made	我高兴地看到我们的进展，
over the past nine months	这是在过去的九个月中取得的，
in streamlining our budget processes, crafting our Capital Master Plan	涉及精简预算程序、制定基本建设总计划
and putting our financial house in order.	以及整治财务等方面。

句2： We also sincerely hope that the Lebanese people through national reconciliation will be able to restore political and social stability by electing their new president in accordance with their constitutional process.

笔译译文： 我们也真诚希望，黎巴嫩人民能够通过民族和解，按照黎巴嫩宪法程序选举产生黎巴嫩新总统，恢复政治和社会稳定。

视译译文：

断　　句	译　　文
We also sincerely hope	我们也真诚希望，
that the Lebanese people through national reconciliation	黎巴嫩人民通过民族和解，

（待续）

262

（续上表）

断　句	译　文
will be able to restore political and social stability	能够恢复政治和社会稳定，
by electing their new president	为此，要选举新总统，
in accordance with their constitutional process.	选举要符合宪法程序。

句 3：　　We again urge the authorities in Myanmar to exercise utmost restraint, to engage without delay in dialog with all the relevant parties to the national reconciliation process on the issues of concern to the people of Myanmar.

笔译译文：　我们再次敦促缅甸当局在最大程度上实行克制，立即与缅甸民族和解进程有关的各方就缅甸人民所关心的问题进行对话。

视译译文：

断　句	译　文
We again urge the authorities in Myanmar	我们再次敦促缅甸当局
to exercise utmost restraint,	实行最大限度的克制，
to engage without delay in dialog	立即展开对话，
with all the relevant parties to the national reconciliation process	同所有与实现民族和解进程相关的各方
on the issues of concern to the people of Myanmar.	商议缅甸人民所关心的问题。

句 4：　　From my first day in office, I have stressed the importance of disarmament, as mandated most recently in the General Assembly's support for my proposal to establish an Office of Disarmament Affairs.

笔译译文：　我从就职第一天起，就在强调裁军的重要性。大会最近表示支持我提出的设立裁军事务厅的建议，再次确认了这一任务。

视译译文：

断 句	译 文
From my first day in office,	我从就职的第一天起，
I have stressed the importance of disarmament,	就在强调裁军的重要性。
as mandated most recently in the General Assembly's	这在最近的联合国大会上得以确认，
support for my proposal	支持我的建议，
to establish an Office of Disarmament Affairs.	同意建立裁军事务厅。

4 参考译文

构建更强有力的联合国，建设更美好的世界

潘基文

纽约，2007 年

很高兴并且很荣幸能和各位共同出席我们第六十二届大会一般性辩论的开幕式。我相信今后的一年将是我们历史上最具挑战的一年。同时我确信，我们一起努力，将能使这一年成为最成功的年份之一。

我们有了一个良好的开端。上星期，我们主办了千年发展目标非洲指导小组的高级别会议——这是一个明确的优先事项。世界领导人还举行了会议，讨论在中东、阿富汗、达尔富尔和伊拉克等问题上前进的道路。昨天，我们开了一次关于气候变化的极其成功的会议。我们的目标是振作我们的努力，在一个框架，即联合国的框架下协调我们的行动，以便我们团结如一地共同对付全球变暖问题。这本身就是一项伟大的事业。我希望我们将以这种方式在今后共同合作。

展望今后的一年和未来，我们可以看到一系列艰巨的挑战。这些问题是没有边界的，是任何国家，无论大小贫富，都不能够独力解决的。与以往相比，我们现在生活在一个更需要集体行动的时代。许多时候，好像是人人都要求联合国做所有的事情。当然，我们不可能事事都做出成果。但是，这不能成为一无所为的借口。因此，我讲话的主题就是：构建更强有力的联合国，建设更美好的世界。

　　我们这个不断变化的世界，需要一个更强有力的联合国。大家都知道，一个坚强有力，而且享有权能的秘书处的重要性。我的愿景是建立一个注重结果的行政机构，一个效率高、方向明、求实效、讲问责的行政机构，一个彰显优秀、诚信，以服务全球公益为荣的行政机构。为实现这一愿景，我们必须进行自我的现代化。我们联合国内部的气候需要变化。我们需要重新思考我们的工作方式。我们的主题应当是精简化、合理化和授权。为了不辜负世界对我们的高度期望，我们要变得更迅速、更灵活和更有流动性。我们要少讲豪言壮语，而更注重结果——更注重把事情做成。

　　我把实施大会先前核准的旨在提高透明度、加强问责制和提高效率的管理改革列为重中之重。我高兴地看到，在过去九个月中，我们在精简预算程序、制定基本建设总计划和整治财务情况方面取得了进展。我尤其感谢已足额缴付年度预算摊款的 102 国政府。

　　通过共同努力，我们成功改组了我们的维和行动，一共影响到 18 个多国特派团的 10 万多名联合国人员。我打算通过加强政治事务部来承续这一努力。我们在应对危机方面必须更加积极主动。周密计划和妥善执行的预防性外交能够挽救许多生命，防止许多悲剧的发生。这是宪章给联合国规定的核心职责之一。

　　我将竭尽全力结束达尔富尔悲剧。苏丹政府必须信守诺言，加入全面和平谈判，实行停火。我们也必须在结束南北长期内战的协定的基础上向前推进，并为 2009 年的选举做好准备。达尔富尔危机的发生，有很多原因。这一危机的任何持久解决办法，都必须解决所有这些问题——安全、政治、资源、水、人道主义、发展等各方面问题。同在其他地方一样，我们在这里必须解决导致冲突的根源问题，无论这些问题多么复杂，多么盘根错节。

　　中东和平对于该区域和全世界的稳定至关重要。我们知道需要的是什么：终止暴力，结束占领，建立一个内部和平且与以色列和平相处的巴勒斯坦国，以色列与阿拉伯各国实现全面区域和平。随着阿拉伯各国和美国重新发挥领头作用，加上四方代表托尼·布莱尔先生的积极努力，推动谋求和平新努力的要素正在形成。

　　我们也真诚希望，黎巴嫩人民能够通过民族和解，按照黎巴嫩宪法程序选举产生黎巴嫩新总统，恢复政治和社会稳定。

　　伊拉克现在已经成为全世界的问题。安全理事会最近通过第 1770 号决议，联合国据此能发挥重要作用，推动政治谈判和民族和解，以及为伊拉克人民提供人道主义援助。但我们认识到，联合国工作人员的安全和保障是首要的考虑。

在阿富汗，我们必须更有效地与我们的伙伴合作，解决贩运毒品和资助恐怖主义的问题。

我们密切关注缅甸的事态发展。我们再次敦促缅甸当局在最大程度上实行克制，立即与缅甸民族和解进程所有有关各方就缅甸人民所关心的问题进行对话。在这方面，预期我的特使不久将能访问缅甸。

我从就职的第一天起，就强调裁军的重要性。大会最近表示支持我提出的设立裁军事务厅的建议，再次确认了这一任务。我们必须注入新的活力，努力停止大规模杀伤性武器及相关技术的扩散，特别是防止这种材料落入恐怖分子手中。最近在朝鲜民主主义人民共和国问题上取得的进展使我很受鼓舞。我衷心希望即将举行的朝韩首脑会晤将为朝鲜半岛的和平、安全以及最终和平统一创造历史性势头。我深信我们将通过谈判与伊朗伊斯兰共和国达成解决办法。我们的最终目标仍然是彻底销毁大规模杀伤性武器。如果我们失败，有一天这些武器就会消灭我们。

对待政治，如同对待生活，我们联合国都必须把目光放长看远。当我们处理当前事务的时候，我们也必须放眼未来。我在昨天的讲话中说，气候变化是我们时代的一个决定性议题。我们大家都同意，现在正是采取行动的时机。让我们一起参加巴厘岛会议，创造一个突破。

我们也都同意，全球变暖问题的解决，不能以牺牲经济发展为代价。经济发展是联合国工作的第二根支柱。不能把发展与社会公平问题放在次要地位，认为没有和平与安全问题那么重要。今年是千年发展目标进程的中间点。我们已经取得了一些成功。世界各地有空前多的人摆脱了贫穷。但是，全球化的浪潮并没有使所有人都享受到水涨船高的好处。非洲的情况最为严重，那里住着被世界银行一位经济学家称为世界上最穷的"底层 10 亿人"的大多数。我们必须认真注意这些有特殊需要的国家。我们必须关注世界上最贫穷国家人民的呼声，因为他们往往是被忽视的人群。因此，我在本月早些时候召集了千年发展目标非洲指导小组，将主要多边发展组织的领导人汇聚一堂。

只要我们能够帮助那些最贫穷的国家脱离它们深陷的困境，我们的千年发展目标仍然是可以实现的。这些困境，有的是由于治理不善，还有则是疾病和恶劣的卫生保健所造成的。我们不能容忍艾滋病毒／艾滋病这一当代祸害的继续存在。同样不可容忍的是，每年有将近 1,000 万儿童在五岁生日之前死亡，大部分死于疟疾之类可以预防的疾病。这是世界道德良心上的一道疤痕。

这并不是说，这些国家应该也能够自己做的事情，也要由我们来越俎代庖。"亚洲奇迹"证明，发展之所以能够成功，大多归因于明智的选择和严格的执行。从我们自己来说，我们必须设法使我们的多边发展方案更加有效和连贯，将我们在卫生、教育、农业、基础设施各方面的努力更好地结合起来，以期做出更好的成果。对捐助国而言，他们必须作出更多努力，履行在援助、减免债务和市场准入方面的承诺。开放、公平和非歧视性的贸易与金融体系，对非洲及其他地区每一个发展中国家的未来都至关重要。这就是为什么我们必须竭尽全力，推动以发展和"贸易援助"为重点的多哈发展议程。

联合国的第三大支柱——人权，已被写成庄严的《世界人权宣言》。2008年是该《宣言》通过的 60 周年纪念。人权理事会必须高举人权火炬，始终如一、不偏不倚地在全世界履行其职责。我将努力把我们的保护责任理念从言词化为行动，确保及时采取行动，使各地人群免遭种族灭绝、种族清洗或危害人类的罪行之害。我们的各个国际法庭，从卢旺达到塞拉利昂，正在继续进行工作，很快也会在黎巴嫩开展工作。有罪不罚的时代已经终结。与此同时，英勇无畏、矢志不移的联合国人道主义工作人员，全力拯救生命。这些人员协助保护平民使之免受武装民兵掠夺，保护儿童使之免受饥饿，保护妇女使之免受可耻暴力的侵犯。

今年没有发生 2004 年海啸那样大规模的自然灾害。但洪水、旱灾和极端天气，或许因气候变化而变得更为凶猛，给千百万人民带来痛苦和磨难。这是联合国工作的前线。我们一定向那些无力自救的人伸出援手。

面对我们面前各种艰巨的挑战，我常常感到力不从心。人们对我们的期望很高，要忠实、高效地实现这些期望，就需要我们十分的努力和自律。我们必须改变联合国的办事方式，要更注重结果而非官僚程序，这需要耐心、坚持和勇气。历史的钟摆正在荡向对我们有利的方向。多边主义再次兴起。一个日趋相互依存的世界认识到，明天的各种挑战，最好是通过联合国来处理。事实上，也只能通过联合国来处理。谢谢。

四、自主训练

请在 15 分钟之内迅速阅读下面的讲话，了解大意。学生可组成对子练习，互相监控对视译技巧的掌握情况、视译质量和现场表现，或以边视译边录音的形式进行个人练习。视译时要保持正常语速，译文要顺畅达意。如遇难句，可在首次视译后参照"实战练习"中难句分析与视译处理的方法进行练习，找出解决方法。

The Hong Kong Special Administrative Region
at 10 Years—an American Perspective

US Consul-General James B. Cunningham

2007

It is a great pleasure to be here today. I want to thank the Better Hong Kong Foundation for inviting me to share an American perspective on Hong Kong after 10 years as a Special Administrative Region of China. I am particularly pleased to be addressing a Better Hong Kong Foundation audience. The Foundation was created in 1995 by a group of Hong Kong's influential business and community leaders for the expressive purpose of enhancing public confidence in Hong Kong's future. You have done good work, and I am pleased that the United States enjoys a close relationship with you in support of that goal.

As you may know, I am a newcomer to Hong Kong with a fresh perspective. But my first exposure to the remarkable road you have been on came more than 20 years ago. My wife and I were befriended in Europe by a Chinese couple from Hong Kong who were living abroad temporarily. Even then they were greatly concerned about Hong Kong's return to China, and they eventually decided to leave beforehand. Two or three years before 1997, there was a surge of concern in the international press over the territory's future: dire predictions and expressions of worry were the common currency of public discussion. In June of 1995, Fortune magazine ran this cover story: "The Death of Hong Kong". It was in that business- and investment-unfriendly climate that the Foundation was created to help restore confidence in the territory.

In looking at this magazine cover 12 years later, I recall Mark Twain's comment when someone told him that his obituary had been published in New York. He responded, "The reports of my death are greatly exaggerated." Hong Kong too has exceeded expectations, and the Better Hong Kong Foundation has helped build greater international understanding between East and West by promoting understanding of Hong Kong, its relationship with the Chinese mainland, and the unique "one country, two systems" model. In discussing Hong Kong on the occasion of the 10-year anniversary of the establishment of the Special Administrative Region, I hope to contribute to the mutual understanding the Foundation seeks to develop.

Let me begin by saying that looking back over the last 10 years, the United States believes that "one country, two systems" has been a success for China, especially for Hong Kong...

I would also like to state unequivocally that my government wants Hong Kong and the "one country, two systems" model to succeed. Before and since 1997, the implementation of this historic experiment has been of great interest to the international community. After 10 years, we continue to have great hopes for Hong Kong's future. This is more than a thing of mere words, because the US has a measurable stake in Hong Kong's success. As Asia's world city, Hong Kong plays an important role which benefits China, the US and many others in the globalized, interdependent 21st century. America itself has no small stake in Hong Kong. It is our 15th largest export market. 60,000 US citizens reside here, and a million more Americans visit each year. 1,200 US firms have local and regional offices here—which, by the way, employ 10% of Hong Kong's workforce. US direct investment in Hong Kong totals 38 billion US dollars.

Looking back over the past 10 years, Hong Kong, like much of the rest of Asia, has faced its share of trials. But Hong Kong has been able to rebound—decidedly so. Economic growth over the last three years has been strong (GDP grew by 6.5% in 2006), and polls show the Hong Kong people are generally optimistic about the future and about their role in China. The United States shares that optimism and congratulates Hong Kong on being on the path to success. We have strong expectations that Hong Kong will continue on that high road.

There is good reason for this positive forecast. After 10 years of Chinese sovereignty, Hong Kong remains the most open and developed part of China. The central government has generally respected its commitment to maintain a high degree of autonomy for Hong Kong, and has acted over the years in concrete ways to support Hong Kong's economic development and prosperity. The Closer Economic Partnership Arrangement, the introduction and expansion of the individual visitor scheme, the growing cooperation within the Pan-Pearl River Delta region and the liberalization of rules on the use of Renminbi in business and finance remain important elements of Hong Kong's past and future economic success. Hong Kong's role as an international financial center has strengthened in the last 10 years. Hong Kong's market capitalization is now three and a half times what it was in 1997. The territory is the number one source of capital for China, raising 43 billion US dollars in 2006. Hong Kong remains an important economy which exercises active membership in the World Trade Organization and in the Asia-Pacific Economic Cooperation (APEC) forum.

Once again this year, for the 13th straight year, the Heritage Foundation recognized the Hong Kong SAR[1] as having the highest level of economic freedom in the world. Just last week, the Japan Center for Economic Research ranked Hong Kong first out of 50 world economies in 2006 in the areas of competitiveness, internationalization, and finance.

Importantly, though, Hong Kong serves as an example of more than just an economic success story. Hong Kong remains a model Chinese society that observes the rule of law, follows free and fair market principles, allows unfettered entrepreneurial activity, and respects freedom and human rights, including religious freedom. Its political system is evolving, and public participation in civic affairs is growing. Hong Kong has survived and thrived over the years by repeatedly adapting to changing economic and political circumstances, and redefining itself. It must continue to do so to remain stable, prosperous and competitive. In a rapidly changing global economy, the status quo is not enough.

...

That said, our evaluation of the progress over the past 10 years is positive, and we are optimistic about the next 10 years—as Americans usually are. Hong Kong is an open, vibrant, and sophisticated society. It has much to contribute to China, and to offer to the rest of the world as an international city. People here continue to anticipate the future, and to plan for change. I have been fortunate to make dozens of Hong Kong friends in my time here; they are proudly Chinese, and see no contradiction between love of their country and the pursuit of Hong Kong's economic and political development. "One country, two systems" is working, despite the earlier doubts and the predictable difficulties. There is no doubt in my mind that it can continue to do so. The United States is a friend with a sincere hope for and strong interest in Hong Kong's success, and, more broadly, China's success.

Let me close by presenting a more positive bookend to my earlier, pessimistic visual aid. Here is a more recent graphic: the March 2007 *Time* magazine cover touting "A Vision for Hong Kong". The United States' vision for Hong Kong's future is bright indeed. We see a Hong Kong that is part of a prosperous, stable, and confident China, and which contributes to its country and the world by continuing to

---

1   Special Administrative Region.

be a leading light in economic freedoms, civil liberties and respect for human rights. We see a Hong Kong that continues to adapt and respond to changes. We envision a Hong Kong that draws strength from its Chinese heritage as well as the Western culture, a Hong Kong that has found its own voice, and is a positive, dynamic force in China's development on all fronts.

第12单元

It 句式的视译

基本技巧：
• 将以 It 作为先行主语的句子译为汉
  语的"是"字句。

一、技巧讲解：It 句式的视译

我们这里所说的 It 句式，是指以 It 做主语的句子。这类句子在英语中很多，但基本上分为两种。第一种是 It 有具体的意义，比如 It is raining（天下雨了）。第二种是 It 没有具体的意义，只是起到形式上的主语作用，亦称为先行主语 It。（张道真，2007：480-481）我们在这里主要讨论第二种，因为这种句子会以 It 代替真实主语，而将真实主语移到句子的后面。比如 It is our duty to serve the people，这里的真实主语是 to serve the people 这个短语。

以 It 作形式主语的句子有三种基本形态。第一，不定式是真实主语。比如上面所举的例子。第二，动名词是真实主语，比如，It is no use arguing with him. 第三，从句作真实主语，比如，It happened that we were all at home that day.

以 It 作形式主语的句子，往往其真实主语比较长，这也正是英语句子要使用一个先行主语 It 的原因之一。这种句子在笔译中并不困难，只要按照句子的原意翻译过来，并将句子结构做较大的调整，即将真实主语调整到句首，取消先行主语 It。但是在视译中，由于真实主语较长，而在汉语中没有这种先行主语的句式，所以，翻译上会有一定的困难。这种困难主要来自语序调整。比如 It is easy to criticize others. 我们一般译为："批评别人是容易的。"（张道真，2007：480）这个句子的翻译是将不定式作为真实主语的部分置于句首。如果我们考虑到视译的时间问题和语序原则，就会将这个句子译为："容易的是批评别人。"

　　再考虑上文中举的几个例子，都可以用这种带"是"的汉语句子翻译出来。It is our duty to serve the people. 这个句子我们可以译为："我们的责任是为人民服务。"It is no use arguing with him. 译为："没有用处的是与他进行辩论。"It happened that we were all at home that day. 译为："碰巧的是那天我们都在家。"

　　所以，在视译中，以 It 作形式主语引导的句子在大部分情况下，可以译为汉语的"是"字句式。下面我们举几个典型的例子说明以 It 为先行主语的句子的视译方法。

例 1：　　It is important not to be easily satisfied.
译文 1：　不要轻易满足是很重要的。
译文 2：　重要的是不要轻易满足。
【讲解】　这是一个以 It 为先行主语的句子，谓语是形容词，真实主语是动词不定式。我们将先行主语和谓语译为"重要的是"，然后将真实主语依次译出。

例 2：　　It is our privilege to visit your country.
译文 1：　访问贵国是一大荣幸。（张道真，2007：480）
译文 2：　非常荣幸的是能够访问贵国。
【讲解】　这是一个"it is + 名词"的句式，笔译将其置于句尾。在视译中，我们将 It is our privilege 译为"非常荣幸的是"，其后依次译出。

例 3：　　It is a pity that he does not swim.
译文 1：　他不会游泳，真遗憾。（薄冰，2006：566）
译文 2：　遗憾的是他不会游泳。
【讲解】　这也是一个"It is + 名词"的句式，后面跟一个作为真实主语的从句，译法同上。许多英语句子是用先行主语 It 引导的。下面列出这类句子的基本句式：

　　1）It is + 名词：It is a pity / a shame / an honor / a good thing, …

　　2）It is + 形容词：It is clear / important / good / doubtful / understood / ridiculous / absurd, …

　　3）It + 动词：It doesn't matter / makes no difference, …

　　在视译中，处理这类句子有一个规则，就是将先行主语及谓语照原来语序先行译出，然后以"是"与后面的真实主语连接。上面我们举的三个例子，都是采用了这种方法。当 It 后面的谓语是形容词或名词的时候，尤其如此。汉语的"是"字句在视译中十分有用，可以比较灵活地与后面的部分连接，使句子不但能够按照原来的语序顺译，也更符合汉语习惯。我们再举几个例子加以说明。

例 4：　It is important that we should speak politely.
译文 1：我们说话要有礼貌，这是很重要的。（薄冰，2006：374）
译文 2：重要的是，我们说话要有礼貌。

例 5：　It is strange to see so many people are doing the same thing.
译文 1：看到这么多人都在做同一件事情，真是很奇怪。
译文 2：奇怪的是，看到这么多人都在做同一件事情。

例 6：　It is necessary that English majors speak English every day.
译文 1：英语专业的学生要天天讲英语，这是很有必要的。
译文 2：很有必要的是，英语专业的学生要天天讲英语。

例 7：　It is a shame that they have lost the game.
译文 1：他们输掉了比赛，真是遗憾。
译文 2：遗憾的是，他们输掉了比赛。

　　还有一类 It 引导的句子，就是 It is said/reported/rumored 等。这类句子可以译为"所说的是"、"所报道的是"、"所言传的是"，但通常使用"据"字句来翻译更符合汉语习惯，如"据说"、"据报"、"据传"等。这种类型的句子笔译与视译相同。比如 It is reported that as many as 100,000 people joined in the demonstration. 它的笔译和视译都译为："据报，有 10 万人参加了示威游行。"
　　处理以先行词 It 引导的句子，关键是将汉语中的"是"字句用好。具体来讲就是不译 It，而是将它后面具有实际意义的词先行译出，然后用"是"将其与后面的部分连接起来，按顺序译出。

二、语段视译

1 词汇与表达
在进行语段视译前，请先预习以下词汇与表达。

demo	样碟
big label	大公司
equity	股本
platinum	白金销量（即 100 万张唱片的销量）
debut	首次演出
deliverance	释放

2 视译语段

请在 3 分钟之内迅速阅读下面的语段，了解大意，然后结合所学要点进行视译练习。视译时要保持正常语速，译文要顺畅达意。

A London-based pop singer is raising funds to kick-start his career by selling shares in himself on Internet auction site eBay. In just three days, Shayan has raised 9,000 pounds from buyers in London, New York and Toronto. Shayan insists the scheme is a way of avoiding the traditional route of sending demos to major labels. "The most difficult thing is to get people's attention," he says. Speculative buyers are offered the chance to invest 3,000 pounds in return for a 0.25% equity share in anything the 27-year-old singer-songwriter earns over his entire career. The shares remain valid for 70 years after the artist's death, and can be transferred to the buyer's children. "People are investing on risk," admits Sahyan. "But it's a very sensible investment proposition. Over the past five years, 300 albums have broken platinum." Aside from the eBay sales, the singer has secured some impressive backing. His debut album, *Deliverance*, is released on his own label with distribution through Universal. A private investor has spent 100,000 pounds on recording and marketing it. （摘自《英语学习》，2005 年第 12 期，第 7 至 8 页）

原译文：伦敦流行歌手沙洋正在为启动职业生涯筹资，办法是在拍卖网站 eBay 上出售"自我股份"。不过三天功夫，他已经从伦敦、纽约和多伦多的买家那里筹到了 9,000 英镑。沙洋坚称，这种办法可以让他绕过传统路线，不用向那些大唱片公司寄送样碟。他说："最难的事情是引起人们的注意。"沙洋给投机买家们提供了机会。3,000 英镑的投入就可以换到这位 27 岁的歌手兼歌曲写手整个职业生涯所有收入的 0.25%。所获股份在这位歌手死后 70 年依然有效，买家还可以把它转到自己孩子名下。"人们的投资是有风险的，"沙洋承认，"但这是一桩相当明智的投资主意。过去五年里，有 300 张专辑突破了白金销量（即 100 万张的销量）。"除了从 eBay 取得的收入之外，这位歌手还从别处得到了一些相当强劲的支持。他已经用自己的品牌推出了首张专辑《释放》，由环球公司负责发行。一名私人投资者为专辑的录制和发行投入了 10 万英镑。（冰尘译）

3　视译译文

	断　句	译　文
1	A London-based pop singer is raising funds	有位伦敦的流行歌手正在筹集资金，
2	to kick-start his career	以便开始自己的职业生涯，
3	by selling shares in himself	方法是出售自我股份，
4	on Internet auction site eBay.	并且是在拍卖网 eBay 上出售。
5	In just three days,	仅仅用了三天，
6	Shayan has raised 9,000 pounds	这位叫沙洋的歌手就筹到 9,000 英镑，
7	from buyers in London, New York and Toronto.	买家来自伦敦、纽约和多伦多。
8	Shayan insists	沙洋坚持说，
9	the scheme is a way of avoiding the traditional route	这样做可以避开传统的方式，
10	of sending demos to major labels.	不必将样碟送到大唱片公司。
11	"The most difficult thing is	"最困难的事情
12	to get people's attention,"	就是引起人们的注意，"
13	he says.	沙洋这样说。
14	Speculative buyers are offered the chance	投机买家因此得到了机会，

（待续）

（续上表）

断 句	译 文
15	to invest 3,000 pounds	他们投资 3,000 英镑，
16	in return for a 0.25% equity share in anything	就可以得到 0.25% 的回报，
17	the 27-year-old singer-songwriter	也就是这位 27 岁的歌手兼歌曲作者
18	earns over his entire career.	整个职业生涯所有收入的 0.25%。
19	The shares remain valid	股份会长期有效，
20	for 70 years after the artist's death,	在歌手去世后 70 年内仍然如此，
21	and can be transferred to the buyer's children.	还可以转到购买者子女名下。
22	"People are investing on risk,"	"人们的投资是有风险的，"
23	admits Sahyan.	沙洋承认这一点。
24	"But it's a very sensible investment proposition.	"但这是一个十分明智的投资决定。
25	Over the past five years,	在过去五年里，
26	300 albums have broken platinum."	300 张专辑突破了白金销量。"
27	Aside from the eBay sales,	除了从 eBay 得到的收入之外，
28	the singer has secured some impressive backing.	这位歌手还得到了强有力的支持。
29	His debut album, *Deliverance*,	他的首张专辑名为《释放》，
30	is released on his own label	是用自己的品牌推出的，
31	with distribution through Universal.	发行人是环球公司。
32	A private investor has spent 100,000 pounds	有位私人投资者投入了 10 万英镑，
33	on recording and marketing it.	录制和发行了这张专辑。

4　视译点评

1. 原文第二句：In just three days, // Shayan has raised 9,000 pounds // from buyers in London, New York and Toronto.

　　原译文把后置状语 from buyers in London, New York and Toronto 译成状语"从伦敦、纽约和多伦多的买家那里"，置于谓语和宾语"筹到了 9,000 英镑"之前。视译时，从 from 处另译一个分句，按照原文语序，译为"买家来自伦敦、纽约和多伦多"。

2. 原文第三句：Shayan insists // the scheme is a way of avoiding the traditional route // of sending demos to major labels.

　　视译时，可译成三个分句，其中第三个部分的介词短语 of sending demos to major labels 作为前面 avoid 的宾语的一部分，要增添表示否定意思的词"不必"，使前后意思连贯，即："不必将样碟送到大唱片公司"。

3. 原文第五句：Speculative buyers are offered the chance // to invest 3,000 pounds // in return for a 0.25% equity share in anything // the 27-year-old singer-songwriter // earns over his entire career.

　　此句较长，断句后第三、四、五个类意群不易处理。原译文把 anything 引导的后置定语从句译作汉语前置定语："这位 27 岁的歌手兼歌曲写手整个职业生涯所有收入的"，以此来限定 0.25%。视译要避免作这样大的语序调整，因此，第三个类意群视译时可译成："就能得到 0.25% 的回报"，然后在译第四个类意群时添加"也就是"，使这部分成为前一分句的解释："也就是这位 27 岁的歌手兼歌曲作者整个职业生涯所有收入的 0.25%"。

三、实战练习

1　词汇与表达

　　请先熟悉以下词汇与表达，并适当地运用在视译中。

Davos	达沃斯（瑞士地名）
hang in the balance	未定，处于危急中
Chancellor Merkel	默克尔总理（德国）
multilateralism	多边主义

Gleneagles	格伦伊格尔斯庄园
G8 Summit	八国集团峰会
Kofi Annan	科菲·安南（第七任联大秘书长）
emission	排放
carbon dependence	对含碳燃料的依赖
quantum	总量
quotient	份额
governor	州长（美国）
binding cap	上限
atavistic	古老的
proselytize	说服他人转变宗教或政治信仰
buffet	冲击
failed state	失败国家
abyss	深渊
Gaza	加沙地带
the West Bank	约旦河西岸

2 实战课文

请在 15 分钟之内迅速阅读下面的讲话，了解大意。视译时要保持正常语速，译文要顺畅达意。

Speech to the World Economic Forum[1] (Excerpt 1)
Tony Blair
Davos, 2007

Despite the multiple challenges we face in the world today, I am optimistic. Mind you, in my job, you have to be. It is true that each of the three issues—world trade, climate change, Africa—that have dominated Davos, hangs in the balance. But on each, there is progress that would have been unimaginable even a short time back. Let me briefly state where I think we are on each issue and then give a broader context for my optimism; and end with an analysis of what we have to do.

On the WTO, within the past few days I have held discussions with President Bush, President Lula and Chancellor Merkel. We had a great discussion with trade

---

1　原文参见 http://www.weforum.org/pdf/AM_2007/blair.pdf。

Ministers under Pascal Lamy's expert eye yesterday. "Cautious optimism" was how it was described. I think it is now more likely than not, though by no means certain, that we will reach a deal within the next few months. Countries are moving closer together; there is a recognition of political energy and drive; and an increased recognition of the dire consequences of failure. A trade deal would be a big boost to the notion of multilateralism; help the world's poorest escape their poverty; and achieve an impact on overall trade and business, three times the amount of the last trade round. **This is a critical priority for me in the coming period and that determination, I am pleased to say, is shared by the other major players in the negotiation. (句 1)**

Of course Africa would be a central beneficiary of such a deal. It is sometimes too easy to be pessimistic about Africa. But just think of what progress there has been. HIV/AIDs treatment now being given to 1.6 million. $100 billion of debt wiped out, enabling countries like Tanzania to transform primary education. Fifty democratic elections in Africa in the last five years. And six major wars have ended. We made commitments, not least on aid at the Gleneagles G8 Summit in July 2005. We must honor them. **We will have the first meeting of the Africa Progress Panel which will monitor our commitments under Kofi Annan's leadership in Berlin later this year. (句 2)**

The other topic at the top of the Gleneagles agenda was climate change. Kyoto was an extraordinary achievement, over 100 countries coming to an agreement with profound implications for their future economic growth. But in reality, even if implemented—and Britain is one of the few nations that will hit, indeed exceed our Kyoto targets—it would only stabilize emissions. In truth, we need them cut, probably by an order of 60% by 2050—something we have now set as a UK domestic target. **Moreover, whatever we do—Britain accounts for around 2% of total emissions—any agreement that does not have binding commitments from America, China and India is not one that can deliver. (句 3)**

Fortunately I believe we are, potentially, on the verge of a breakthrough. Chancellor Merkel is providing excellent G8 leadership. China and India are participating constructively in the "G8+5" process Gleneagles established. They know that they will suffer if the environment degrades further. They have every imperative to be part of a deal, provided it is one that allows them to grow their economies so that they can spread the prosperity they are creating to the millions in those countries still in poverty.

And the mood in the US is in the process of a quantum shift. The President's State of the Union address built on his "addiction to oil" speech last year and set the first US targets for a reduction in petrol consumption. Many individual American states—notably California, with whose Governor I signed a bilateral agreement on this subject last year—are setting targets for reducing emissions and taking far-reaching action to achieve them. American businesses—including many of their major power companies—have become advocates of a binding cap and trade system.

The German G8 Presidency gives us an opportunity to agree at least the principles of a new binding international agreement to come into effect when the Kyoto Protocol expires in 2012;（句 4）but one which is more radical than Kyoto and more comprehensive, one which this time, includes all the major countries of the world. It is a prize of tantalizing significance and I think it is possible.

So across all three issues, there are signs of hope. But this is part of a bigger shift in the politics of the global community. It is in this shift that the real possibilities of progress lie. What is really happening is that nations—even the most great—are realizing that they cannot pursue their narrow national interests without invoking broader global values. They are obliged to recognize that interdependence is the defining characteristic of the early 21st century world.

These three topics which have dominated Davos in 2007 are all global in their impact, their political relevance and in their prospective solutions. The Shifting Power Equation, the title of Davos this year, is in part, obviously, about emerging new powers; but it is equally about the fact that power over global issues can only be effectively wielded today by global alliances, based on global values.

There is also the curious mix of moral cause and strategic interest. We know we have a clear interest in combating climate change; but we feel it too, as a moral duty to successive generations as well as our own. Business is here in Davos not simply to talk about commerce, industrial trends, competitive challenges, but also about its role in tackling the great issues of the day. It has moved way beyond traditional notions of corporate responsibility. Business believes that it, too, has a strategic interest in the moral cause.

The world today is in a kind of perpetual global conversation. Campaigns are begun and intensified almost instantly. Tragedy or injustice, like war, leaps into our living rooms, assaulting our senses, bringing us to a judgment on events that may be thousands of miles away but of which we feel a part. This can happen in a malign way, as when an atavistic terrorist ideology uses the Internet to recruit or proselytize; or in a benign way, as the magnificent Live Aid showed in awakening the conscience of the world over Africa. Either way, it is a reality and it has a profound impact. Individuals become part of mass movements for change and action. Political leaders find that the time quotient between foreign and domestic affairs alters dramatically. Business gets involved in politics, not as partisans of a political party, but as important actors in global debate.

Above all, nations find that they need to confront and deal with challenges that simply do not admit of resolution without powerful alliances of other nations. And every nation, even the most powerful, is obliged to find such alliances or find their own interests buffeted and diminished. That is why we call it interdependence. It is the ultimate joining together of self-interest and community interest. Afghanistan was a failed state, its people living in misery and poverty but in days gone by it would have stayed that way without the world much noticing. September 11th brought it to our notice in the most unforeseen but catastrophic way. Look how the world has changed because of it. We know Africa's plight is shameful in a world of plenty. But I have never shrunk from confessing another motive. I believe if we let Somalia or Sudan slip further into the abyss, the effect of their fall will not stay within their region, never mind their nation. **I will argue for the presence of peace in Palestine on its own terms; but there is no question that its absence has consequences on the streets of cities in Britain amongst people who have never been near Gaza or the West Bank.**（句 5）

And, of course, there is climate change. Assume even a possibility of its threat being real. It would be madness not to act to prevent its realization—just as a precaution. Its challenge is the supreme expression of interdependence. America and China, even if they had no other reason for a relationship and they have many, would need one simply for this alone. To this add economic globalization, which offers, in general, such immense opportunity but whose effects, in particular, can be random and savage. So just take these three issues: climate change, Africa and world trade. Work out what is at stake: the future of the planet, the death or life of millions of people every year, the ability to spread the life chances of globalization, the single greatest economic engine of our time, more evenly.

3 难句分析和视译处理

句1： This is a critical priority for me in the coming period and that determination, I am pleased to say, is shared by the other major players in the negotiation.

笔译译文： 在今后的一段时期内这将成为我工作的重中之重。我很高兴参与谈判的其他主要各方与我有着相同的决心。

视译译文：

断　句	译　文
This is a critical priority for me	这是我工作的重中之重
in the coming period	今后的一段时期内都是如此。
and that determination,	我有决心，
I am pleased to say,	也很高兴看到，
is shared by the other major players	其他的主要参与各方也有同样的决心
in the negotiation.	共同搞好谈判。

句2： We will have the first meeting of the Africa Progress Panel which will monitor our commitments under Kofi Annan's leadership in Berlin later this year.

笔译译文： 今年晚些时候，在柏林我们将在科菲·安南的领导下举行第一次非洲进步专题研究会，监督我们履行承诺的情况。

视译译文：

断　句	译　文
We will have the first meeting	我们将召开首次会议
of the Africa Progress Panel	也就是非洲进步小组的会议，
which will monitor our commitments	来监督我们履行承诺的情况。
under Kofi Annan's leadership	会议由科菲·安南召集，
in Berlin later this year.	今年晚些时候在柏林举行。

句3： Moreover, whatever we do—Britain accounts for around 2% of total emissions—any agreement that does not have binding commitments from America, China and India is not one that can deliver.

笔译译文： 另外，不论英国采取什么措施，英国只占全球排放量的 2%。任何没有美国、中国、印度承诺履行的条约都不会产生实际效果。

视译译文：

断　句	译　文
Moreover,	另外，
whatever we do—	不论英国采取什么措施——
Britain accounts for around 2% of total emissions—	英国毕竟只占全球排放量的约 2%——
any agreement	任何协议，
that does not have binding commitments	如果缺少约束性的承诺，
from America, China and India	缺少美国、中国和印度的承诺，
is not one that can deliver.	就不会有任何效果。

句 4： The German G8 Presidency gives us an opportunity to agree at least the principles of a new binding international agreement to come into effect when the Kyoto Protocol expires in 2012.

笔译译文： 在德国担任 G8 轮值主席国期间，我们有机会至少就一项新的具有约束力的国际协议的原则部分达成一致。该协议将在《京都议定书》于 2012 年到期后正式生效。

视译译文：

断　句	译　文
The German G8 Presidency	德国担任 G8 轮值主席国，
gives us an opportunity	给了我们一个机会
to agree at least the principles	至少能够就原则达成一致，
of a new binding international agreement	以形成新的具有约束力的国际协议，
to come into effect	新协议的生效时间是在
when the Kyoto Protocol expires in 2012.	《京都议定书》2012 年到期之后。

句5： I will argue for the presence of peace in Palestine on its own terms; but there is no question that its absence has consequences on the streets of cities in Britain amongst people who have never been near Gaza or the West Bank.

笔译译文： 我赞成为巴勒斯坦按其自身要求实现和平，但毫无疑问，缺乏和平的巴勒斯坦也会影响到英国大街上那些从未去过加沙地带或约旦河西岸的民众。

视译译文：

断　句	译　文
I will argue	我赞成，
for the presence of peace in Palestine	在巴勒斯坦实现和平，
on its own terms；	要依照巴勒斯坦自己的要求去做。
but there is no question	但毫无疑问，
that its absence has consequences	没有和平就会造成危害，
on the streets of cities in Britain amongst people	会危及到英国城市大街上的平民，
who have never been near Gaza or the West Bank.	虽然他们从未到过加沙地带或约旦河西岸一带。

4 参考译文

世界经济论坛上的讲话（节选 1）

托尼·布莱尔

达沃斯，2007 年

尽管当今世界面临诸多挑战，我依然乐观。身为首相，我也必须乐观。的确，达沃斯的三大主要议题，世界贸易、气候变化、非洲，每一个都充满了变数。但是，我们在每一个问题上都取得了不久前还无法想象的进展。请让我先简要地谈谈我对每个问题的进展的看法，然后说明让我乐观的大背景，最后分析一下我们应采取的措施。

关于世贸组织，在过去的几天里我与布什总统、卢拉总统和默克尔总理进行了讨论。我们昨天与各贸易部长以及该问题的专家帕斯卡尔·拉米一起展开了很好的讨论。可以用"谨慎的乐观"来描述我们的心态。我认为现在很可能——当然不是说绝对会——在接下来的几个月内达成一项协议。各国间的分歧正在缩小，政治力量正重新开始发挥作用。人们也更清楚地认识到该进程如若失败会产生怎样的可怕后果。如能达成贸易协议，将极大促进多边主义的发展，帮助世界最穷苦的人们摆脱贫困，对整个贸易和商业产生积极影响，其成果会是上一轮世贸谈判的三倍。在今后的一段时期内这将成为我工作的重中之重。我很高兴参与谈判的其他主要各方与我有着相同的决心。

当然，非洲将成为这一协议的主要受益者。有时我们很轻易就对非洲持悲观态度。但想想我们取得的进展吧。160 万人已得到艾滋病毒／艾滋病治疗。1,000 亿美元债务被免除。这使坦桑尼亚等国能够改善其初等教育。非洲过去五年内共举行了 50 次民主选举，结束了六场战争。我们做出了承诺，特别是 2005 年 7 月在（苏格兰"鹰谷"）格伦伊格尔斯庄园举行的八国峰会上做出的提供援助的承诺。我们必须履行这些承诺。今年晚些时候，在柏林我们将在科菲·安南的领导下举行第一次非洲进步专题研究会，监督我们履行承诺的情况。

格伦伊格尔斯峰会的议程表上的另一个首要议题就是气候变化。《京都议定书》是一项伟大的成就。100 多个国家达成了对他们的未来发展有着深远影响的协议。但现实中，该协议即使得到落实也只能使排放量保持稳定，不再上升，而英国是为数不多的会真正达到并超越《京都议定书》目标的国家之一。事实上，我们必须减少排放量，到 2050 年前要大约减少 60%——这已被设为英国国内目标。不过，不论英国采取什么措施，英国只占全球排放量的 2%。任何没有美国、中国、印度参与的约束性条约都不会产生实际效果。

幸运的是，我相信我们很有可能即将取得突破。默克尔总理担任八国集团轮值主席以来工作非常出色。中国和印度积极地参与了格伦伊格尔斯峰会建立的"G8+5"对话。中印两国知道，如果环境进一步恶化，他们也将深受其害。因此，只要能让两国的经济继续发展，使其创造的繁荣能够惠及国内上百万贫困人民，中印两国就有参与这一进程的迫切需要。

美国民众的态度正在发生实质性的转变。去年布什总统的国情咨文以美国有"石油之瘾"为主题，而今年的国情咨文第一次设定了减少石油使用的目标。在美国，许多州都在设定减少排放量的具体目标并为实现完成这些目标采取意义深远的行动。尤其是加利福尼亚州，去年我曾与其州长签署了关于该问题的双边协议。美国商业——包括许多重要的电力公司——也倡导设立有约束力的温室气体减排最高限额并建立相关的交易机制。

在德国担任 G8 轮值主席国期间，我们有机会至少就一项新的具有约束力的国际协议的原则部分达成一致。该协议将在《京都议定书》于 2012 年到期后正式生效。但它比《京都议定书》动作更大，更全面。参与者将包括所有主要国家。这将是了不起的成就，而且我相信这是可能做到的。

因此，这三个问题都有希望得到解决。这是国际社会政治变化的一部分，真正的进展可能正伴随着变化到来。事实上，各国——甚至最强大的国家——都逐步意识到如果不接受更为广泛的全球价值观，就不可能谋求本国狭隘的国家利益。他们必须认识到互相依存是 21 世纪初世界的首要特征。

这三大主导着 2007 年达沃斯论坛的议题影响着全球，其政治影响和未来的解决方案也关乎全世界。"变化中的权力格局"作为本年度达沃斯的主题，在一定程度上，明显地反映了对正在崛起的大国的关注，但它也证明在处理全球事务方面，任何强大的力量只有依靠建立在全球价值观基础上的全球同盟才能发挥作用。

这里既有道德原因也有战略利益。我们知道迎战气候变化与我们自身的利害关系，但我们还认为这是我们为了子孙后代，也是为我们自己所应承担的道德义务。在达沃斯，商界人士不仅讨论商贸、行业趋势、竞争与挑战，他们也讨论商界在解决当今重大问题时的作用。这种作用已经远远超出了以往对公司责任的认识。商业界也相信，道德原因中含有战略利益。

当今世界处于不断的全球对话中。各种运动的开始和发展都发生在瞬息之间。悲剧或不公正，比如战争等，通过传媒进入了我们家中，冲击着我们的感官，迫使我们对那些发生在万里之遥却令我们感同身受的事件做出评判。这可以是坏事，例如，反潮流的恐怖主义意识形态利用网络来招募人马或蛊惑人们改变信仰。也可以是好事，例如规模宏大的巨星义助非洲慈善演唱会唤醒了全世界对非洲的良知。无论如何，这都是现实，都将带来深远的影响。个人力量也纷纷加入到要求变化和行动的大众运动中来。政治领袖处理国内外事务的时间比例发生了巨大变化。商界人士不是以某个政党成员的形式，而是作为全球讨论的重要参与者也参与到政治中来。

总之，各国都认识到只有依靠与其他国家结成强大的联盟，共同寻求解决方案，才能应对各种挑战。所有国家，既便是最强大的国家，也必须找到同盟才能保全自己的利益。这就是我们所说的互相依存。这是为了自身利益和集体利益而结盟的最高形式。阿富汗曾是一个失败的国家，其人民生活在痛苦与贫穷之中。他们本来会持续这种生活，不被世界所关注。但是 9 · 11 事件这场根本不可预见的大灾难使我们聚焦阿富汗。看看这一事件使当今世界发生了多么大的变化。我们知道非洲的困境使富足的世界感到羞耻。但我从未否认还有另一个动机。我相信如果我们任索马里或苏丹继续滑向深渊，它们的灾难不仅会影响这一地区，也不仅只关系到这两国的人民。我赞成在巴勒斯坦按照其自己的要求实现和平，但毫无疑问，缺乏和平的巴勒斯坦也会影响到那些走在英国城市的大街上，从未去过加沙地带或约旦河西岸的民众。

当然，气候变化问题也是如此。我们即使仅仅假设其潜在威胁有可能是真实的，为了预防起见，凡是正常人都会采取行动防止这种威胁成为现实。气候变化带来的挑战最能体现世界各国的互相依存。美国与中国即使找不到其他建立关系的理由——当然，有许多理由支持这种关系——仅仅为了应对气候变化，两国也会进行合作。合作的理由还要加上经济全球化。总的来说，全球化提供了大量的机会，然而其影响可能难以控制且具有破坏性。那么，就来看看这三大问题——气候变化、非洲和世界贸易涉及哪些利害关系：这个星球的未来、每年数百万人的存亡、全球化——这个时代最强劲的经济推动力能否使更多的人分享它带来的生活机遇。

四、自主训练

请在 15 分钟之内迅速阅读下面的讲话，了解大意。学生可组成对子练习，互相监控对视译技巧的掌握情况、视译质量和现场表现，或以边视译边录音的形式进行个人练习。视译时要保持正常语速，译文要顺畅达意。如遇难句，可在首次视译后参照"实战练习"中难句分析与视译处理的方法进行练习，找出解决方法。

Speech to the World Economic Forum (Excerpt 2)
Tony Blair
Davos, 2007

Consider what is at stake in these issues. Then consider how hard we have found it to put the right alliances in place; reach agreement; and take the appropriate measures to get the job done. This is my major reflection on 10 years of trying to meet these challenges, 10 years in which, as a deliberate policy, Britain has been at the forefront, for better or worse, of each of these major global issues. Interdependence is an accepted fact. It is giving rise to a great yearning for a sense of global purpose, underpinned by global values, to overcome challenges, global in nature.

But we are woefully short of the instruments to make multilateral action effective. We acknowledge the interdependent reality. We can sketch the purpose and describe the values. What we lack is capacity, capability, the concerted means to act. We need a multilateralism that is muscular. Instead, too often, it is disjointed, imbued with the right ideas but the wrong or inadequate methods of achieving them. None of this should make us underestimate what has been done. But there is too often a yawning gap between our description of an issue's importance and the matching capability to determine it. In this regard, there is often an easy and lazy critique that puts this down to an absence of political will. In my experience there is, usually, not a problem of political will. By and large it's there. It is translating that will into action that is the problem. Why? Because it requires focus, time, energy and commitment, and though individual leaders and nations can provide those qualities intermittently, sustaining them over time, with all the other pressures it is just practically impossible.

Global purpose, underpinned by global values requires global instruments of effective multilateral action. A UNSC[1] without Germany, Japan, Brazil or India, to say nothing of any African or Islamic nation, will, in time, not merely lose legitimacy in the eyes of the world, but seriously inhibit effective action. By all means let us have some form of bridging mechanism—perhaps semi-permanent status without a veto—to a reformed Council; but get it done. Likewise with reform within the UN—greater power to the Secretary General, merging agencies, … But reform now has to happen. There is a powerful case for merging the IMF and World Bank and for increasing the influence of the developing countries within them. The G8 is already well on its way to metamorphosis into G8+5. At G8+5, it can be a forum for agreement between the most powerful nations with a true modern global reach. But sooner or later, the metamorphosis should be complete. We need to make the regional blocs more effective.

I strongly believe in changing the rules of the EU to build efficacy in Europe's power. The EU at 27 cannot operate within the system used for an EU of 15 countries. It would hugely help the cause of Africa if the AU became a strong and cohesive voice and instrument of Africa's interests.

1　United Nations Security Council.

However, this is not just about governmental institutions. Into the void between identifying an issue's importance and securing the means of acting on it, has increasingly stepped the non-governmental and non-state actors. The resource of the Gates Foundation is being put to the eradication of malaria—a preventable disease which kills one million a year. The Grameen Bank, founded by Mohammed Yunus has pioneered micro-credit projects which now have over 80 million recipients, the majority of them women. It is a partnership between governments, private markets, NGOs and faith groups that is providing immunization that will save five million children's lives and those of a further five million adults. The agenda on climate change is increasingly being set by coalitions of business, most recently the group of US companies calling for tougher action but also setting out practical ways of doing it. All of this is great, ground-breaking work. But in a sense it is laying bare the paucity of the instruments to effect change, which we have at our disposal. In 1999 in Chicago I called for a doctrine of international community, in which we accept that a modern foreign policy cannot work except on the basis of shared common values. These values gave us not just a right but a duty to act in order to protect people at risk. I meant it in the context of Kosovo and ethnic cleansing. But of course its application goes far wider. The common theme that runs through such apparently disparate issues like the struggle against terrorism or poverty in Africa is that both require active measures of intervention. Indeed the very consequence of interdependence is the necessity to intervene, in coalition with others, in order to prevent danger or injustice that may originate outside our borders but ultimately will affect us within them.

So, today, we see the establishment of a proper democratic state of Palestine as benefiting not just the people of Palestine and Israel but the wider Middle East and the world. We know, too, that if Central Africa is given over to conflict it will at some stage be a global threat. Likewise if Iraq or Afghanistan falls back into failed states exporting violence, we will suffer the impact. But we know also that none of these desirable objectives will occur without our active intervention. We are familiar with military intervention; the path of aid and development is well trodden. But the concept of nation-building—by which I mean the construction of the capacity for effective self-government within a country—is still in its infancy. The proper infrastructure of government—functioning commercial and legal systems, health and education ministries that can actually administer, economic authorities that have real authority; police and military that perform the tasks they should under proper rules of governance: these things often seem less exciting and motivating than direct intervention to cure disease or alleviate poverty, but in reality they are the life blood of true progress for nations struggling to be nations. Aid for trade is at least as important as any other part of the world trade deal. Why? Because it builds capacity. There is a whole new dimension to international intervention that needs development. It is in building capacity that the fate of Palestine, Iraq, Afghanistan or any of poorest or war-ravaged African nations will obtain their salvation. Everything else—worthy and essential though it is—fails unless the systems of self-government and therefore self-help are brought into being. These are new skills the international community must develop.

There is a further element to it. We need proper, well-constructed means of conflict resolution and peace-keeping. What is happening in Darfur today is a scandal; not a problem, a scandal. Hundreds of thousands die or live lives of unbelievable risk and misery because we cannot assemble a proper peace agreement, properly enforced, with the full weight of the international community behind it. I know there are a host of political reasons that are colliding with our good intent. But the real problem, again, is the absence of a sustained international focus, with the capacity to keep at it, report back credibly and trigger action, if nothing happens. Not all of this requires us to go back to traditional institutions of international governance like the United Nations. Non-state actors can play a role here too. But the point is very simple: if we are to intervene successfully, we have to have the capability to do so. Therefore a key and new part of our international dialog must now be strengthening the instruments and institutions, those between governments but also those within broader civic society, that can build capacity. We need new networks, new relationships between countries and between people which mobilize the practical means of bringing change into being. There is an urgency here. What is remarkable about Davos this year—and this has been true for some years now—is the degree of consensus around a values-based international agenda. It is what makes me optimistic. There is a true sense of global responsibility. But ours is not the only narrative competing for the world's attention. There is another. It may be—is—based on a total perversion of Islam; but it has shown itself capable of playing cleverly on the injustice, poverty and alienation felt by many whose lifestyles are a world away from ours. We believe we are doing our best to confront the world's problems and to lift the scourge from the backs of so many millions whose lives are blighted. But this counter-ideology mocks our efforts, disputes our motives, turns our good faith into bad.

And there is yet another narrative. In 20 years, or sooner, there will be new powers, new constellations of authority, with strong intentions and powerful means of advancing them. What values will govern that new world? Will they be global values, commonly shared or will the world revert to spheres of interest, to competing power-plays in which the lesser or struggling nations are the victims? If the narrative we believe in—a world of tolerance, freedom, openness and justice for all—is to be credible, it has to be effective. The best answer to fear is always hope. But hope requires belief. And belief comes only from words turned into deeds. So take these issues: Africa, climate change, world trade. Imagine over the coming months the world agrees and over the coming years, it acts. Think how attractive our story of the world's progress would be. Then think of failure and who will weep and who will rejoice. Think of all of this. Then let us agree. Then let us act.

第13单元

There+be 句式的视译

> 基本技巧：
> - 将 There+be 句式译为以"有"字引导的汉语句式。

一、技巧讲解：There+be 的视译

在英语中，There+be 句式是一种常见的结构，表示"存在"、"有"的意思。There+be 句式类似形式主语，真实主语是它后面的名词。There+be 句式在主语后面常常有一个状语，表示时间或地点。比较典型的 There+be 句式是 There is a cup on the desk. 在笔译中，一般要颠倒语序，将状语置于汉语句子的句首，即"桌子上有一个茶杯。"

如果 There+be 句式的句子本身很短，视译中不会出现什么困难。比如上面的句子，完全可以在译员一目可及的范围之内，即便是做语序调整，也很容易。但问题是，在实际的视译中，这类句子往往有一些其他成分插在句子之中，使得整个句子很长，超出了一目可及的范围，这就加大了视译难度。比如，There are several workers, hundreds of students, and many villagers singing and dancing at the construction site. 笔译译文为："工地上有几个工人，几百个学生，还有许多村民在唱歌跳舞。"由于将状语"工地上"置于句首，我们就必须读完整个句子才能将其译出。这显然不符合视译的要求。在这种情况下，我们需要将句子顺次译出，即"有几个工人，几百个学生，还有许多村民，在工地上唱歌跳舞。"

所以，在遇到 There+be 句式的时候，要按照顺序，一般将 There+be 译为"有"，然后根据句子的顺序，接着往下翻译。我们举几个例子予以说明。

例 1： There's been a gentleman here asking to see you.

译文 1：这儿有位先生要见你。（张道真，2002：486）

译文 2：有位先生在这里，他要见你。

【讲解】 这是一个典型的 There+be 句式。我们先将句子根据类意群分为两个视译单位，即：There's been a gentleman here // asking to see you. 然后，以"有"字开头，加入适当的汉语量词（位、个、些等），先将后面的真实主语译出"有位先生在这里"；再另起一句，将原句中的分词短语译出"他要见你"。在第二个分句里，加入了主语"他"，使句子更加通顺。

例 2： There are dozens of reasons why I must go.

译文 1：我有种种必须离职的理由。（张道真，2002：486）

译文 2：有很多理由，所以我必须离职。

【讲解】 这个句子是一个主从复合句，包含一个以 why 引导的同位语从句。我们先将 There+be 部分以"有"字句译出，然后依照定语从句的译法，另起一句将从句译出，并且加入"所以"将前后连接起来，使句子更加顺妥。

例 3： There appeared to be a war between his heart and his mind.

译文 1：他的情感和理智之间似乎有一场斗争。（张道真，2002：488）

译文 2：似乎有场战争，在他的情感和理智之间展开。

【讲解】 这是一个带有较长的介词短语的 There+be 的变形句式，仍然以"有"字句式来处理，并分成两部分来做视译，appear to be 译为"似乎有"。第二个分句加入汉语动词"展开"使句子顺畅。

例 4： There is not any body in an absolute state of rest in the world.

译文 1：世界上没有处于绝对静止状态的任何物体。（陈定安，1998：165）

译文 2：没有任何物体处于绝对静止状态，在这个世界上是没有的。

【讲解】 有时候，由于中间插入的部分较长，视译译员无法将原句中的时间状语或其他修饰成分迅速调整到句子的其他位置，只能按照顺序译出。这样，原来句尾的修饰语就成为视译难点。在这种情况下，有一种化解的办法，就是再加一个稍有重复的短语或是短句，将其译出。在例 4 译文中，我们使用了"在这个世界上是没有的"来补足原句的意思。再如，There are now published thousands and millions of books every year. 原译文为："现在每年出版上亿册书。"（薄冰，2006：506）在视译中，我们很难一下子看完全句，往往下意识地在 every year 之前停下来。所以，我们可以将这个句子译为："现在有上亿册书出版，每年如此。"方法也是加上一个短语，补足原义。

关于 There+be 句式的视译，我们一般将 There+be 译为"有"，再将 There+be 原句中真实主语后面的状语或其他附加成分另作一句独立译出，必要时加连接成分使译文通顺妥帖。

二、语段视译

1　词汇与表达

在进行语段视译前，请先预习以下词汇与表达。

revenue	收入，岁入
evasion of duties	逃税
convert	转变，改变

2　视译语段

请在 3 分钟之内迅速阅读下面的语段，了解大意，然后结合所学要点进行视译练习。视译时要保持正常语速，译文要顺畅达意。

Yet the taxation of trade has its disadvantages. If taxes on commerce are too high, they may have the effect of reducing the volume of trade and hence the amount of revenue. The high duty on English wool exports in the 14th century may well have been a factor in the sector's decline. High import duties, on the other hand, encourage smuggling. Even an island state like Britain found it impossible to prevent large-scale evasion of duties in the 18th century, when the figure of "Smuggler Bill" attained heroic status and as many as 20,000 people were involved in illegal trade. More importantly, import duties discriminate against foreign goods which might otherwise be cheaper than those which are domestically produced. From a liberal perspective, tariffs are not only a burden on consumers; they also diminish the efficiency of the international economy as a whole by sheltering from competition mediocre firms that happened to be on the right side of a national border. It was the practical argument that lower tariffs would increase trade volumes, allied to a distinctly Protestant view of the economy as divinely ordained and self regulating mechanism, which converted the majority of the British political elite to free trade. (摘自《英语学习》, 2005 年第 3 期, 第 73 页)

原译文: 但是对贸易征税也有不利之处。商业税若定得过高, 就可能会导致贸易量降低, 进而收入下降。14 世纪英国羊毛出口征收的高关税也许是这一行业逐渐衰退的一个原因。另一方面, 高进口关税也鼓励了走私。在 18 世纪, 即便像英国这样的岛国也发现防止大规模逃税是不可能的。当时的走私贸易额惊人, 有多达两万人在从事非法贸易。更重要的是, 进口关税歧视外国货, 它们本来可能会比本国货要便宜些。从自由主义的观点来看, 关税不仅是消费者的负担, 而且因为它庇护本国劣等商家免遭竞争, 还从总体上降低了国际经济的效率。低关税会增加贸易额的实用论点, 加上典型的新教观点——经济是神授的、自我调节的机制, 使得英国大部分政治精英都转而信仰自由贸易了。(宏刚译)

3 视译译文

	断 句	译 文
1	Yet the taxation of trade	但是贸易征税,
2	has its disadvantages.	也有不利之处。
3	If taxes on commerce are too high,	如果商业税定得太高,
4	they may have the effect	就可能产生一种后果,
5	of reducing the volume of trade	这就是降低贸易量,
6	and hence the amount of revenue.	因而也就减少了收入。
7	The high duty on English wool exports	英国羊毛出口税太高,
8	in the 14th century	这是 14 世纪的状况,
9	may well have been a factor	也很可能是一个原因,
10	in the sector's decline.	导致了这个行业的衰退。
11	High import duties,	高进口税,

(待续)

（续上表）

	断　句	译　文
12	on the other hand,	从另外一个方面来看，
13	encourage smuggling.	会鼓励走私。
14	Even an island state like Britain	即便是一个像英国这样的岛国，
15	found it impossible	也不可能
16	to prevent large-scale evasion of duties	制止大规模逃税，
17	in the 18th century,	在 18 世纪，
18	when the figure of "Smuggler Bill" attained heroic status	英国走私款额高得惊人，
19	and as many as 20,000 people were involved in illegal trade.	多达两万人从事非法贸易。
20	More importantly,	更重要的是，
21	import duties discriminate against foreign goods	进口税歧视外国货物，
22	which might otherwise be cheaper	外国货本来可以比较便宜，
23	than those which are domestically produced.	而国产货却相对昂贵。
24	From a liberal perspective,	根据自由主义的观点，
25	tariffs are not only a burden on consumers;	关税不仅增加了消费者的负担，
26	they also diminish the efficiency	而且降低了效率，
27	of the international economy as a whole	降低了整个国际经济的效率，
28	by sheltering from competition	因为受它庇护而免于竞争的是
29	mediocre firms	那些平庸的公司，
30	that happened to be on the right side of a national border.	仅仅因为这些公司是本国公司而已。

（待续）

（续上表）

	断 句	译 文
31	It was the practical argument	一种实用主义的论点是，
32	that lower tariffs would increase trade volumcs,	降低关税会增加贸易额。
33	allied to a distinctly Protestant view	同时还存在一种典型的新教观点，
34	of the economy as divinely ordained	认为经济受到上帝的管理，
35	and self regulating mechanism,	是自我调节的机制。
36	which converted the majority of the British political elite	这就使得大部分英国的政治精英
37	to free trade.	开始信仰自由贸易。

4 视译点评

1. 原文第二句：If taxes on commerce are too high, // they may have the effect // of reducing the volume of trade // and hence the amount of revenue.

这是个条件句，主句并不复杂，但宾语 the effect of reducing the volume of trade and hence the amount of revenue 较长，原译文根据全句意思将谓语和宾语的中心词 have the effect 译为一个动词"导致"，使译文顺畅达意。但在视译时，译员习惯在一目可及的范围内处理，这样读到 effect 处可能会自然停顿下来，所以可以将 have the effect 单独译出，即"就可能产生一种后果"，然后通过添加"这就是"连接后面部分。

2. 原文第三句：The high duty on English wool exports // in the 14th century // may well have been a factor // in the sector's decline.

此句虽然是个简单句，但是主语和宾语中的介词短语在笔译时都需要作一定的语序调整，才更符合汉语表达习惯，所以原译文将"14 世纪"这个时间状语置于句首，将 on English wool exports 译为前置定语"英国羊毛出口征收的"以修饰"高关税"，将原文句尾的 in the sector's decline 提前，并把介词短语中的 the sector 译成修饰"一个原因"的主谓结构定语的主语，其中的名词 decline 译成"逐渐衰退"，作谓语。然而，视译时此句按类意群可断为四部分：The high duty on English wool exports // in the 14th century // may well have been a factor // in the sector's decline. 每部分单独译成一个汉语分句，即："英国羊毛出口税太高，// 这是 14 世纪的状况，// 很可能是一个原因，// 导致了这个行业的衰退。"通过把定语 high 译为谓语"太高"，添加连接语"这是"，保持了原文的语序。

3. 原文第五句：Even an island state like Britain // found it impossible // to prevent large-scale evasion of duties // in the 18th century, // when the figure of "Smuggler Bill" attained heroic status // and as many as 20,000 people were involved in illegal trade.

　　与原译文比较，在视译 found it impossible to prevent large-scale evasion of duties 时，我们没有采用"发现……是不可能的"的句式，没有把 it 替代的部分 to prevent large-scale evasion of duties 译作"发现"的宾语，从而避免了语序的调整，灵活地将这种表达译成汉语"无法"，不但意思相同，而且易于连接。同样，视译译文中"在 18 世纪"这个时间状语不仅保持在原位，没有被调整到句首，而且成为修饰后面 when 引导的从句的时间状语。虽然对于此句的主句来说，时间的界定没有像调整到句首后那么清楚，但是整句的意思没有因此受到影响。视译 as many as 20,000 people were involved in illegal trade 时，可译成"多达多少人做某事"的汉语句式，其中的被动式 were involved 译成主动式"从事"或"参与"。

4. 原文第六句：More importantly, // import duties discriminate against foreign goods // which might otherwise be cheaper // than those which are domestically produced.

　　此句中有英文形容词的比较级结构 A is cheaper than B。汉译时通常要调整语序，译为"甲比乙要便宜些"。由于原文中 B 部分较长，语序调整会增加视译的困难，所以视译时，将英语的比较级结构一分为二，分别译成两个分句："外国货本来可以比较便宜"和"而国产货却相对昂贵"。这样就有效地保持了原文中比较的意思。

5. 原文第七句：… they also diminish the efficiency // of the international economy as a whole // by sheltering from competition // mediocre firms // that happened to be on the right side of a national border.

　　原译文："……而且因为它庇护本国劣等商家免遭竞争，还从总体上降低了国际经济的效率。"其中，把原文中 by 引导的表示方式的状语译为表示原因的状语，并且按照汉语的表达方式置于表示结果的分句之前。对于 firms 的限定性后置定语从句 that happened to be on the right side of a national border，原译文把从句的意思概括地译成定语"本国（的）"，置于中心词"商家"之前。另外，原译文把原文主句句尾的状语短语 as a whole 调整到句首，译为"从总体上"。这么多的调整在视译时是难以做到的，既会影响口译的速度，也不利于译文的顺畅。因此，此句视译时要分为五个视译单位，依次译作："而且降低了效率 // 降低了整个国际经济的效率，// 因为受它庇护而免于竞争的是 // 那些平庸的公司，// 仅仅因为这些公司是本国公司而已。"笔者对第二个视译单位里的固定搭配词组——shelter A from B 的变体 shelter from B A——中的 from competition 采用了变通的方法，先行译出，然后用"是"字句连接后面的分句，使整个句子通顺易懂。

6. 原文第八句：It was the practical argument // that lower tariffs would increase trade volumes, ...

原句中主句的译文"低关税会增加贸易额的实用论点"调整了原文语序，把同位语从句 that lower tariffs would increase trade volumes 译为汉语主谓结构的定语："低关税会增加贸易额的"。视译译文则利用汉语的"是"字句结构"一种实用主义的论点是"，自然地连接起后面由原句同位语从句转变的句子——"降低关税会增加贸易额"。

三、实战练习

1 词汇与表达

请先熟悉以下词汇与表达，并适当地运用在视译中。

UNEP（United Nations Environment Program）	联合国环境规划署
executive director	行政主任
World Environment Day	世界环境日
ecosystem	生态系统
glacier	冰河，冰川
greenhouse gas	温室气体
early warning system	早期预警系统
ocean circulation	大洋环流
polar region	极地
methane	甲烷

permafrost	永冻土
outback	内陆
Rio de Janeiro	里约热内卢（巴西城市）
profligate burning	低效用燃烧
fossil fuel	矿物燃料
PricewaterhouseCoopers	普华永道（公司名）
zero-emission	零排放
coal-fired power station	燃煤发电站
displaced people	背井离乡的人们
intergovernmental	政府间
civil society	公民社会，市民社会
carbon market	碳汇交易市场
Nairobi	内罗毕（肯尼亚首都）
Clean Development Mechanism	清洁发展机制，缩写为 CDM
sub-Saharan Africa	撒哈拉沙漠以南的非洲

2　实战课文

请在 15 分钟之内迅速阅读下面的讲话，了解大意。视译时要保持正常语速，译文要顺畅达意。

World Environment Day
UN under Secretary-General, UNEP Executive Director
Achim Steiner

2007

World Environment Day 2007 focuses on the challenges facing the people and ecosystems of the Arctic and Antarctic as a result of rapid environmental and climatic change. （句 1）In doing so it also links to the wider world where glaciers are shrinking and an increasing number of extreme weather events are triggering more frequent droughts and floods.

In focusing on the polar regions we hold up a mirror to the accelerating impacts sweeping the whole planet from the release of greenhouse gases into the atmosphere. These seemingly remote regions vividly illustrate the interconnectedness of all life on the Earth—bringing home to the six billion people alive today how mutually reliant and linked we all are to landscapes and ecosystems both near and far.

The Arctic and Antarctica may be the Earth's climate early warning system—feeling the heat first—but we know it does not end there. Ocean circulation, the key driver of regional and global weather systems, is inextricably linked with melting and freezing processes in and around the poles. The polar regions are also a kind of protective shield, reflecting heat back into space that would otherwise be absorbed on the Earth. There is also growing concern over so-called "positive feedbacks" including the potential release of massive amounts of the powerful greenhouse gas methane, which is stored in the Arctic permafrost.

So, what happens in the Arctic and the Antarctic as a result of climate change is of direct interest to us all—from someone living in the Congo River Basin, the Australian outback and in rural China, to suburban dwellers in Berlin, New Delhi, Rio de Janeiro or Washington, D.C.

At the same time, the actions of those living outside the polar regions is of direct interest to Arctic peoples. **The vast majority of emissions that are contributing to melting ice are being generated on the roads and in the factories, homes and offices of the industrialized and, increasingly, the rapidly industrializing economies.（句 2 ）**

We are currently locked into a vicious and ever widening circle. Our common responsibility is to make it a virtuous one—to underline that overcoming the profligate burning of fossil fuels is not a burden but an opportunity. Switching to a cleaner and more efficient development path can not only liberate us from the overarching threat of climate change, it can free us from dependency on a finite and, some might say, politically disruptive resource.

There are signs that this switch can—and is indeed starting to—occur as a result of several central factors finally coming into play. Firstly the economics of inaction and the economic benefits of action have in recent months moved to the fore. **A review by Sir Nicholas Stern, published in advance of the climate convention talks held in Nairobi in late 2006, has changed the landscape forever in this respect. (句 3)** It states that if no action is taken, we risk raising average global temperatures by more than 5℃ from pre-industrial levels, and this would lead to the equivalent of a minimum loss of 5% of GDP annually.

In contrast, the costs of acting to reduce greenhouse gas emissions to avoid the worst impacts could cost as little as 1% of global GDP each year. The US firm PricewaterhouseCoopers recently concluded that the world would have to sacrifice just one year's economic growth over the next four decades to reduce carbon emissions sufficiently to curb global warming.

The Stern Review also estimates that reducing emissions would actually make the world better off. One estimate indicates that, over time, a shift to a low carbon global economy would trigger benefits of $2.5 trillion a year. Findings like this take climate change beyond the portfolio of the environment minister and firmly into the in-tray of the world's finance ministers and heads of state.

The second factor is the issue of energy security—or, one might say, energy insecurity—due to the global dependence on fossil fuels. Countries are increasingly recognizing that the benefits of renewable energy sources, low- or zero-emission coal-fired power stations and energy efficiency extend beyond the atmosphere to national security.

Others are also starting to grasp another notion of security, which includes the link between extreme weather events like floods and droughts to wider national and regional issues.

Climate change is magnifying existing disparities between rich and poor and aggravating tensions over fragile or increasingly scarce natural resources such as productive land and freshwater. It increases the potential to create a new class of displaced people known collectively as environmental refugees.

You do not have to take my word for that. Cristina Narbona, the Spanish environment minister, was asked at the recent climate change talks why her country was investing in a new partnership between the UNEP and the UN Development Program (UNDP) to assist Africa adapt to climate change. Her response was clear. Spain links the increasing numbers of people from Africa who are risking life and limb in flimsy boats to sail to the Canary Islands with climate change impacts.

Finally, the science of climate change is now indisputable, and has been further underlined in the latest reports of the Intergovernmental Panel on Climate Change released in February this year. The findings put a full stop behind the scientific debate as to whether humankind is influencing the climate and now beg the question of what we are going to do about it.

Collective and decisive political will is the final—and still missing—piece in the jigsaw puzzle. While many sectors of society are moving to address climate change—including local authorities, industry, the financial sector and civil society— the collective political process is moving frustratingly slowly.

At the climate change meeting in Nairobi some steps were taken. **The UNEP** and UNDP's just-mentioned new partnership aims to assist developing countries to secure a share of the clean energy projects that are starting to flow from the Kyoto Protocol's Clean Development Mechanism. （句 4） It will also offer a rapid response so countries in sub-Saharan Africa and elsewhere can insulate their economies against climate changes that are already underway.

Furthermore, the Kyoto Protocol's Adaptation Fund was agreed, and there were other positive signs, not least on issues like avoided deforestation where there was productive and fulsome debate. However, no agreement was achieved on the deep and sustained cuts in greenhouse gas emissions needed to stabilize the atmosphere, an agreement which is also vital for maintaining confidence and investment in the blossoming carbon markets. （句 5） If Nairobi was not the place, then where and when will this action on deeper cuts in a post-2012 world emerge?

It was John Tyndall, the English physicist, who first recognized the power of carbon dioxide and water vapor to change the Earth's climate. That was over 100 years ago in his seminal paper of 1863. We cannot wait another 100 years to act. Indeed there are some respected observers who claim we have as little as a decade or so to do so. Six months from now, on the Indonesian Island of Bali, governments will resume the climate talks. I sincerely hope that Bali will be the watershed where science, security issues and economics combine to produce wide-ranging political action.

The theme for this year's World Environment Day is Melting Ice: A Hot Topic? Thus it is fitting that the main celebrations are being hosted by Norway on the edge of the Arctic Circle. The logo underlines the global theme by asking a polar bear, an African farmer, a Pacific islander, an insurer and businessman, two indigenous children and ultimately "Yourself" the rhetorical question of whether indeed this is the topic of our time.

Perhaps we should have added a further person—namely a politician. World Environment Day has at its heart the empowerment of the individual citizen. The UNEP urges everyone to embrace this year's theme and put the question to their political leaders and democratically elected representatives: just how much hotter does this topic need to become before governments across the globe finally act?

3 难句分析与视译处理

句 1：　　　World Environment Day 2007 focuses on the challenges facing the people and ecosystems of the Arctic and Antarctic as a result of rapid environmental and climatic change.

笔译译文： 环境和气候的快速变化给人类与南北两极的生态系统都带来了挑战。因此，2007 年世界环境日的焦点问题是我们将如何面对这些挑战。

视译译文：

断　句	译　文
World Environment Day 2007	2007 年世界环境日，
focuses on the challenges	集中讨论诸多挑战，
facing the people and	这些挑战威胁人类，
ecosystems of the Arctic and Antarctic	也威胁南北两极的生态系统，
as a result of rapid environmental and climatic change.	引发挑战的是迅速的环境和气候变化。

句 2： The vast majority of emissions that are contributing to melting ice are being generated on the roads and in the factories, homes and offices of the industrialized and, increasingly, the rapidly industrializing economies.

笔译译文： 工业化经济体和正在快速工业化的经济体的交通工具、工厂、住宅和办公场所是绝大部分温室气体的排放者，造成冰雪的融化。

视译译文：

断　句	译　文
The vast majority of emissions	绝大部分温室气体排放出来，
that are contributing to melting ice	造成了冰雪的融化，
are being generated	这些气体大都来自
on the roads and in the factories, homes and offices	交通工具、工厂、住宅以及办公场所，
of the industrialized and,	工业化国家情景如此，
increasingly, the rapidly industrializing economies.	迅速工业化的经济体也越来越是如此。

句 3： A review by Sir Nicholas Stern, published in advance of the climate convention talks held in Nairobi in late 2006, has changed the landscape forever in this respect.

笔译译文： 2006 年后期在内罗毕举行气候公约会谈之前，尼古拉斯·斯特恩爵士发表的一篇评论永久地改变了人们对这一点的认识。

视译译文：

断　句	译　文
A review by Sir Nicholas Stern,	尼古拉斯·斯特恩爵士写了一篇评论，
published in advance of the climate convention talks	发表在气候公约会谈之前，
held in Nairobi in late 2006,	会谈是 2006 年晚些时候在内罗毕举行的，
has changed the landscape forever	他的评论永久地改变了人们的认识，
in this respect.	改变了人们对气候变化的认识。

句 4： The UNEP and UNDP's just-mentioned new partnership aims to assist developing countries to secure a share of the clean energy projects that are starting to flow from the Kyoto Protocol's Clean Development Mechanism.

笔译译文： 之前提到的联合国环境规划署和联合国开发计划署的新合作项目，旨在协助发展中国家参与由《京都议定书》的清洁发展机制所启动的清洁能源项目。

视译译文：

断　句	译　文
The UNEP and UNDP's	联合国环境规划署和开发计划署，
just-mentioned new partnership	设立了我们刚刚提到的合作项目，
to assist developing countries	目的是帮助发展中国家，

（待续）

（续上表）

断　句	译　文
to secure a share of the clean energy projects	保证他们能够参与清洁能源项目，
that are starting to flow	这些项目刚刚开始启动，
from the Kyoto Protocol's Clean Development Mechanism.	是《京都议定书》清洁发展机制下的项目。

句 5：　However, no agreement was achieved on the deep and sustained cuts in greenhouse gas emissions needed to stabilize the atmosphere, an agreement which is also vital for maintaining confidence and investment in the blossoming carbon markets.

笔译译文：　然而，会议并未能就大幅度并持久减少温室气体排放量以稳定大气达成协议，而这一协议对于保持人们对繁荣的碳汇交易市场的信心和投资来说至关重要。

视译译文：

断　句	译　文
However, no agreement was achieved	然而，没有能够达成协议，
on the deep and sustained cuts	以大幅度并持久减少
in greenhouse gas emissions	温室气体排放量，
needed to stabilize the atmosphere,	而我们需要这样的协议来稳定大气层，
an agreement which is also vital	达成这样一个协议也是至关重要的，
for maintaining confidence and investment	因为它有助于保持人们的信心和投资，
in the blossoming carbon markets.	使繁荣的碳汇交易市场得以发展。

4 参考译文

世界环境日

联合国副秘书长，联合国环境规划署执行主任
阿齐姆·施泰纳
2007 年

环境和气候的快速变化给人类与南北两极的生态系统都带来了挑战。因此，2007 年世界环境日的焦点问题是我们将如何面对这些挑战。与此同时，今年的世界环境日还将关注世界其他存在着冰川减少、极端恶劣天气增多的地区。极端的气候使得旱涝灾害更为频繁。

两极地区反映出由于温室气体大量进入大气，不断增强的影响遍及全球。两极地区看似遥远，却深刻反映出地球上的生命彼此息息相关这一事实，并让今天生活在这世界上的 60 亿人清楚地认识到，无论与我们距离是远是近，任何地方的环境和生态系统都与我们密切相关。

北极和南极可以成为地球气候的早期预警系统，因为这两个地方最先感受到热流。但我们也知道其作用并非仅止于此。作为地区及全球天气系统变化的主要原动力，洋流与两极内及其周围的冰融与冰冻有着密不可分的联系。两极还像一个保护伞，将本来会被地球吸收的热量反射到太空。此外，人们也越来越担忧一种被称为"正反馈"的现象，例如，储存在北极的永冻土中极具威力的温室气体甲烷可能会由于北极冰融而大量释放。

由上可知，气候变化在南北极引起的变化与我们每个人都存在直接的利害关系，无论你生活在刚果河盆地、澳洲内陆、中国农村，还是住在柏林、新德里、里约热内卢或华盛顿特区的郊区。

与此同时，极圈外的居民的生活方式也直接影响到北极圈内的居民。工业化经济体和正在快速工业化的经济体的交通工具、工厂、住宅和办公场所是绝大部分温室气体的排放者，造成了冰雪的融化。

目前我们被困在恶性循环之中，而这种循环还在不断扩大。我们共同的职责是将恶性循环变为一种良性循环。我们要强调的是，消除对矿物燃料的低效使用不是负担，而是一次契机。如果我们能转而采取一条更清洁，更高效的发展之路，我们不但能从气候变化的阴霾下解脱出来，还能摆脱对石油这种储量有限、还被称之为具有政治破坏力的能源的依赖。

有迹象表明，由于一些重要因素终于开始发挥作用，这种转变能够而且确实已开始出现了。首要因素是，在最近几个月里，不采取行动的代价和采取行

动所带来的经济利益逐渐为世人所关注。2006 年末在内罗毕举行气候公约会谈之前，尼古拉斯·斯特恩爵士发表的一篇评论永久地改变了人们对这一点的认识。该评论称，如不采取任何行动，我们很可能面临全球平均气温比工业化之前至少上升 5℃ 的危险，其后果相当于每年至少损失 5% 的 GDP。

相反，若采取行动来减少温室气体排放以防造成最严重的破坏，其年均成本只是全球 GDP 的 1%。美国公司普华永道最近的结论称，在接下来的 40 年，全世界只需牺牲一年的经济增长，而由此减少的碳排放量足以控制全球气候变暖。

斯特恩的文章还预计减少排放量会使世界更加富裕。其中一项估计指出，随着时间推移，世界向低碳经济的转型将带来每年 25,000 亿美元的益处。诸如此类的发现使解决气候变化不再仅仅是环境部长的任务，而是真正进入了世界各国财政部长甚至国家首脑的议程。

其次，全世界对矿物燃料的极度依赖使得能源安全问题也成为了主要因素之一，也有人称之为"能源不安全问题"。各国已越来越清晰地认识到可再生能源的好处。建造低排放或零排放的燃煤发电厂和提高能源使用效率不仅关乎大气质量，更关系到国家安全。

人们也开始明白另一类安全问题，包括极端恶劣气候如洪水和干旱与更广泛的国家和地区问题之间的关联。

气候变化严重地扩大了现有的贫富差距，加剧了由于可耕地和淡水等脆弱且越来越稀缺的自然资源引发的紧张局面，增加了出现一个被统称为"环境难民"的新群体的可能性，这些人迫于自然灾害而背井离乡。

我的话或许不足为信。但最近在关于气候变化的谈话中，西班牙环境部长克里斯蒂娜·纳尔博纳作出了十分明确的回答。关于西班牙为何要对联合国环境规划署和联合国开发计划署的一项新的援助非洲应对气候变化的合作项目进行投资，她说越来越多的非洲人受到气候变化引发的灾害的影响，他们不惜冒着失去生命或残疾的危险，乘着简陋的船只逃到加那利群岛上。因此，西班牙认为这些难民与气候变化的影响有关。

最后一点，有关气候变化的科学研究不容置疑，并在今年 2 月发布的最新的联合国政府间气候变化工作小组报告中得到进一步强调。研究结果彻底结束了关于人类是否影响了气候的科学辩论，并迫切要求我们给出对策。

如今，万事俱备，只欠坚定的集体政治意愿。虽然地方机构、各行各业、金融部门和公民社会等社会各界纷纷采取行动应对气候异常，但集体的政治进程却发展缓慢，令人沮丧。

内罗毕召开的有关气候变化的会议已经采用了几种方案。之前提到的联合国环境规划署和联合国开发计划署的新合作项目，旨在协助发展中国家参与由《京都议定书》的清洁发展机制启动的清洁能源项目。该合作项目还将为撒哈拉沙漠以南的非洲及其他地区提供快速应对方案，以保护他们的经济免受气候变化带来的危害。合作已经在实施中。

另外，会议同意成立《京都议定书》适应基金。还有其他积极的现象，尤其是在遏制森林砍伐等问题上，展开了大量的卓有成效的辩论。然而，会议并未能就大幅度并持久减少温室气体排放量以稳定大气达成协议，而这一协议对于保持人们对繁荣的碳汇交易市场的信心和投资来说至关重要。既然内罗毕没能就此达成协议，那么等到 2012 年后究竟在何时何地才能就进一步减排达成协议呢？

英国物理学家约翰·廷德耳最先发现二氧化碳和水蒸气能够改变地球气候。100 多年前，他把这一发现记在 1863 年的研究报告里。我们不能再等上100 年了。事实上，一些备受尊敬的观察者告诫我们必须在 10 年左右的时间内采取行动。半年后，各国政府将在印度尼西亚的巴厘岛重新召开气候会议。我衷心希望巴厘岛能成为一个新起点，让科学、安全问题和经济学共同促成广泛的政府行动。

今年世界环境日的主题是：冰层融化应成为热点问题吗？因此，位于北极圈边缘的挪威也就理所当然地成为主要庆祝活动的主办国。为凸显主题的全球性，该项活动的会标图案是分别向一头北极熊、一位非洲农民、一位太平洋海岛居民、一位从事保险业的商人、两名当地的儿童及"您"提出了设问：这难道不是我们这一时代的重点议题吗？

也许我们还应该在这些人里再加上一位政治家。世界环境日的本质就是赋予每位公民行动的力量。联合国环境规划署鼓励每个人响应今年的主题并向他们的政治领袖和民主选举出的代表们提出这个问题：这个话题究竟要热到什么程度，才能使全球各国政府最终采取行动呢？

四、自主训练

请在 15 分钟之内迅速阅读下面的讲话，了解大意。学生可组成对子练习，互相监控对视译技巧的掌握情况、视译质量和现场表现，或以边视译边录音的形式进行个人练习。视译时要保持正常语速，译文要顺畅达意。如遇难句，可在首次视译后参照"实战练习"中难句分析与视译处理的方法进行练习，找出解决方法。

Address to the Luncheon in Honor of His Excellency Mr. Wen Jiabao, Premier of the People's Republic of China

John Howard

Canberra, 2006

It is with great warmth and enthusiasm that I welcome you here today, Mr. Premier, as a further token of the remarkable way in which relations between our two countries has developed over the last decade. We began our day, as you will recall, walking very early in the morning as is my customary wont and I was delighted that you joined me on that walk and we chose to traverse the R.G. Menzies Walk; a walk around the lake in Canberra named after Australia's longest serving Prime Minister. And as I pointed out to you the photograph and the biographical details of Robert Gordon Menzies as Prime Minister of Australia, I thought to myself of the remarkable changes that have taken place in our two countries since his retirement in 1966 and the remarkable changes of course that have taken place in attitudes amongst the political leadership of either political persuasion in this country toward China.

And I had cause to reflect, as I did in our discussion today, that of all the important relationships that Australia has, and we have many and it is not my purpose today to engage the rather pointless exercise of trying to prioritize relationships, we do have a very important relationship with China. But I think it is accurate to say that of all the important relationships Australia has with other countries, none has undergone a greater transformation over the last decade or more as has our relationship with China. And that development is grounded in a number of things. It is grounded in common sense; it is grounded in realism of both the opportunities of our relationship, but also the limitations of it. It is also grounded in a frank recognition of the differences that exist historically, culturally and politically between our two countries.

And the fact that we have both, particularly over recent years, but I suspect for a long time in different ways, we have both recognized that we are fundamentally different in so many ways, but that in an ironic sense, has enabled us to build rather more effectively on the things that we have in common and the strengths that we can derive from the relationship.

Australia of course is the sixth most continuous democracy in the world and therefore our political system is very different from that of China's. But the growth and development of China is truly historic. And as I said in a speech I gave in New York at the time of the General Assembly gathering last September, I believe that the economic expansion and the outward development of China is not only good for China, it is also very good for the world. And it follows from that, that we welcome China's growth and China's development. We see it in a positive light. We do not see any merit at all in any policy of containment toward China; rather we see it very much in the interests of this country, the interests of our region and indeed the interests of the world to be an active partner in that long journey that China has begun to undertake toward realizing her full potential.

Of course the growth of Australia's economic relationship with China has been truly astounding. There are many figures that can be individually a metaphor for this but perhaps none is better than to say that our exports to China have quadrupled in the last decade. Now that has been largely, but not entirely driven by the remarkable expansion in the resource sector. China's growing demand for energy to underpin and guarantee her economic growth and development demands satisfaction. And Australia, providentially, has the resources to assist that process.

But it would be wrong to see the economic relationship between Australia and China exclusively in terms of resource development, important though that is. Shortly before this lunch I gathered together some of the business leaders of our country who have very heavy investments and involvement in China and it covered the whole gamut of our trading capacity. We had, of course, leaders of resource companies, we also had vice chancellors of universities, managing partners of large legal firms, of insurance companies; and it was a reminder that this is a very broad relationship.

China is Australia's largest source of students. It is the second largest source of migrants. It is the most rapidly growing, or one of the most rapidly growing rather, sources of tourism and it's estimated by some that the number of Chinese tourists coming to Australia by the year 2010 will exceed the number coming from Japan.

Now all of those things illustrate the breadth of the relationship. It's also a relationship built very much upon people-to-people links. I've often told Chinese leaders that the combination of Cantonese and Mandarin now represents the most widely spoken foreign language in this country, that Chinese bulk very large in many parts of metropolitan Australia and most particularly in Sydney.

There's a growing appetite for Chinese culture and an understanding of both the culture and the language of this remarkable country. I'm very pleased to note that a partnership between Asialink, the University of Melbourne and the Chinese government will see the establishment of the Confucius Institute in Melbourne in the near future. And this will enable a greater understanding of, and a greater appreciation of, the Chinese language and Chinese culture.

China is asserting her legitimate interest as a significant power; now the third most powerful economy in the world. And in the process of asserting, those legitimate interests, of course, carry as part of the international community and a leading player in the international community, the responsibilities of that authority and that position. And amongst the many things that the Premier and I discussed earlier today were the challenges faced by the major powers; the permanent members, perhaps more accurately described, of the United Nations, by the nuclear issues concerning Iran.

And we agreed how very important it was to try and solve this problem through the processes of the United Nations and the International Atomic Energy Agency. And that can best indeed, perhaps only be achieved, if there is unity of purpose between and amongst the five members, permanent members of the United Nations Security Council.

We in Australia recognize very much the positive contribution that China (has made), as the nation having potentially the greatest influence on the DPRK, (and) the role that China has played in encouraging a sensible resolution of that challenge. We are still a long way from a solution and we continue to encourage China to exercise her undoubted influence on the DPRK, an influence that exceeds that of any other country. Not only in our region but potentially around the world, of course, the relationship between China and the United States is crucial. As all of you will know, Australia has never played down or in any sense apologized for the closeness of our relationship with the United States. That relationship is deep; it's based on history and shared values and it's arguably stronger now than ever before.

But the strength and the depth of that relationship in no way affects or will it affect the capacity of Australia to interact with and form a close and lasting partnership and friendship with China. I take the optimistic view, not only in our region but also around the world of relations between the United States and China. I do not subscribe to the school to which some belong of an inevitable breakdown leading to potential conflict. I rather take the view that common sense will prevail not only in relation to Taiwan but in relation to the wider interests of those two societies. The history of recent times suggests that there is a greater realization of the need for that on all sides and it remains as part of our continuing commitment to the One China Policy, which I had the opportunity of reaffirming today in my discussions with the Premier, it remains our very strong exhortation to all concerned that we should maintain the lowest possible temperatures in relation to matters across the Taiwan Strait.

Mr. Premier, you come here as a leader of the largest nation numerically in the world, you come here as a leader of a nation with which Australians have not only a growing interest but a growing fascination. There is much that we can build together, we do have differences and our willingness over the years to frankly recognize those differences and not pretend otherwise and to not engage in phoney embraces of common attitudes and common values that simply don't exist, has been, I believe, the secret of the success of the relationship. In my personal experience I have not forgotten a meeting I had with the former President of China Jiang Zemin in the margins of the first APEC meeting that I attended in Manila in 1996 that took place in the wake of a rather difficult period in the relationship between Australia and China. At that meeting both of us identified the need to focus on those things where we could find common ground and whilst in no way retreating from our respective positions in relation to other issues, not to allow those differences to contaminate the broader relationship and that has been the approach that the government and I believe the people in the business community of Australia have taken over the years.

Our relationship with China is broad, it's growing; the presence here today of so many business leaders is testament to the strength of the economic relationship. But as all relationships will tell us, it's those deeper people-to-people links that are very important. They are substantial they are growing and they are respectful on both sides so far as Australia and China are concerned. To you sir, as somebody who's had a very successful, interesting and remarkable political career in your own country, any student of recent Chinese political history will read your resume, if I might put it that way, with great admiration and great appreciation. Your personality, your engaged commitment to the cause of better relations between our two countries is something that I very deeply appreciate.

We welcome you here for what you are as an individual leader but also for what you represent as a leader of a remarkable nation which is destined to play an even greater role in the affairs of the world and a nation with which Australia seeks to build an ever-closer and more effective and more permanent partnership.

长句的视译（I）

基本技巧：
- 拆分长句，依序顺译。

一、技巧讲解：长句的视译

　　长句在翻译中是较难处理的。由于长句的句法关系比较复杂，各个部分之间又存在内在的逻辑关系，对于有充分时间处理的笔译人员来说，也不是容易的事情。所以，笔译教材往往将长句的处理分为几个步骤。比如，许建平提出，长句的翻译要"分为理解、表达两个阶段共七个具体的处理步骤。理解阶段可分为四个步骤：1）扼要拟出全句的轮廓；2）根据上下文和全句内容领会其要旨；3）辨清该长句的主从结构；4）找出各句之间的从属关系。表达阶段可分为三个步骤：1）试将每个划开的单句逐一翻译；2）将译出的句子进行调整、组合；3）对译文进行加工润色。"（许建平，2000：156）

　　这样做对于笔译来说是非常实用的。但是对于同传和视译人员，由于时间的限制，这样反复思考和斟酌则是不可能的。他们必须边听边做，或是边看边做，要跟随发言人的速度，没有可能先将全句听完或看完。虽然有经验的会议翻译都有一定的预测能力，在听到一部分内容之后，预测句子其后的内容和结构，但毕竟还是要顺着原文，一点点译出。这说明，长句对视译人员来说更加困难。

　　对于长句的翻译处理，笔译人员会遵从几种有效的方法。比如，张培基等提出了四种翻译长句的方法，即：顺序法、逆序法、分译法、综合法。（张培基，1980：155-164）许建平提出了六种方法，即：内嵌法、切分法、倒置法、拆分法、插入法、重组法。（许建平，2000：156-190）宋天锡等也提出了四种译法：拆离法、改变顺序法、插入法、重组法。（宋天锡，2000：249-259）从这些不同的方法中，我们可以看出，长句的处理确实是翻译的难点。这些方法在笔译中也是综合使用，根据长句的具体情况，使用不同的方法。

根据这些方法的基本特征，我们发现有些在视译中是无法使用的。原因是大多都要求译员读懂全句，理解各个部分的关系，而在视译中，译员无法做到的恰恰是读完全句。最多看到第五、六个词的时候，译员就必须开始翻译了。当然，这些翻译方法有的是具有借鉴意义的。下面我们以张培基先生的四种方法为例，看看哪些可以用到视译之中，哪些无法用到视译之中。

首先是顺序法。张培基先生对顺序法的定义是："有些英语长句所叙述的一连串动作基本上是按动作发生的时间先后安排，有些英语长句的内容是按照逻辑关系安排。这与汉语表达方法比较一致，因此翻译时一般可按照原文顺序译出。"（张培基，1980：156）我们来看张先生给出的一个例子：On August 1, the gunboat began her mission, which was, in the eyes of the defenders, a provocative act and seemed to be part of the overall assault which had begun on July 31. 原译文是："8 月 1 日炮舰开始执行任务。在防御者看来，这是一次挑衅行动，而且似乎是 7 月 31 日开始的全面攻击的一个组成部分。"

译者将原来的长句分成三个部分：On August 1, the gunboat began her mission, // which was, in the eyes of the defenders, a provocative act // and seemed to be part of the overall assault which had begun on July 31. 然后根据这三个部分，依次译出。从总体上来看，这是比较符合视译原则的。当然，译者只是根据原文的逻辑关系来分，并没有考虑各个部分的长度。

其次是逆序法，即"有些英语长句的表达次序与汉语表达习惯不同，甚至完全相反，这时就必须从原文后面译起，逆着原文的顺序翻译。"（张培基，1980：158）也就是说，这样的句子要做语序上的大调整。我们也来看看张培基先生举的例子：And I take heart from the fact that the enemy, which boasts that it can occupy the strategic point in a couple of hours, has not yet been able to take even the outlying regions, because of the stiff resistance that gets in the way. 原译文是："由于受到顽强抵抗阻挡着，吹嘘能在几个小时就占领战略要地的敌人甚至还没有占领外围地带，这一事实使我增强了信心。"

译者是将原语序完全颠倒之后译出的。这样的处理，对于笔译人员来说，是正常的，也是合理的。但是对于视译人员来说，则无法做到。越是长句，越要顺译。所以，逆序法不适用于视译和同传。

　　第三是分译法。"有时英语长句中主句或从句与修饰语间的关系不十分密切，翻译时可按汉语多用短句的习惯，把长句的从句或短语化为句子，分开来叙述；为使语意连贯，有时还可以适当增加词语。"（张培基，1980：160-161）所举的例子是：The president said at a press conference dominated by questions on yesterday's election results that he could not explain why the Republicans had suffered such a widespread defeat, which in the end would deprive the Republican Party of long-held superiority in the House. 原译文是："在一次记者招待会上，问题集中于昨天的选举结果，总统就此发了言。他说他不能够解释为什么共和党遭到了这样大的失败。这种情况最终会使共和党失去在众议院中长期享有的优势。"

　　译者根据意思将原句拆分成三个单句：1）总统发言；2）总统不能解释共和党的失败；3）失败可能导致的结果。拆句分译是符合视译原则的。并且拆句分译也是视译处理长句的基本技巧之一。视译与笔译不同的是，笔译往往根据意思进行拆句分译，而视译要在兼顾长度的情况下拆句分译。比如，笔译可以将 The president said at a press conference dominated by questions on yesterday's election results 作为第一个拆分部分，但在视译中，这仍然太长，仍须进一步拆分。

　　第四种是综合法。"有些英语长句顺译或逆译都感到不便，分译也有困难，这时就应仔细斟酌，或按时间先后，或按逻辑顺序，有顺有逆、有主有次地对应全句进行综合处理。"（张培基，1980：162）所举的例子是：By the middle of the year, he warned, the Soviet Union would overtake the United States in the number of land-based strategic missiles, the result of a massive Soviet effort beginning in the mid-1960s, after the Cuban fiasco, to achieve at least parity and possibly superiority in nuclear weapons. 原译文为："他警告说，到本年年中，苏联将在陆上发射的战略导弹的数量上超过美国，因为苏联在古巴事件中遭到失败之后，从 20 世纪 60 年代中期起就大力发展导弹，目的是为了在核武器方面至少达到同美国均等，并力争超过美国。"

　　译者在这一句中使用了顺序法、逆序法、分译法等不同的技巧，所以称之为综合法。对于笔译人员来说，综合法是常用的。实际上，任何一个长句的处理，可能都要兼用各种不同的方法。纵观以上四种基本方法，顺序法和分译法比较符合视译的要求。但是，决定视译的顺序及如何分译的主要依据是我们在第二单元中所讲的视译单位。所以，视译中长句处理的基本技巧是：拆分长句，顺次译出。也就是以视译单位为基本拆分依据，然后按照拆分后的单位顺序译出。我们在下一单元里会详细解释。这里只举一个例子简单说明。

我们以上面用过的句子为例：And I take heart from the fact that the enemy, which boasts that it can occupy the strategic point in a couple of hours, has not yet been able to take even the outlying regions, because of the stiff resistance that gets in the way. 在翻译这个句子的时候，译者使用了逆序法，将原句顺序做了很大的调整。如果不做这样大的调整，是否可以译出原句呢？

我们先将原句用视译单位拆分开来，即将原句断为八个类意群：And I take heart from the fact // that the enemy, which boasts // that it can occupy the strategic point // in a couple of hours, // has not yet been able // to take even the outlying regions, // because of the stiff resistance // that gets in the way. 然后照此顺序依次译出："我的信心大增，// 因为敌人曾吹嘘，// 可以占领战略要地，// 并且只消几个小时。// 但现在甚至仍未能 // 占领外围地带。// 这是由于我们顽强的抵抗，// 阻止了他们的前进。"

总之，视译长句仍然需要把握视译的基本原则，那就是依序顺译。

二、语段视译

1 词汇与表达

在进行语段视译前，请先预习以下词汇与表达。

wear off	消失
Nonconformist Memorial Hall	新教纪念馆
apostle	信徒
draw a red herring across the trail	转移对主要问题的注意力
gospel	真理，经典

2 视译语段

请在 3 分钟之内迅速阅读下面的语段，了解大意，然后结合所学要点进行视译练习。视译时要保持正常语速，译文要顺畅达意。

At all these meetings I took part in the debates. My excessive nervousness soon wore off. One of the public meetings I haunted was at the Nonconformist Memorial Hall in Farringdon Street in 1884. The speaker of the evening, very handsome and eloquent, was Henry George, American apostle of Land Nationalization and Single Tax. He struck me dumb and turned me to economics. I read his *Progress and Poverty*, and went to a meeting of Hyndman's Marxist Democratic Federation, where I rose and I protested against its drawing a red herring across the trail blazed by George. I was contemptuously dismissed as a novice who had not read the great first volume of Marx's *Capital*. I promptly read it, and returned to announce my complete conversion by it. Immediately contempt changed to awe; for Hyndman's disciples had not read the book themselves, it being then accessible only in Deville's French version in the British Museum reading room, my daily resort. From that hour I was a speaker with a gospel, no longer an apprentice trying to master the art of public speaking.[1]（庄绎传，1999：98-99）

原译文：在所有这些集会上，我都参加辩论。过分紧张的心情不久也就消失了。1884 年我参加过一次公众集会，那是在法灵顿大街新教纪念馆举行的。那天晚上讲演的是亨利·乔治，他人品出众，口若悬河，是个主张实行土地国有化和单一税制的美国人。他的讲话使我瞠目结舌，同时也使我转向经济学。我看了他的《进步与贫困》，又去参加海德门的马克思主义组织"民主联盟"举行的会议。会上我起来发言，指责他们节外生枝，破坏了乔治开辟的道路。他们轻蔑地说我是个新手，连马克思的《资本论》第一卷这部重要著作都没有读过。我随即读了《资本论》第一卷，又来参加会议的时候，就宣布我在它的影响下，彻底改变了自己的信仰。轻蔑顿时变成了敬畏，因为海德门的信徒们并没有读过这本书，当时这本书只有德维尔的法文译本，放在不列颠博物馆的阅览室里。我每天就呆在那里。从这时候起，我成了一个按照经书讲话的人，而不再是一心想掌握演说艺术的小学生了。

3　视译译文

	断　句	译　文
1	At all these meetings	在所有这些集会上，
2	I took part in the debates.	我都参加了辩论，
3	My excessive nervousness soon wore off.	过分紧张的心情不久也就消失了。

（待续）

1　较原文略有删改。

（续上表）

	断　句	译　文
4	One of the public meetings I haunted was	有一次公众集会我也参加了，
5	at the Nonconformist Memorial Hall in Farringdon Street	那是在位于法灵顿大街的新教纪念馆举行的，
6	in 1884.	时间是 1884 年。
7	The speaker of the evening,	那天晚上的讲演人
8	very handsome and eloquent,	人品出众，口若悬河，
9	was Henry George,	他叫亨利·乔治，
10	American apostle	是个美国人，
11	of Land Nationalization and Single Tax.	主张实行土地国有化和单一税制。
12	He struck me dumb	他的讲话使我瞠目结舌，
13	and turned me to economics.	同时也使我转向经济学。
14	I read his *Progress and Poverty*,	我看了他的《进步与贫困》，
15	and went to a meeting	又去参加了一个会议，
16	of Hyndman's Marxist Democratic Federation,	会议是海德门的马克思主义组织"民主联盟"举办的。
17	where I rose and I protested against	会上我站起来发言指责他们，
18	its drawing a red herring across the trail	说他们转移视线、偏离正路，
19	blazed by George.	也就是偏离了乔治开辟的道路。
20	I was contemptuously dismissed as a novice	我被他们轻蔑地说成新手，
21	who had not read the great first volume of Marx's *Capital*.	说我连马克思的《资本论》第一卷这部大作都没有读过。
22	I promptly read it,	我随即读了《资本论》第一卷，

（待续）

（续上表）

	断　句	译　文
23	and returned to announce my complete conversion by it.	又来参加会议，宣布这本书彻底改变了我的信仰。
24	Immediately contempt changed to awe;	顿时轻蔑变成了敬畏，
25	for Hyndman's disciples had not read the book themselves,	因为海德门的信徒们没有读过这本书，
26	it being then accessible only in Deville's French version	当时这本书只有德维尔的法文译本，
27	in the British Museum reading room,	放在不列颠博物馆的阅览室里。
28	my daily resort.	而我每天都会到那里去。
29	From that hour	从那时候起，
30	I was a speaker with a gospel,	我成了一个引经据典的讲演人，
31	no longer an apprentice	我不再是一个小学生，
32	trying to master the art of public speaking.	一个学习演说艺术的小学生了。

4　视译点评

1. 原文第三句：One of the public meetings I haunted was // at the Nonconformist Memorial Hall in Farringdon Street // in 1884.

原译文将此句句尾的时间状语 in 1884 置于句首，并将主语中的后置限定性定语从句 I haunted 译为主语和谓语，同时，把主语中被限定的中心词 One of the public meetings 译为该句的宾语。视译时，不作调整，而是通过添加"有"字将原句主语译为一个分句"有一次公众集会我也参加了"，把原句的谓语和地点时间表语分成两个视译单位，在原句谓语前添加指示代词"那"构成另一个分句，译为"那是在位于法灵顿大街的新教纪念馆举行的"，"时间是 1884 年"。由于这一句的地点状语较长，也可以将地点状语本身分为两个视译单位：at the Nonconformist Memorial Hall // in Farringdon Street，译为"那是在新教纪念馆举行的，纪念馆位于法灵顿大街"。

2. 原文第四句：The speaker of the evening, // very handsome and eloquent, // was Henry George, // American apostle // of Land Nationalization and Single Tax.

句中表语的同位语较长。原译文把其中作后置定语 of Land Nationalization and Single Tax 的介词短语按汉语中定语的位置放在中心词之前，译为"主张实行土地国有化和单一税制的美国人"。采用这种处理方法需要读完整个同位语才能开始翻译。视译时，为了节省时间，可以先将同位语的中心词译成一个分句"是个美国人"，然后把 apostle 译作动词"主张"，把作后置定语的介词短语译为它的宾语"实行土地国有化和单一税制"，形成另一分句。

3. 原文第六句：I read his *Progress and Poverty*, // and went to a meeting // of Hyndman's Marxist Democratic Federation, // where I rose and I protested against // its drawing a red herring across the trail // blazed by George.

虽然这是一个长句，但是视译时，按照视译单位依次译成句子困难不大，只是句尾的后置过去分词定语 blazed by George 是一个难点。可以另分一句，译为："也就是乔治开辟的道路。"

4. 原文第九句：Immediately contempt changed to awe; // for Hyndman's disciples had not read the book themselves, // it being then accessible only in Deville's French version // in the British Museum reading room, // my daily resort.

此句中，表示原因的独立成分较长，其中又包含了两个介词短语和一个同位语，会给视译造成困难。原译文将这部分分成两个句子，依序译成："当时这本书只有德维尔的法文译本，放在不列颠博物馆的阅览室里"和"我每天就呆在那里"。这种处理方法与视译原则一致，但是在视译同位语 my daily resort 时，加上"而"字能够更好地使听众理解整句的逻辑关系。

三、实战练习

1 词汇与表达

请先熟悉以下词汇与表达，并适当地运用在视译中。

the Heritage Foundation	（美国）传统基金会
US-China SED（Strategic Economic Dialog）	美中经济战略对话
genesis	诞生

brokerage	经纪业
proprietary training	独立经营培训
QFII（Qualified Foreign Institutional Investors）	合格境外机构投资人
QDII（Qualified Domestic Institutional Investors）	合格境内机构投资人
debit card	借记卡
non-life insurer	非人寿保险
counterfeit goods	假冒商品
precautionary savings	预防性存款
market-determined exchange rate	市场化汇率

2 实战课文

请在 15 分钟之内迅速阅读下面的讲话，了解大意。视译时要保持正常语速，译文要顺畅达意。

China and the Strategic Economic Dialog

Treasury Secretary of the United States   Henry M. Paulson

Washington, D.C., 2007

It's a pleasure to be here this morning to talk about the US-China economic relationship. Prior to the first Strategic Economic Dialog meeting in Beijing last December, Heritage Foundation published a "Web Memo" offering insights and advice about the SED. One of the points made was that American officials should not approach the dialog as an opportunity to lecture Chinese officials. In a similar vein, I won't approach our time this morning as an opportunity to lecture you, given the depth of Heritage's expertise on China. I look forward to sharing my views, and to hearing about yours during the discussion following my remarks.

You are certainly familiar with the genesis of the SED. In August 2006, President Bush and President Hu agreed to create an on-going forum to manage our economic relationship, for our mutual benefit, on a long-term strategic basis. We held our inaugural meeting in Beijing, continued our efforts through a series of meetings among Chinese and US officials, and held the second meeting two weeks ago here in Washington, D.C.. This dialog is important because we must get this relationship right. An open, honest economic relationship between our two countries is important to the future of the global economy.

For over 30 years, the Heritage Foundation has been formulating and promoting free market public policies. There is much common ground in your commitment to the principles of free enterprise and the over-riding objectives of broad-based economic engagement with China. **Across the spectrum of economic issues, I believe it is in the best interest of the United States, China and the rest of the world that China move more quickly to adopt market-based reforms.** （句1）And that is one of the primary objectives of the SED to speed the pace of reform in China.

We who believe in open economies are swimming against a strong protectionist tide these days. As I explained to the Chinese, a large section of the American public doesn't believe that the benefits of trade are being shared equally between or within our two countries, and Congress reflects that view. The Chinese delegation had the opportunity to meet with Congressional leaders during their visit. I think the meetings were mutually respectful, and it was beneficial for the Chinese to personally meet those who have such serious concerns.

Protectionism isn't a growing force only in the United States. It is playing a role in domestic politics in China as well. This fall, the Communist Party of China will hold its 17th Party Congress, to determine changes in leadership. This may impact many aspects of national policy, including the pace of economic reform in China.

The task of the SED is long-term, and that is difficult in a town where short-termism is the order of the day. A newspaper headline at the conclusion of the recent SED meeting said that it did not "resolve major issues". This, in my opinion, misses the point. The dialog is an on-going process. To get results, we must build relationships, and take smaller, deliberate steps forward together to create momentum for greater change. Through candid discussions, we will ease, rather than increase, tensions and get to solutions and action.

The second SED meeting produced tangible results that have laid the groundwork for greater progress. In particular, we made notable progress on civil aviation, energy and the environment, and financial services. **We announced a new air services agreement that will make it easier, cheaper, and more convenient to fly people and to ship goods between the US and China.** （句2）Over the next several years, we estimate that this agreement will stimulate some $5 billion in new business for our airlines as they take advantage of growing travel between our two countries. In addition to doubling the number of passenger flights over the next five years, by 2011 we will have full air cargo services available. Our future goal is to get a fully liberalized agreement in place, just as the United States recently accomplished with the European Union.

We also made progress in fostering further development of China's financial markets, an area which is crucial to China's transition to a market-based economy. The Chinese will remove a block of entry on new foreign securities firms and resume licensing securities companies this year. They will also allow foreign securities firms to expand into brokerage, proprietary training and fund management businesses. They will increase the quotas for Qualified Foreign Institutional Investors (QFIIs) from $10 billion to $30 billion, and remove restrictions on the types of investments that Qualified Domestic Institutional Investors (QDIIs) can make outside of China. **Together, these agreements will expand opportunities for US financial services firms and, by allowing greater financial flows, help create the basis for moving more quickly to a market-determined exchange rate. （句 3 ）**

China will also allow foreign-invested banks, including US banks, to offer their own brand of Renminbi-denominated credit and debit cards, and will complete decisions on pending applications for US non-life-insurers to convert into subsidiaries by the first of August.

Our discussions also focused on increasing government transparency and intellectual property rights. We signed an agreement to strengthen the enforcement of intellectual property laws, and to maintain an exchange between our respective Customs staff to share experiences on counterfeit goods and seizures.

Through the SED, we also collaborated on a series of policies to help promote energy security and protect the environment, which will affect not only our two countries but nations around the world. In particular, we reached agreements that will create demand and incentives for the rapid development and deployment of clean and efficient energy technology. We also agreed to work together as part of the WTO Doha negotiations to discuss reducing or eliminating tariffs in order to increase access to important environmental technologies.

I again pressed the Chinese to increase the flexibility of their exchange rate in the short term and to transition to a market-determined exchange rate in the medium term. The Chinese have taken some steps, and they can do more. While currency reform is not going to eliminate our trade deficit, a market-determined exchange rate that reflects the underlying fundamentals of the Chinese economy is one component of the actions needed to address imbalances.

Rebalancing China's growth to be less dependent on exports is key to reducing China's trade surplus, and assuring that China can continue to grow in the future without generating large imbalances. Moving more quickly to embrace competition and market principles will also spread the benefits of China's robust growth to all of China's people. Just as important is addressing the structural reasons why Chinese households save so much and consume so little. Precautionary savings rates would likely decrease, and consumption increase, if there were a stronger social safety net. Competitive retail financial services would allow the Chinese public to insure against risk, finance major expenditures like education, and garner a higher return on their savings. **Investments driven by market signals and expected profitability, rather than by administrative guidance, combined with a reduction in precautionary savings, would shift the economy from its infrastructure and export manufacturing focus and spread prosperity more widely. (句 4)** This can only be beneficial, and China's consumption and import level can only increase.

The question, of course, is how do we get there? We will have our third SED meeting in December. Between now and then, we will continue to actively work on the trade agenda, on opening markets, increasing transparency and innovation, rebalancing growth and promoting energy efficiency and security, as well as environmental protection measures. We will continue our focus on financial services, moving at a faster pace toward a market-driven currency and expanding US access in the services sector. We have room to be more creative and accomplish a good deal more.

As I said at the opening of the recent SED meeting, Americans are impatient to see real change. Today, China is part-way between an administered economy and a market-based one. I think that the greater risk for China is in moving too slowly, not in moving too quickly, and I have tried to impress that upon the Chinese at every opportunity. **I view my job as working with Vice-Premier Wu Yi to continue a constructive relationship that speeds our pace forward on the long-term strategic road, while building confidence and encouraging both sides to overcome hurdles and focus on achievements. (句 5)**

3 难句分析与视译处理

句 1： Across the spectrum of economic issues, I believe it is in the best interest of the United States, China and the rest of the world that

China move more quickly to adopt market-based reforms.

笔译译文：纵观所有经济问题，我相信中国加快市场经济改革最符合美国、中国以及世界其他各国的利益。

视译译文：

	断　句	译　文
1	Across the spectrum of economic issues,	纵观所有经济问题，
2	I believe	我相信
3	it is in the best interest of	最有利于
4	the United States, China and the rest of the world	美国、中国以及世界的做法是
5	that China move more quickly	中国加快转型
6	to adopt market-based reforms.	实行市场经济改革。

句 2：We announced a new air services agreement that will make it easier, cheaper, and more convenient to fly people and to ship goods between the US and China.

笔译译文：我们宣布了一项新的航空服务协议，从而使中美间的客运和货运更方便、更便宜、更快捷。

视译译文：

断　句	译　文
We announced a new air services agreement	我们宣布了一项新的航空服务协议，
that will make it easier, cheaper, and more convenient	以便提供更方便、更便宜、更快捷的服务，
to fly people and to ship goods between the US and China.	促进美中两国的客运和货运。

句 3：Together, these agreements will expand opportunities for US financial services firms and, by allowing greater financial flows, help create the basis for moving more quickly to a market-determined exchange rate.

笔译译文： 以上协议将扩大美国金融服务公司的商机，而且通过允许金融流动增加为汇率更快市场化创造了条件。

视译译文：

断　句	译　文
Together, these agreements will expand opportunities	以上协议将扩大商机，
for US financial services firms and,	使美国金融服务公司得益，
by allowing greater financial flows,	还可以通过促进更多金融流动的方式，
help create the basis	创造条件，
for moving more quickly to a market-determined exchange rate.	更快地实现汇率的市场化。

句4： Investments driven by market signals and expected profitability, rather than by administrative guidance, combined with a reduction in precautionary savings, would shift the economy from its infrastructure and export manufacturing focus and spread prosperity more widely.

笔译译文： 如果根据市场信号和预期获利进行投资，而非按照行政导向投资，再加上预防性储蓄的减少，这将使经济发展摆脱靠基础设施建设和以出口制造业产品为主的现状，并使更多地区繁荣起来。

视译译文：

断　句	译　文
Investments driven by market signals	投资要以市场信号为牵引，
and expected profitability,	要以预期获利为动力，
rather than by administrative guidance,	而不是根据行政导向投资，
combined with a reduction in precautionary savings,	再加上减少预防性储蓄，

（待续）

（续上表）

断　句	译　文
would shift the economy	这会使经济
from its infrastructure and export manufacturing focus	不再以基础设施建设和出口制造业为主，
and spread prosperity more widely.	也会使更多的地区繁荣起来。

句 5：　　I view my job as working with Vice-Premier Wu Yi to continue a constructive relationship that speeds our pace forward on the long-term strategic road, while building confidence and encouraging both sides to overcome hurdles and focus on achievements.

笔译译文：　我的工作就是与吴仪副总理合作，继续推动利于我们沿着长期战略之路快速前进的建设性伙伴关系，建立信心、鼓励双方战胜困难、着眼成果。

视译译文：

断　句	译　文
I view my job as working with Vice-Premier Wu Yi	我的工作就是与吴仪副总理一起
to continue a constructive relationship	继续推进建设性伙伴关系，
that speeds our pace forward	这样才能加快步伐，
on the long-term strategic road,	沿着长期战略之路前进，
while building confidence	同时，我们要建立信心，
and encouraging both sides	并鼓励双方
to overcome hurdles and focus on achievements.	克服困难，着眼成果。

参考译文

中国与经济战略对话

美国财政部长　亨利·M.保尔森

华盛顿特区，2007 年

　　我十分荣幸今天早上能在此谈谈中美经济关系。第一届经济战略对话于去年 12 月在北京召开前，传统基金会发表了一篇"网络备忘录"，提出了关于经济战略对话的见解和建议。其中一点是，美国官员不应把这一对话看作是对中国官员进行说教的机会。同样，我今天早上也不会对你们进行说教，因为我知道传统基金会对中国的研究是相当有深度的。我期待与你们分享我的观点，并希望在我演讲后从讨论中听到你们的意见。

　　你们对经济战略对话的诞生肯定不陌生。2006 年 8 月，布什总统和胡主席一致同意以长期战略为基础，本着双方互惠的原则，建立一个持久的论坛来处理两国间的经济关系。我们在北京举行了首轮对话，之后中美官员间又进行了一系列会谈。两周前在华盛顿这里举行了第二轮对话。这种对话很重要，因为我们必须使中美经济关系健康发展。两国间是否能形成公开坦诚的经济关系对全球经济的未来至关重要。

　　30 多年以来，传统基金会致力于制定和倡导自由市场的公共政策。你们坚持企业自由经营的相关原则，并把与中国进行广泛的经济接触作为压倒一切的目标，这两者间有共通之处。纵观所有经济问题，我相信中国加快市场经济改革最符合美国、中国以及世界其他各国的利益。因此，推动中国加快改革也是经济战略对话的主要目的之一。

　　我们这些奉行经济开放的人如今正顶着保护主义的强大逆流前行。正如我向中国人所解释的那样，很大一部分美国公众不相信我们两国间或两国内享有同等的贸易利益。国会也反映了这一点。中方代表团在他们访美期间得到机会与国会领导人会面。我认为会议中双方彼此尊重。能够与他们这些对中美贸易充满担忧的人亲自会面对中方而言相当有益。

　　保护主义势力不仅在美国逐渐壮大，它也影响着中国的国内政治。今年秋天，中国共产党将举行第十七届党代会，届时将举行领导班子的换届选举。这将影响到国内政策的方方面面，包括中国经济改革的步伐。

　　经济战略对话的任务是长期的，这对于一个日常只重视短期目标的小城尤为困难。最近这次经济战略对话会议结束时，一家报纸的头条称经济战略对话未"解决任何重大问题"。在我看来，这根本是无的放矢。该对话是一个不断推进的过程。要取得成效，我们必须先建立关系，有计划地小步前进，共同创造更大的变革势头。通过开展真诚的讨论，我们将缓和而非加重紧张情绪，从而找到对策并采取行动。

　　第二届经济战略对话取得的有形成果为争取更大的进展打下了基础。特别值得一提的是，我们在民航、能源和环境以及金融服务几方面取得了显著进展。我们宣布了一项新的航空服务协议，从而使中美间的客运和货运更方便、更便宜、更快捷。接下来几年内，由于两国间的往来会愈加频繁，我们预计该协议将为我们的航空公司带来约 50 亿美元的新生意。除了未来的五年内将客运航班数量翻一番之外，到 2011 年我们将提供全面的空中货运服务。我们未来的目标是像美国最近与欧盟达成的协议一样，与中国达成一项全面开放的协议。

　　我们在巩固中国金融市场的未来发展方面也取得了进展。金融市场对中国向市场经济转型而言尤为关键。中国今年将为新的外国证券公司的进入扫除一道障碍并恢复向证券公司发放许可证。他们还将允许外国证券公司把在中国的业务扩大到经纪人业务、独立经营培训和基金管理等方面。他们将把合格的境外机构投资者（简称 QFII）的配额从 100 亿美元提高到 300 亿美元，并解除对合格境内投资者（简称 QDII）在中国以外投资种类的限制。以上协议将扩大美国金融服务公司的商机，而且通过允许金融流动增加为汇率更快市场化创造了条件。

　　中方还将允许包括美国银行在内的外资银行发行本银行的人民币储蓄卡和信用卡，并将在 8 月 1 日前就美国财险公司分支机构转为子公司的申请做出决定。

　　我们的讨论还涉及提高政府工作透明度以及保护知识产权。我们签署了有关加强知识产权法实施的协议和关于继续两国海关官员交流，分享查处收缴假冒商品经验的协议。

　　通过开展经济战略对话，我们还就一系列保障能源安全和保护环境的政策进行了合作。这不仅将影响到中美两国，还将影响世界其他各国。特别是我们达成了几项协议，决定将创造需求和建立奖励机制来鼓励快速开发和应用清洁高效的能源技术。双方还同意作为多哈世贸组织谈判的一个部分，共同讨论如何通过减少，乃至取消关税，增加重要环保技术的获取途径。

　　我再次要求中方在短期内提高其汇率的灵活性并在中期内向汇率市场化过渡。中国已经采取了一些步骤，但他们还有行动的空间。虽然货币改革不能消除我们的贸易逆差，但是，反映中国经济的重要原则的汇率机制市场化是解决贸易不平衡问题的方法之一。

　　调节中国的经济增长，降低其对出口的依赖是减少中国的贸易顺差的关键，并能确保中国未来的持续增长，避免大幅度失衡。加快引入竞争机制，采取市场原则也将使中国人民能够分享中国经济腾飞产生的好处。同样重要的是找到中国家庭存款高、消费少的社会经济结构方面的原因。如果建立起牢固的社会保障网，预防性存款比率将有可能降低，而消费将会增加。竞争力强的现有零售金融服务将使中国大众能规避风险，能负担大笔用于教育等方面的开销，并用他们的积蓄进行投资，获得高回报。如果根据市场信号和预期获利进行投资，而非按照行政导向投资，再加上预防性储蓄的减少，这将使经济发展摆脱靠基础设施建设和以出口制造业产品为主的现状，并使更多地区繁荣起来。这样做有百利而无一害，中国的消费和进口水平也只会提高，不会下降。

　　当然需要解决的问题是：我们具体该怎么做才能实现上述目标呢？我们将于12月举行第三届经济战略对话。在此之前，我们将继续积极合作，制定有关贸易议程，开放市场，提高透明度，鼓励创新，平衡增长，提高能源使用率，保障能源安全和采取环保措施的政策。我们将继续聚焦金融业，加快推进汇率市场化，并扩大美国在服务业所占比例。我们有足够空间来开发创造力并取得更大的成功。

　　正如我在最近这次经济战略对话会议开幕时所说，美国已经迫不及待地希望看到真正的变化了。今天，中国正处于政府指导经济和市场经济之间，我认为中国面临的更大的风险是前进得太慢，而非太快。我已经利用每个机会来使中方加深这一认识。我的工作就是与吴仪副总理合作，继续推动利于我们沿着长期战略之路快速前进的建设性伙伴关系，建立信心、鼓励双方战胜困难、着眼成果。

四、自主训练

　　请在15分钟之内迅速阅读下面的讲话，了解大意。学生可组成对子练习，互相监控对视译技巧的掌握情况、视译质量和现场表现，或以边视译边录音的形式进行个人练习。视译时要保持正常语速，译文要顺畅达意。如遇难句，可在首次视译后参照"实战练习"中难句分析与视译处理的方法进行练习，找出解决方法。

ASEAN-China Relations: Harmony and Development
Secretary-General of ASEAN Ong Keng Yong
Singapore, 2006

I am honored to join you this morning and share my thoughts with you. This is the Commemorative Symposium to mark the 15th Anniversary of ASEAN-China Dialog Relations. The theme of the symposium "Harmony and Development" is fascinating. This is because these two concepts are both contradictory and complementary at the same time. Please also allow me to express my sincere congratulations to the organizer of this event, the East Asian Institute in Singapore, for the warm welcome and excellent arrangements made for this Symposium.

Having participated in the Commemorative Summit to mark the 15th Anniversary of ASEAN-China Dialog Relations on 30 October, 2006, in Nanning, I observe the increasingly close relationship between the leaders of ASEAN member countries and China. Regular high-level dialogs and consultations among the leaders will help in building mutual trust, confidence and comfort, thus allowing a free-flow and frank discussion and exchange of views on issues of common interest. Such atmosphere will certainly serve well for the continuous nurturing of ASEAN-China relations.

Building a Strong Foundation

The historical links between Southeast Asia and China date back to centuries during which individual countries of this region and China carried out trade, cultural interactions and sea voyages. Collectively, as ASEAN, the relationship between countries in Southeast Asia and China started to open up in the year 1991. At the early stage, the relations progressed gradually as both sides worked toward achieving a significant level of comfort and confidence. ASEAN and China have always managed to find innovative ways and means to deal with challenges and move the relationship forward.

Now, 15 years later one could observe that ASEAN-China relationship has matured. Cooperation has developed in breadth and depth, covering various areas of collaboration, in politics and security, economics and trade, socio-culture and people-to-people interaction. The relationship reached a higher level with the signing of the Joint Declaration on Strategic Partnership for Peace and Prosperity in October

2003 and the adoption of a five-year ASEAN-China Plan of Action to implement the Joint Declaration in November 2004 by the leaders of ASEAN and China. These important documents provide the guide and road map for advancing cooperation between the two sides.

Supporting and Complementary Role

ASEAN and China are playing the supporting and complementary role in each other's socio-economic development and in maintaining peace and stability in the region. Many would argue that China is a strong competitor of ASEAN with far-reaching impact on the latter's strategic outlook and economic prosperity. On the contrary, ASEAN views the fast growth of China and its development as a positive phenomenon spurring ASEAN to integrate economically in a faster pace. ASEAN believes that both sides could tap on the complementarities for mutual gains.

ASEAN views China as a close neighbor and an important dialog partner with tremendous potential to offer. With its rapid economic growth and a population of about 1.3 billion people, China is a huge consumer of ASEAN products and also a source of future FDI to the region. In addition, ASEAN is benefiting from the large number of Chinese tourists visiting the region and vice versa. The arrival of tourists from China averaged 3 million in 2004 and 2005.

China is also supporting ASEAN's integration through the promotion of trade and investment in the region. In addition, it supports various regional integration schemes. China contributed $1 million to the ASEAN Development Fund and pledged another $1 million for the implementation of Initiative for ASEAN Integration (IAI) projects. Furthermore, China is involved in the ASEAN-Mekong Basin Development Cooperation (AMBDC), the Brunei Indonesia Malaysia Philippines-East ASEAN Growth Area (BIMP-EAGA) and other sub-regional economic initiatives.

ASEAN is now vigorously embarking on its integration and community building efforts to push ahead to make this region a single market and production base with free flow of goods, services, investment and skilled labor, and freer flow of capital. All this will further contribute to the enhancement of ASEAN's economic base, which in turn will also benefit China.

Enhancing Economic Partnership

Economic cooperation has grown rapidly, especially after the signing of the

Framework Agreement on Comprehensive Economic Cooperation (CEC), which provides for the establishment of an ASEAN-China Free Trade Area, scheduled for 2010 for Brunei Darussalam, Indonesia, Malaysia, the Philippines, Singapore, Thailand and China; and for Cambodia, Lao PDR[1], Myanmar and Viet Nam to join by 2015.

According to ASEAN's statistics, total trade between ASEAN and China grew by 27% from $89 billion in 2004 to $113 billion in 2005. The contribution of total ASEAN-China trade to the total ASEAN trade with the world also increased from 8.3% in 2004 to 9.3% in 2005. However, China's foreign direct investment to ASEAN declined by 15% from $670 million in 2004 to $570 million in 2005. Cumulative (1999-2005) China's FDI to ASEAN amounted to $1.4 billion. Certainly, more Chinese companies can invest substantively in the industrial and job creating sectors of ASEAN's economies.

The Agreements on Trade in Goods (TIG) and Dispute Settlement Mechanism under the Framework Agreement on CEC were signed in November 2004. The Agreement on TIG had come into force on 20 July, 2005. Business transactions and the flow of FDI are expected to increase as a result of the entering into force of the Agreement on TIG and the reduction and elimination of tariffs. The Agreement on Trade in Services between ASEAN and China is expected to be signed soon. Negotiations on the agreement on investment are ongoing.

One area for both sides to work on is infrastructure development to accelerate ASEAN's economic growth. China's investment here will also narrow the development gaps among ASEAN member countries. A good systematic approach will be beneficial to China's inner provinces such as Yunnan, Sichuan, etc.

Promoting People-to-People Exchange

On socio-cultural cooperation, there have been several activities organized in ASEAN and China to enhance people-to-people exchanges and promote public awareness among the peoples of ASEAN and China. While, the business sector has established several events such as the annual ASEAN-China Expo and ASEAN-China Business and Investment Summit to help match-making, networking and expanding business linkages, more is needed to be done to ensure other sections of

---

1 Lao People's Democratic Republic.

the population—government officials, youth, civil society and intellectuals—could interact to comprehensively strengthen ASEAN-China dialog partnership.

Basically, information on ASEAN and China must be more effectively disseminated to all segments of the society. More websites, greater news coverage and documentaries should be made available to reach out to a large spectrum of audiences, both in ASEAN and China. China's announcement at the ASEAN-China Commemorative Summit in October 2006 in Nanning that it would invite 1,000 youth from ASEAN member countries to visit China and its offer to train 8,000 ASEAN professionals in different fields in the coming five years are a good gesture in fostering people-to-people interaction, especially among the young people.

Moving into the Future

The ASEAN-China dialog partnership has developed steadily over the past 15 years. The broad-based cooperation is guided by well-thought-out plans and a long-term vision. To a large extent, strong political will on both sides ensure that the relations are properly nurtured and strengthened in a calibrated manner.

However, ASEAN and China should not take their past accomplishments for granted since the region and the world are constantly changing. As such the relationship would face various new opportunities and challenges, and the way forward would be for ASEAN and China to continue to build upon their achievements. It is also vital for both sides to manage potential challenges with utmost care by taking into account the overall state of the relationship and the bigger strategic picture.

In the coming years, ASEAN and China will continue to strengthen their cooperation and implement what both sides have committed to do, especially the realization of the FTA[1] so that it would bring about more tangible benefits to the peoples of ASEAN and China. Moreover, both sides will have to work closely to address challenges facing the region such as transnational crime and terrorism, SARS, avian influenza and natural disasters.

With rapid developments in the region, ASEAN has initiated new ideas such as the East Asia Summit (EAS) and the FTA strategy to manage regional affairs and challenges. China's support for ASEAN's initiative is essential for their

---

1　Free Trade Agreement.

success. A cohesive and strong ASEAN is in China's own interest. Narrowing the developmental gap among ASEAN member countries is a key strategy for a cohesive and strong ASEAN. China can play a big role in this ASEAN endeavor.

Looking into the immediate future, another idea worth deliberating is how ASEAN and China should pursue the envisioned East Asia community. This visionary concept is firing the imagination of many scholars and thinkers. The question is how to evolve the multi-faceted and multi-layered existing relationships revolving around the region into a community-based feeling without arousing undue stress and tension. The ASEAN Plus Three framework and mechanisms have been developed over the past 10 years. They must be built upon and a greater value-add obtained from them while the vast potential of the EAS is tapped. I trust that participants to this symposium will add valuable views and share ideas on how to advance and move ASEAN-China strategic partnership forward.

第15单元

长句的视译（Ⅱ）

基本技巧：
• 拆分长句，依序顺译。

一、技巧讲解：长句的视译

在前一单元里，我们谈到了英语长句的笔译技巧。不少学者提出了许多关于长句的翻译技巧，这些技巧给了我们很多启发。但是，在视译中，由于翻译时间和翻译要求的限制，所以，有些技巧是无法使用的。即便是比较符合视译要求的翻译技巧，比如顺序法和分译法，也需要根据视译的特点，以不同的理念加以借鉴，而不能直接照搬。

本单元我们仍然讨论视译中长句的具体处理技巧，主要是通过一些实际的例子来说明。虽然在各种会议的发言中，长句并不占很大比重，但是，长句毕竟不时出现，在训练中更要从严从难，练习好长句的视译。

视译的长句处理基本技巧是"拆分顺译"。所谓"拆分"，就是根据视译单位断句。无论多长的句子，都只能将其拆分成一目可及的视译单位，然后充分使用其他视译技巧，将长句译完。所谓"顺译"，就是按照原来句子的顺序，依从拆分后的视译单位，逐个译出。正如我们在第一单元中所说，由于汉语的高度灵活性，这样做是可行的、合理的。并且，也只有这样做，才能符合视译的要求，争取速度，顺利完成翻译。

下面我们举一些例子来说明长句视译的"拆分顺译"技巧。

例1： Captured documents which we have obtained from individuals who had been infiltrated through this corridor plus prison-of-war reports that we have obtained in recent months led us to believe that the volume of infiltration has expanded substantially.

译文 1: 我们从经由这个走廊渗透进来的人身上缴获的文件，加上近几个月从战俘那里得到的口供，使我们相信，渗透的规模确实扩大了。（张培基，1980：157-158）

译文 2: 缴获的文件是从一些人身上得到的，他们通过这个走廊渗透进来，另外还有战俘的口供，都是近几个月得到的，这些使我们相信，渗透的规模扩大了许多。

【讲解】 这是个很复杂的长句：一个主句，三个定语从句，一个宾语从句。主语 captured documents 附带了两个定语从句：1) which we have obtained from individuals; 2) who had been infiltrated through this corridor。另外还有一个附加语 plus prisoner-of-war reports，而在这个附加语中又有一个定语从句 that we have obtained in recent months。句子的宾语是一个复合成分，其中又包含一个宾语从句 that the volume of infiltration has expanded substantially。

译文 1 是笔译译文，虽然是按照顺序法译的，但顺序的依据是意思，亦即译者将句子根据意思分为四个部分，分别是：1) 我们从经由这个走廊渗透进来的人身上缴获的文件；2) 加上近几个月从战俘那里得到的口供；3) 使我们相信；4) 渗透的规模确实扩大了。但是，在视译中，我们不可能完全根据意思来拆分，笔译译文中，除了第三部分之外，其他部分都有大幅度的语序调整，这也不符合视译要求。

译文 2 是视译译文。译文 2 的做法是，首先要根据视译单位断句，然后按照顺序依次译出。我们把这个长句分为七个类意群：Captured documents // which we have obtained from individuals // who had been infiltrated through this corridor // plus prison-of-war reports // that we have obtained in recent months // led us to believe // that the volume of infiltration has expanded substantially. 然后按顺序译出：“缴获的文件 // 是从一些人身上得到的，// 他们通过这个走廊渗透进来；// 另外还有战俘的口供，// 都是近几个月得到的。// 这些使我们相信，// 渗透的规模扩大了许多。”

例 2: A great number of graduate students were driven into the intellectual slum when in the United States the intellectual poor became the classic poor, the poor under the rather romantic guise of Beat Generation, a real phenomenon in the late 1950s.

译文 1：20 世纪 50 年代后期出现了一个真正的奇观：穷知识分子以"垮掉的一代"这种颇为浪漫的姿态出现而成为美国典型的穷人。正是在这个时候，大批大学毕业生被赶进了知识分子贫民窟。（许建平，2000：177）

译文 2：大批大学毕业生被赶进了知识分子贫民窟。当时在美国，贫穷知识分子变成了典型的穷人，身上还披着"垮掉的一代"的浪漫外衣，这就是 20 世纪 50 年代后期的真实现象。

【讲解】 这也是一个很复杂的句子，其中虽然只包含一个状语从句，但修饰语很多，使句子的翻译，尤其是顺译，成为比较困难的事情。所以译文 1 采用了逆序法，对原句结构做了很大的调整。在视译中，我们仍然需要基本按照原句语序译出。我们还是先根据视译单位断句，将句子拆分为六个类意群：A great number of graduate students // were driven into the intellectual slum // when in the United States // the intellectual poor became the classic poor, // the poor under the rather romantic guise of Beat Generation, // a real phenomenon in the late 1950s. 然后依序译出："大批大学毕业生 // 被赶进了知识分子贫民窟。// 当时在美国，// 贫穷知识分子变成了典型的穷人，// 身上还披着"垮掉的一代"的浪漫外衣，// 这就是 20 世纪 50 年代后期的真实现象。"

例 3：The poor are the first to experience technological progress as a curse which destroys the old muscles-power jobs that previous generations used as a means to fight their way out of poverty.

译文 1：对于以往的几代人来说，旧式的体力劳动是一种用以摆脱贫困的手段，而技术的进步则摧毁了穷人赖以谋生的体力劳动。因此，首先体验到技术进步之害的是穷人。

译文 2：穷人是首先体验技术革新之苦的人。技术革新摧毁了旧式的体力劳动机会，而以前几代穷人都是靠体力劳动来摆脱贫困的。

【讲解】 这是一个复合长句，包含两个定语从句以及其他许多修饰成分。译文 1 对语序进行的大幅度调整，基本上是原来的句首成为译文句尾，原来的句尾成为译文句首。即便是这样的句子，仍然可以依序译出。当然，我们首先要断句如下：The poor are the first // to experience technological progress as a curse // which destroys the old muscles-power jobs // that previous generations used as a means // to fight their way out of poverty. 然后依序译出：" 穷人是首先 // 体验技术革新之苦的人。// 技术革新摧毁了旧式的体力劳动机会，// 而以前几代穷人都是靠体力劳动 // 来摆脱贫困的。"

例 4： At the opening banquet, Nixon seemed to have paraphrased his host's position by saying: "There are of course some who believe that the mere act of saying a statement of principles or a diplomatic conference will bring lasted peace. This is naïve."

译文 1： 尼克松在欢迎宴会上说：" 当然，有些人认为只要发表一项原则声明或举行一次外交会议就能带来持久和平。这真是天真的想法。" 尼克松的这番话似乎是在阐述东道国的立场。（宋天锡，2000：255）

译文 2： 在欢迎宴会上，尼克松似乎是在复述东道国的主场，因为他这样说：" 有人当然会认为，只要发表一个原则声明或是召开一次外交会议就会带来持久和平。这种想法是天真的。"

【讲解】 这个句子包含一个用作状语的介词短语 by saying... 和一个很长的直接引语。因为这个状语难以处理，所以，译者调整了语序，首先译出以这个介词短语引出的直接引语，然后将原文主句放在后面译出。但在视译中，我们可以按照视译原则来做。首先，我们按照视译单位拆分句子：At the opening banquet, // Nixon seemed to have paraphrased his host's position // by saying: // "There are of course some who believe // that the mere act of saying a statement of principles // or a diplomatic conference // will bring lasted peace. // This is naïve." 然后依序译出：" 在欢迎宴会上，// 尼克松似乎是在复述东道国的立场，// 因为他这样说：// '有人当然会认为，// 只要发表一个原则声明 // 或是召开一次外交会议 // 就会带来持久和平。// 这种想法是天真的。'"

总之，对于长句的视译，我们首先要有信心，按照视译要求，采用视译技巧，按顺序翻译是可能的。然后再按照视译单位来拆分句子，依次译出。不管多长和多复杂的句子，都是可以这样处理的。经反复练习，逐步熟练起来，就会养成良好的视译习惯，并且会越来越得心应手。

二、语段视译

1 词汇与表达

在进行语段视译前，请先预习以下词汇与表达。

"universal nation"	"有感召力的普世国家"
acculturation	同化过程
discrete	无关联的
Polyglot	多种语言的混用
monoclonal	单克隆的
Babel	巴别塔（通天塔）

2 视译语段

请在 3 分钟之内迅速阅读下面的语段，了解大意，然后结合所学要点进行视译练习。视译时要保持正常语速，译文要顺畅达意。

One of the major reasons for America's great success as the world's first "universal nation", for its astonishing and unmatched capacity for assimilating immigrants, has been that an automatic part of acculturation was the acquisition of English. And yet during the great immigration debate now raging in Congress, the people's representatives cannot make up their minds whether the current dominance of English should be declared a national asset, worthy of enshrinement in law. Polyglot is fine. When immigrants, like those in Brooklyn, are members of a myriad of linguistic communities, each tiny and discrete, there is no threat to the common culture. But all of that changes when you have an enormous linguistically monoclonal immigration as we do today from Latin America. Then you get not Brooklyn's successful Babel but Canada's restive Quebec. Monoclonal immigration is new for the US, and it changes things radically. If at the turn of the 20th century, Ellis Island had greeted teeming masses speaking not 50 languages but just, say German, America might not have enjoyed the same success at assimilation and national unity that it has.[1]（摘自《英语学习》，2006 年第 12 期，第 24 至 26 页）

1　较原文有删改。

原译文：美国是世界上第一个"有感召力的普世国家"，取得了巨大成功，在移民同化方面表现出惊人的、无与伦比的能力，主要原因之一就在于（移民）学会英语成为同化过程中自然而然的一部分。现在国会正就移民问题进行激烈的辩论，当前英语的主导地位是否应被宣布为国家财富，值得以法律的形式神圣化——对此，人民代表们拿不定主意。多种通用语是好事。如果移民都像布鲁克林的移民一样，分属众多彼此不相关联的语言小群体，那么对共同文化毫无威胁。但是，当某种人数众多、讲单一语种的移民群体涌入美国时，一切都会不同。而我们今天的确有这样一个群体自拉美而来。接踵而来的将不是布鲁克林成功的巴别城，而是加拿大动荡不安的魁北克了。单一语种移民对于美国来说是全新的现象，会带来根本性的变化。如果19世纪与20世纪之交涌入埃利斯岛的移民说的不是50种语言，而只是一种，比如说德语，美国可能就不会在同化移民和民族统一上取得今天的成功。（韦元等译）

3 视译译文

	断 句	译 文
1	One of the major reasons	有许多原因，
2	for America's great success	使美国取得巨大成功，
3	as the world's first "universal nation",	成为世界上第一个"有感召力的普世国家"，
4	for its astonishing and unmatched capacity	使它具有惊人的巨大能力，
5	for assimilating immigrants,	同化来自各国的移民。
6	has been that	其中一个主要原因在于，
7	an automatic part of acculturation	同化过程中自然而然的一部分
8	was the acquisition of English.	是使移民学会英语。
9	And yet during the great immigration debate now raging in Congress,	现在移民问题成为国会激烈辩论的主题，
10	the people's representatives cannot make up their minds	民选的议员们拿不定主意的是，

（待续）

（续上表）

	断　句	译　文
11	whether the current dominance of English	是否当前英语的主导地位
12	should be declared a national asset,	应被宣布为国家的财富，
13	worthy of enshrinement in law.	是否值得以法律的形式神圣化。
14	Polyglot is fine.	讲多种语言是好事。
15	When immigrants, like those in Brooklyn,	如果移民都像布鲁克林的移民一样，
16	are members of a myriad of linguistic communities,	分属许多语言群体，
17	each tiny and discrete,	每个群体很小而且互无关联，
18	there is no threat to the common culture.	那就不会威胁到共同文化。
19	But all of that changes	但现在一切都不同了，
20	when you have an enormous linguistically monoclonal immigration	因为涌入美国的是大量讲单一语种的移民群体，
21	as we do today from Latin America.	就像今天来自拉美的移民。
22	Then you get not Brooklyn's successful Babel	结果自然不是布鲁克林成功的巴别城，
23	but Canada's restive Quebec.	而是加拿大动荡不安的魁北克了。
24	Monoclonal immigration is new for the US,	单一语种移民对于美国来说是全新的现象，
25	and it changes things radically.	会带来剧烈的变化。
26	If at the turn of the 20th century,	如果 19 世纪与 20 世纪之交，
27	Ellis Island had greeted teeming masses speaking not 50 languages	埃利斯岛迎来的移民说的不是 50 种语言，
28	but just, say German,	而只是一种，比如说德语，

（待续）

（续上表）

	断　句	译　文
29	America might not have enjoyed the same success	美国可能就不会取得如此的成就，
30	at assimilation and national unity that it has.	在同化移民和民族统一方面就不会有今天的成功。

4　视译点评

1. 原文第一句：One of the major reasons // for America's great success // as the world's first "universal nation", // for its astonishing and unmatched capacity // for assimilating immigrants, // has been that // an automatic part of acculturation // was the acquisition of English.

　　此句主语部分很长，含有两个并列的、由 for 引导的介词短语，系动词 has been 之后的表语是从句。原译文对全句的语序进行了较大的调整，这样的语序调整使译文意思既忠实于原文，又符合汉语的表达习惯。但是在视译中，这种大调整是不可能的事情。视译要尽量保持原文语序，以视译单位断句后依序译出，比如，句子主语的前半部分是 One of the major reasons // for America's great success // as the world's first "universal nation"，这是个名词词组，可划分为三个视译单位，采取了三个技巧：1) 用增添动词"有"字做引导；2) 把介词"for"译成汉语动词"使"；3) 把介词"as"译成汉语动词"成为"。对应视译译文为："<u>有</u>许多原因，//<u>使</u>美国取得巨大成功，//<u>成为</u>世界上第一个有感召力的普世国家。"原来的长名词词组，被分为三个视译单位，每一个视译单位译成一个汉语动词引导的短句，听起来也很顺耳。

2. 原文第二句：And yet during the great immigration debate now raging in Congress, // the people's representatives cannot make up their minds // whether the current dominance of English // should be declared a national asset, // worthy of enshrinement in law.

　　原译文也是做了很大的语序调整，把原文中的主句 the people's representatives cannot make up their minds 调整到整个句子的句尾："现在国会正就移民问题进行激烈的辩论，当前英语的主导地位是否应被宣布为国家财富，值得以法律的形式神圣化——对此，人民代表们拿不定主意。"视译译文没有调整语序，通过译员语气的变化使听众明白含有"是否"的两个问题：

"当前英语的主导地位是否应被宣布为国家财富"，和"是否值得以法律的形式神圣化"是民选议员辩论的两个问题。

3. 原文第五句：But all of that changes // when you have an enormous linguistically monoclonal immigration // as we do today from Latin America.

　　笔译把说明结果的原文主句"一切都会不同"放在说明条件的从句"但是，当某种人数众多、讲单一语种的移民群体涌入美国时"之后，符合汉语的逻辑表达习惯，同时将原文条件状语中的状语部分 as we do today from Latin America 单独译成一个分句："而我们今天的确有这样一个群体自拉美而来。"视译不作语序调整，利用汉语状语位置的灵活性，把 when 引导的条件从句译成"因为"引导的分句，放在主句之后，意思清楚明白，as 引导的状语从句与笔译译文一样处理，保留在原位。

4. 原文第八句：If at the turn of the 20th century, // Ellis Island had greeted teeming masses speaking not 50 languages // but just, say German, // American might not have enjoyed the same success // at assimilation and national unity that it has.

　　此句主句的笔译做了语序调整，把介词短语 at assimilation and national unity that it has 按照汉语此类状语的位置放在谓语之前，译为"在同化移民和民族统一上取得今天的成功"。视译尽量保持原文语序，把原文主句分解为两个视译单位：America might not have enjoyed the same success // at assimilation and national unity that it has，然后依次分别译为两个分句："美国可能就不会取得如此的成就"和"在同化移民和民族统一方面就不会有今天的成功"。

三、实战练习

1　词汇与表达

　　请先熟悉以下词汇与表达，并适当地运用在视译中。

Bertrand Russell	伯特兰·罗素
political upheaval	政治动乱
fear-monger	散布恐怖情绪的人
periphery	周边

in a nutshell	概括地说
broadband subscriber	宽带上网用户
supertanker	超级油轮
coal-fired power station	燃煤发电站
antagonistic	愤怒的
constituency	选民
value chain	价值链
league	等级，种类

2 实战课文

请在 15 分钟之内迅速阅读下面的讲话，了解大意。视译时要保持正常语速，译文要顺畅达意。

Europe and China: Partnership, Competition and Leadership (Excerpt 1)
Mandelson

Beijing, 2006

An Intelligent Understanding of the Question of China

Almost exactly 86 years ago this month, in 1920, before Tsinghua University moved to Changsha and then back here to Beijing, the outstanding British philosopher and political thinker Bertrand Russell gave a lecture here at this university. It was part of his year in China lecturing on China's future development at the end of which he wrote a book about his impressions. He called the book *The Problem of China* and I searched out a copy while I was preparing for this lecture. Partly because I wanted to see what an educated European and Englishman might have made of China those eight decades ago. Partly because I wondered what advice he had for his fellow Europeans in seeking a partnership with China.

It's a very dated book, but some words from the introduction leapt off the page at me. Russell wrote: "China has an ancient civilization which is now undergoing a very rapid process of change... Chinese problems, even if they affected no one outside China, would be of vast importance, since the Chinese constitute a quarter of the human race. In fact, however, all the world will be vitally affected by the development of Chinese affairs. This makes it important to Europe, almost as much as to Asia, that there should be an intelligent understanding of the questions raised by China, even if, as yet, definitive answers are difficult to give."

I think we are now moving toward those definitive answers. Back in 1920 Russell sensed that China was on the verge of integrating into the international system of nation states. **He knew that it was looking for a way to balance rapid industrialization with the preservation of the social and cultural balances in what was then a largely agricultural society.（句 1）**

But what strikes me is that these words could nevertheless have been written yesterday. In fact, they almost certainly were written in some variation yesterday in a European or America newspaper or journal, or spoken by a politician or a policymaker. These questions are on everyone's lips.

The course of the 20th century, and the course of war and political upheaval in China have delayed China's full integration into the international system. **But we have now come back to a point where the need for an intelligent understanding of the questions raised by China's growing weight and confidence are [is] once again at the forefront of debate.（句 2）**

Today I would like to offer some tentative answers. In a positive way, because I am a "China optimist", not a China fear-monger. This is the spirit and attitude of the European Commission's recently published policy on China which is the basis of my approach. You can sum it up like this: Europe and China are competitors. We are also partners. Together, we share global responsibilities.

China Comes Back to the Center

For the rest of the world it is now unarguable that China's temporary move to the periphery of the international system is over. In a nutshell—and this is the core of my remarks—you could identify any global problem we face and you will find that China is an essential part of the solution, with a role in framing the international agenda and assuming new leadership responsibilities as it does so.

China's international isolation ended for all intents and purposes in 1978 with the Deng Xiaoping reforms and the reasoning that if the Chinese economy could develop the market mechanisms necessary to produce sufficient surplus for export it could spend the income on modernization at home.（句 3） That simple economic idea when applied by, and to, the genius of more than a billion Chinese has become the engine for the single fastest economic transformation the world has ever seen. China's economy has been growing at around 9% a year for two decades and its share of global GDP has risen 10-fold. This has powered China's emergence at the heart of the global economy and the international trading system.

As China and the other emerging economies catch up with the developed world, we are witnessing the creation of a truly multi-polar economic world, and politics is following closely behind. China is an active geopolitical player not just across Asia but increasingly in Africa and also in Latin America. Its competitive exports are restructuring all our economies and changing the dynamics of global trade. It is impacting on every continent.

It is no longer possible for China to shut out the world or behave as if it were outside the system looking in. China's decision to accept a full stake in the existing international trading and collective security system will help decide how effective those systems are or, indeed, whether they continue to exist in their current form. That's why China has no option but to choose effective leadership and shared responsibility in the world.

In growing into its global role, China has not rewritten or bent the laws of economics. The same export led growth and heavy capital investment produced the same results three decades ago in the Republic of Korea and China's Taiwan, and they are producing the same results today in Malaysia and Viet Nam. But the difference in China is one of sheer scale.

China today welds more steel, pours more concrete and burns more coal than any other country in the world. Twenty years ago Europe traded almost nothing with China. Today China is Europe's single biggest source of manufactured goods. By the end of this decade China will be the largest exporter in the world.

This economic growth has lifted more people out of poverty more quickly than any economy in history, which is something we should all celebrate. Last year 80 million Chinese people bought a new cellphone, and China has more broadband subscribers than any other market in the world outside the United States, which means that all of you will live lives your grandparents could not even dream of.

China's policymakers and leaders have recognized that this rapid economic change is creating huge social and environmental challenges. Economic inequality and regional disparities will be a growing source of social pressure, as will the projected tide of internal migration to China's growing cities, which is projected to reach 300 million people by the middle of this century.

But the challenges are not only domestic. The rest of us are not idle spectators in this process, because it will have profound implications for our lives, our economies and our shared environment. It is right that Chinese policymakers combine confidence and pride in China's growth with a sober sense of the immense social and environmental challenges that lie ahead. China is a supertanker, but it is steering through narrow straits. And those straits are peopled by those living on and around this and every other continent.

China's Future, Everyone's Future

So, my essential point today is that Europe and the rest of the world have a huge investment in working with China as it sets its course. How the European Union and the United States, in particular, respond to China's rise and to the shift it has provoked in the global geopolitical and economic architecture will be as decisive as China's own choices.

And I say European Union advisedly because challenges like energy security, the environment and migration are subjects where only collective European action can be effective—not just that of individual European nations. Here the European Commission has to give leadership. China needs a continental partner in Europe; Europe needs a continental policy on China.

And both of us need the active engagement of the United States. For this reason it is immensely significant that the US has moved to foster greater strategic engagement with China, a move cemented during the US Treasury Secretary Hank Paulson's recent visit here.

One very fundamental reason for this shift is clear. China is now the largest foreign owner of US government and corporate debt after Japan. The economic interlocking is deepening every year. China operates both as a manufacturing finishing shop for Asian and foreign companies and as a sizeable export market for European and US capital. China's growth is dependent on Chinese and foreign-owned companies in China exporting to the huge markets of the United States and Europe. This is why those who think that in trade it is easy to or even possible—let alone desirable—to target one particular country's goods are living increasingly behind the times.

But—and this is the point I want to underline—our interdependence is also ultimately a political one. We have a joint stake in managing the global economy and maintaining a stable and equitable world. And China is now in a position not only to accept new responsibility in these areas, but also to show strong leadership. I want China to do so.

For example, as a member of the WTO China is guaranteed open and stable access to global markets. But China could do more in return, for example by playing a much more active role in helping to steer the WTO negotiations in the Doha Round.

In its international diplomacy China has been increasingly rising to the vocation implied by its permanent seat on the UN Security Council. It has taken the lead as a mediator with the DPRK. It has also contributed to the UN-mandated peace-keeping force in Lebanon.

Last weekend's Sino-African Summit here in Beijing was a reminder that China's appetite for energy resources and raw materials has provoked a flow of Chinese investment and engagement beyond its continental frontiers, especially in Africa. Now China's presence in Africa should evolve into a wide and responsible contribution to Africa's development challenges. I welcome the steps in this direction that China has announced.

In every sphere, we are seeing fresh evidence that global challenges do not respect national borders, and nowhere is this more obvious than in respect of the world's energy resources and the related issue of climate change. Europe and the United States have a huge responsibility to set a good example. **But a country like China that produces a new coal-fired power station every week, and might be the world's biggest emitter of carbon dioxide by 2030, is a country with a central role in addressing the emergency of climate change. (句 4)**

China is already a net energy importer and its energy needs will continue to grow. China's energy policy will have to reflect our joint responsibility for managing what is both a finite resource and the key element in climate change. **The incontrovertible evidence assembled in the UK and published in the report by the international economist, Sir Nicholas Stern on the economics of climate change leave us in little doubt that global warming is an issue for humankind of a political order of magnitude probably greater than any other. (句 5)**

But the same logic of responsibility and leadership applies to migration, or organized crime, or international terrorism. These are questions on which China has not only major national interests but also clear international responsibilities—and a new capacity to act.

3　难句分析与视译处理

句 1：　He knew that it was looking for a way to balance rapid industrialization with the preservation of the social and cultural balances in what was then a largely agricultural society.

笔译译文：　他知道中国当时作为一个基本还处于农业社会的国家，正在寻找一条既能够快速实现工业化又可以保持其社会和文化平衡的道路。

视译译文：

断　句	译　文
He knew	他知道
that it was looking for a way	中国正在寻找一条道路，
to balance rapid industrialization	希望能够实现快速工业化
with the preservation of the social and cultural balances	同时又能保持社会和文化的平衡发展，
in what was then a largely agricultural society.	而中国当时还基本上是一个农业社会。

句 2：　But we have now come back to a point where the need for an intelligent understanding of the questions raised by China's growing weight and confidence are [is] once again at the forefront of debate.

笔译译文：　但是，我们现在又回到了这样一个时刻：如何明智地认识中国不断增强的重要性和信心再次成为了争论的焦点。

视译译文：

断　句	译　文
But we have now come back to a point	但我们现在又回到了这样一个时刻，
where the need for an intelligent understanding of the questions	需要明智地认识一些问题，
raised by China's growing weight and confidence	这是伴随着中国不断增强的重要性和信心而产生的，
are [is] once again at the forefront of debate.	这再次成为了争论的焦点。

句3： China's international isolation ended for all intents and purposes in 1978 with the Deng Xiaoping reforms and the reasoning that if the Chinese economy could develop the market mechanisms necessary to produce sufficient surplus for export it could spend the income on modernization at home.

笔译译文： 1978 年邓小平开始的改革全面结束了中国与世界隔离的状态，开放的理由是中国经济发展市场机制才能产生足够的赢余出口，如果这样，中国就可以将出口的收益投入国内现代化建设。

视译译文：

断　句	译　文
China's international isolation ended for all intents and purposes	中国与国际社会隔离的状态全面结束了，
in 1978 with the Deng Xiaoping reforms	因为 1978 年邓小平开始进行改革开放。
and the reasoning that	改革的理由是
if the Chinese economy could develop the market mechanisms	如果中国经济能够发展市场机制，
necessary to produce sufficient surplus for export	就可以产生足够的赢余出口，
it could spend the income on modernization at home.	那么，中国就可以将出口的收益投入国内现代化建设。

句4： But a country like China that produces a new coal-fired power station every week, and might be the world's biggest emitter of carbon dioxide by 2030, is a country with a central role in addressing the emergency of climate change.

笔译译文： 但是像中国这样一个每周都有新的燃煤发电站建成的国家，到 2030 年可能将成为世界最大的二氧化碳排放国，所以中国在应对气候变化这个亟待解决的问题上需要发挥关键作用。

视译译文：

断　句	译　文
But a country like China	但是像中国这样一个国家，
that produces a new coal-fired power station every week,	不断修建新的燃煤发电站，每周建一座，
and might be the world's biggest emitter of carbon dioxide	可能将成为世界最大的二氧化碳排放国，
by 2030,	到 2030 年时就会如此。
is a country with a central role	因此，中国需要发挥关键作用，
in addressing the emergency of climate change.	积极应对亟待解决的气候变化问题。

句 5：　The incontrovertible evidence assembled in the UK and published in the report by the international economist, Sir Nicholas Stern on the economics of climate change leave us in little doubt that global warming is an issue for humankind of a political order of magnitude probably greater than any other.

笔译译文：　英国收集的无可置疑的证据和国际经济学家尼古拉·斯特恩爵士发表的有关气候变化经济学报告使我们完全相信全球变暖是人类面临的关乎政治秩序的一件头等要事。

视译译文：

断　句	译　文
The incontrovertible evidence assembled in the UK	英国收集了确切的证据，
and published in the report	也有报告公布了同样的证据，
by the international economist, Sir Nicholas Stern	作者是国际经济学家尼古拉·斯特恩爵士，
on the economics of climate change	他的报告讨论气候变化的经济学。
leave us in little doubt	这些证据都使我们确信：

（待续）

(续上表)

断　句	译　文
that global warming is an issue for humankind	全球变暖是全人类面临的问题，
of a political order	关系到政治秩序，
of magnitude probably greater than any other.	是头等重要的事情。

4　参考译文

欧洲与中国：合作伙伴、竞争对手、领导力量（节选 1）
曼德尔森
北京，2006 年

对中国问题的明智理解

　　大约整整 86 年前的这个月，即在清华大学搬到长沙后又迁回北京之前的 1920 年，杰出的英国哲学家和政治思想家伯特兰·罗素来到清华大学演讲。那也是他当年就中国的未来发表演讲的一部分，之后他著书讲述了他的印象。这本书的书名是《中国问题》。我在准备此次演讲时找到了这本书。一方面，我想了解一个欧洲有识之士，一个英国人在 80 年前是如何解读中国的，另一方面，我想知道他在如何与中国建立伙伴关系方面给他的欧洲同伴提出了什么忠告。

　　虽然这是本旧书，但是引言中的一段文字跃入了我的眼帘，罗素写道："中国是一个正在经历飞速变化的文明古国……由于中国拥有全世界四分之一的人口，中国问题即便对中国以外的人没有任何影响，也是十分重要的。实际上，全世界都将受到中国事务发展的重大影响。因此，即使很难确定地回答中国提出的问题，而且至今都尚未得出确定的答案，仍然需要对这些问题有一个明智的认识，这对欧洲而言很重要，对亚洲也是如此。"

　　我认为现在我们正在接近那些确定答案。早在 1920 年罗素就察觉到中国很快就会融入民族国家的国际体系。他知道中国当时作为一个基本还处于农业社会的国家，正在寻找一条既能够快速实现工业化又可以保持其社会和文化平衡的道路。

　　然而，真正触动我的是罗素的这段话就像刚刚写于昨天。其实，我几乎可以肯定，在昨天的欧美报纸或杂志上一定印有类似的观点，政界人士或决策者也一定发表过这样的看法。大家都在谈论这些问题。

在 20 世纪，中国的国内战乱和政治动荡延误了中国全面融入国际体系的进程。但是，我们现在又回到了这样一个时刻：如何明智地认识中国不断增加的重要性和信心再次成为了争论的焦点。

今天，我想提出几个可以进一步探讨的答案。从积极意义上讲，我是"中国乐观派"，不是恐华论的散布者。欧盟委员会最近发表的对华政策也体现了这种精神和态度，是我的态度的基础。简单地讲：欧洲和中国既是竞争对手，同时又是合作伙伴。我们共同分担全球责任。

中国重返世界中心

对于全世界，中国暂时处于国际体系边缘的状况已经结束，这是不容置疑的事实。一句话，中国在确定国际议程和承担新的领导责任方面发挥的作用已经使其成为了解决我们面对的任何全球性问题的关键。这就是我的核心观点。

1978 年邓小平开始的改革全面结束了中国与世界隔离的状态，开放的理由是中国经济发展市场机制才能产生足够出口赢余，如果这样，中国就可以将出口的收益投入国内现代化建设。当这个简单的经济学原理在中国得以贯彻实施，十几亿中国人民的智慧推动了世界有史以来最快的经济转变。中国的经济 20 年来一直保持每年约 9% 的增长速度。中国占世界 GDP 的份额增长了 10 倍。这样的增长动力使中国跻身于全球经济和国际贸易体系的中心。

随着中国和其他新兴的经济体赶上发达国家，我们看到真正的多极经济世界的创立，而多极政治世界的创立正在紧随其后。中国不仅在亚洲是积极的地缘政治的参与者，在非洲和拉丁美洲它在发挥越来越大的作用。中国出口货物的竞争力正在重组我们的经济，改变着全球贸易的动态，其影响遍及世界各大洲。

中国不再可能置身于世界之外，也不可能像体系外的观望者那样行事。中国决定完全接受现行国际贸易和集体安全体系中的利害关系，这对于这些体系的有效性至关重要，或者说，有助于确定这些体系是否会以现在的形式继续存在。所以，中国没有其他选择，只能选择在全世界发挥有效的领导作用，承担共同的责任。

在中国逐步发挥其全球作用的过程中，中国没有改写或任意歪曲经济法则。30 年前，在韩国和中国台湾地区，同样的出口带动的经济增长和大量的资本投资取得了同样的成果。现在，在马来西亚和越南也正在产生同样的效果。而中国的不同之处则在于其巨大的规模。

中国现在比世界上的其他国家焊接更多的钢材，浇灌更多的水泥，燃烧更多的煤炭。20 年前，欧洲与中国几乎没有任何贸易往来。现在中国是欧洲最大的制造业货物的来源。本 10 年末，中国将成为世界最大的出口国。

从速度上看，中国的经济增长在帮助更多的人摆脱贫困方面超过了历史上任何经济体，这是值得我们大家庆祝的幸事。去年，8,000 万中国人购买了新手机。中国现在拥有的宽带使用者数量超过了美国以外的任何市场。这意味着你们未来的生活是你们的祖父母根本就梦想不到的。

中国的决策者和领导人已经认识到飞速的经济变革正在带来巨大的社会和环境方面的挑战，经济不平等和地区间发展不平衡会造成越来越大的社会压力，同样，预计可能出现的国内移民潮涌入不断扩大的城市也会加剧此类问题，移民数量在本世纪中期预计将达到 3 亿之多。

但是，挑战并不仅仅来自国内。我们其他的人在这个过程中不能袖手旁观，因为这些都将对我们的生活、经济以及我们共有的环境产生深刻的影响。中国的决策者既对中国的发展满怀信心和自豪，同时又对所面临的巨大的社会和环境方面的挑战有着清醒的认识，这是正确的。中国是一艘正在狭隘的海峡中行驶的超级油轮，而海峡两岸居住着亚洲和其他洲的人民。

中国的未来，大家的未来

因此，我今天的基本观点是欧洲以及全世界在中国确定航线时与其合作是一笔巨大的投资。特别是欧盟和美国如何对中国的崛起做出反应，如何应对中国在全球地缘政治和经济结构中引发的变化，这将与中国自己作出的选择一样至关重要。

我说到欧盟是因为对于像能源安全、环境问题、移民问题这样的挑战只有依靠欧洲的集体行动才能取得成效——不能仅靠欧洲各国单独的努力。在这方面，欧盟委员会必须担当领导责任。中国在欧洲需要洲级合作伙伴，欧洲对中国也需要大洲政策。

我们双方都需要美国积极的参与。因此，美国开始加强与中国进行更多的战略接触具有重大意义，美国财政部长汉克·保尔森最近的访华又进一步强化了美国的举措。

出现这种根本转变的原因之一很清楚，中国现在是仅次于日本的美国政府和企业债务的最大的外国债主。经济上的相互联结正在逐年加深。中国是亚洲公司和其他外国公司的制造工序的最后一站，也是欧洲和美国资本的规模巨大的出口市场。中国的发展有赖于中国公司和在华的外国公司对美国和欧洲的庞大市场的出口。所以，那些认为开展贸易时，只盯住一个国家的商品既容易，可能又可取（更别说他们愿意了）的人们正变得越来越落伍，落后于时代的发展。

但是，我想强调这样一点——我们的相互依存最终也是政治上的相互依存。我们在管理全球经济和维持一个稳定平等的世界方面的利益息息相关。中国现在不仅要在这些方面承担新的责任，还要显示出强大的领导力量。我希望中国这样做。

例如，身为世贸组织的成员，中国拥有自由稳定的国际市场准入权。但是中国可以为此作出更多的贡献，比如，在多哈回合的世贸谈判中帮助把握方向，发挥更多的积极作用。

在国际事务中，中国已经越来越多地承担起联合国安理会常任理事国的职责，在与朝鲜民主主义人民共和国的谈判中中国作为调解方发挥了领导作用，为联合国派驻黎巴嫩的维和部队也作出了贡献。

上周末在北京举行的中非首脑峰会使人想到中国对能源和原材料的需求已经使中国的投资和活动源源不断地跨越洲际分界线，特别是在非洲。中国在非洲应当对非洲发展所面临的挑战作出贡献，广泛地承担起相应的责任。我欢迎中国宣布的相关举措。

我们在方方面面都看到生动的示例说明全球性挑战无视国界。然而，最明显的例子就是世界能源和与其相关的气候变化问题。欧洲和美国在发挥表率作用方面负有重大的责任。但是像中国这样一个每周都有新的燃煤发电站建成的国家，到 2030 年可能将成为世界最大的二氧化碳排放国，所以中国在应对气候变化这个亟待解决的问题上需要发挥关键作用。

中国已经是一个能源净进口国，其能源需求还会不断增长。中国的能源政策应该体现我们在管理有限的资源和控制引发气候变化的关键因素方面的共同责任。英国收集的无可置疑的证据和国际经济学家尼古拉·斯特恩发表的有关气候变化的经济学报告使我们完全相信：全球变暖是人类面临的关乎政治秩序的一件头等要事。

但是，对待移民问题、有组织犯罪、国际恐怖主义也需要同样的责任和领导作用。在这些问题上，中国不仅有重大的国家利益，也有明确的国际责任——以及新的行动能力。

四、自主训练

请在 15 分钟之内迅速阅读下面的讲话，了解大意。学生可组成对子练习，互相监控对视译技巧的掌握情况、视译质量和现场表现，或以边视译边录音的形式进行个人练习。视译时要保持正常语速，译文要顺畅达意。如遇难句，可在首次视译后参照"实战练习"中难句分析与视译处理的方法进行练习，找出解决方法。

Europe and China: Partnership, Competition and Leadership (Excerpt 2)

Mandelson

Beijing, 2006

China, Europe and the United States

In this context, I want to develop my belief that on all of these questions China, Europe and the United States should maintain a closer dialog and have the potential to act more in concert, offering the three poles of a global response. Such a partnership would demand a new order of engagement between us.

Two developments should be stressed. The first is, as I have noted, Treasury Secretary Paulson's signaling—indeed from this very podium—of new engagement in US policy toward China which will commit the US administration to taking on powerful antagonistic constituencies in the United States.

The second development is the European Union's renewal of its own clear call for partnership with China. I am here in Beijing to present to my Chinese counterparts the new policy documents that the European Union has recently published that set out our future political and trade and investment agenda with China. This includes the launch of negotiations on a new Partnership and Cooperation Agreement between China and the European Union, and a radically updated set of agreements on trade and investment, which I am discussing with Minister Bo Xilai this week. I believe he shares my tough-minded but positive vision of where we need to take this.

Because this new EU-China strategy contains the now familiar but demanding messages on human rights and improved market access, it has been seen by many as a hard line. And it is tough where it needs to be, in areas like social and political freedoms, intellectual property rights and fair trade. But it is emphatically a message of partnership and joint responsibility.

And from that perspective our often difficult debate on issues like fundamental rights and market access must be seen not as the totality of our relationship, but as the frank dialog that is needed to allow us both to build a partnership for global challenges but also to help ensure China's own internal stability—for the region and for the world's sake. We have backed the "Harmonious Society" concept and ongoing efforts to reform and open up. I believe Europe, as an intelligent critic, will be above all a constructive ally of reform.

Managing Our Commercial Relationship

I want, in the concluding section of my remarks, to focus on our commercial relationship not only because this is my own area of responsibility but because, if our trading relationship is not handled properly, it is capable of seriously impeding—even jeopardizing—the development of our wider relationship.

China's rise has exerted serious pressure on many European industries, especially in labor intensive manufacturing. European companies are being forced to adjust, to move up the value chain and invest in their comparative advantages in design and high-tech, high quality production.

China is forcing us to compete harder both for our own markets and for export markets. China is the major challenge for almost any exporting European business that still wants to be a business in 10 years' time. But the economic evidence suggests China is actually a globalization success story for Europe. Why? Because many European companies also invest and produce here. Our importers and retailers buy here.

Competitively priced inputs from China have also lowered costs for European processing industries and cheap Chinese goods have lowered costs for European consumers, which has kept a downward pressure on inflation and interest rates. One study in the Netherlands suggested that cheaper Chinese goods save the average European household about €300 every year—and those benefits accrue mainly to poor households in Europe who most value the savings.

Most importantly, China is also a growing magnet for our own trade and investment, not least because China's growing numbers of discerning middle class consumers are a key market for the things that Europe produces best. Take my word for it—if you are not already doing so, in 10 years' time you'll all be drinking European wine and eating French cheese, wearing smart Italian clothes and shoes and driving German cars. And much else besides.

I am the first to accept that China is already far ahead of almost all other emerging economies in opening its market to trade. But China's benchmark is not to be found in the developing world. By 2010 China will be the world's biggest exporter. It plays in a different league. The expectations are higher.

Five years after its accession to the WTO, despite a lot of implementation work, China has still not fulfilled some of its commitments and the EU will push to see these met. China can still do more to open its markets and liberalize trade in services and investment. And it will gain from that, as liberalization translates into higher living standards.

Europe has no interest in challenging the exercise of legitimate comparative advantage in labor or production costs. That is tough competition but it is fair competition and we will respect it. But Europe will defend itself against unfair trade—just as China does all the time, and just as we are entitled to do under WTO rules.

Europe also needs to see tougher action on counterfeiting in China, which is a ball and chain on EU competitiveness and a growing problem for China itself. Last month China overtook Germany to become the world's fifth biggest filer for patents. So increasingly the Chinese government is seeing a joint interest in fighting this illegal activity—but we need to see more enforcement of the law.

There are other structural trade barrier issues that Europe will continue to urge China to address. The focus on export-led growth rather than domestic consumer demand, and high levels of precautionary saving by Chinese consumers restrain the important development of a growing consumer economy and act as a brake and barrier to others' exports to China which would rebalance trade.

This no doubt sounds like another list of foreign complaints and demands. But our recent trade and investment strategy makes it clear that there are responsibilities on both sides. Europe for its part must commit to helping China assume full market economy status and offering open and fair access to China's exports, and it must adjust to the tough Chinese competitive challenge. We have to take on our own protectionists, because we cannot demand openness from China from behind barriers of our own.

Conclusion: Europe and China

In other words, the challenge for Europe and China lies in balancing partnership with competition and a frank debate on values with a clear understanding that we make up between us a quarter of humanity, and that we share a fragile and threatened planet. Our current political contact, and the infrastructure of our bilateral political relationship, is not yet strong enough, or intensive enough, in my view, to bear the weight and challenges of this partnership. This needs to change.

I've always suspected that part of Europe's problem in dealing with China begins with incomprehension. We studied Confucianism. We modeled our civil services on the mandarins of Chinese government. We imported your porcelain and then we imported the tea to drink from it. But the understanding of China in Europe is still too often as two-dimensional as the lacquered images of China on a porcelain tea cup. That will also have to change.

This university was founded to prepare students to travel and study abroad. In the 21st century—which will be your century—it must take up that vocation. And Europe needs to send its own in return. The flow of knowledge and experience, and the building of trust between China and Europe is [are] the foundation [foundations] of effective partnership.

What is absolutely fundamental—and Bertrand Russell was at least right about this in 1920 and it is even more true now—is that the whole world will be affected by Chinese affairs. However we frame the questions raised by China's dramatic rise, the one thing we know for sure is that all our destinies are intertwined. China and Europe have no choice but to answer those questions together. And we must join urgently with others in doing so.

附录一

自主训练参考答案

第 1 单元

美国国务卿科林 · 鲍威尔接受中央电视台专访（节选 2）

国务卿 我们并不想指责中国，告诉中国必须按我们的方式做。但我想遵守国际准则会使中国受益。我相信中国应该遵守国际社会的准则，不是因为我们指责中国，而是因为我们认为中国更完全地达到国际社会标准既符合中国人民的利益，也符合中国的利益。我们对自己也有检讨。美国是一个多年来一直都存在人权方面问题的国家。我就是一个最好的例子。40年前像我这样一个黑人根本不能想象可以当上国务卿，而现在我已经坐在国务卿的位子上了。所以我们已经发生了变化，这是因为我们的人民清楚地知道，如果我们要忠实于我们的价值观，那么我们就必须使之应用到所有美国人身上。我想这就是国际准则——这是追求更高目标、更高标准的准则。我们认为中国人民将从中受益。我们并不是在对中国人民说教。我希望中国人民能够认识到我们有时在这些问题上的推进不是要责怪或惩罚，而是要鼓励中国向我们相信对中国和中国人民有利的方向发展。

主持人 我认为，我们的确需要更多对话，也许，今天的对话能够有助于这个长期的过程。

国务卿 在我将同贵国领导人进行的会谈中，我们将讨论人权问题，以及在人权问题上我们双方再次开始对话的机会。

主持人 国务卿先生，中国希望与美国建立建设性的合作关系，并且我们非常重视尼克松总统 70 年代初访华以来美中之间签订的所有联合公报。并且，在 1998 年，美国政府以"三不"重申了对台湾的立场，所以，我想知道，你能不能明确地告诉我，这一立场有没有变化？

国务卿 在布什领导下的美国政府的立场是：我们相信《与台湾关系法》及随后

的三个联合公报，是我们与中国关系的基础，是一个足够牢固的基础，让我们朝着积极的方向前进。

主持人　让我们转过来谈谈全球性问题。我们知道有些专家和分析人士说美国的全球问题战略，在某些问题上倾向于变得更加僵化了，如在《京都议定书》、反弹道导弹、国家导弹防御系统和其他问题上。我的问题是，美国政府是如何看当今世界的？

国务卿　我们认为世界在经济上和政治上越来越相互关联。我们并不是在孤立自己，不像有些人所说的那样正在走向单边主义。我们仍是北大西洋公约组织、联合国和世界贸易组织中的积极成员。我们有活跃的同盟，我们在太平洋有所存在，在欧洲有所存在，所以，我们并不是走向孤立，更不是朝着单边主义前进。同时，当出现像《京都议定书》这样的问题时，当我们认为我们坚持或批准这样的议定书并非最符合美国利益时，或者坦率地讲，并非最符合全世界的利益时——因为我们认为《京都议定书》并非是解决全球气候变暖的正确方法——我们认为我们应该发表看法、明确立场，即便这样做看上去是在自我孤立。如果你相信你的立场，你应该表达出来，即使这样做会因为与大多数其他国家想法相悖而受到批评。这正是我们的政治制度所赋予我们的职责之一。而且因为我们所处的地位，我们做这些判断非常引人注目，因为人们说美国正在试图走向单边，但实际不是这样。但当我们的利益与其他人的利益有所不同时，我认为重要的是说出来，尽量解释我们的观点。

导弹防御问题也同样是这种情况。这不仅仅是导弹防御。我们对世界的观察使我们认识到，我们所生活的世界已经不是冷战世界，我们互相指向对方的大量的核武器不再是必需。所以，与俄罗斯一道，我们想减少在我们彼此的军火库中的战略进攻性武器数量；同时，我们注意到，有来自于一些国家的另外一些危险。那些国家，出于他们自己的原因，已经开始发展大规模杀伤性武器和运载这些武器的导弹。我们认为，发展防御这些武器的方法非常明智。所以，这就是我们进行导弹防御的原因，但这一计划被这个有 30 年历史的、1972 年签订的《反弹道导弹条约》所约束。所以，我们正在与俄罗斯一道工作，寻求摆脱这个条约束缚的方法，以便我们能够发展导弹防御来制衡和对付这些新的威胁。

主持人　但有些人认为，美国这样做是在幻想出某种实际上并非构成急迫威胁的敌人。而同时，退出 1972 年的条约将对全球军控形势产生严重后果。

国务卿　我们认为不会。我们认为，1972 年的条约是出于另外一个时代的要求，当时我们力图阻止战略进攻性武器的发展，但那种发展已经停止了。现在的情况正向相反的方向发展，如普京总统和布什总统一周前在热那亚所谈，我们所拥有的进攻性武器数量还可以进一步削减。但数量减少并非因为《反弹道导弹条约》的存在，而是因为不再需要这么多。所以，《反弹道导弹条约》是为了另外一个时代的需要，另外一种不再存在的政治环境的需要。我们不应让这个条约成为采取有关导弹防御的明智合理之举的障碍。我认为，我们将能说服俄罗斯领导人，我也希望能说服中国领导人，使他们相信我们的导弹防御计划对他们的核威慑并不构成威胁。

主持人　你将与中国领导人探讨这一问题吗？

国务卿　我相信这个题目在讨论中会出现。

主持人　国务卿先生，我这儿有一个小礼物，或者说是一个小秘密，但我不打算送给你。这是你的自传《我的美国之路》。这是中文版。我想这对我来说有点贵，将近 30 元人民币。我在这本书中读到了你的经历。你想表达的似乎是：对于一名军人，一名士兵来说，战争并不是最终目的，和平才是。所以，我想问，您在军队中服役 30 多年，作为一名军人，战争与和平、士兵与和平的关系是怎样的？你能不能告诉我一些简单的想法？

国务卿　我认为任何一个头脑健全的士兵都不希望看到战争，因为他们知道战争的后果，战争所带来的破坏，战争会夺去生命。因此美国军队的原则是：保持强大以维护和平、避免战争。如果因为无从选择而不得已要打仗，那就争取以最小的伤亡速战速决，以避免造成更多不必要的破坏。士兵们非常向往和平。我现在没有穿军装，而穿着西服，但同样向往和平。道理是一样的，我正在努力运用自己在军队中所学到的领导才能、管理方法、在世界各地从军所获得的经验以及担任国家安全顾问所获取的经验，以此来帮助我担任一个向往和平的国务卿。

主持人　这是否对你的个人世界观和看待生活的态度的转变有所影响？

国务卿　没有，我对世界与生活的看法是一如既往的渴望和平、寻求朋友、寻找希望，尽我个人所能，尽我的国家所能去帮助世界上那些依然遭受苦难的人们——那些食不果腹的人们，那些疾病缠身的人们，那些无家可归的人们。美国是地球上最慷慨的国家之一。如我刚才所言，美国不需要敌人。我们不需要敌人，我们也不想要敌人，我们希望帮助别人。我们希望帮助中国，我们希望帮助中国利用 21 世纪信息技术世界的良机加入国际市场。我们希望中国与我们进行贸易，让美国的产品进入中国，让中国的产品进入美国。让我们在一种相互尊重的氛围中共享彼此的文化与价值观，而不是一方压倒另一方。我们理解法治与人权的重要性。如果像我，像你们的领导人和布什总统以及其他所有领导人这样的人都准备利用这一点，通过合作，而不是通过对抗，那么展现在我们面前的就是一个光明的未来。现在回到你原先的问题上，答案就是：友好、合作、协作、融洽相处，找到我们利益的共同点与能够共同合作的领域，再找到我们的分歧点，让我们共同就这些分歧进行磋商，把它们变成我们共同关注的问题。

主持人 国务卿先生，我从这本书中看到，您上次来中国是 70 年代初期，将近 30 年以前。那是很久以前了。现在，作为国务卿又来到这里，您对中国有没有一个很好的、全面的看法？实际上，中国在过去的 20 到 30 年间发展十分迅速，发生了那么巨大的变化。

国务卿 从我上次到中国访问约 30 年以来，中国发生了巨大的变化。那是我第一次访问中国，1983 年我也来过这里。即便是当时，也可以看到中国开始发生的变化，但远不如 1983 年至 2001 年之间发生的变化那么显著。我祝贺中国人民、中国领导人所展现出的活力和敢于冒险的精神，以及跨入一个新世界而摒弃一些无效果的和无益于中国人民的行事程序与方式的愿望。在你们的领导人应付 21 世纪的挑战的时候，我期待着这种变革继续进行。你们可以确信，在我们两国共同前进的同时，美国将随时准备与中国领导人合作与共事。

第 2 单元

后危机时代世界经济（节选 2）

约翰·利普斯基

2008 年 11 月 17 日

完善全球金融体系

在种种迫在眉睫的挑战以外，此次金融危机昭示至少三个与全球金融结构相关的领域有待我们开拓新思维，采取新举措。首先，必须完善金融管理制度的设计。其次，必须开辟更好的途径评估系统风险。第三，必须建立更为有效的、协调的行动机制，以便降低并及时应对危机风险。

此次危机暴露了当前国内国际监管框架的局限性。开放的金融市场可降低资金成本，并由此带来丰厚的收益。但将这一潜能变成现实需要更加有效的监管。金融领域的创新与融合使得各种冲击在各类资产与各种经济体中传播的速度加快，范围扩大，这一点已显露无遗。尽管如此，监管措施仍仅限于单个金融机构层面，而并未充分考虑到国内机构的行为之于整个体系与世界的影响。此外，宏观谨慎政策手段并未充分考虑到工商与金融周期，导致杠杆过度发展。

因此，当前的挑战便是在避免增加不必要负担的同时，设计出新的规则与制度，以降低系统风险，完善金融中介机制，并且适当调整管理和监督范围。

——更为有效的资金及流动性的要求有助于使各类金融机构对风险应对自如，特别是那些高度关联的机构。逆景气循环宏观谨慎制度似乎是减少系统风险的有效途径。更好地利用统一管理的清算所和有组织的交易所可以提高金融基础设施抵御交易对手失败的能力。

——我们需要进一步在全球范围内协调监管体系，以保证监管范围适当。此次危机凸显了活跃在全球范围内的金融机构与面向国内的监管者之间的矛盾。这一矛盾同时存在于危机预防与应对的能力中。在解决那些总部设在相对较小国家的国际银行的问题时，此矛盾尤为突出。

——更为详实的、实用的信息将有助于同时提高市场参与者与领导层二者评估系统风险的能力。这就要求对透明度、公开度以及报告制度进行审查。同时，信息需求可被更为广泛地应用于各类机构，其中包括保险公司以及各类资产负债表外的实体。

此次危机充分表明，人们将为未能及早发现风险而付出沉重的代价。甄别风险更为有效的途径需要制定政策的关键性人物紧密配合，将分散于国际及国家各个层面的宏观金融信息与专业知识集中汇总。

——所有早期预警系统都始于全球金融与经济发展相关信息的日趋完善，与实现更好的监管体制如出一辙。更有效的风险评估还意味着加强宏观金融分析，以及不断改进早期预警系统。

——实行早期预警与监控同样需要寻求合理的激励机制，兼顾自发开展经济脆弱程度评估的国家与被强制进行此项评估的国家。这样，人们就需要对不同模型是否奏效做出评判，有的模型依靠"荣辱感"，"服从或解释"发挥效力，有的则有赖于约束性承诺。

——私营经济需要改进其风险管理机制，这是由于事实已经证明：现实世界与传统模型相比，前者更是风险四伏。为实现这一目标，人们可能需要创建新型商业形式，而并非仅仅建立新的机制。经过改良的管理框架应当为实现这一目标提供恰当的激励。

20 国集团行动计划

实际上，此次峰会本着脚踏实地的精神提出了上述所有问题。与会各国高瞻远瞩，在意识到短期内加强全球需求的基础上，通过了一项全面的"改革原则实施金融和经济改革行动计划"。即将成立的工作组将在以下五大领域推进政策改革：提高透明度并完善问责制、加强良好的监管、促进金融市场的诚信、强化国际合作以及改革国际金融机构。

与会各国在上述各方面均就一系列短期议题取得共识，并有望在 2009 年 3 月底前提出具体改革方案，以供研究。各国还敲定了一套中期行动计划，由工作组日后落实。计划包括 20 国集团成员以及各种国际实体需要采纳的大约 50 项具体步骤。其中半数以上计划将于明年第一季度内成形。

峰会行动计划有的放矢地应对各项重要挑战。峰会公报行动计划要求各国达成新的共识，内容涉及复合证券估价、信用评级机构职责审查、改善信用违约掉期市场与其他店头衍生品市场基础设施。此外，行动计划要求审查风险管理措施标准以及改善流动性风险管理标准。

同时，行动计划要求国际货币基金组织与扩大后的金融稳定论坛及标准制定机构通力合作，针对缓解当前体系中明显的顺景气循环提出建议，并改进现有规则的适用范围。除此以外，国际货币基金组织应担负起提高各国法规协调性、加强国际监管合作的重任。为实现这一目标，监督者受命为所有大型跨国金融机构建立监督"学院"。峰会公报还承诺 20 国实行"金融部门评估计划"报告，此份报告由国际货币基金组织与世界银行共同完成。截至目前，与会国中除两个以外均已实行"金融部门评估计划"报告或实行在即。

当然，20 国集团不懈努力的成果究竟如何尚未见分晓，特别是实现短期目标的期限自然是在美国新一任总统就职以后。但值得一提的是，各国已经认清最为重要的各项具体挑战，明确了政治上广获支持的任务，并为达成具体方案设定了确切的期限。国际上这一领域内的"利益攸关者"有望依行动计划不断为实施决定性的行动施加压力，使各国不至于空怀良好的意愿。

国际货币基金组织的作用

在结束本次演讲前，我愿谈谈适逢挑战，国际货币基金组织所发挥的作用。

——首先，国际货币基金组织一如既往地进行常规性多边与双边监管，为成员国提供政策建议与技术援助。

——第二，国际货币基金组织已及时采取行动，帮助在此次危机中受到重创的新兴经济体，以及大幅放缓的发达经济体。随着危机不断深化蔓延，国际货币基金组织以流动资金的形式拨款，总额超过 2,000 亿美元，以帮助成员国弥补资金短缺。在近来几周内，已有一些国家向国际货币基金组织寻求金融援助，其中包括匈牙利、冰岛和乌克兰，此外还有多项计划尚在磋商中。

——第三，随着创造新政策工具的需要日趋明显，国际货币基金组织已另辟蹊径，充分利用其资源。日前，基金组织已向低收入成员国放宽了外生冲击贷款的发放条件。同时，我此前提到的"短期流动贷款工具"使宏观经济强健、政策实施历来连贯的国家有机会优先从组织获得庞大的资源，助其缓解可自我调整的短期外部流动性压力，避免造成国际收支差额问题。

——第四，尽管组织可通过与成员国间现有的借款安排获得额外的资源，但随着危机日益蔓延，各国资源总和是否足以满足成员国的需求仍成为一个严峻的问题。寻求一条更为系统的保障国际流动资金供给的途径应成为当前的重中之重。这可能需要借助各国为国际货币基金组织的援助项目共同出资（匈牙利便是一例），或是增加组织可用于贷款的资源。对第一种方案而言，将组织可用于借贷的资源增加一倍不失为明智之举，尽管目前看来现有资源足以应对当前形势。

基金组织已采取多项步骤以完善金融体系。我们已经开始加强早期预警能力，这与组织促进世界金融稳定的核心使命并行不悖。但是，我们需要更好地理解金融部门发展与宏观经济状况间的关联（例如，货币政策与风险承担间的关系）。因此，我们率先对这一领域展开研究。我们还需开发更新更好的运作手段加强宏观金融监管。国际货币基金组织热切希望能加强与这一领域其他组织的合作。

在上周末的峰会中，国际货币基金组织的作用自然也成为一项重要议题。无论是在峰会上，双边谈判中，还是峰会宣言里，20 国领导人均表明他们希望未来国际货币基金组织可以在应对危机、总结经验、加强监管以及重建国际金融结构等方面扮演关键角色。具体而言，各国领导人：

——坚决支持国际货币基金组织就危机控制与危机应对所发挥的作用，例如推行新的"短期流动贷款工具"；同时他们要求基金组织不断审查、调整其贷款机制。

——一致同意保证基金组织拥有充足的资源，以发挥其作用。日本政府就此做出承诺，再额外提供 1,000 亿美元，充实基金组织用于借贷的资源，并号召其他各国也出手相助，使现有流动资金储备翻一番。

——要求基金组织对所有成员国开展大力、公平的监管，对其金融部门给予更多关注，并且为宏观金融政策提供更强有力的建议。为此，20 国均承诺加入金融领域评估项目。

——要求基金组织与扩大后的金融稳定论坛通力合作，以更好地将监管行动纳入宏观谨慎分析中，同时提高早期预警能力。

——要求基金组织领导各国从当前危机中吸取经验教训，并且依照两机构领导人于上周签署的协议，与金融稳定论坛全面加强合作。

——呼吁基金组织参与建议的制定，缓解金融系统顺景气循环。

——号召基金组织为制定、实施符合国际标准的新法规创造条件。

各国领导人同时强调他们希望亲眼目睹对布雷顿森林体系进行改革。他们特别强调，有必要保证在这一体系以及整个国际体系中新兴经济体与发展中经济体可获得更多的发言权与代表性。

结论

今天我在此着力向各位描绘了一幅宏伟蓝图。各国最高领导人已一致认可，我们需在众多领域立刻展开行动，重新为全球经济与金融系统打下坚实的基础。人们无需夸大其词，主张建立新体系。各国现已就通过改革消除现有体系中的弊端达成广泛共识，并且这些改革工程浩大。宏观经济政策行动，特别是财政政策与广大国家休戚相关，其必要性也在与日俱增。金融领域政策改革必须继续推行，并视具体情况加以调整。我们必须同舟共济，巩固全球金融结构。为此，我们需重新检验管理中存在的漏洞，采用新式手段发现薄弱环节，防微杜渐。同时充分意识到实现金融一体化和提供跨国资金支持对于制定法规、开创预防及应对危机的新机制均具有重要意义。

20 国集团金融市场和世界经济峰会向世人传达了一条前所未有的政治信息——为抵御当前来势汹汹的金融危机，应对诸多方面史无前例的挑战，各国就采取广泛行动达成共识，其力量与日俱增。不论如何衡量，峰会上制定的目标都堪称宏伟。我与国际货币基金组织的诸位同事已做好准备，协助 20 国领导人制定详尽的实施方案，以便将今天我们共同关注的问题，共同面临的挑战落实为具体行动。最重要的是，国际货币基金组织已准备就绪，我们将利用金融资源与专业知识，为铸就后危机时代更为强健的全球经济助一臂之力。

第 3 单元

在联合国教科文组织教育领导人论坛的讲话

美国教育部长玛格丽特·斯佩林斯
巴黎，2008 年

拉尔夫，谢谢你热情的介绍，感谢你在微软为建立超越技术合作的伙伴关系方面所作的工作。对于我的朋友格里·埃利奥特以及其他来自微软公司的各位，感谢你们为大会成功召开所作的贡献。我知道现在对诸位来说是一个过渡时期。你们将要失去比尔·盖茨这个伟大的领导者。然而，微软的损失却是教育界的收获。他的思想和奉献令人倍感激动。

松浦总干事，感谢您对联合国教科文组织的领导，由于您的领导，该组织向世界发出了教育界的最强音。您的工作非常出色。美国为与您在教育方面的合作深感自豪。

让我对我们的主办城市和国家也表示感谢。有些人爱说"巴黎之春"。作为一个历史专业的学生，我喜欢在 7 月 4 日和巴士底日之间的时间到访巴黎。你们的国家支持了美国革命，教育了我们的国父们，并向我们赠送了自由这一"礼物"，我们对此永远感激不尽。

教育是个矛盾体。优质的教育能够开启无数机会的大门，团结人民。然而，相当一部分的教育活动是独自开展的，人们在图书馆或教室的四壁内安静地学习。我想，技术也是一样。科技人员远离尘嚣，写编码，完善软件，度过漫长的岁月。他们为我们提供了在以毫微秒计算的瞬间就能与世界各地人民交流的能力。

技术革命为高等教育的改进及其扩展提供了金色的机遇。现在，我们必须使高等教育变得更容易获得，更支付得起，且更加负责。

但是，我们现在不再像从前那样享受身处世外桃源的舒适。不展望未来我们就不能从历史中学习——未来的远景宽阔无比、包罗万象——建立在个人的选择和需求的基础之上。所以，在2005年，我为了利用这一宝贵时机，召集了"高等教育的未来"大会。我们邀请学术界、私营部门以及政府的最优秀、最具聪明才干的领导者齐聚一堂，共同制定一个面向未来的计划——嘉宾包括微软公司的埃利奥特。

《对领导者的考验》这份报告要求大专院校从"以声誉为重的体系向以业绩为基础的体系转变"。报告引起了重视，也收到了许多的评论。有的说："我们比你干这行的时间要长得多"——他们说得对！有些美国大学有着三百多年的历史。也有的说我们拥有"世界上最好的高等教育体系"——这样的夸耀不绝于耳，致使我们常常忘记了其他国家在多么努力地进行竞争。还有些人说："不要告诉我该怎么做好我的工作。我自己知道该怎么做。"

我承认我们在教育社会精英方面成效卓著。我们一直擅长帮助那些一出生就可以接受教育的人得到更好的机会。但是，仅仅这些已经不再是我们唯一的工作了。我们现在必须做更多的事情，要远远超过过去。我不想告诉大学该如何办学。但是，身为教育部长，我的确想让他们知道，作为三分之一的投资者，我们在联邦政府层面到底有什么期望——我们是真正的伙伴——在美国高等教育领域合作。

我们期望大学：

破除障碍，改变阻碍进步的习惯；

通过教育更多来自不同经济、文化背景的人，建立人力资本；

通过技术的应用和创新来推动变化，赋予学生权力；

继续强调卓越的研究和学识，同时培育与私营部门和慈善机构的伙伴关系。

高等教育办学必须更加灵活、内容更加充实、一切工作更加以学生为本，只有这样才能保证持续取得成绩，这也正是大会的期待。

因此，我要求我们的大专院校尽快采纳高等教育委员会的建议。这些建议包括大学与高中之间在课程开设方面进行更多的合作并建立联盟。我们需要大学新生为取得成功做好准备，而不是让他们为价格昂贵又耗费时间的补习课程所拖累。

另一个建议是关注非传统型的学习者，比如在竞争激烈的全球经济形势下，为增强自身竞争优势重返校园的成人学生。

我们还要更加重视社区大学的学生。这些学生往往边工作边学习。社区大学在提供灵活的学习机会方面发挥了先锋作用，他们以技术为基础，根据消费者的需求和当地对劳动力的要求设计课程。所以，我们的大约 1,400 万本科生中有一半是在社区大学学习。

总之，我们的高等教育需要更多的信息和透明度。

几年前，我在帮助我女儿选择大学时发现有很多对最好的"派对学校"的指南，但是，鲜有比如关于"毕业后最好的前景"方面的材料。我们能够在网上购买汽车，能够找到价格、耗油量、甚至置杯架的数量。但是，常常很难找到有关四年学位的真正成本，或者获得学士学位平均所需时间的信息。我认为应该把不断上涨的学费的一部分投资给那些通过"点击"便可以选择正确的学校的更好的数据信息系统——使选择更加容易，使信息更容易获得。

我知道你们也深有同感。联合国教科文组织已经增开了一个新的窗口，用以提供各国高等教育的相互比较以及最新信息。

现在应该是跳出我们的舒适区，敞开学术界的大门，开始为改进现状进行合作的时候了。我对于前景持乐观态度，为什么？因为我们正在努力——正在帮助小学生和中学生为上大学和未来的人生做好准备。

六年前，布什总统签署同意《不让一个孩子掉队法案》成为法律，该法案并没有告诉学校应该如何办学，但是，它的确让学校明白了社会对于它们的期望是什么。首先要使每个孩子在阅读和数学方面达到年级及格水平，或更为出色。与教科文组织的"人人受教育"运动一样，我们最后给自己设定了真正时限：2014 年。当然，我还没有碰到愿意等到那时的父母！

这条法律是对过去的教育体系的回应，这种体系曾经出色地培养过一些学生，但却使其他学生感到无望，前途渺茫。后者主要是居住在美国城市的中心的，来自少数民族裔和低收入家庭的学生。这样的体制出现了机能障碍，著名的 1983 年的报告《危险之中的国度》把此现象称之为"高涨的平庸趋势"。所以，我们努力前进，破除障碍，改变习惯，引领趋势。

我们发现我们把期望值定得越高，我们的儿童和教员就越勤奋地为实现目标而努力。我们还发现衡量和公布考试成绩和其他信息后，学校和社区都更加努力以帮助儿童进步。现在，阅读和数学的分数都在提高，少数民族裔和白人学生之间的"成绩差别"终于开始在相当程度上缩小。我们认识到，有衡量标准就能出成效。这就是开发人力资本的意思。

这对成人同样适用。请记住，并不是只有学生弃学，在五年里也有一半的教员离职。所以，我们设立了一个 1 亿美元的教师激励基金，旨在奖励工作优异的教员。我们还让学生的家长有权得到更好的信息和更多的选择，包括课后活动和免费辅导，我们甚至还为学生提供去教育质量较好的公立学校上学的交通工具。

最后，我们认识到 90% 的快速增长的工作职位都要求中学水平以上的培训或教育——特别是在科学、数学和技术方面。两年前，我们开始对那些学习严谨的科学和数学方面的课程或在科学和数学领域深造的大学生进行奖励，给予他们特别的助学金。仅在第一年就奖励了 4 亿多助学金，有 36 万学生受益，许多人经济上并不富裕，他们在这些充满挑战的课程和领域中取得了优异的分数。

总之，我们正在将我们教育的重心从通用的传统做法转向对个体需求的重视——使教育比以往任何时候都更具流动性，更相互关联，更了解技术。

在美国，从"危险之中的国度"到"硕果累累的国家"用了整整 18 年时间。如今，我们再次不能高枕无忧了。当今世界变化得太快。

高等教育必须紧跟我们在小学和中学教育体系中已经形成的走向开放、透明、承担责任的发展趋势。这是解决比尔·盖茨称之为"规模问题"的唯一办法，是能够帮助尽可能多的人的唯一办法。

梅特卡夫定律提出，随着一个网络的使用人数的增加，该网络的价值呈几何数增长。因此，最好的技术是能够惠及最多人的技术，使用者继而在使用中改进技术。

"创新杯"决赛选手路易斯·塞耶斯说得很精彩："没有人能告诉我们，我们不能做某件事。……如果我们不喜欢，我们就改变它。当有一天结束之时，我们明白是我们创造了它。"我们就是这样建立起一个全球合作的平台。合作与孤立背道而驰，而合作恰恰是我们现今的需要！

学生并不在乎公立还是私立，盈利还是非盈利的标签。他们真正关心的学校是否便利，他们是否负担得起，教育质量如何，学校是否关心他们的需求——以及成绩。

我们任何人都不能对我们的人力资本置之不理。联合国宣布教育为基本人权已经 60 年了，而现在全世界还有大约 8 亿人不识字，其中三分之二是妇女。几乎四个儿童中就有一个不能完成只有五年的基础教育。

让我们承诺把高质量的教育资源给予他们。让我们宣誓使高等教育成为全球变化和合作的新世纪的中心工作。通过共同努力，我们能够为未来开辟道路，为今天树立榜样。

谢谢各位、谢谢微软公司和联合国教科文组织，感谢你们让我们关注这个重要的话题。让我们行动起来。我们不会失去什么，却将获得一个世界。

第 4 单元

经济全球化（节选 2）
马尔科姆·弗雷泽
2000 年

　　乔治·索罗斯已对我们发出过警告。他写道："尽管我已经在金融市场上赚了钱，但现在我担心，自由放任的资本主义任意大肆扩张，以及市场价值观影响到我们生活的各个方面，这会危及到我们这个开放和民主的社会。……过多的竞争，过少的合作，会导致令人难以忍受的不平等和不稳定。自由放任的资本主义的信条是，公共利益是通过对个人利益的无穷追求实现的。除非我们能认识到有某种共同利益需要置于个人的特别利益之上，否则，我们目前的系统……就很可能会崩溃。"索罗斯的个人经历告诉我们，我们不能对他的警告置若罔闻。金融市场，特别是外汇市场和股票市场，已经变得日益变幻莫测，对冲基金的运作也愈加不可预测，这一切都表明，我们要认真地对待它们向我们提出的挑战。具体地说，这些挑战主要来自两个方面：其一是在一个全球化的市场中如何保持某种形式的平等和合理的竞争，其二是如何在金融市场内部建立稳定性。

　　我们迫切需要建立一个国际机构，由它在一个全球化的环境下制定公平贸易的规则。中等规模或小规模的国家将是这一创举的最大的获益者。如果一个国家还想继续保持其吸引国际投资的竞争力，那么，现有的那些为保证公平贸易而设立的国家机构就大都变得无足轻重。 还有更为重要的一点，我们需要建立一个更加稳定的汇率体制。对于新兴市场和发达工业国家的货币应采取不同的态度。我们确实需要减少金融市场的短期变化和不稳定性，但同时，从中期时段看，又需要有足够的灵活性进行调整，要适当处理好两者兼容的关系。

　　美元和欧元将占领世界金融市场的大半壁江山。因此，大西洋两岸的货币汇率的稳定性对世界的稳定至关重要。但在亚洲地区，由于日元和人民币具有非常重要的地位，它们对美元和欧元的比率的稳定性也具有极为重要的意义。世界各个主要货币的代表应经常磋商，协调其基本政策目标，达成共识，实现汇率的更大稳定性。如果大国之间已经建立了更大的稳定性，就应该允许其他国家，尤其是那些开放市场规模不大的国家选择自己的汇率体制。没有一种体制是放之四海皆古适用的，所以，选定的体制应有利于减少不稳定性，鼓励投资，对变化的环境具有必要的灵活性。

　　现有的金融系统极为脆弱，无论在强度和深度上都需要大大加强。这就需要建立审慎监督的国际框架，对国际金融交易进行有效监督。这对于创造足够的国际资金流动性，同时减少出借方和借款方不顾一切的冒险行为都至关重要。在建立这一监督系统的过程中，必须要有七国集团以外的其他国家，特别是发展中国家和经济体制转型国家的参与，同时还需要建立一个权威的国际管理机构。这一权威管理机构应为各种金融管理形式设立最佳惯例标准，监督各个金融机构遵守这些标准，协调各个机构之间的行为，以减少违规者带来的危害。除了审慎的监督制度以外，还需要制定信息披露、市场控制和跨国界合并的国际标准。实行审慎管理方面的最佳做法不仅需要政治承诺，而且还需要专业的技术。在这方面，许多国家需要帮助。

在国际金融市场中，短期和长期资金流动之间要保持某种平衡。一个国家的金融发展状况以及资金在其市场中出入的速度之间要保持一致性，这一点同样重要。国际货币基金组织要求其所有成员国之间实现国际收支资本项目的完全自由兑换，这其实是错误的。在某种情形下，一些新兴市场限制短期资金的流入，并阻止国民手中的资本逃逸，这种做法是恰当的。在这方面，智利已经树立了良好的榜样。这样做也可以缓解最近发生的亚洲金融危机的严重程度。

国际货币基金组织应继续在适当的条件下帮助处于金融危机中的国家。但是，在这种情况下，国际货币基金组织应更多地考虑到这个国家的历史及其具体的经济状况，而不应像在印度尼西亚所做的那样，包揽世界银行对长期发展问题所承担的责任。

国际货币基金组织的资金来源应该得到加强，以便它在需要的时候可以给有关国家提供应急基金，帮助它们避免危机。要避免危机的发生，及时得到足够的资金帮助是极为重要的。寻找途径，鼓励国际货币基金组织帮助避免危机的发生，而不仅仅是在危机发生后对危机做出反应，这一点至关重要。在任何为保持资金流动性而做的安排中，国际货币基金组织在帮助陷于困境的国家时应注意不要免除借贷方的责任。在某些情形下，国际货币基金组织的紧急财政援助对借款方的帮助甚至超过了对困难国家本身的援助。借款方要自己承担风险。

作为对上述论述的补充，我想就亚太地区提出两点具体的建议。从某些方面来看，这一地区比起世界其他地区，在结构和组织方面都存在更多的问题。在北美和南美地区，有一个北美自由贸易协定组织，这一组织最终覆盖整个美洲地区是意想之中的事。另外，美洲地区还有一个美洲国家组织。欧洲则有欧洲联盟，正在一天天地成长壮大。在我们这个地区，也建立了亚太经济合作组织，旨在推动和促进自由贸易。亚太经合组织创建时的初衷是比世界贸易组织动作更快一步。最初致力于推动亚太经合组织的国家只想把它的影响力限制在东亚和东南亚地区。后来，美国想介入，环太平洋地区的其他国家也想介入，现在，它们都已成了亚太经合组织的成员国，但它们的利益却有极大的差异。成员扩大后，亚太经合组织作为追求自由贸易的领头羊的地位受到了削弱。由于成员国数量众多，利益分散，很难充分和有效地推进东亚和东南亚的特殊利益。

　　我们自己这个地区应该更多地关注本地区的利益和地区问题。要达到这个目的，首先，我们可以组织由所有东亚和东南亚国家领导人参加的政治会议，这个会议当然得将澳大利亚和新西兰包括在内，每年举行一次。会议要设自己的秘书处。这个会议需要处理一系列重要的问题，如：亚太经合组织达到自己的目的了吗？东亚和东南亚应该寻求更加快速和有效的发展之路吗？这一会议还可以讨论安全问题，当然，安全问题不是这个论坛的议题。本地区内国家的利益不一定与本地区外国家的利益一致。有时候，这些因素会转移国家的注意力，使其对自身的安全问题没有足够的关注。从长期来看，同一地区国家间的关系是唯一可行的和持久的安全保证。

　　就经济事务方面来看，这样一个论坛也可以从实际操作方面进行考察，这是最初由日本提出的建议。亚洲金融危机开始之时，日本曾建议在本地区内建立一个基金会，名字可以叫做亚洲货币基金组织。建立这样一个基金的目的显然是为了促进地区金融市场的稳定，增加透明度，鼓励所有国家对资本市场的操作保持适当的审慎监督和管理。有了日本、中国以及本地区内其他国家的资源，建立这样一个基金是可行的。

　　由于美国希望继续保持其在国际货币基金组织中的主导地位，这一建议一直没有得到认真的考虑。但是，如果我们考察了国际货币基金组织和美国国会的关系，了解了美国国会如何将自己的意愿强加于国际货币基金组织的政策之上，我们就会更想建立一个独立的货币基金组织。总之，公司全球化和金融市场全球化已经日益成为一种全球现象，其产生的长期影响也尚未被我们完全了解，在这样一个具有高度竞争性的世界里，中国和亚洲为推进本地区的利益可以做许多事情。

第 5 单元

经济全球化——中国与亚洲（节选 2）

李光耀

北京，2000 年

互联网与新经济

　　数字革命已经席卷整个发达国家世界。电脑促成了互联网的发展。随着通讯、电脑与媒体的整合，互联网将成为一个威力强大的多媒体网络。这些发展引发了美国的"新经济"。电脑和互联网使得美国的国内生产总值每年增加 0.4 至 0.6 个百分点。资讯科技与互联网也成为传统经济里的公司借以提高生产力与利润的强有力工具。它们现在可以同时与多个供应商直接联系，也可以核查最新的销售量与存货，并直接与顾客接洽，从而减低成本，提高生产力。在这方面，欧洲、日本和新兴工业经济体都落后了好几年。

其他国家，如中国，已经发觉到这种发展，而且正尽快建立新经济所需的基础设施。1999 年，中国的互联网用户已经增加四倍多，达到 900 万，使中国成为互联网十大使用国之一。根据中国社会科学院的预测，如果以每年 100% 的增长速度计算，互联网用户数目将在 2003 年达到 6,000 万。然而，中国目前在互联网主机、电话线与个人电脑渗透率方面还是落在大多数东亚经济体的后头。

数字革命可以把中国的长期增长率每年提高一至三个百分点。因此，中国应尽快增加电脑与互联网的使用。中国政府一直都在发展资讯基础设施，并扩大和加深其资本市场。中国已经在北京、上海、广东、深圳和天津等地建立了好几个高科技和互联网产业园。然而，要使数码科技达到最高的价值，政府必须解除对电信市场的控制。中国已答应在加入世贸组织时，开放这个领域，并在两年内让外资拥有高达 50% 的股权。中国也答应在加入世贸组织后六年内解除对电信服务提供者的所有限制。

资本市场

任何一个国家若要让企业家大展鸿图，就必须发展其资本市场。虽然中国拥有高储蓄率（1998 年占国内生产总值的 42%），但只有很小一部分流进私人企业，流入高科技创业公司的储蓄更是少之又少。银行体系由国有银行支配，这些银行很少提供资金给私人企业，尤其是高科技创业公司。截至 1999 年底，中国的证券市场资本总额只占国内生产总值的 33%，是世界上占有率最低的国家之一，也落在东盟国家与印度之后。到今年二月，在上海与深圳证券交易所挂牌的大多数公司都是国有企业。中国证监会给予国有企业优先上市权的做法使新的创业公司难有机会。

科技教育

要在高科技领域取得成功的主要因素是教育制度。中国劳动队伍的低教育水平是一个障碍。中国的劳动队伍中有 12% 是文盲，35% 仅受过小学教育，只有 3.5% 受过高等教育。在每年的学生大军中，只有 6% 最终升入高等学府。因此，中国制定了"211 计划"（在这项计划下，中国将设立 100 所世界级大学，以应付 21 世纪的高科技人力需求）。

必须记住的重要一点是，能创立高科技创业公司的并不是政府官员或国有企业，而是私人个体。他们需要那些在新科技时代成长、对硅谷和其他地方的发展了如指掌的监管人员给予协助。五十岁开外的政府官员并不了解这场数码革命的潜能。

互联网的新一代须起主导作用。

在新加坡,政治领导人都是四五十岁左右的人。但他们对数码的见识却比不上那些二三十岁的、富有创造力和生产力的年轻一代。一般来说,新网络公司都是由二十多岁的年轻人创立起来的。为了制造一个有利的环境和促进更多新互联网公司的创立,新加坡挑选了一些在互联网时代长大的三十多岁的人担任监管人员。他们更了解这种科技的潜能,而且在思想方面也同二十多岁的年轻人比较接近。他们在监管方面会比较宽容,让有创造力的人才可以发挥所长。

中国拥有一批懂得充分利用全球化和新经济的人才。中国一直都在经济、管理和电脑方面培养有才干的大学毕业生。中国最宝贵的资产是成千上万杰出的年轻人,他们二三十岁、曾在海外,特别是美国求学和工作过。他们之中有许多目前是在中国国内担任中低级职位或仍然逗留在国外。在今后的二三十年里,他们会升到政府和商界的高层,对当代世界的最新发展有充分的认识和了解。他们会使中国在治理国家和经营企业方面迎头赶上美国、日本和欧盟国家。

中国已经做出了战略性的决定,这个决定对中国本身和世界都有深远的经济与地缘政治的影响。中国企业将向先进国家学习,同时也将同它们合作及竞争。全球性的竞争将促使中国国内的企业提高效率和生产力,但创新的过程也会淘汰过时的工厂,导致失业和由此带来的各种社会问题。然而,这最终会使中国脱颖而出,成为 21 世纪全球货物、服务、资金、人才以及思想等交流的最主要参与者之一。

第 6 单元

在中美创新大会上的发言(节选)

美国商务部长　卡洛斯·M.古铁雷斯
北京,2007年

非常高兴能够在本周来到北京。每一次到访北京,总能看到变化,从迎接奥运会的施工建设到大吊车打造的城市新面貌都在不断变化。这些变化不仅标志着中国国内的巨大变化,也标志着中国与世界关系的变化。

本周晚些时候我将参加商贸联合委员会的会议和经济战略对话。这两个会议是我们两国政府间重要的双边对话。随着两国关系的发展,我们也将面临更多的机遇和挑战。本周我们希望就对两国都很重要的问题展开讨论。这次大会正是这个讨论的组成部分——实际上是五月在华盛顿特区举行的经济战略对话会议的成果,是对开拓创新对于在全球范围创造充满活力的、健康的、不断发展的经济的重要性的认可。

当今世界的竞争比以往任何时候都激烈。中国同印度和俄罗斯在过去的20几年间成为了全球经济的全面参与者，有30亿消费者融入了世界经济。你们通过改变中国的经济发展方式使新的想法、新的消费者以及新的竞争者大批涌现，给全球市场带来了巨大的变革。

20年前，贸易仅占世界经济的17%，而今天大约有30%的增长；

20年前，世界经济总值只有15万亿美元，而今天估计已达48万亿。

由于贸易壁垒的消除及各国对待新人新思维的开放姿态，创新型社会层出不穷。在美国，我们的市场经济帮助促进了创业文化和创新精神。纳米技术、生物燃料、信息技术的领先推动我们的经济向前发展，使我们不断保持竞争优势。事实上，世界经济论坛最近将美国经济列为全世界最具竞争力的经济，这在很大程度上是由于我们鼓励创新的能力。这种能力激发的思想和开发的精良产品大大丰富了美国的社会经济生活，创造财富并带来高水平的生活。

发现者、发明家、创造者以及敢冒风险的开拓者在我们的经济进步中发挥了不可或缺的作用。30年前，Google、Dell、Cisco、eBay这样的公司并不存在，但是它们都创立于美国——一个鼓励和奖励创新和才智的国家。美国人每年注册成百上千万的专利，数量多于任何其他的国家。美国创新产业的出口量占到美国出口总量的一半以上。这些产业代表美国经济增长的40%，为1,800万美国人提供工作，而这些人的工资比美国平均工资高40%。

我们这些政府工作人员并不创造经济增长，不创造工作岗位，不分配资本，也不推出新产品。这一切都是私营部门的创新者和企业家的功劳。我们认为政府的作用就是创造持续成功的环境。INSEAD，欧洲的优秀商学院之一，把美国列为全球创新的龙头老大。他们指的是我们由尖端技术、商业市场和资本以及顶级学术研究机构构成的"创新环境"。但是，同一研究也指出了威胁我们领先地位的各种因素——其中最大的问题是教育，我们需要"自己培养更多的科学家和工程师"。这就是我们努力促进开展更多科研、激励创新、加强教育系统的原因：

我们成倍增加了激励创新的联邦科研资金；

我们已经提议建立永久的鼓励私营部门开展研究的研发税务积分；

我们正在加强公共教育系统，特别是在数学和科学方面。

我们在这些领域继续努力的同时，为了保持发展势头，我们已经采纳并在继续促进一些重要的原则。今天我们提出的问题是，"保证创新环境的持续发展需要那些条件？"

首先，我们要继续开放全球市场。我们两国的经济都已经受益于更多的国际接触。美国和中国必须共同努力抵制我们各自国内不断抬头的保护主义逆流。我们必须向我们的民众表明自由公平贸易能为我们的经济带来的好处。我们必须表明我们将使我们的贸易伙伴对履行开放市场的承诺担负责任。我们也必须向他们表明加重经济负担并有损于创造就业机会的过度控制管理是危险的。这不仅对美国是重要的，对中国的全球伙伴也是如此。

我们相信对于创新型经济，尊重知识产权至关重要，无论对于我们自己的经济还是我们的贸易伙伴都是如此。所以，尊重知识产权一直是我们双边和多边谈判以及协议的重要组成部分。一贯地、透明地、公平公正地执行管理知识产权的规则能够激励人们创新。没有明确的规则，没有强有力的执法，任何国家都不能如愿以偿地实现经济的全面发展，也不能建立起强大的、知名的、受人尊敬的品牌，而这样的品牌正是发达经济的标志。

不执行知识产权保护，社会就不能企望创新带动的经济增长。这是我们与中国发展关系时遇到的主要挑战之一。尽管近期中国在出台要求计算机预先安装正版操作软件的新规定，承诺加入世界知识产权组织等方面已经取得了一些进步，但还需要做出更多的努力。我们认为中国仍然需要跨越这道障碍才能真正成为一个开放的创新型社会。去年，在中国，中国自己的专利注册多于外国的专利注册。显然，有效的知识产权保护对于中国的创新人士来说利害攸关。重要的是，缺少执行知识产权保护所造成的影响并不仅仅限于经济领域。比如，假药危害着受骗上当的人们的健康和安全，有时甚至害人致死。

保证产品的安全对于创新型社会的发展至关重要。消费者不会购买令他们害怕担心的东西。我们认识到以科学的、透明开放的方式管理我们面临的挑战是正确的。我们还认识到产品安全问题并非靠在边境设立检查就能一了百了，必须从生产的源头就建立起安检机制。此刻，对于中国来说是个转折点。每个国家都要对自己如何保证本国公司产品的安全做出选择。中国——以及我们所有的贸易伙伴——都必须为保证自己的产品安全尽力尽责。

有关商业和投资的法规的透明度和可预测性是另一个关键，能够向我们两国内潜在的合作伙伴发出积极的信号。资本分配者寻找安全的、可预测的市场，他们小心翼翼地注意存有不确定因素的地方。开放社会敞开大门欢迎外国投资和外国公司的竞争。只有当真正的竞争受到欢迎时，经济才能从中受益。允许外国公司带来新产品和新服务能够给消费者提供更多的选择，并且加强国内市场。为投资者增加市场的可预测性、透明度和可靠性将使中国对美国公司更具吸引力，尤其是对美国的出口产品。

只有根据市场需求，在达成共识和自愿的基础上制定标准，开放社会才能受益。强大的、创新型经济要求建立灵活的调控体系，以支持市场为导向的技术标准。这些标准应该允许所有利益攸关方，包括私营部门参与标准的制定。与其他任何国家相比，中国从全球标准中受益最多。中国一直能够按照全球标准开发产品并在世界各地进行销售。全球标准创造了一种使创新人士能够展开合作的共同语言。

我们越来越关注政府授权制定的专门技术标准的施行情况。这种做法也许在短时期能够提供竞争优势，但实际上它阻碍或限制合作。这些规定不仅会限制产品的发展，也会减少消费选择。在开放的市场经济社会里消费者掌握着真正的权力。让消费者做出最能满足他们需求的选择吧。在美国，政府不挑选谁是赢家谁是输家，确定产品或技术的赢家和输家的是消费者，而不是政府。

政府在营造鼓励创新环境方面担负着重要的责任。我们教育儿童，保持低税收，开放新市场，资助基础研究，保证联邦政府规定的合理性并且保护知识产权。这样，私营部门在这种环境里就能够创造工作岗位，分配资本，推出使消费者、经济体以及国家受益的新产品和新服务。

这些原则是创新型社会的基础。全面地吸纳这些原则将帮助中国继续从先进的发展中经济体向先进的发达经济体迈进。这些原则也将帮助我们创造一种可持续的、互惠互利的关系。中国领导人发出的信号表示他们理解这一点。上个月，温家宝总理做了一个题为"只有开放兼容，国家才能富强"的讲话。他说："中国近30年的发展告诉我们，现在的世界是开放的世界，任何一个国家要发展，孤立起来，闭关自守是不可能的。"我们希望这一认识能够在我们本周的讨论中得到体现。开放是未来我们两国关系的核心。坚持开放不易，但是这是必要的。创新产生变化，而变化是艰难的，我们必须与各种企图开倒车的势力进行斗争。

我们有责任找到共同创造有利于可持续的、开放的、互惠互利的关系的方法，而这种关系的确立有赖于创新人士队伍的不断壮大。历史表明国家通过挑选赢家或输家的做法所采取的冒进的产业政策最终都以削弱自己的竞争力，导致市场疲软而告终，此举无助于市场的发展。

中国必须表明自己在全球经济中是负责任的利益攸关方。全世界都在注视着中国。中国日益增强的重要地位赋予中国政府和中国的工商领导者重大的责任。一个繁荣的中国符合美国的利益，同样，一个昌盛的美国也最有利于中国。通过合作，我们两国能够实现双赢，能够将我们的创造力变为造福大家的产品。

第7单元

21世纪对领导者的挑战（节选2）
吉米·卡特

我的列位继任者和美国公众已经接受了这一观点。开明的个人利益已然盛行，美国公私各部门为促进中国的经济发展做了不少工作。

自 1979 年开始，美国人民迎来了 10 万多名中国访问学者和留学生到我国的大学和学院，其中相当数目的人得到美国的资助。许多人已回到中国报效祖国，将来还会有数以千计的人回到中国。这方面的交流让我引以为自豪，并且我希望将来这种交流能够得到进一步发展。

在中华人民共和国的非市场经济尚不充分具备加入世界银行和国际货币基金组织的条件时，美国就同意中国成为其成员国。

美国市场对中国商品开放。美国人消费掉中国出口总量的近 40%。美国的公司和金融机构对中国进行大量投资，美国公司还特别慷慨地促进对中国实施技术转让。

我们欢迎中国更多地参与世界事务的政策，但却受到美国有些人轻率的谴责。他们力图限制美国同中国的贸易和外交联系。他们惧怕中国经济发展以及可能随之而来的军事力量的渐增。对于这些人，我要说：与其对抗受到排斥的中国的种种危险，或做削弱、孤立中国的劳而无功之事，还不如展望繁荣、友好的中国所能带来的挑战和机遇。

总而言之，1972 年以来美国历届政府都认识到：一个安全、不断现代化的、有效施行仁政的中国，一个有助于全球及区域稳定、繁荣的中国，符合美国的利益。这样的中国也正是中国政府和人民所希望的。同样，我认为，一个安全、经济健全、领导有方并奉行建设性外交政策的美国也符合中国的利益。我坚信，中国领导人若能依照以上看法发表一项声明，将会受到美国人民的欢迎。这一论述究竟意味着什么？要回答这一问题，我们不可沉湎于过去，而必须展望未来。《上海公报》、外交关系正常化以及 1982 年关于售台武器的协定等文件仍然具有约束力，但我们不可过分纠缠我们已经走过的这段历程。相反，我们必须探索前面的领域。

全人类和各国政府也正面临着人口和技术变革所引起的一系列类似的问题。这些问题是前所未有的，却鲜为人们理解。例如，在全世界范围内，交通、通讯变得易如反掌：电视、圆盘式卫星天线、传真机、个人电脑和电子通讯的日益普及，正在改变着人们的希冀和渴望。政府不仅不能阻止这些技术变革，相反，政府必须学会利用新技术所带来的机遇。

这些发展还意味着：在未来的岁月里，国家安全、经济增长和有效领导将和20 世纪有着概念上的区别。这些变革已经显而易见了。例如，在安全领域，技术变革正在改变着武器和军事战略。任何国家都不能借恫吓邻邦、使其感到不安来有效实现自身的安全。有不安全感的人们越来越容易获得大规模杀伤性武器。在经济领域，各国认识到，在全球经济一体化的情况下，很难制定独立的增长战略。政治经济领导人越来越多地受制于外部力量和体制的约束。如果他们试图解脱国际金融和商业力量的制约，那么他们国家的经济就会停滞不前。

世界各地领导人遵守国际行为准则的情况，日益成为人们评判其业绩的依据。请允许我试举几例：

各国如果不对国际组织尽财政义务，就会受到批评，美国不缴纳联合国会费便是一例。

各国背离公认的国际商业做法，就会受到孤立。围绕《赫尔姆斯—伯顿法》的争议，使美国正在认识到这一点。

各国如果违背国际公认的人权准则，或者似乎拒不给予少数民族及宗教信仰上属于少数的群体以基本自由，那就会受到特别仔细的监察。

鉴于这些变革，要在21世纪美中两国、以至于任何国家有效地施行仁政，需要哪些条件呢？人性显然不会改变。所有的人仍然会有共同的愿望：衣食无忧，居所不愁；不用担心随时随地会有暴力行为、任意逮捕和遭受酷刑；有信仰自由；享受言论和集会自由并参与自治。满足上述愿望是促进人权的精髓所在。我们的宪法、法律以及我们两国自愿签署的若干国际公约和盟约，让我们有义务对这些愿望做出回应。

但是，21世纪的有效治理将不仅仅要求政府保护公民的人权不受侵犯。在以下各方面也需要采取积极行动：

为日益增多的老年公民提供福利；

通过人道手段，解决各国国内和国际上史无前例的人口迁移所带来的后果；

加强法治；

改进解决内乱的技术措施；

让公民参与影响到他们生活的重大政策的决策过程；

制定有效措施，确保政府有充分的收入；

尽管全球经济似乎在加剧国际间和各国内部的不平等，仍然要防止收入分配上出现极度不公平；

在市场调控和放手任其发展之间找到适当的平衡点；

在中央、省级和地方政府之间适当分配权力。

人口和技术方面的挑战提出了诸多问题，上述各项是其中的一部分。如果不能迎战这些有关治理的挑战，我们两国就都不会有稳定和繁荣。中美两国必须解决这些问题，才能保证我们的国家在21世纪能有效施行仁政。我们两国认识到自身的不足，从各自的传统和国际义务出发，正在施政管理的方方面面进行实验。例如，美国在其福利制度方面下放权力，增加市场竞争力，调整联邦政府和州政府之间的权力分配。中国在进行农村选举，扩大法治，活跃议会机构，发展市场经济和改进城市管理。在我们两国，这些改革还只是刚刚起步。我们需要创造性的思想，考虑世界各地政府和社会如何才能最大地获益于技术变革、经济一体化和多极化对21世纪的影响。最佳答案可能不会来自各国的中央政府，而是来自地方；可能不仅仅由政府提供，而且也会由私营部门提供。

我们两国尽管具体方式有所不同，但都未能实现我们的期望、尽到自己的义务。我们双方进行自我评估并对对方做出评价，是件有益的事。只要别人提出的意见是建设性的，而不是骄傲自大、自以为是，我们中的任何一方就应当欢迎对方指出自己的缺点。如果一方取得了进展，另一方应加以赞许。中美两国在近年来关于人权的讨论中忽略了这些简单的道理。

我提议，卡特中心可以作为一个平台，在那里我们两国有影响的人士可以聚会，在平等和相互尊重的基础上，就 21 世纪的挑战交流思想。我们在分头探讨适合各自国情和历史的解决方法时，可以相互学习不少东西。就人权和领导方法展开广泛的对话和合作，有助于增进相互信任、消除那些可能在我们之间造成分裂的战略、经济和文化等方面的分歧。让我们携手共建美好明天，造福两国人民、造福全人类！让我们再次踏上我和邓小平 20 年前所开始的旅程！

第8单元

建立中美经济关系合作新习惯（节选）
艾伦·F. 霍尔默大使
清华大学，2007年

我们变化中的经济关系

中国在世界舞台上的再度崛起是近年来最有影响的地缘政治事件之一。现在几乎在所有的问题上，从贸易到国家安全，再到气候变化，几乎在所有的地方，从朝鲜到伊朗再到苏丹，中美的利益都越来越多地重叠在一起。中国已经与全球经济如此充分地融合在一起，因此，中国经济所发生的一切都会影响到国际社会。

合作性的、建设性的、坦诚的中美关系对于理解和回应中国的发展是至关重要的，这表现在各个可能的方面上。当我纵观中美经济关系的时候，我发现这一关系正在步入一个新阶段。

首先，中美经济的互相依赖程度正在加深。在越来越多的经济及由经济引发的问题上，我们都更加需要彼此。在过去的五年间，据美国方面的数据，美国对中国的出口额已经从 180 亿美元增长到了 520 亿美元，而美国从中国的进口额也从 1,020 亿美元增长到 2,870 亿美元。此外，美国和中国也正塑造着全球的能源和环境趋势，当然同时也为其所塑造。这种塑造与被塑造引发了不容忽视的经济后果。比如说，我们这两个国家是世界上最大的能源消费者和温室气体排放者。

其次，贸易和投资曾经在很大程度上是双边关系稳定的原因，但是现在，它也正日益成为双方关系紧张的原因。这种状况影响了中美两国各自国内对于参与经济全球化益处的共识。上世纪 80 年代，我首次深入参与国际贸易问题，那时我们和中国尚未有明显的贸易紧张状况，主要是因为那个时候我们还没有很多的双边贸易关系。从某种意义上讲，我们的贸易紧张正反映了我们关系的成熟及双边贸易与投资的迅速增长。我们需要确保能够有效处理这些紧张关系，使双边经济关系平稳发展。

在 WTO 的框架内处理平等和主权经济体的贸易争端是一个正常机制。根据 WTO 的统计数据，从 1994 年 WTO 成立以来，已经有 99 宗案例对美国提出指控，而美国也对 28 个国家提出了 88 宗指控。在中国方面，有五宗案例是美国针对中国提出的，两宗是中国针对美国提出的。欧盟向美国提出的指控最多（共 31 宗），其次是加拿大（共 14 宗）。

对持续上升的贸易量的忧虑体现在几个方面，这也是我将要说到的我们面临的第三个动因的原由：经济民族主义和保护主义正在我们两个国家抬头。这些情绪可能会对领导者施加压力，使他们无法采取符合中美两国人民和经济长期利益的措施。

在应对全球化方面，两国的决策者必须压制住一时冲动，不能为片面追求短期和被误导的政策效应而抛弃开放经济的长期奋斗的利益。例如，布什政府一直反对国会提出的会产生反作用的并对美经济产生威胁的有关中国外汇管理方面的议案。与此同时，在中国的国际收支经常项目顺差持续大规模增长，并对外汇市场进行长期大规模干预的情况下，中国在美国对华出口和投资方面所设的壁垒使美国难以维持经济开放。

相互依赖性的加深、在经济政策共识上的紧张状态及经济保护主义的抬头——中美经济关系的这三点新趋势是我们共同面临的问题，需要我们双方合作解决。

化解复杂情况，建立合作新习惯

这些动因促成了 2006 年布什总统和胡锦涛主席建立战略经济对话（SED）。他们对这一个论坛提出了设想，在一致强调长期战略关系的重要性的基础之上，为两国政府在高层面上的交流提供便利。

化解我们的复杂情况，不断增加互助关系确实棘手，而且要求在合适的时间就合适的问题，用合适的方式与合适的人对话。很久以前我学到，不管是什么样的对话，如果你想有所收获，那么最重要的就是尽量设身处地为他人着想，试着站在他人的角度上去看世界。这样你才能达到一致，获得双赢，而且达成的一致既能促进双方共同的利益，又能经得住时间的考验。战略经济对话正体现了这样一种方式。

SED 作为中美关系中起领导作用的新的机制，已经为华盛顿和北京的决策者提供了有效的渠道。通过这种做法，我们重建了稳定繁荣的经济互动的基础。就 SED 而言，美国有三大核心目标。

建立合作新习惯

首先，通过这一框架，我们正以建立双边合作新习惯的方式推动中美关系前进。我们已经制订出一个大的议程，内容涵盖交叉经济和因经济发展引发的重大问题，如监管透明度、能源节省、环境保护、创新、食品和产品安全，以及重大的经济问题，如汇率和宏观经济政策、市场准入、金融市场发展和开放。

我们敦促双方各个层次各个方面的政府官员开展更为多样的互动活动，打破妨碍有效交流和成果产生的烟囱管式的传统官僚体制。与此同时，我们通过连续高层次的互动设定目标并保证它们的贯彻实施。

虽然如此，好的过程并不一定保证取得好的结果。中国和美国高级官员之间展开的对话，虽然有用，但不能为了对话而对话，也不能让领导人对于有分歧的政题"一笔带过"。它的意义在于设定目标，明确结果和完善实际解决方案。

直接沟通交流正是如此：在中美关系史上，它一直以减少误会、排除误解的方式使两国关系平稳发展。通过这种交流，它帮助我们向中国发出信号：我们欢迎一个自信、和平、繁荣的中国的崛起。脆弱的、不安全的中国并非美国的经济及安全利益所在。

加快中国经济转型

第二，我们共同的政策应加快中国下一轮"改革开放"的进程，这一点极其重要。中国经济增长的速度是有目共睹的，但还需要不断努力。

中国的最高领导已经认识到他们所面临的一个重大难题，即如何在不再处于初级经济增长阶段的情况下采取必要的大胆措施。我们非常赞同目前的领导班子所做的努力，他们正在将现有经济转型为更加以市场为导向的、更少依赖于低附加值的制造业出口的，更多依赖于中国人民的技术和才智的，更少物质投入和自然资源消耗型的经济。

中国面临的重大风险之一就是政府的行动不够迅速，无法及时采取政策手段处理其经济增长模式所带来的经济和社会的不平衡。没有强有力的政策调整，中国的经济增长道路就不会持久，这也是中国的领导层公开声明的。我们鼓励关键性的改革，帮助中国化解经济增长过快所带来的问题，包括金融市场开放和调整增长使其获得平衡的规划。中国已经向世界证明它可以发展得很快，但是它能同样证明它可以用不同的方式发展吗？能不能在发展的同时既重数量又重质量？能不能最终获得可持续性的发展？

中国需要采取果断的结构性政策来转变其经济增长方式，目前其经济增长方式的特点还是重工业多、能源消耗高、资金密集、依赖出口，应转变为更依赖国内市场及服务产品的经济增长方式，国民收入中家庭收入的份额也应当增加。为了让市场力量有效地调节经济，让繁荣发展惠及所有的中国人，中国需要有更为灵活的价格机制，这包括更加灵活的、市场驱动的汇率。汇率灵活可以使货币政策——这一指导经济最有力的手段——集中在保证价格和金融稳定方面。

另外，人民币汇率正在被越来越多的国家视为不公平竞争的原因之一。越来越多的国家领导人和多边机构在呼吁货币升值。上个月在华盛顿举行的国际货币基金组织年会上，达成了一份联合公报，要求人民币汇率机制更加灵活。

IMF 联合公报明确了在保持全球发展的同时，有序地解决全球发展不平衡问题是各国共同的责任。就美国而言，就有一些需要做的事情，其中如采取行动推动美国的国家存款，包括不断巩固其财政。我很高兴地宣布我们正在取得进步，尽管我们要做的工作还没完成。根据最新的数据，美国联邦预算赤字下降了一半左右，从 2005 年到 2007 年间，由占 GDP 的 2% 下降到 1%。

中国未来能否成功的关键在于它是否愿意加快以市场为基础的经济改革的步伐。履行甚至是超越它对 WTO 所做出的承诺，抵制保护主义的情绪，开放其经济，使其产品特别是服务，走向更广的国际竞争，会有助于调整经济平衡，使更多的中国人从经济繁荣中受惠。这些改革目前以及今后都会受到影响力不断增大的中国工商界的抵制。在我看来，中国长期经济安全的最大危险不在于中国开放得太快，而在于保护主义的盛行和改革步伐太慢。

鼓励中国在国际往来中承担起责任

第三，也是最后一点，我们支持中国积极担负起作为一支全球经济力量的责任。我们欢迎中国加入重要的国际金融机构，并给予中国更强的话语权。从 2006 年经济战略对话初创以来，我们支持中国加入了泛美开发银行 (IADB) 和设在巴黎的金融行动专责委员会（FATF）。我们也强烈支持中国在国际货币基金组织和世界银行里拥有更多的投票权。更多的参与可以使中国从这些机构中获益，不过，北京也应当意识到作为一个更积极的参与者的责任这一点十分重要。

对许多最贫穷国家而言，中国已成为他们重要的国外援助国。我们希望与中国——一个新的并受欢迎的参与者——携手在多边关系中努力保证对外援助和贷款切实促进可持续发展。

在中美经济关系的新时代，我们的商业活动要求有新的发展措施。我们正在通过创造政治空间和发展机制能力来迎接这些挑战，以保证我们双边经济关系的长久稳定。

第9单元

欧洲在体育运动方面的作用

欧洲事务部长　吉姆·墨菲
伦敦，2008年

我非常高兴出席今天上午的会议。本次大会是在各利益攸关方结束长达几周的会议和讨论之时召开的，有待解答的问题是：我们如何使欧盟作为一个区域机构共同应对欧洲乃至世界在 21 世纪面临的挑战？我们查看了欧洲在信仰、气候变化、社会事务等方面的作用。我期待我们今天能就欧洲在体育运动方面的作用展开对话。

你们或许会问：欧盟与体育运动有什么关系？

有两个关系。

第一，因为我们是以《里斯本条约》为背景考虑这些问题，而《里斯本条约》在某些方面对体育运动意义重大。

第二，体育运动作为一种团结的力量在欧洲乃至欧洲之外的地区都发挥着较为广泛的作用，体育运动从广义上讲是创造健康社会的手段。

让我们首先看看《里斯本条约》对体育运动有什么作用。这个条约被媒体的一些部门妖魔化了，可以说，故事被装扮成了事实。但是，尽管我今天并不是要在此为条约辩护，我还是要向在场的任何爱好体育运动的欧元怀疑论者明确地指出：《里斯本条约》不允许欧盟协调有关体育运动的规定。这就是说，在条约的诸多方面欧盟的投入都受到严格限制，体育运动便是其中之一。欧盟在这方面的投入仅限于对国家层面采取的行动进行补充或添加。

该条约的作用是允许欧盟机构在远远超过现在情况的基础上从体制方面承认体育运动的特殊本质，也就是说体育运动在欧洲不应该受害于更广的欧盟立法在无意间造成的后果。

特殊性和自治的问题还有待于正在进行的辩论的结果。我知道一些人原本希望在条约中看到更多的保证。人们在谈论这些问题并且辩论还在继续，这很好。比如今年，欧洲理事会正在对自治进行充分的调查。

但是，除了特殊性和自治的复杂性，条约将首次承认体育运动在欧洲社会的重要作用。条约的批准将允许对体育运动项目进行欧盟特定的持续资助，计划在 2009 年进行试点。这应该会结束为了适应不同的资助来源而操纵体育运动项目的这种令人有点生疑的做法——比如，以"旅游"项目为名资助奥地利和捷克共和国的北欧两项滑雪队——从而承认体育运动应当因其本身得到资助。

我希望我们将看到欧盟体育计划的发展，看到体育与健康和教育等相关的政策之间建立更多的联系。为此，我下面要谈谈体育运动为什么与我这个欧洲部长有关系的第二个原因——这是因为体育运动在社会具有较为广泛的作用。

体育与健康和教育等政策之间的联系对在座的各位是显而易见的。我所在的格拉斯哥选区非常清楚地证明了体育对年轻人的吸引力，因为体育运动能够鼓舞人——无论你是观众还是参与者。年轻人需要受到鼓舞，体育运动恰恰提供他们所需的行为准则——体育包含着团队合作、公平竞争以及竭尽全力做到最好；体育帮助人自信，学会新的技能，强壮体魄，使才能得到认可和发展。体育为不同的天赋和兴趣提供了这么多不同的机会——我们只需看看这个会场，就能看到所有体育运动项目的代表，从冰球到马术，从举重到滑翔运动。

毫无疑问，在基层支持体育运动是增加社区凝聚力的一种有效的方式。历史上，许多重要的欧洲体育运动俱乐部都植根于当地的教会和工作场所。体育运动能跨越文化、政治及经济方面的鸿沟，足球可能就是最好的例证——全球有 7 亿多人观看了 2006 世界杯决赛。正如我刚才谈到的，体育运动包括了大量的各种各样的活动，欧盟就有 70 万个运动俱乐部和协会。难怪英国奥林匹克协会把体育运动称作欧洲最大的社会运动。

这一点很重要。因为我们现在在欧洲所看到的种种分歧与我们更为熟悉的历史上国家间的分歧毫无关系。我现在谈的是富人与穷人之间的矛盾，是各个社会里不同文化和宗教群体之间的内部矛盾。我们还需要在这些方面做出很多的努力，但是毫无疑问的是体育运动作为一种力量可以发挥团结作用。体育运动是能够战胜那种认为人可以以不同的文化、宗教或经济背景来划分的狭隘的信条的一种共同兴趣。我最近访问了萨拉热窝。在那里我有机会代表英国使馆足球队与波斯尼亚的议员们踢了一场足球。我有两个收获：第一，这是一个证明体育运动实质上是一种团结的力量的好机会；第二，我的膝盖受了重伤。

在国家层面，人民对体育运动的热爱能够成为表明他们身份的强有力的公开声明。1995 年，纳尔逊·曼德拉在南非举行的橄榄球世界杯决赛上身着南非国家队的"跳羚"队衫，这一姿态影响之大丝毫不亚于他的任何讲话。他的做法让所有南非人民为他们的国民身份感到自豪，并向世界传递了这样的信息，即新南非将是一个让其所有的公民具有归属感的国家。

但是，对一个比以往任何时期流动性都更强，文化都更加多元化的欧洲来讲，各个国家对体育运动的热爱有着什么样的影响呢？我认为高尔夫莱德杯赛以及十柱保龄球赛是体育赛事中唯一几项能够使欧洲人团结起来，共同为一支球队呐喊加油的项目，对此，我欢迎今天在座的体育运动专家多多指正。

我们能够重新考虑诺曼·特比特的板球实验。我们大多数人都会记得特比特勋爵天真且错误的建议，他认为能否改变人们对所喜爱的体育运动的忠诚是衡量一体化是否成功的标准。我不知道现在旅居海外的 550 万英国人有多少人还喜欢板球。

　　或许我们可以提出这样的论点，的确，尽管没有什么能像在体育赛场上取得胜利一样激发起民族自豪感，但是体育运动给予了人们更大的奖励，这就是可以看到健康的比赛在不同的群体和社会之间架起桥梁。

　　体育不会将我们分开。体育把我们团结在一起——甚至在我们互为竞争对手时也是如此。这对于欧洲也是一样。27 个国家更多地为了他们的共同目标而团结在一起，而不是因为各自的国家利益而相互隔离。

　　世界已经改变，我认为世界变得更加美好：便利的国际旅行和通讯革命使世界变小。但是，与此并存的现实是主宰媒体的问题影响着我们，无论我们生活在世界的什么地方——不断高攀的食品价格和油价、气候变化、冲突。这些是我们需要共同应对的挑战。我们需要开放眼界，结成联盟，确认共同的目标，发展包容的社会，使人们感到他们同属于一个更为广大的全世界的人类社会。这就是我希望欧盟能够帮助我们取得的成果，而体育运动恰恰能够帮助我们实现这些目标。

　　让我们不要忘记国际性体育运动是早在发明"全球化"一词之前我们就享有的伟大的全球化机会之一。创立于 1894 年的国际奥委会比联合国早建 50 多年，国际足联自第一次世界大战起就一直存在。

　　认可体育运动在欧洲社会的作用是《里斯本条约》的一个鲜明的优点，对此，我认为即便最强硬的欧元怀疑论者也会表示支持。

第 10 单元

2005 年诺贝尔奖演说辞（节选 2）
国际原子能机构总干事，诺贝尔和平奖获得者
穆罕默德·埃尔巴拉迪博士

　　不管你们相信进化论、智能设计论还是上帝造物论，有一点是肯定的。人类自有史以来，一直以宗教、意识形态、种族的种种借口在战争中相互残杀。任何一个文明都从未自愿放弃过最强有力的武器。今天我们似乎已经同意彼此分享现代科技，但是我们仍然拒绝承认我们价值观中的核心价值是共同的。

　　我本人是埃及穆斯林，在开罗和纽约接受教育，现在居住在维也纳。我和我的妻子在北部世界居住了半生的时间，其余的时间在南部世界度过。我们亲身体会到了人类大家庭的独特本质以及我们共同拥有的价值观。莎士比亚在《威尼斯商人》中通过提问道出了人类大家庭中每一位的心声："你们要是用刀剑扎我们，我们不是也会出血吗？你们要是搔我们的痒，我们不是也会笑起来吗？你们要是

给我们下毒，我们不是也会被毒死吗？你们要是欺侮了我们，我们难道不会复仇吗？"而且，请大家不要忘记：

没有任何一种宗教的基础不是宽容，没有任何一种宗教不珍视人类神圣的生命。

犹太教告诫我们重视人类生命的美丽和欢乐。

基督教告诫我们待邻如待己。

伊斯兰教认为，不公正地杀死一个人就相当于屠杀整个人类。

印度教把整个宇宙视为一个大家庭。

佛教号召我们珍视万物合一。

有人可能会说，如果一个社会构筑在宽容和珍视圣洁的人类生命之上，认为边界、民族和意识形态都无足轻重，那未免太过理想化。但是对此我要说，这不是理想主义，相反这恰恰是现实主义，因为历史告诉我们战争几乎从未解决过人类的分歧。武力不能使旧的伤口愈合，而只能造成的新的伤痛。

我刚才谈了我们要如何与不当使用核能源作斗争。现在我还想告诉大家，这种能源可以怎样为人类造福。

在国际原子能机构，我们每天都在各大洲忙于利用核技术和放射性技术为人类服务。在越南，由于国际原子能机构的帮助，农民们种出的大米具有更高的营养价值。在整个拉丁美洲，核技术正在帮助人们绘制地下含水层的地图，以便可持续地管理当地的供水。在加纳，一台新的放疗机在为数千名病人治疗癌症。在南太平洋，日本科学家采用核技术研究气候变化。印度正在兴建8个新的核电站，为不断壮大的民族提供清洁电力。这个例子刚好证明越来越多人的希望核能源将在世界范围内快速投入广泛使用。这些，以及数以千计的其他项目实现着原子能机构的理想：和平利用原子能。

但是正是由于核能和核技术的利用日益广泛，所以最大限度保护核安全也变得至关重要。切尔诺贝利事故以后，我们在全球努力提高核设施的安全性能。2001年9月恐怖袭击以后，我们更加注意核安全。在这两方面，我们都建立了一个由法律准则和性能标准构成的国际网络。但是我们最显而易见的影响还是在核活动现场。我们向世界各地派遣了百余支由国际专家组成的核查小组来确保核活动的安全性。

我为国际原子能机构的2,300名辛勤工作的员工感到自豪，今天我也要和他们分享这份荣誉。其中有些人也随我来到了现场。我们来自90多个国家，这为我们的工作带来不同的视角。我们的多样性正是我们的优势所在。我们的权限十分有限，预算也不多，而且我们没有军队。但是，正是由于我们的坚定信念赋予了我们力量，我们将始终敢于向强权讲真话，我们也将始终独立客观地完成我们的使命。诺贝尔和平奖于我们而言是强有力的信息，它敦促我们持之以恒地为安全和发展工作。持久的和平并不单单是成就，而是一种氛围、一个过程、一份事业。

　　今天我在这里为大家描绘的图景可能有些悲观。但是最后我要告诉大家我为什么仍然充满希望。这是因为，全球化积极的一面正促使不同的国家和民族之间在政治上、经济上和社会上相互依存，而使战争成为一个越来越难以接受的选择。在欧盟的 25 个成员国之间，经济和社会政治如此地相互依存，这使得用武力解决分歧变得非常荒谬。同样，对于拥有来自欧洲、中亚和北美的 55 个成员国的欧洲安全与合作组织也是如此。那么，这样的范例通过创造性的多边机制和积极的国际协作，能不能在全世界范围内推广呢？整个世界将会因此成为强者公平，弱者安全的典范。

　　我充满希望还因为公民社会正在变得更加信息灵通，而且也越发活跃。他们正在敦促政府进行变化——创造基于多样性、宽容和公平的民主社会。公民社会也提出了创造性的解决问题的办法。他们提高人的思想觉悟、筹集捐款，而且致力于把公民精神从地方推向全球。他们努力使人类大家庭更加亲近。与以往任何时候相比，我们现在有更多的机会来肯定地回答那个亘古不变的问题："我能守护我的兄弟吗？"我们现在需要转变心理，拥有一种全新的心态，我们应该能够视大洋彼岸的陌生人为自己的近邻。

　　最后，我充满希望是因为我在我的孩子及他们那一代人身上看到了希望。我19 岁的时候第一次出国。我的孩子们比我更幸运，他们还是婴儿的时候就已经开始接触外国文化，并成长在一个多元文化环境中。我敢肯定地讲，我的儿子和女儿完全看不到肤色、种族和国籍的差异。他们并不觉得他们的朋友济子、马福坡（音）、贾斯廷、绍洛和胡萨姆之间有什么区别，对于他们来说，这些人都是他们同伴，是他们要好的朋友。通过旅行、媒体和通信，全球化可以帮助我们把彼此仅仅看作人类的一员，就像我的孩子和他们的同龄人那样。

　　想象一下吧，如果各国用等同于制造战争机器的金钱来促进发展的话，那将会是怎样的情况呢？让我们想象一个人人有自由有尊严的世界吧。让我们想象一个我们为死去的儿童伤心流泪的世界吧，无论他们是死在达尔富尔地区还是在温哥华。让我们想象一个我们可以通过外交和对话而不是炸弹和子弹解决分歧的世界吧。想象一下，如果唯一的核武器只是陈列在博物馆里的文物。想象一下，我们可以留给子孙后代什么遗产。

　　想象一下吧，其实，这样的一个世界就在我们的手中。

第 11 单元

美国人对香港回归 10 周年的看法

美国总领事　詹姆斯 ·B. 郭明翰
2007 年

非常荣幸今天能来到这里。我要感谢香港明天更好基金会邀请我在香港成为中国的特别行政区 10 年之际从一个美国人的视角谈谈我的感受。我尤其高兴与香港明天更好基金会的听众交流。该基金会于 1995 年由一批香港具有影响力的商界和社团领袖创建，旨在巩固公众对香港未来的信心。你们成绩斐然，而我很高兴美国为支持同样的目标与你们构筑了亲密的关系。

你们或许知道，我初到香港，对香港的概念是全新的。但是我第一次接触到你们了不起的发展历程是在 20 多年前。我和我的妻子在欧洲结交了一对来自香港的中国夫妇。他们当时暂居海外。即便是那时，他们都非常担心香港的回归。最终他们决定在回归之前离开香港。1997 前的两三年间，国际媒体纷纷表示了对这块土地未来的担忧，公众讨论中经常充斥着大胆的预言和焦虑担忧。1995 年 6 月，《财富》杂志的封面报道题为"香港之死"。而正是在这种商业和投资都处于逆境的时候，为帮助恢复人们对香港地区的信心，这个基金会成立了。

12 年后当我再次看到这本杂志封面的时候，我回忆起马克 · 吐温的一句话。当得知他的讣告被刊登在纽约的报刊上时，他说："有关我去世的报道是夸大其词。"香港同样令人出乎意料。香港明天更好基金会通过使大家更好地理解香港，香港与内地的关系以及"一国两制"的模式，促进了东西方彼此之间更深的了解。在香港特别行政区成立 10 周年之际谈香港，我希望为基金会在加深互相了解方面的努力做出贡献。

首先，我想说，回首过去的 10 年，美国相信"一国两制"对于中国，特别是香港而言是成功的。……

我还想明确地说美国政府希望香港和"一国两制"的模式继续取得成功。1997 年前后，国际社会以极大的兴趣关注这一具有历史意义的试验。10 年后，我们依然对香港的未来充满希望。这不只是说说而已，因为香港的成功关乎美国的重大利益。在全球化、互相依存的 21 世纪中，香港作为亚洲的国际都市，发挥着极大的作用，有利于中国、美国和许多其他国家。美国自身在香港的相关利益就不小。这里是我们的第 15 大出口市场。6 万名美国公民居住在这里，每年有超过 100 万美国人到访香港。1,200 家美国公司在此有驻港和地区办事处，并且雇佣了香港 10% 的劳动力。美国在香港的直接投资共计 380 亿美元。

回首过去的 10 年，香港就像许多亚洲的其他地区一样，也曾经历了许多考验。但是香港已经复苏——这是毋庸置疑的。过去三年内经济增长非常强劲（2006 年的 GDP 增长率为 6.5%），民意测验显示香港人总体对未来以及他们在中国扮演的角色表示乐观。美国持同样的乐观态度，并祝贺香港走向成功。我们非常期待香港在这条成功之路上继续走下去。

我们有充分理由做出这种积极的预言。中国重新行使对香港的主权 10 年后，香港依然是中国最开放、最发达的地区。中央政府总的来说履行了其维护香港高度自治的承诺，并多年来以具体行动支持香港的经济发展与繁荣。"内地与香港关于建立更紧密经贸关系的安排"，开始并扩大"个人游"计划，增加泛珠江三角洲内的合作以及在商业和金融业内放宽对人民币使用规定的限制依然是香港过去和未来经济成功的重要因素。香港作为国际金融中心的角色在过去 10 年也得到巩固。香港的市场资本化程度是其 1997 年的 3.5 倍。该地区是中国最大的资本来源，2006 年共筹集 430 亿美元。中国香港在世界贸易组织和亚太经合组织内仍然积极发挥着成员作用，是其中重要的经济体。

传统基金会今年再一次，也是连续第 13 年认为香港特别行政区享有全世界最高程度的经济自由。上周，日本经济研究中心在竞争力、国际化程度以及金融业发展方面，把中国香港排在 2006 年度 50 大经济体的首位。

重要的是，香港不仅仅是经济成功的典范。香港在遵从法治，遵循公平自由的市场原则，允许不受约束的企业活动，并尊重自由和人权，包括宗教自由方面依然是华人社会的模范。香港的政治制度还在前进，且公众越来越多地参与到公民事务中来。香港依靠反复适应变化的经济和政治情况和不断调整自我定位，经受住了过去几年的考验并重新繁荣起来。香港要保持稳定、繁荣，保持其强大的竞争力，就必须继续这样走下去。在急速变化的全球经济面前，仅仅保持现状是不够的。

……

尽管如此，我们对过去 10 年的进程的评价依然是积极的，而且我们对未来 10 年依然乐观——就像美国人向来乐观一样。香港社会是一个开放、活跃、成熟的社会。它可以为中国作许多贡献，同时，香港作为一个国际都市，也可以为世界其他地区带来好处。这里的人们依然期待未来，并继续筹划改变。我非常幸运能在这些日子里结交许多香港朋友。他们是自豪的中国人，并且认为他们对祖国的爱和对香港政治经济发展的追求并不相互矛盾。"一国两制"卓有成效，尽管当初对此存在着怀疑并预见了种种困难。我认为，毫无疑问"一国两制"可以继续有效地发挥作用。美国是你们的朋友，诚挚地希望香港成功，并对此表示极大兴趣。推而广之，美国对中国的成功也是如此。

最后，让我为我开始播放的悲观的视频补充一个积极的材料。这是近期发布的图像：2007 年 3 月出版的《时代》杂志，封面醒目地写着"展望香港的未来"。

美国预测香港的未来是非常光明的。我们希望未来的香港是繁荣、稳定且自信的中国的一部分，并且以经济自由，公民自由和尊重人权的领航形象为自己的国家和全世界作出贡献。我们希望未来的香港继续适应并应对变化。我们希望未来的香港从中华民族的传统和西方文化中汲取力量，发出自己的声音，成为中国全面发展进程中一支积极向上、生气勃勃的力量。

第 12 单元

世界经济论坛上的讲话（节选 2）

托尼·布莱尔

达沃斯，2007年

我们先考虑一下这些问题牵涉的利害关系，再想一想，为了建立正确的同盟，达成协议，为了采取适当措施解决问题我们遇到了多少困难。这是我对 10 年来为应对挑战所作的努力的重要总结。10 年来，遵循我们制定的政策，英国不计得失，在解决每一个重大全球问题时始终站在最前列。互相依存是大家都已接受的事实。大家为了战胜全球性挑战，渴望寻求一个以全球价值观为基础的共同的全球目标。

但我们苦于没有使多边行动生效的机制。我们已意识到互相依存这一现实。我们能描绘出目标和价值观。我们缺少的是采取行动的能力和共同行动的方式。我们需要强有力的多边机制。然而，现实往往是：我们的多边行动相互脱节，用意良好却由于方法不当或手段不足无法取胜。但这些都不应使我们低估我们的努力。我们往往把某个问题描述得极为重要，却没有作出相应的努力去解决问题，两者间存在着很大的差距。在这方面，往往会有评论轻易地把它归结为缺乏政治意愿。以我的经验来看，问题通常不在于缺乏政治意愿。总的来说，我们是有政治意愿的，问题是我们的决心经常不能转化为行动。这是为什么呢？因为行动要求注意力集中，需要时间、精力和坚持不懈的努力。虽然领导人和国家自身有能力长期坚持做到这一点，但是，实际上，他们面临的各种其他压力让他们根本无法采取行动。

以全球价值观为基础的全球共同目标需要全球机制才能产生有效的多边行动。联合国安理会如果没有德国、日本、巴西或印度的参与——更不用提没有非洲国家和伊斯兰国家的参与，不仅会在全世界眼里丧失合法性，而且会严重破坏行动的有效性。我们当然可以制定某种形式的过渡机制，比如设置不具备否决权的准常任席位，然后再过渡到一个经过改革的安理会。但一定要完成改革。对于联合国内部的改革也是一样，要赋予秘书长更大的权力，合并机构，……但是，现在就必须开始改革。要求合并国际货币基金组织和世界银行，并且提高这两个机构内发展中国家的影响力是有充分的理由的。G8 峰会正逐渐转变为 G8+5 峰会。G8+5 峰会可以成为一个论坛，使最强大的国家在此达成真正具有现代的全球影响力的协议。但是，这一转变迟早都必须完成。我们需要使地区组织发挥更大作用。

我深信，要提高欧盟的执行力就必须修改欧盟的规章。现在有 27 个成员国的欧盟难以在原来只有 15 个成员国时建立的体制中运作。如果非盟能成为一个强大而统一的声音，并为非洲谋求利益，这将非常有助于非洲现状的改善。

但是，这不仅仅是政府机构的责任。对于确定某一问题的重要性与确保应对行动方面的差距，非政府与非国家的力量的介入在不断增加。盖茨基金的资源被用于消灭疟疾。这是一种可预防的疾病，每年约导致 100 万人死亡。由穆罕默德·尤努斯建立的格莱珉银行，率先启动了小额信贷业务，已有超过 8,000 万借贷者，其中大部分是女性。正是由于政府、私有市场、非政府组织和宗教团体间开展的一项提供免疫服务的合作，500 万儿童和 500 万成年人将得以生存。越来越多的商业联盟正在制定应对气候变化的日程表。最近美国企业联盟除呼吁采取更有力的行动之外，还在制定切实可行的方案。所有这些都是了不起的突破性成就。但就某种意义而言，这也暴露出我们现在缺乏有效办法和机制。1999 年在芝加哥，我曾呼吁建立这样一个国际社会的信条：我们承认当代外交政策只有基于共同的价值观才能发挥作用。这些价值观赋予我们的不仅有权力，还有义务，要求我们采取行动保护处于危难中的人们，我是指在科索沃事件和种族清洗的情况下采取行动。当然，该信条的适用范围还更广。一些看似毫不相干的问题，如反恐斗争和非洲贫困，其实有着相同之处。这两者都要求主动干预。事实上，互相依存使干预成为必要的手段——以联盟的方式来阻止危险或不公正的发生。虽然这些问题很可能发生在国外，但最终会影响到国家内部。

因此，如今我们认为，建立一个合理民主的巴勒斯坦国不仅符合巴勒斯坦和以色列人民的利益，也符合广大中东地区和全世界的利益。我们也知道，如果中非陷入冲突之中，总有一天会威胁全球。同样的，如果伊拉克或阿富汗重新成为失败的国家并输出暴力，我们也将成为受害者。但是我们知道，除非我们积极干预，否则这些充满良好愿望的目标都不会实现。我们对如何实行军事干预了如指掌，对如何进行援助和促进发展也驾轻就熟。但对于国家重建——我指的是在一个国家建立一个有充分能力发挥作用的自主政府——依然处于摸索阶段。政府治理的基础设施——能够发挥作用的商贸和法律体系，能够管理到位的卫生部和教育部，有真正权威的经济部门，能够依照治理法规履行职责的警察和军队，这些往往看似乏味无趣，不如通过直接干预来治疗疾病或消除贫困来得痛快，但事实上，这是保证这些国家为成为名副其实的国家努力奋斗，取得进步的关键。贸易援助的重要性决不低于世贸协定的其他内容。为什么？因为贸易援助能发展国力。

国际干预是有待开发的一片全新的领域。只有发展国力，巴勒斯坦、伊拉克、阿富汗和任何最贫困的或处于战乱中的非洲国家的命运才能得到拯救。其他所有帮助尽管也是必需且宝贵的，但在没有自治政府和自助体系的情况下都不能起到作用。国际社会必须开发这些新的方法。

还有一点，我们需要恰当的、完善的解决冲突和维持和平的方法。如今发生在达尔富尔的一切是丑闻——不是问题而是丑闻。成千上万的人死去，或者生活在难以置信的危险和痛苦之中，只因我们无法达成适当的和平协议，不能正常执行这种协议，也缺乏整个国际社会的全力支持。我知道有许多政治原因与我们良好的意愿相左，但问题的真正实质仍在于缺乏持久的国际关注，当无人制止事态发展时，我们没有坚持不懈的努力，缺乏发回真实的事态报告并采取行动的能力。并非所有这些都需要我们求助于像联合国这样的传统形式的国际治理机构。非政府组织和个人也可以发挥作用。问题是如果我们希望干预成功，我们就必须有行动能力。因此，我们的国际对话的一个新的关键是：必须以加强体制和手段为主。这不仅指政府间也包括存在于民间的能增加实力的体制与手段。我们需要构筑新的关系网，新的国家间合作关系以及人与人之间的合作关系，从而调动起各种切实可行的手段来使变化成为现实。时间紧迫，时不我待。今年的达沃斯论坛的意义就在于大家就一个基于共同价值观建立的国际议程达成了较深层次的共识，而这也是达沃斯历年的特点。正是这一点让我乐观。这体现了真正的全球责任感。但是，我们争取世界关注的声音并不是唯一的。还有一个声音。它也许是对伊斯兰教的歪曲滥用，但这个声音能狡猾地利用许多生活方式与我们有着天壤之别的人们所感受到的不公正、贫困以及隔离。我们相信我们正竭尽全力应对世界面临的问题，努力除去成百上千万人背上的枷锁，帮助他们摆脱苦难。但这种反动的意识形态嘲笑我们的努力，歪曲我们的动机，丑化我们的美好信念。

还有另一种可能。20年后，或者在更短的时间内，有着强大的意志和手段来实现其意愿的新的强国将诞生，新的势力结构也将生成。这个新世界会以什么样的价值观为指导呢？是人类共享的全球价值观呢？还是要把世界重新分割成势力范围，回到大国权力角逐，弱小国家饱受其害的状况呢？如果我们坚信的未来——一个宽容的、自由、开放且公正的世界——令人信服，它就必须成为现实。对于恐惧，最好的回应永远是希望。但要有希望，首先就要有信仰。只有实践诺言才能维护信仰。因此，让我们关注非洲、气候变化、世界贸易这三大问题。让我们设想一下，如若在未来的几个月内这世界将达成共识，在未来的几年里整个世界将采取行动，那将是怎样的前景啊？想一想我们对世界进步的构想是多么吸引人，再想想我们如果失败，谁会悲伤，谁会高兴。仔细想一想吧。最后，让我们达成共识，让我们行动起来。

第13单元

欢迎中华人民共和国国务院总理温家宝访澳的午餐会致辞

约翰·霍华德
堪培拉，2006年

总理先生，我非常热烈地欢迎您的到来。我们两国关系在过去10年间有了长足发展，这一成绩在今天得到了进一步验证。您一定还记得，今天我习惯性地晨起散步，让我高兴的是您也加入进来，而且我们还一块穿过 R.G. 孟席斯小路，堪培拉这条环湖小路是以澳大利亚执政最久的总理名字命名的。我把罗伯特·戈登·孟席斯的照片指给您看，并向您讲起他作为澳大利亚总理的生平故事，那时，我不由得在心里暗暗感叹，自1966年他退休后，澳中两国都发生了巨大变化，而且我国两党领导人对中国的态度也有了很大转变。

正如在我们今天的谈话中一样，我很自然地想到很多对澳大利亚而言很重要的国家间关系，不过我今天讲话的目的并不是给这些关系进行毫无意义的排序，我们与中国的关系十分重要。不过更准确地说，比起澳大利亚和其他国家的关系，澳中关系在过去的10年或更长时间内发生的变化最大。这一变化的产生有着很多原因。变化产生于我们的共识，基于两国关系既有机遇又有局限的现实主义，同时也在于双方坦率地承认两国历史、文化和政治方面存在的差异。

我认为，在很长一段时间内，特别是近几年，我们都以不同方式认识到双方在诸多方面有着根本差异。但有趣的是，正是这一认识恰恰使我们更加有效地利用双方的共同点以及双边关系给我们带来的益处。

澳大利亚的民主传统在世界历史上排名第六，因此我们的政治体系和中国差异很大。但是，中国的成长进步确实是历史性的。正如去年9月我在纽约联大演讲时所说，我相信，中国的经济进步和外向型发展不仅有益于中国，同时也有益于世界。因此，我们欢迎中国的成长和发展。我们是从一个积极的角度看待这一问题的。我们认为，任何遏制中国的政策都毫无意义，不仅这样，我们还要在中国充分发挥其巨大潜力的长征路上成为一个积极的伙伴，这不仅有利于我国，有利于我们这个地区，更有利于整个世界。

澳中经济关系的巨大发展让人惊叹。单就很多数字而言就可以证明这一点，但最鲜明的是澳大利亚对华出口量在过去10年间翻了两翻。原材料市场的巨大发展为此做出很大贡献。为巩固和保证经济发展，中国对能源日益扩大的需求亟待满足。幸运的是，澳大利亚恰好拥有丰富的资源来促进中国的发展。

但是，尽管两国在原材料领域的关系很重要，澳中经济关系绝不仅仅局限于此。就在这个午餐会之前，我召集了一些本国的商界领导人物，他们都在中国有很多投资和业务，这些商务活动涵盖了我国贸易行业的方方面面。我们邀请了原材料公司的领导，同时也有大学的副校长，大型法律顾问公司和保险公司的合伙人，而这也刚好证明我们两国的经济往来十分广泛。

澳大利亚留学生中来自中国的人数最多，中国同时也是澳大利亚第二大移民输入国。在澳大利亚旅游业中，中国游客人数增长最快，或更准确地说，中国游客是增长最快的游客群体之一。据估计，中国入澳游客数到 2010 年将超过日本来澳游客。

所有这些都证明，我们两国关系涉及范围十分广泛，而且尤其是基于人民对人民的联系。我曾数次向中国领导人说起，广东话和普通话合起来看是目前澳大利亚使用最多的外语，中国人大量居住在澳大利亚的大城市里，特别是悉尼。

澳大利亚对中国文化的热爱与日俱增，国内了解中国文化和汉语的人也越来越多。我很高兴地注意到，墨尔本大学亚洲联系中心和中国政府之间的合作很快就要有可喜的结果，就在不远的将来，墨尔本大学将建立孔子研究中心。这将进一步促进澳大利亚了解和欣赏中国的语言和文化。

作为一个大国，特别是世界第三大经济体，中国正在坚定不移地维护它的合法权益。在维护这些权益的过程中，中国同样也要承担其作为国际社会一分子和重要参与者的相应责任。今天总理先生和我的讨论涉及很多问题，其中就有世界主要大国，或者更准确地说是联合国安理会常任理事国所面临的包括伊朗核问题在内的各种挑战。

我们一致认为，通过联合国和国际原子能机构努力解决这一问题十分重要。而要实现这一愿望，最好需要，或者说必须要联合国安理会五个常任理事国统一目的，取得一致意见。

澳大利亚十分认可中国在这一过程中所作出的积极贡献。中国对朝鲜的潜在影响最大，在促进朝鲜问题的合理解决方面中国发挥了积极作用。目前我们还远远没有解决这个问题，因此我们也期待中国继续利用其对朝鲜不可比拟和不容置疑的影响促进问题圆满解决。中美关系不仅在我们这个地区，而且在整个世界都是至关重要的。正如大家所知，澳大利亚从来没有故意淡化澳美之间的亲密关系，也从来没有要为这种紧密关系表示什么歉意。澳美关系十分深厚，因为它是基于历史和两国共同的价值观念。而且澳美关系现在比以往更加牢固。

但是，澳美关系现在没有，将来也绝对不会影响澳大利亚与中国交往并建立持久紧密的伙伴关系和友谊。无论在本地区内还是世界范围，我对中美关系都非常乐观。我并不认同某些人所宣传的中美关系终将破裂并引起冲突的说法。我认为不论是在台湾问题上还是中美两国广泛利益上，共识终将成为主流。近期历史表明，各方面都越来越需要共识。这也是我们始终坚持一个中国政策的原因之一，在今天与总理先生的会谈中我也再次确认了这一点。我们对各相关方的一致立场是尽量使涉及台湾海峡问题的事务降温。

总理先生，您今天作为世界上人口最多的国家的领导人来到这里。澳大利亚人民对贵国的兴趣和热爱与日俱增。我们两国可以共同努力的事情很多。澳中两国确实存在很大差异，但我认为，我们两国关系良好的秘诀在于多年以来我们都愿意坦率承认彼此之间的差异而不是故意遮掩这些差异，我们也没有虚情假意地接受根本不存在的共同态度和价值观。在我个人的经历中，我始终无法忘怀1996年在马尼拉召开的第一届亚太经合组织会议上我与中国国家主席江泽民的会晤。当时的澳中关系刚刚经历过一段非常艰难的时期。在那次会晤中，我们一致认为双方应该在可以达成共识的方面集中精力，没有必要对各自在其他问题上所持的不同立场作出让步，这些分歧不应该影响我们广泛的双边关系。我和政府都认为，这也正是澳大利亚商界人士多年以来所遵循的策略。

我们同中国的关系是广泛的，并且还在不断发展。今天出席会议的这么多位商业领袖证明了我们两国经济关系的强大。但正如所有关系所表明的那样，只有在人民与人民之间建立起深层联系才至关重要。就澳中关系来讲，人民之间的关系实实在在，这种关系在日益壮大，而且双方都给予高度重视。总理先生，您在贵国有着十分成功而有意义的政治生涯，我可以说，研究中国政治历史的学生都将怀着崇敬爱戴的心情阅读您的履历。我非常钦佩你的人格魅力，也感谢您为促进澳中关系所付出的坚持不懈的努力。

我们今天欢迎您的到访，不仅因为您是一位领导者，更因为您是一个注定将在国际事务中日益发挥重大作用的伟大国家的领导人。澳大利亚希望同这个国家建立更加亲密、有效和持久的伙伴关系。

第14单元

东盟一中国关系：和谐与发展

东盟秘书长 王景荣
新加坡，2006年

很荣幸今天上午能够和大家一起分享我的一点想法。本次纪念座谈会是为了纪念中国东盟对话关系15周年。本次会议的主题——"和谐与发展"——非常有意思，因为这两个概念既对立又统一。请允许我衷心祝贺大会主办方，新加坡东亚思想库，感谢你们的热烈欢迎，感谢你们为本次会议所作的周密安排。

2006年10月30日我在南宁参加了中国东盟对话关系15周年纪念峰会，在那次会议上我注意到东盟成员国领导人同中国领导人的关系越来越密切。定期的高层对话和领导人之间的协商探讨将帮助我们建立相互信任，增强对彼此的信心，使关系更融洽，从而促进双方对共同关心的话题进行更为自由和坦诚的讨论，交换彼此看法。这样一种氛围对于东盟—中国关系的健康发展十分有利。

建立坚实基础

东南亚和中国的历史联系可以追溯到几个世纪以前，当时东南亚地区的国家各自同中国开展贸易、文化交流，进行航海活动。东盟作为一个整体同中国的关系始于1991年。早期阶段，双方努力建立融洽关系和高度信任，促进双边关系逐步发展。东盟和中国不断探索创新途径应对挑战，推动关系向前发展。

现在，大家都可以看到15年后的今天，东盟—中国关系已经十分成熟。双方合作不断深化，合作领域也不断扩大，遍及政治和安全、经济和贸易、社会文化和民众交往等各个方面。2003年10月双方签署了中国与东盟面向和平与繁荣的战略合作伙伴关系联合宣言。双方领导人为了具体实施联合宣言又于2004年11月通过了东盟—中国五年行动计划。双边关系此时已经达到了一个新的高度。这些重要文件为促进双边合作指引了方向并规划了路线。

互助互补

东盟和中国在彼此社会经济发展及维护地区和平稳定事务中发挥着互助互补的作用。很多人会认为，中国是对东盟的战略观和经济发展有着深远影响的强有力的竞争对手。其实恰恰相反，东盟认为中国的迅速发展为加快东盟的经济一体化提供了积极的氛围和动力。东盟坚信双方都可以充分利用这种互补关系，从中受益。

东盟视中国为近邻，而且是一个有着巨大潜力的重要对话伙伴。经济飞快发展并拥有13亿人口的中国是东盟产品的巨大消费市场，也是未来东盟地区外商直接投资的主要来源。另外，大量的中国游客也使东盟受益，反之亦然。2004年和2005年，中国游客平均人数达到300万。

中国同样也通过贸易和投资推动东盟的一体化。另外，中国也为各项地区一体化计划提供支持。中国为东盟发展基金会提供了100万美元的资金，并承诺为东盟一体化项目的实施另外提供100万美元。同时中国也参与了东盟—湄公河流域开发合作、文莱—印尼—马来西亚—菲律宾—东盟东部经济增长区和其他次区域经济项目。

为使本地区早日成为商品、服务、投资、技术劳动力和资本自由流通的单一市场和生产基地，东盟正在积极推进一体化和共同体建设。这些都将进一步促进东盟经济基础的发展，而中国也将从中受益。

发展经济合作伙伴关系

经济合作关系发展迅速，特别是在签订了全面经济合作框架协议之后。该协议规定建立东盟中国自由贸易区，计划文莱、印度尼西亚、马来西亚、菲律宾、新加坡、泰国和中国将在 2010 年加入其中，柬埔寨、老挝人民民主共和国、缅甸和越南在 2015 年也将加入进来。

根据东盟的数字统计，中国东盟贸易 2004 贸易额为 890 亿美元，2005 年为 1,130 亿美元，上升 27%。东盟中国贸易占东盟世界贸易的比重从 2004 年的 8.3% 增长到 2005 年的 9.3%。但是，中国在东盟的外商直接投资却从 2004 年的 6.7 亿美元减少到 2005 年的 5.7 亿，下降了 15%。1999 年至 2005 年中国在东盟的外商直接投资累计达到 14 亿美元。当然，越来越多的中国企业会在东盟的产业领域和其他创造就业机会的领域进行更多的投资。

2004 年 11 月，双方签署了全面经济合作框架协议下的货物贸易协议和争端解决机制协议。其中货物贸易协议于 2005 年 7 月 20 日生效。该协议的生效和关税的削减有望增加双边商贸交易，促进外商直接投资的自由流动。中国东盟服务贸易协议也将很快签署。双方正在就协议中关于投资的部分进行谈判。

为了加速东盟的经济增长，东盟基础设施建设需要双方共同的努力。中国的投资将缩小东盟成员国之间的发展差距。建立良好的体系也将有利于中国云南、四川等内陆省份的发展。

推动民间交往

在社会文化合作方面，为了促进民间交流，提高东盟和中国民众的思想意识，东盟和中国已经组织了许多活动。同时，商业界也组织了很多活动，如东盟中国博览会，东盟中国商务与投资峰会，以帮助双方找到合适的合作伙伴，建立联系网络，扩大商业联系。不过，在其他方面还有很多工作要做，如政府官员、青年人、公民社会和知识分子等方面，这样才能促进东盟中国对话伙伴关系的全面互动和发展。

最重要的是要使社会的方方面面能够更多地了解到关于中国和东盟的信息。我们需要更多的网站、新闻报道和纪录片来为东盟和中国的广大受众提供信息。2006 年 10 月在南宁召开的东盟—中国纪念峰会上，中国宣布邀请 1,000 名来自东盟成员国的青年访问中国，并在未来五年内为东盟培训 8,000 名各行各业的专业人士。这对于促进民众交往，特别是青年人的交往是十分有利的。

走向未来

东盟—中国对话关系在过去 15 年间稳步发展。精心制定的计划和远见卓识指导着这种广泛合作。双方的政治意愿在很大程度上确保双边关系得以健康适度地发展和加强。

但是，因为我们这个地区乃至整个世界都在不断变化，因此东盟和中国不能为过去的成绩沾沾自喜。我们的双边关系会不断面对各种新的机遇和挑战，要推动关系向前发展就要再接再厉，继续奋斗。另外，双方同时还要从双边关系整体状况和战略宏图出发，小心谨慎地处理各种潜在挑战，这一点至关重要。

在未来几年，东盟和中国还将继续加强合作，将双方的承诺付诸实践，特别是要建立自由贸易协定，为东盟和中国人民带来更多实惠。另外，双方还要密切合作，共同应对本地区所面临的跨国犯罪、恐怖主义、非典、禽流感和自然灾害等种种挑战。

随着本地区的飞速发展，东盟为了管理地区事务和应对挑战，提出了诸如东亚峰会和自由贸易区等计划。中国对这些计划的支持是东盟成功的关键。一个有凝聚力的强大的东盟也符合中国的自身利益。缩小东盟成员国之间的发展差距是建设一个团结的强大的东盟的关键策略。中国在这项事业中能够发挥很大作用。

近期最值得探讨的一个问题是东盟和中国如何共同建设人们脑海中勾勒的东亚共同体。这个理念激发了很多学者和思想家的想象力。问题的关键是，如何使现在这种围绕本地区所形成的多方面多层次关系，发展成为以共同体为基础的感情，而又不会引起不必要的紧张和压力？东盟 10+3 框架和机制在过去 10 年间有了一定发展。我们应该在此基础上继续发展，并且在开发东亚峰会巨大潜力的同时从这一框架获取更大价值。我相信本次会议的与会者都将为促进东盟—中国战略伙伴关系交换看法，提出宝贵的建议。

第 15 单元

欧洲与中国：合作伙伴、竞争对手、领导力量（节选 2）

曼德尔森
北京，2006 年

中国、欧洲和美国

我相信对于所有这些问题中国、欧洲和美国应当坚持开展更加密切的对话，有可能以更加一致的步调采取行动，成为全球应对方案的三大支柱。这样的合作伙伴关系将在我们之间建立起新的接触规则。

我想有必要强调两个进展。第一是我刚才已经提到过的美国财政部部长保尔森发出的信号——就在这个讲台上——是关于美国对华的新接触政策，而这一政策会使美国政府需要对付本国内强大的、态度对立的选民们。

第二个进展有关欧盟再次明确地要求与中国继续伙伴关系。我此次来京的目的就是向我的中国同行呈交欧盟近期公布的确定我们未来与中国开展政治、贸易及投资合作的议程。其中包括启动就一项新的欧盟中国伙伴关系与合作协议和一套已经快速更新的有关贸易和投资的协议的谈判。我和薄熙来部长本周将对此进行讨论。我相信他和我一样决心坚定并对我们努力的方向抱有同样的希望。

新的欧盟—中国战略包括大家熟悉的欧盟在人权和改善市场准入方面的严格的要求，所以很多人认为它代表强硬路线。这个战略在需要强硬的社会政治自由、知识产权保护以及公平贸易方面态度强硬。但是，它强调的是伙伴关系和共同责任。

从这个角度看，不应该把我们经常就有关基本权益和市场准入所展开的艰难的辩论看作是双方关系的全部，而应看作是我们为了应对全球挑战，并为了本地区乃至全世界的利益，帮助确保中国自身国内稳定进行地必要的坦诚对话。我们一直支持"和谐社会"的理念，支持中国进行改革开放的工作。我相信作为一个明智的批评家，欧洲首先会成为一个支持改革的建设性盟友。

管理我们之间的商业关系

在结束讲话之前，我想重点谈一下我们的贸易关系，这不仅是因为我主管贸易，而且也因为我们的贸易关系处理得不太好——有可能严重地阻碍，甚至破坏我们关系的广泛发展。

中国的崛起给欧洲许多的产业，特别是劳动密集型的制造业造成了严重的压力。欧洲公司被迫进行调整，提高价值链，并且对自身具有相对优势的设计、高科技和高品质生产进行投资。

为了保住我们自己的市场和出口市场，中国正在迫使我们进行更加激烈的竞争。中国对于所有仍希望在未来 10 年有所发展的欧洲出口业构成主要的挑战。但是从经济角度看，中国对于欧洲实际上是全球化成功的例证。为什么这样讲呢，因为许多欧洲公司也在中国投资和生产。我们的进口商和零售商都在中国采购。

来自中国的进口产品，价格上具有竞争优势，已经降低了欧洲加工产业的成本。便宜的中国货物降低了欧洲消费者的成本，也一直有助于降低通货膨胀和利息率的压力。荷兰的一项研究表明价格便宜的中国货物每年为一般的欧洲家庭节约大约 300 欧元，欧洲的贫困家庭是主要的受益者，他们非常看重节约的开支。

最重要的是，中国对我们贸易和投资吸引力越来越大，尤其是因为中国不断壮大的有品位的中产阶级消费群体是欧洲最佳产品的重要市场。我敢说，既便你们现在没有这样做，10 年后你们都会喝着欧洲的葡萄酒，吃着法国奶酪，穿着漂亮的意大利服装和鞋，开着德国轿车，你们的消费会远远超出这些。

我是第一个认为中国已经在开放本国市场方面远远领先于其他新兴经济体的

人。但是，不应当按发展中国家来要求中国。到 2010 年中国将成为全世界最大的出口国。地位不同，期望自然要高。

中国入世后的五年中，尽管已经做了许多努力，但是仍然有部分承诺尚未得到兑现。欧盟将会推动中国履行这些承诺。中国在开放市场，放宽服务业和投资领域方面还有可能做更多的努力。贸易自由有利于提高人民的生活水平，所以中国本身也会从中受益。

欧洲无意挑战中国在劳动力和生产成本方面的合理竞争优势。那方面的竞争是残酷的，但也是公平的。我们对此表示尊重。但是欧洲要保护自己免遭不公平竞争——就像中国一直所做的一样，因为按照世贸组织的规定，我们都有权这么做。

欧洲还需要看到中国在打击假冒商品方面采取更加严厉的行动。假冒商品不但制约了欧洲的竞争力，对中国也是一个日益严重的问题。上个月中国超过德国成为了世界第五大专利申请国。所以，中国政府也日益认识到我们在打击这一非法行动方面有着共同的利益——但是，我们需要看到更多的执法行动。

欧洲还将继续督促中国处理其他结构性贸易壁垒。注重以出口带动经济增长而不重视国内消费需求，以及中国消费者高水平的预防性存款都限制了重要的增长型消费经济的发展，也阻碍了可以对贸易起到平衡作用的外国对华出口贸易。

毫无疑问，这些听起来很像外国人一连串的抱怨和要求。但是，我们最近的贸易和投资战略清楚地表明我们双方都要承担责任。欧洲自己必须致力于帮助中国取得完全市场经济地位，给予中国开放公平的对欧出口市场，欧洲必须适应中国严峻的竞争挑战。我们必须同欧洲内的保护主义者做斗争，因为我们不能躲在我们自己的壁垒后面要求中国提供开放的市场。

结论：欧洲与中国

换句话说，欧洲与中国面临的挑战在于如何平衡双方之间的伙伴关系和竞争关系。我们要就价值观展开坦诚的辩论，但是我们首先需要清楚地认识到我们双方人口之和占世界总人口的四分之一，而且我们共享一个脆弱并且正在受到威胁的星球。我认为我们现在的政治联系，以及双边政治关系的基础还并不牢固，难以承受这种伙伴关系带来的压力和挑战。需要改变这种情况。

我一直怀疑欧洲与中国打交道中出现的问题在一定程度上是由于不理解造成的。我们研究儒学。我们依照中国的政府部门建立了文官制度。我们进口中国瓷器，又进口了茶叶并开始饮茶。但是，我们对中国的了解往往只是平面的，就像茶杯上画的中国画。这也需要变化。

清华大学当初创立的目的是帮助学生出国旅游和学习。在 21 世纪，这个你们的世纪，清华应当起到这样的作用。欧洲也需要送自己的学生到中国旅游学习。不断的相互了解和亲身经历以及中欧之间建立的信任是富有成效的关系的基础。

　　最根本的是，整个世界都将受到中国事务的影响。伯特兰 · 罗素在 1920 年认识到这点至少是对的，那么，现在就更是如此。无论我们怎样对待中国惊人的崛起带给我们的问题，我们知道有一点是肯定的，那就是我们的命运息息相关。欧洲和中国别无选择，只有共同回答这些问题。我们也迫切需要与其他的国家和人们一起共同回答这些问题。

附录二
主要参考书目

薄冰主编. 高级英语语法. 北京：世界知识出版社，2006.

蔡基刚编著. 英汉汉英段落翻译与实践. 上海：复旦大学出版社，2001.

陈德彰编著. 英汉翻译入门. 北京：外语教学与研究出版社，2005.

陈定安编著. 英汉比较与翻译（增订版）. 北京：中国对外翻译出版公司，1998.

陈文伯著. 英汉翻译技法与练习. 北京：世界知识出版社，1998.

崔长青，张碧竹著. 翻译的要素. 苏州：苏州大学出版社，2007.

德利尔，J. 著，孙惠双译. 翻译理论与翻译教学法. 北京：国际文化出版公司，
    1988.

方梦之编著. 英汉翻译基础教程. 北京：中国出版集团中国对外翻译出版公司，
    2008.

浩瀚，马光主编. 轻松掌握英语翻译. 北京：中国古籍出版社，2001.

华先发主编. 新实用英译汉教程. 武汉：湖北教育出版社，2000.

黄龙著. 翻译技巧指导. 沈阳：辽宁人民出版社，1986.

吉尔，D. 著，刘和平等译. 笔译训练指南. 北京：中国出版集团中国对外翻译出
    版公司，2008.

勒代雷，M. 著，刘和平译. 释意学派口笔译理论. 北京：中国对外翻译出版公
    司，2001.

彭长江主编. 英汉-汉英翻译教程. 长沙：湖南师范大学出版社，2002.

秦亚青. 浅谈英中视译. 外交学院学报，1987(1).

塞莱斯科维奇，D.，勒代雷M. 著，阎素伟等译. 口译训练指南. 北京：中国出
    版集团中国对外翻译出版公司，2007.

思果著. 翻译研究. 北京：中国对外翻译出版公司，2001.

斯诺，E. 著，董乐山译. 西行漫记. 北京：外语教学与研究出版社，2005.

宋天锡编著. 英汉互译实用教程. 北京：国防工业出版社，2003.

宋天锡，袁江，袁东娥编著．英汉互译实用教材．北京：国防工业出版社，2000．

王恩冕编著．大学英汉翻译教程．北京：对外经济贸易大学出版社，2004．

王佐良著．翻译：思考与试笔．北京：外语教学与研究出版社，1989．

温秀颖等编著．英语翻译教程．天津：南开大学出版社，2001．

许建平编著．英汉互译实践与技巧．北京：清华大学出版社，2000．

杨承淑著．口译教学研究：理论与实践．北京：中国对外翻译出版公司，2006．

叶子南著．高级英汉翻译理论与实践．北京：清华大学出版社，2001．

张道真编著．实用英语语法．北京：商务印书馆，1979．

张道真编著．实用英语语法（最新版）．北京：外语教学与研究出版社，2007．

张培基，喻云根，李宗杰，彭谟禹编著．英汉翻译教程．上海：上海外语教育出
　　　版社，1980．

中国对外翻译出版公司选编．翻译理论与翻译技巧论文集．北京：中国对外翻译
　　　出版公司，1983．

钟述孔著．英汉翻译手册．北京：商务印书馆，1980．

朱佩芬编著．实用英汉口译技巧．上海：华东理工大学出版社，1995．

庄绎传编著．英汉翻译教程（辅导用书）．北京：外语教学与研究出版社，1999．